The Forming
of an American Tradition

The Forming

of an

American Tradition

A Re-examination of
COLONIAL PRESBYTERIANISM

Leonard J. Trinterud

BOOKS FOR LIBRARIES PRESS
FREEPORT, NEW YORK

STANDARD BOOK NUMBER:

8369-5450-5

LIBRARY OF CONGRESS CATALOG CARD NUMBER:

78-124262

PRINTED IN THE UNITED STATES OF AMERICA

To My Mother

PREFACE

As the Presbyterian Church in the United States of America approaches the 250th anniversary of its founding, it becomes increasingly clear that the entire history of the Church has been shaped by that which its founding fathers thought and did during its first half century, 1706–1758. No valid understanding of American Presbyterianism is possible apart from a thorough comprehension of the Church's life in these formative years. The purpose of this volume, accordingly, is to re-examine colonial Presbyterianism in order to make more clear the native genius of American Presbyterianism.

The study here presented falls into two parts. Part I is intended to show that Presbyterianism came to the American colonies by a series of transplantations from several sources, principally from New England and Ulster. The blending of the divergent allegiances and concerns of these various Presbyterianisms became a fiery ordeal of ecclesiastical controversy and spiritual awakening. In the ordeal, however, there was born a new order, an American understanding of Presbyterianism. Part II undertakes to describe how this American Church understood and conducted its mission in the late colonial era, through the Revolutionary War, and in the years of crisis following that war. During these years the Church itself was profoundly altered by forces working both from within and from without. The Church that emerged at the beginning of the republican era was not the Church of 1758, and the early years of the nineteenth century were to witness a severe struggle over whether to accept the norms of 1758 or the norms of the contemporary Church.

The period covered in this study is over a century, and the available sources have presented somewhat of a problem. For the period prior to the Great Awakening original sources are meager, and they do not become adequate for some phases of the Church's life during the entire colonial era. Fortunately, however, more original sources are available now than at any time subsequent to the Revolutionary War. Moreover, these sources are quite sufficient to provide us with a rather clear picture of the definitive movements in the Church's history, even though we might wish occasionally for more details. While careful account has been taken of the relevant secondary materials, original sources, manuscript and printed, have controlled the entire study back of this volume. Consequently the documentation is confined largely to the primary materials. The limitations of space, however, have made it necessary to keep the documentation to a minimum.

My debt to the previous historians of the Church is large. Of these, Charles A. Briggs and Richard Webster have been drawn upon most heavily. E. H. Gillett, Charles Hodge, and William Hill have often served as guides into fruitful restudies of the primary sources, in addition to being useful as secondary authorities. To the writings of several recent American Church historians, Guy S. Klett, William Warren Sweet, Wesley M. Gewehr, and Charles H. Maxson, my obligations, acknowledged and unacknowledged, are great. For the general background of American history during the colonial era, I have used the works of many. Especially large is my debt to the many books and articles of Evarts B. Greene, T. J. Wertenbaker, James Truslow Adams, Edward Channing, and Charles M. Andrews. It has not been possible in a work of this nature to acknowledge adequately this debt, real though it is.

Greater than my debt to the literature of historical research is my debt to those who make such researches possible. Beyond all others is my debt to Princeton Theological Seminary and to its president, John A. Mackay. This study was begun under a fellowship granted by the seminary, and carried forward during two widely separated subsequent periods of residence on that historic Presbyterian campus. Except for Princeton's incomparable library, and its splendid staff, headed by Dr. Kenneth S. Gapp, this volume could not have been written. No statement could chronicle the kindnesses which Dr. Gapp and his staff have extended to me. Great also is my obligation to The Presbyterian Historical Society of Philadelphia, and to its Research Historian, Guy S. Klett. Much that I might have missed has been called to my attention by Mr. Klett. Mrs. Catherine R. Klett transcribed for me all the extant manuscript sermons of William Tennent, Sr., a service for which I am most grateful. Dr. Charles A. Anderson, the Director of The Presbyterian Historical Society; his predecessor, the late Thomas C. Pears, Jr.; and the entire staff of the Society have been of constant assistance.

The resources of many other libraries as well have been used in the research out of which this study has been written. To these libraries, and to their staffs, I owe much. Principally, I am indebted: in Philadelphia, to the Historical Society of Pennsylvania, the Library Company of Philadelphia, and the Library of the University of Pennsylvania; in Princeton, to the Library of Princeton University; in New Brunswick, to the Sage Library of New Brunswick Theological Seminary and the Library of Rutgers University; in New York City, to the New York Public Library and the Library of Union Theological Seminary; in the Boston area, to the Congregational Library, the Boston Atheneum, the Boston Public Library, the Massachusetts Historical Society, the libraries of Harvard University, including the Andover-Harvard Theological Library, and the American Antiquarian Society; in Chicago, to the Virginia Library of McCormick Theological Seminary, the libraries of the University of Chicago, and the Newberry Library; in Pasadena, to the Huntington Library; and in Pittsburgh, to the Library of Western Theological Seminary.

Several libraries that were not visited in person have been most helpful in answering inquiries and in furnishing photostats and microfilms of items in their collections: the Library of Congress; the libraries of Union Theological Seminary in Richmond, Yale University, and Dartmouth College; and the British Museum.

During the writing of this history the manuscript was read in whole or in part by several friends, each of whom aided me greatly by his counsel, and none of whom is responsible for what has finally been written: Guy S. Klett, of The Presbyterian Historical Society; Professor Ernest T. Thompson, of Union Theological Seminary, Richmond, Virginia; William Warren Sweet, the dean of the historians of the American Church; Professor Robert Hastings Nichols, of Union Theological Seminary, New York City. My wife has shared much of the labor involved in this study, making it our common task.

To my successor in the editor's chair at The Westminster Press, Dr. Paul L. Meacham, and to my former colleagues there, I owe a great debt of thanks for their counsel and assistance.

L. J. T.

McCormick Theological Seminary

TABLE OF CONTENTS

PART I

The Agony of Birth

1

THE CHURCH IN THE WILDERNESS

Presbyterianism in the American colonies sprang from two main sources, English Puritanism and Scottish Presbyterianism. Each of these sources, however, had been modified by passing a time in another country under circumstances that had affected permanently both its life and its thought. The Puritanism from which stemmed so significant a part of American Presbyterianism was largely second- and third-generation New England Puritanism which had been profoundly influenced by colonial life. The Presbyterians of Scottish origin who came to America during the colonial period were mostly from North Ireland. Few came direct from Scotland. Scotch-Irish Presbyterianism, while transplanted originally from Scotland, had been modified in many ways by its experiences of poverty and persecution in Ireland. It was inevitable, therefore, that American Presbyterianism would arise without any one clear-cut pattern, and that in the attempt to establish for it forms and standards the original sources as well as the modified sources would all make their claims. A number of subsidiary sources also would make their contributions, Huguenot, Dutch, Welsh, and German. Finally the American wilderness itself would challenge all these older traditions and practices, and the Presbyterianism of America would emerge as something differing from all its sources.

Puritans began migrating to the American colonies in large numbers before English Puritanism had been broken permanently into two distinct bodies, Presbyterian and Congregational. While Independent or Congregational tendencies predominated among these early American Puritans, leanings toward Presbyterian forms were also present and were often pronounced. Events in England, such as the work of the Westminster Assembly of Divines, the Protectorate of Cromwell, the Restoration of 1660 and the Ejection of 1662, together with the development of thought and practice in the colonies themselves, gradually separated American Puritanism into several groups. By the close of the seventeenth century the Independent-Congregational pattern was almost, though not wholly, unchallenged in Massachusetts Bay Colony. In Connecticut, Congregationalism showed strong Presbyterian tendencies which were to become more pronounced as the eighteenth century advanced. Nearly all the Puritan churches of Long Island and New Jersey had been planted from Connecticut, and showed even more marked tendencies toward Presbyterian usages than did the mother colony. It was only among these Puritan churches on Long Island and to the southward that Presbyterian tendencies became strong enough to lead to the erection of specifically Presbyterian churches.

Thus by the close of the seventeenth century American Presbyterianism in most areas was as yet undifferentiated from its English Puritan antecedents. Congregational Puritans and Presbyterian Puritans were still bound together by their common ties, and scattered about on Long Island, in the Jerseys, and in New York, Pennsylvania (including Delaware), Maryland, Virginia, and South Carolina. Into most of those Puritan congregations, except perhaps into those of Long Island, Scotch-Irish and Scottish immigrants had begun to come. Though Presbyterian in background, these new immigrants did not always make the existing church that they joined definitely Presbyterian. Even the convictions of the minister were not enough to make one of these churches take its place firmly in the Presbyterian or the Congregationalist way. Predominantly Congregationalist churches received Scottish and Scotch-Irish members and even Scottish Presbyterian preachers, yet remained Independent in persuasion. So also Presbyterian Puritan congregations received reinforcements from Scotland and Ireland and yet called avowedly Congregationalist ministers. The differences between Congregationalists and Presbyterians had not yet been driven to the point of causing a rupture within their ranks.

The issues upon which Puritanism in England had finally divided into Congregationalists and Presbyterians grew out of two seemingly irreconcilable concepts of the Church. To those of the Congregationalist persuasion, the Church of Christ on earth existed only in its individual congregations. The Church Universal was but the totality of these congregations. To the Presbyterian wing of Puritanism, the Church Universal transcended all its many local manifestations, being an entity greater even than the sum of all its parts. It was the one body of Christ. From these two starting points each group went on to differ with the other on a number of crucial issues.

Church membership for the Congregationalists was a matter of utmost gravity. He who was admitted to membership in a local congregation must be one whom the members of the church judged had received of God those renewing graces that alone could make one eligible for membership in the church. The whole church (i.e., the local congregation) must hear the prospective member's account of God's work in his soul and determine whether or not, in their judgment, he had been made fit for membership. The clergy and deacons could in no wise perform this task on the church's behalf. The consensus of the whole church must be expressed. Infallibility in this judging of persons' saving graces was never professed in Congregationalism, but the feeling was that the church must judge as best it could and act upon its judgment. The responsibility was squarely upon them.

Among Presbyterians the conviction was strongly held that in the final analysis the elect of God were known to him alone. These then were the real Church, the universal body of Christ transcending all its local manifestations. In admitting a person to the local congregation, the Presbyterians felt obligated to claim no more than that, in a charitable judgment, they had reason, based upon an examination of his faith and life by the minister and the elders who represented the people, to hope that God had numbered him within the great Church Universal. If that possibility was credible, the person ought to be allowed to join the local congregation and partake of the means of grace there offered. Admission was ever to the whole Church of Christ, and this authority to admit the local church professed to exercise, through its officers, by divine appointment.

The office of the ministry was also understood differently in each group. The Congregationalists, for whom the Church was the local congregations only, held that each church existed completely and essentially without any officers (Thomas Hooker). Out of its own body it was to select and ordain its pastors, teachers, deacons, and other officers. Whenever a minister left his flock, he ceased to be a minister. In a neighboring congregation he might speak, but not as a minister. No ministerial functions were rightfully his beyond the bounds of his own congregation. He was a minister of that local church, ordained by it and for it.[1]

The Presbyterians, on the other hand, ordained men to the ministry of the Church Universal. Wherever they went, whether in one local congregation or another, whether presently with a charge or without one, these men were in the sacred office for life. Their ordination was by other ministers, who ordained them by virtue of an authority that they professed to hold on behalf of the Universal Church. They expected that all other (non-Presbyterian) churches also would recognize these men as ministers of Christ, not merely as Presbyterian ministers.

From such divergent views concerning the Church and the ministry, it was natural that quite different conceptions should arise also concerning the relationship between the clergy and the laity within the Church. To the Congregationalist, the real Church was the laity, and the ministers stood upon a par with the laity as individuals within the one body. True, theirs was the important task of teaching, preaching, exhorting, and visitation, but these were all within the realm of persuasion and loving pastoral care. Whenever an issue involved " the keys to the Kingdom " (entrance to the Church) or church discipline, decency and expedition warranted the clergy's drafting of the agenda for a meeting of "the brotherhood " (all the male members of the congregation), and some advisory or exploratory counseling with the prospective member or the supposedly refractory member. The brotherhood alone, however, among whom the clergy had their place only as equals, could determine any issue relating to " the keys " or to discipline. They were the Church, and such matters were for the Church to determine.

To the Presbyterian, these matters assumed a very different aspect. The ministry who functioned in a local church exercised an office in behalf of the whole Church of Christ. The people were not to exercise their prerogatives directly, but, by divine appointment, through chosen elders who were peculiarly fitted to exercise such weighty responsibilities for the Universal Church. Quite apart from his objections on principle, the average Presbyterian feared that in practice the uninformed and unorganized laity under Congregationalist usage would soon fall completely under the influence of the clergy. A bench of elders would stand over against the clergy as an authentic voice of the people. Yet, since they served as elders in the Church of Christ, the elders were not the mere creatures of their electors. These elders, then, together with the minister as moderator only, were to exercise the power of the keys and church discipline, doing so in the name of whole body of Christ. They did not act merely on behalf of the local congregation.

From these two divergent doctrines of the nature of the Church sprang, of necessity, several severe practical problems. Neither group thought that unregenerate people should be admitted to Church membership. But their very different views as to the conditions of membership led the Congregationalists and Presbyterians farther and farther apart. Neither group believed that the sacraments were " general " means of grace, open to any and all indiscriminately. Both believed that only members of the Church should participate in the sacraments. Every celebration of the Lord's Supper and every baptism of a child, therefore, only made more clear the basic distinction between Congregationalist and Presbyterian. In a Presbyterian church the Lord's Supper would be observed regularly, preferably quarterly, and most of the members of the congregation would attend and participate. Frequently members of neighboring congregations would attend also, and participate. The sacramental services in the Presbyterian congregations tended to be great occasions, attended by large numbers. In a Congregationalist church the number of full members was generally very low in the seventeenth and early eighteenth century. Most of the people of a community would "attend meeting," but few attempted to qualify for membership. Consequently a Communion service would be open to only a small handful of people. The tendency was, therefore, to celebrate the Sacrament only at rare intervals, and after the retirement from the sanctuary of most of the congregation. In the one branch of Puritanism the Sacrament was a holy festival, often held out-of-doors because of the number who participated. In the other branch the Sacrament was a solemn ordinance, observed by half a dozen or ten who were the true Church. The same problem arose in principle regarding Baptism. Church members only might claim for their children the privilege of being baptized. Again, who might vote in calling a pastor for the congregation? Each group would answer, "All members may vote." But in one congregation a very few might vote; in the other several hundred might be qualified.

Another great issue that agitated Puritanism, and the issue which was the direct occasion of finally separating British Puritanism into Congregationalists and Presbyterians, was again an outgrowth of the two differing concepts of the Church. What was the province and place of the higher councils of the Church? For the Congregationalist, the answer was as simple as it was categorical. The Church existed completely and essentially in every local congregation. A council of churches was therefore only quantitatively superior to any one local church. As such its authority was advisory only, and its province was but the matter stated in the call by which it had been summoned. Any church that felt the need of counsel and advice was free to request it of such other churches as it pleased, and once the council had fulfilled this request, it passed out of existence. Only the local churches existed perpetually in their own right.

To the Presbyterians, the great entity remained at all times the one body of Christ, the Universal Church. No individual congregation could or should stand alone. It was not complete in its own right. It was but a part of the Church Universal and must be subject to discipline in that interest. By divine appointment local churches were to be gathered into presbyteries and these again into higher Church courts. By this ascending order of Church courts, the whole Presbyterian body was to be guided and disciplined in behalf of the Universal Church of which it was but a part. Since the Church Universal existed in its own right, and since the local congregations were in themselves not complete, both the authority and the function of these higher courts made them permanent and self-determining within their respective scopes.

Because of their convictions about the nature of the Church, the Congregationalist Puritans veered more and more toward outright Independency. The Presbyterian Puritans, on the other hand, strove more and more for control and continuance of the national established Church of England. Just to the north of them their Scottish Presbyterian brethren were engaged in a similar struggle. For a short time (1640–1660) the Presbyterian wing of English Puritanism appeared to be achieving their goal. In their day of triumphant rebuilding, their closest spiritual ties became those with their Scottish Presbyterian brethren rather than those with their English Congregationalist Puritan brethren. After 1653, as the Congregationalist-Independent wing grew vastly stronger, the ideal of a national Church became even more deeply rooted in the Presbyterian party. When the episcopal Church of England was restored in 1660, the Congregationalist group were at no great spiritual crisis. They had their local " gathered " flocks and could go on. The Presbyterians, contrariwise, were in a serious situation because of their own convictions. Many of their clergy and laity solved the problem by remaining in the national Church. Others became Independents. Those who remained Presbyterians found their way difficult indeed. Their Scottish brethren had achieved a national Church and therefore did not share their problem. Their Congregationalist Puritan brethren continued to co-operate with them in various projects, but refused to accept their distinctive views.

Here and there local unions of the two groups began to take place in the latter part of the seventeenth century. Not until 1691, however, were the Congregationalists and Presbyterians in London brought together. Increase Mather, of Boston, who was in London at the time, joined with two other ministers in sponsoring a plan of union called the " Heads of Agreement." In the discussions, which took place during the period 1690–1691, only ministers took part. The various congregations as such did not participate. The union was essentially a union of ministers, as events were soon to demonstrate. Under this plan the names " Presbyterian " and " Congregationalist " were to be dropped, and the name " United Brethren " was adopted. The Heads of Agreement made no attempt to present a rethinking of the differences between the two groups. Rather, under this scheme, each group agreed that these differences were no barrier to the union. The plan was basically Congregationalist, or, as Cotton Mather said, the truest possible description of New England Congregationalism. Church councils rather than permanent Church courts were recognized. No mention was made of lay representation in these courts. The decision of a Church council was advisory only. A deliberately vague and harmonistic definition of the Church was adopted. No one local church ought to ordain a man to the ministry. A council should be called for so important an act. Local preference was to determine whether or not a man should be reordained when transferring from one pastorate to another. So also, each congregation was to be free to decide whether or not to have ruling elders, and to adopt its own rules for membership and for admission to the sacraments. The ministers agreed to meet together for mutual counsel and assistance, for ordaining candidates for the ministry, and for the maintenance of the Dissenting cause in England. They were to avow their common faith by acknowledging " the Scriptures to be the word of God, the perfect and only Rule of Faith and Practice "; and by agreeing to " own " that the XXXIX Articles of the Church of England, or the Westminster symbols, or the Savoy Confession, was agreeable to the Scriptures.[2]

Although the majority of the Puritans who had migrated to New England had been of Congregationalist persuasions, Presbyterian tendencies and elements had always been found among them. Here and there local congregations functioned on the Presbyterian basis, e.g., Hingham and Newbury in Massachusetts. Moreover, the Cambridge Platform of 1648 embodied some Presbyterian ideas. The office of the ruling elder was recognized, and both the Congregationalist view that the brethren might ordain their own minister and the Presbyterian view that he should be ordained by other ministers were allowed. The Congregationalist view that a minister ought to be reordained when transferring to a new pastorate was defended, but not asserted so strongly as to make reordination always necessary. Already there had begun to appear that working synthesis of the two views which was to produce what one of Congregationalism's greatest historians has called a " Congregationalized Presbyterianism or a Presbyterianized Congregationalism." [3] When, in 1692, Increase Mather returned from England, both he and his son Cotton promoted vigorously the idea that the Heads of Agreement of the United Brethren of London were the best possible description of New England Congregationalism. Not a few were persuaded to concur in this judgment. When, however, the Brattle Street Church was founded, and Benjamin Colman was ordained by London Presbyterians for service as its pastor, the Mathers both objected vigorously.

The Puritan outposts on Long Island and in the other colonies to the southward were of the same mind as the New England churches. In their isolation the Congregational plan of church government seemed preferable. Since most of them were town churches the Congregational ideal made a great appeal, for then the civic and the religious life of the community were both expressions of the faith of the one local church. The peace of these Puritan outposts was shaken only, as a rule, by controversies due to the two contrary usages regarding the sacraments and to the two views of the authority of the minister over against the congregation, i.e., the problem of the eldership. These disputes arose among the Puritans themselves, and also when Scottish and Scotch-Irish Presbyterians, clergy or laity, migrated into the community. On the whole, however, a viable synthesis existed, and functioned well, even in these isolated Puritan churches.

Long Island was perhaps the earliest scene of distinctively Presbyterian endeavor. At Mespat (near Newtown), Francis Doughty, an English Puritan who had been driven out of Taunton, Massachusetts, for his advocacy of Presbyterian views, attempted to establish a Presbyterian colony in 1642. The following year he and his fellow colonists fled to Manhattan because of an Indian war. In New York City he preached from 1643 to 1648, supported by Puritans and by some of the Dutch. He also ministered for a time at Flushing, Long Island. Finally, in 1657, he removed to Maryland in order to escape Governor Stuyvesant's clutches. Richard Denton, another Presbyterian Puritan from England, settled at Wethersfield, Connecticut, in 1640. Later he was at Stamford. In 1644, he removed to Hempstead, Long Island, bringing with him part of his old congregation. Here he followed Presbyterian forms, but not without protests from some in his flock. Denton returned to England in 1658, and thereafter the church seems to have assumed a Congregational character.[4]

Though each of these early Presbyterian beginnings failed to develop into churches of Presbyterian order, the Hempstead Church did contribute to the founding, at Jamaica, Long Island, of what was probably the first permanent Presbyterian church in the new world. Two of Richard Denton's sons, Nathaniel and Daniel, together with other residents at Hempstead, settled at Jamaica in 1656. By 1662 they had secured the preaching services of Zechariah Walker, an unordained man from Massachusetts who had studied for a time at Harvard. No formal church was organized, however, until June 3, 1672, when, on instructions from a town meeting, John Prudden gathered a church " according to the rules of the Gospel in this town." That " the rules of the Gospel in this town " were Presbyterian is evident from several sources.[5] It seems undubitable, therefore, that the Jamaica church was founded as a Presbyterian church.

Despite the firm rooting down of Presbyterianism in this one town on Long Island, several decades were to pass before the Presbyterian way was to gain any real position on the island.[6] Presbyterianism was to be adopted only slowly and sporadically by the descendants of the Puritan settlers of Long Island. Even when other Long Island churches did become Presbyterian, most of their closest ties were with Connecticut, a fact that was to influence deeply the whole course of American Presbyterianism.

Very much like the Long Island churches were those of Westchester County in New York. The churches there also were offshoots of New England Puritanism. Following the Connecticut pattern, they were mildly inclined toward Presbyterian ways. Occasionally men of Presbyterian tendencies occupied their pulpits. Joseph Morgan served three churches in Westchester County — Bedford, East Chester, and Westchester — from 1699 or 1700 to 1704. After returning to Greenwich, Connecticut, where he formerly had been pastor of the Congregational church, he ministered there until 1708. That year he removed to Freehold, New Jersey, and became pastor of the Presbyterian church there.[7]

In the city of New York, Francis Doughty and Richard Denton had preached from time to time to a small group of Puritans and had baptized children without, it seems, formally organizing a church. Twice in the seventeenth century governors of the colony mention Presbyterians and Independents. In 1678, Governor Andros wrote to the Council of Trade, " There are Religions of all sorts, one Church of England, severall Presbiterians and Independents, Quakers and Anabaptists, of severall sects, some Jews, but Presbiterians and Independents most numerous and substantiall." [8] (Presbyterians here include Dutch Reformed and French Huguenot as well as British Presbyterians.) Governor Dongan's report of 1687 is more explicit: " New York has first a Chaplain belonging to the Fort of the Church of England; secondly a Dutch Calvinist; thirdly a French Calvinist; fourthly a Dutch Lutheran. Here bee not many of the Church of England; a few Roman Catholichs; abundance of Quakers preachers men and women especially; Singing Quakers; Ranting Quakers; Sabbatarians; Anti-Sabbatarians; some Anabaptists; some Independents; some Jews; in short of all sorts of opinions there are some, and the most part, of none at all." [9] However numerous the Puritan group in New York may have been at this time, accordingly, its Independent or Congregational faction was larger than the Presbyterian. No Puritan church, however, was organized by either faction in the city during the seventeenth century.

In the colony of East Jersey the earliest Dissenting churches were the Puritan churches at Newark and Elizabethtown, both organized by settlers from New England. The Newark church was founded in 1667 by the transfer from Branford, Connecticut, of Abraham Pierson and his very decided Congregationalist followers.[10] His son, Abraham, Jr., who became his colleague in 1669 and who succeeded him upon his death, favored Presbyterian ways. After leaving this church, in 1692, he settled in Connecticut, and later became the first rector of Yale College.[11] The Newark church did not become Presbyterian until 1719.

Elizabethtown was settled before Newark, though its church was organized later. The church has at times claimed a date of 1666 for its founding. A more likely date, however, is that of 1668, when Jeremiah Peck began preaching in the town. He was never a regularly settled minister; nor were Seth Fletcher (1680–1682) and John Harriman (1682–1704), who followed him.[12]

The proprietors of the colony of East Jersey included several Scots. The son of one of these proprietors, George Scot, induced the English authorities to allow more than a hundred Scotsmen who had been imprisoned for their participation in the Covenanters' rebellion against Charles II to migrate to East Jersey. On the voyage to America a great number of the passengers, including Scot, perished. The survivors, led by Archibald Riddell, a minister, settled at Woodbridge, New Jersey, in 1686. Here they joined a group of Independents who had maintained a place of worship there since 1675. Riddell became the pastor of the united group on an Independent, or Congregational, basis, serving until 1689, when he returned to Scotland. Samuel Shepherd, from New England, succeeded him on the Congregational plan. Under his successor, Nathaniel Wade, the church became Presbyterian, but not until after the founding of the first presbytery.[13]

Another group of refugee Scots settled in and around Freehold, New Jersey. This region was already somewhat settled by New Englanders, and the two groups worshiped together under the leadership of a Scottish elder, Walter Ker. It has been claimed that the church was organized as a Presbyterian church as early as 1692, but this is doubtful.[14] No ordained minister seems ever to have served it until after the founding of presbytery in 1706. Scottish refugees were intermingled among the New England settlers in a number of other places in East Jersey as well, but no other Presbyterian churches were founded in the colony during the seventeenth century.

In West Jersey colony settlers from New Haven colony provided the nucleus for an early Congregational church at Fairton under the ministry of Thomas Bridge. Under his successor the church became Presbyterian in 1709.[15] In the townships of Maidenhead and Hopewell ground had been given by the proprietors for a church and a burying ground, but no church was formed before the close of the century.

In Philadelphia, the Presbyterians again first appear mingled with another group, this time with the Baptists. As early as February, 1695, a small Baptist congregation was meeting for occasional services in the city. Such Presbyterians and Independents as there were agreed to meet with them, and each group supplied the occasional preacher as they were able. The Presbyterian group grew by immigration more rapidly than the Baptist, and soon the former appealed to the Boston ministers for a pastor. Benjamin Woodbridge was sent, but soon withdrew. His letter of introduction from Governor Danforth of Massachusetts to Governor Markham of Pennsylvania states that he is " sent, not to handle such points as are matters of controversies among the Protestants, but to preach unto as many of all persuasions as the Lord shall make willing to hear. . . ." [16] Evidently it was fully intended that the union with the Baptists was to be preserved by the man whom the Presbyterian group were calling.

When Woodbridge departed, Jedediah Andrews (Harvard, 1695) was sent in his place. Andrews had been brought up in the church at Hingham, Massachusetts, under Peter Hobart, who was Presbyterian in persuasion. He reached Philadelphia in the summer of 1698, and shortly thereafter trouble broke out between the Baptists and the Presbyterians. The Baptists thereupon withdrew from the joint meeting in the Barbados store and the Presbyterians were left in control.[17] Whoever was at fault in the split, Andrews seems to have become quite discouraged during the course of the controversy and for a time thought of returning to New England. Thomas Clayton, the S. P. G. (Society for the Propagation of the Gospel in Foreign Parts) missionary of the Church of England, did what he could to further the dissension and to increase Andrews' discouragement.[18] However, three years later Andrews was ordained pastor in Philadelphia, by whom it is not known. In all probability he was ordained by a council of ministers, called in accordance with New England usage, from Newark, Elizabethtown, and other places to the north.[19]

Delaware was at this time, before 1702, a part of the colony of Pennsylvania. A Presbyterian minister, Samuel Davis, perhaps from Ireland, settled at Lewes in 1698. Here he operated a store and devoted a small part of his time to preaching. He had come to America about 1684 and resided first in Maryland, where Colonel Ninian Beal, a Presbyterian elder of some means, gave him a piece of land. In 1691, or earlier, he became pastor at Snow Hill but was forced to leave there because of some difficulties into which he seems to have fallen.[20] The church at New Castle, Delaware, is older even than that of Lewes. Founded originally as a Dutch Calvinist Church in 1657, the congregation gradually received into its membership English Dissenters, French Huguenots, Scots, and Scotch-Irish. Perhaps as early as 1684 or 1685 it had become an English-speaking Calvinist Church which was essentially Presbyterian. In 1698, John Wilson was sent there from Boston in company with Benjamin Woodbridge, who was going to Philadelphia. He was, however, not permanently settled until 1703.[21]

Farther to the south, in the colony of Maryland, Francis Doughty was preaching as early as 1659. He had fled from New York sometime before August 6, 1657. English Puritans and Scottish Presbyterians came into the colony freely under Lord Baltimore's tolerant policies. His colonial governor at this time was William Stone, a zealous Protestant, and a brother-in-law of Doughty. In 1677, Lord Baltimore wrote to the Privy Council, " The greatest part of the inhabitants of that province (three of four at least) do consist of Praesbiterians, Independants, Anabaptists, and Quakers. those of the church of England as well as those of the Romish being the fewest . . ." [22] Doughty seems not to have settled in any one congregation but to have itinerated in both Virginia and Maryland.[23]

Sometime before April 13, 1669,[24] Doughty was joined by Matthew Hill, an English Presbyterian who had been ejected from a Yorkshire parish in 1662 for nonconformity. Richard Baxter had been instrumental in aiding him to reach America. He settled first in Charles County and then near Port Tobacco. Doughty and Hill had about this same time a colleague of doubtful value. Charles Nicolet, probably of British origin,[25] drew down the wrath of the Upper House of Burgesses and the governor for allowing himself to be used as a mouthpiece for a certain faction on the occasion of his preaching before the Lower House. On April 16, 1669, he was compelled to apologize and shortly thereafter he removed to New England.[26] Matthew Hill suffered also from other grievous troubles, perhaps from inroads by the Quaker missionaries George Fox and William Edmundson, who evangelized that area of Maryland quite successfully in 1672. A very real help to Doughty and Hill were the ruling elders William Durand and Colonel Ninian Beal.[27]

Maryland, Virginia, and Barbados had received a number of Scotch-Irish refugees during the decade 1670–1680. These colonists appealed to the Presbytery of Laggan, in Ireland, for ministers, and William Traill went out to Maryland about 1682. He remained in the colony, perhaps on the eastern shore, until 1688, when he removed to Scotland.

In 1683, Traill was joined by Francis Makemie, a young minister from his former presbytery in Ireland. Makemie did not settle at any one place but itinerated widely along the coasts of Maryland, Virginia, the Carolinas, and Barbados.

While on his many journeys, Makemie became acquainted with Puritan settlers. Through them he began, as early as 1684, a correspondence with Increase Mather. This correspondence he maintained throughout his lifetime. The year 1691 found Makemie in London, where no doubt he met Mather personally and became acquainted with the leaders of the newly formed United Brethren, a group who were to mean much to him and to American Presbyterianism in the years ahead. Makemie's subsequent career reveals on several occasions a basic attitude very much akin to the Heads of Agreement of the United Brethren. From the General Fund of the United Brethren, Makemie was later also to draw substantial financial assistance.

The following year Makemie was resident in Accomac, Virginia, where he had established himself in 1690. Here George Keith, then still a zealous reforming Quaker, visited him in 1692. Makemie had published a catechism to which Keith had many objections.[28] Although he challenged Makemie to a public debate on the matter, Makemie told him to print his sentiments. He did so almost at once, but in what manner is unknown. Makemie prepared *An Answer to George Keith's Libel* in July of that same year and took the manuscript with him on a long-anticipated journey to Philadelphia. Sometime later he sent the work to Increase Mather.[29] Mather had it published in Boston, setting his imprimatur upon it, as required by law, dated March 31, 1694-1695. In it Makemie vindicated his conduct in relation to Keith's challenges and attacks and defended his doctrinal views. Keith's *Libel* itself was incorporated verbatim by Makemie in his *Answer*.

In 1696, Makemie was resident in Barbados. Here he wrote a remarkable work, *Truths in a True Light, a Pastoral Letter to the Reformed Protestants in Barbados* . . . , which was published in Edinburgh in 1699. He argued that the archenemy of the Protestant cause, the Papacy, had always sought to conquer the Protestants by intensifying their differences and triumphing as they cut each other down. He showed that the Dissenters agreed with the Church of England on all the great issues of faith, and urged that among the Dissenters themselves it was folly to magnify such small differences as did exist. Clearly, Makemie was following the policies of the United Brethren of London. From Barbados also he continued his friendly correspondence with Increase Mather.[30]

Meanwhile Josias Mackie, another Scotch-Irish minister, had settled on Elizabeth River, Virginia, in a church that Makemie had occasionally supplied after the death of a former, otherwise now unknown, Scotch-Irish pastor. Mackie cared for this church from about 1691 until his death in 1716.[31] Matthew Hill's work at Patuxent, Maryland, had prospered also. Hill died in 1679, but an elder, Colonel Ninian Beal, had both the zeal and the means needed to carry the church forward. About 1703 this congregation, now a rather strong church of mingled English and Scottish Presbyterians, secured as pastor another Englishman, Nathaniel Taylor.[32]

Another Presbyterian plantation in the American colonies during the seventeenth century was made in South Carolina. Since, however, these Presbyterians never affiliated with those in the middle colonies, their history cannot be discussed here.[33] New England Presbyterianism, as distinct from Congregationalism, also requires special treatment.[34]

The active policy adopted by the Anglican Church about 1700 created for these churches a very serious threat. The S. P. G. received its charter in 1701. This charter defined its mission in terms of a ministry to the colonists, without mention of Indian missions.[35] Its first missionaries were George Keith, now a fiery Anglican, and John Talbot. These men, both polemically inclined, spent two years, 1702–1704, in the colonies on a survey of religious conditions, and in a determined attempt to bring all Dissenters into conformity with the Anglican Church. Moreover, a number of prominent English officials, Governor Cornbury of New York, Lewis Morris of New Jersey, and others, began to urge the establishment of the Anglican Church. The Church of England was already established in Virginia. At an assembly in Burlington, New Jersey, the Anglican clergy in the colonies demanded that in order to qualify for certain offices in the colonies men must receive the Sacrament in the Anglican Church. They had just succeeded in making this conformity a requirement for membership in the colonial assembly of South Carolina. This ambitious program of the Anglicans disturbed deeply all the Dissenters of the middle and southern colonies.

New England also was troubled at this time. In Massachusetts, Governor Andros was threatening the entire New England way, and the Anglican Church had begun to get a foothold. The older English-trained clergy were fast dying off and younger untried colonials were replacing them. Some seem to have had marked Presbyterian tendencies,[36] and even some of the older clergy were persuaded that the more highly centralized Presbyterian form of Church government had become a necessity in view of the dangerous circumstances. In 1705 a convention of ministers met in Boston and drew up a set of Proposals. In these the two principal recommendations were the founding of local ministerial associations and the establishment of permanent, self-per-petuating consociations which would have considerable authority. These Proposals show a marked dependence upon the Heads of Agreement. The recommendation that consociations be formed seemed quite too Presbyterian, and Massachusetts Congregationalists did not follow it. On the other hand, numerous ministers' associations sprang up almost at once, and with little opposition soon took over the powers of licensure and ordination of candidates for the ministry. These associations, by meeting more or less regularly, and by virtue of the powers that controlled entrance into the ministry, did come to exercise a considerable influence, and thereby strengthened Massachusetts Congregationalism in no small measure.[37]

The Puritans and Presbyterians in the other colonies also took steps to strengthen their positions. In Connecticut the Saybrook Platform of 1708 was to combine the scheme of the Heads of Agreement with fifteen additional articles and produce a sort of halfway house between Congregationalism and Presbyterianism. But even before this action the Puritans and Presbyterians in the middle colonies had organized on a more explicitly Presbyterian basis.

After a stay of some years in Barbados, preaching and engaging in trade, Francis Makemie had returned to Accomac County, Virginia, in 1698. The following year he secured from the Accomac court, on the basis of his previous license in Barbados, a license to preach in his own house and in one other some miles distant. Shortly thereafter he seems to have organized churches at Snow Hill, Rehoboth, and several other places in Somerset County, Maryland.[38] Ever a traveler, Makemie made another journey to London sometime during the summer of 1704. Several errands may have called him there. Colonel Anthony Lawson, of the Elizabeth River Presbyterian colony, and others were deeply interested in strengthening their colony. In this interest Makemie published in London, *A Plain and Friendly Persuasive to the Inhabitants of Virginia and Maryland for Promoting Towns and Cohabitation*. Of all the American colonies, he declared, Virginia and Maryland were lagging behind because they had so few towns. Religion, morals, trade, and all other phases of the life of these two colonies were suffering because the completely decentralized plantation life inevitably brought on stagnation. Only by establishing towns could these colonies enjoy a healthy growth.

While in London, Makemie also sought to strengthen the colonial Church. From the General Fund of the United Brethren he secured the promise of money enough to support two ministers in the colonies for a period of two years. Two young Presbyterian ministers, seemingly then resident in London, were secured, John Hampton and George McNish. Hampton, of Scotch-Irish parentage and educated at the University of Glasgow, may have been in the London area since before 1700. McNish, a Scot, was also from the University of Glasgow. Makemie and his two new colleagues arrived in Maryland sometime in 1705.[39]

It was in the midst of such circumstances, then, that a presbytery was founded in the middle colonies. Unfortunately the first page of their record book has disappeared. Who attended the meeting and what was the basis upon which they agreed to organize remains therefore unknown except by inference from later events. The meeting evidently was held at Philadelphia sometime in March of 1706. Seven ministers seem to have attended, or agreed *in absentia* to become members: Francis Makemie, John Hampton, George McNish, Jedediah Andrews, John Wilson, Samuel Davis, and Nathaniel Taylor.

Francis Makemie has traditionally been given the credit for bringing about the organization of the presbytery. He was an inveterate traveler, well acquainted with colonial conditions, and a man of considerable ability. His attitudes toward the English Puritans, as revealed in his associations with the United Brethren, in his *Pastoral Letter* to Barbados, in his friendly correspondence with Increase Mather, and in his general acceptability among the Puritan congregations that he had visited in his numerous travels, made him an ideal leader for the founding of a presbytery which would hold together so many diverse elements. It was unfortunate that he lived to attend only the first two sessions of the presbytery, those of 1706 and 1707.

How much authority this presbytery assumed over their ministers and their congregations is difficult to determine. Since it is certain that no constitution was adopted, and since Makemie refers to the organization as " a meeting of ministers " only, it has been urged at times that the presbytery assumed no authority over either the clergy or the congregations. Yet the presence of elders at the second regular meeting indicates plainly that some congregations at least recognized the presbytery. Moreover, as early as this second meeting, the presbytery assumed the right to require a minister's attendance. The assertion made by John Thomson in 1721 that by common consent the presbytery had adhered to Presbyterian standards was no doubt correct. The more Congregationally minded ministers and people would not see in such a presbytery any very great step beyond the Heads of Agreement of 1690–1691 between the English Presbyterians and Congregationalists. With Increase Mather they might well have felt that the existing differences among Congregationalists themselves were so great that " they who go under the name of Congregational must withdraw Communion from one another as well as from Presbyterians, if differing sentiments about Disciplinary questions, be a sufficient ground for division and separation."[40] The Presbyterians of Scottish and Scotch-Irish origins, who were in the minority among most of the congregations that adhered to the presbytery, gained all that was felt needful in that general Presbyterian patterns were being followed.

The origins of these seven ministers who founded the presbytery have been hotly disputed by various factions within the later Church. It was often asserted by many that the right of certain views and practices to a place in the American Presbyterian Church depended upon whether or not these doctrines and policies were in harmony with those of the founding fathers. The founding fathers must have erected a Church very much like that from which they came. Therefore, if it could be shown that a majority of these seven ministers came from a certain country, then the original charter of American Presbyterianism could readily be reconstructed by studying the Presbyterian Church of that land as it then was. Throughout the nineteenth century recourse was had to this fallacious line of reasoning.[41]

Francis Makemie, the first moderator of the presbytery, was a Scotch-Irishman, with strong ties to both England and New England. Samuel Davis, the merchant-pastor of Lewes, Delaware, probably came from Ireland. Three of the ministers in this newly founded presbytery were from New England. Jedediah Andrews, pastor of the church at Philadelphia, was the son of New England Presbyterians and a graduate of Harvard College. John Wilson, pastor at New Castle, was also from New England. Increase and Cotton Mather had been instrumental in sending him to Delaware, since many New Englanders were settling there on lands purchased by Connecticut. The third pastor from New England was Nathaniel Taylor, of Patuxent, Maryland. George McNish and John Hampton, whom the United Brethren had sent over to the colonies, were the other two charter members of the presbytery. McNish was a Scot and Hampton was Scotch-Irish. If the ministers of this new presbytery were of mixed origins and backgrounds, their congregations were even more so. These congregations had been formed largely from settlers of English origins, from either old or New England. Some had received later admixtures of Scotch-Irish and Scottish members, and a few had received, in addition, members from Dutch, Huguenot, and Welsh churches. Here and there a few German names are found on church lists, indicating accessions from German sources as well.

For many years the closest ties of the presbytery were with New

England and London. Though pleas were sent to Scotland and Ireland also, most of the ministerial recruits and the financial aid that came to the early presbytery were from Boston and London. The minutes of the Synod of Ulster record only one plea from the presbytery in America upon which any action was taken. This plea, received in 1712, met with indifferent handling.[42] The Presbyterian ministers of Dublin, who were much less strict in their adherence to Scotch-Irish Presbyterianism, were, however, of aid to the colonial Church on several occasions. The General Assembly of the Church of Scotland gave the colonial presbytery some assistance, as did also the Synod of Glasgow and various Scottish individuals. Except for such financial aid, however, the presbytery began and continued as a purely indigenous organization. It was not, as has been asserted so often, largely a Scottish and Scotch-Irish Church patterned closely after the Scottish model.

The middle colonies were to be the field of the new American Presbyterian Church. What Presbyterian sentiment there was among the Puritans in New England had adapted itself to the now prevalent "Presbyterianized Congregationalism." The Presbyterians in the colonies south of Virginia were so far removed from those of the middle colonies that several decades were to elapse before a union of these two groups was to become possible. Within the middle colonies growth for the new Church was to come from two sources: the reception of additional existing Puritan churches and the establishment of new churches on the rapidly expanding frontier. The original presbytery seems to have been founded hurriedly, leaving a host of organizational details to be worked out later, and with the full expectation that other churches and other ministers would soon join with the founders.

Though founded in relative obscurity by a few men, American Presbyterianism was thrust suddenly upon the attention of a great part of British colonial America by an incident that befell Makemie a few months after the presbytery was organized. On December 27, 1706, the presbytery held a special meeting at Freehold, New Jersey, for the ordination of John Boyd. Makemie was present at the meeting, and just before, or just after, preached also at Woodbridge, New Jersey. Early in January, he and Hampton went up to New York City, where, at the invitation of the English and Irish Presbyterians, he preached in a private house. From there they went to Newtown, Long Island, in order to preach there. Lord Cornbury, then governor of New York, had both men arrested on a charge of preaching without a license. Not until March 1 were the men able to secure their release on a writ of *habeas corpus*. Even then they were released only until their trial, which was to be held in June. On March 22, the presbytery met at Philadelphia and both men attended. Makemie sought aid from his friends the Boston ministers, who in turn wrote immediately to the United Brethren leaders in London. Hampton was let off at once, but Makemie was tried on June 3, 1707. At his trial he was defended by three of the ablest lawyers of New York. His defense was that he had a license to preach as a Dissenting minister. Though this license had been issued in Barbados, it had been recognized in Virginia, and it was valid in any part of the realm. The court acquitted him, but in vengeful spite Cornbury assessed against Makemie the whole cost of the trial, a sum of £83, 7s., 6d., nearly an average annual salary for a minister. So aroused were the colonists of New York by this vicious act by Cornbury, that a bill was passed by the Assembly the following year forbidding the compelling of a man to pay the costs of prosecuting him. Specific mention of Makemie's case was made at the time. The Assembly also preferred charges in London against Cornbury, and he was recalled in disgrace.[48] Though it cost him sorely, Makemie's trial did bring the infant Presbyterian Church to the favorable attention of many Dissenters in the colonies. The victory that he gained for the Church by standing the trial was his last act on behalf of the new Church. By the next year Makemie was dead.

Though the natural ties of the Puritans of Long Island, New York, and New Jersey were with New England, and more especially with Connecticut, it was apparent that their churches could never be affiliated in any way with the New England churches. In both Massachusetts and Connecticut the churches were established under the colonial governments. In the colonies to the southward the Puritan churches were under other colonial governments. For their churches to be allied with the established churches of the two self-assertive New England colonies would never have been tolerated by their colonial governors or assemblies. These Puritan churches had to remain unorganized in the face of the rising Anglican power in both New York and New Jersey, or else find some means of uniting either among themselves or with some body of like convictions. The Saybrook Platform of 1708 made Connecticut Congregationalism very much like Presbyterianism. The patterns of the new presbytery founded in the middle colonies had not yet been rigidly fixed. Union with this presbytery was accordingly the logical step for all these Puritan congregations.

Interest in the presbytery grew among the Puritan congregations on Long Island. Soon the churches at Newtown, Setauket, Jamaica, and Southhampton joined the presbytery. Goshen also came in. These congregations were made up almost wholly of New Englanders. In New York City a group of Presbyterians organized a church about 1717. It was 1719 before a building could be erected, and even then financial aid from New England was necessary. This New York congregation had members from New England, old England, Scotland, and Ulster.

In the Jerseys, the older New England Puritan churches at Woodbridge, Newark, Elizabethtown, Shrewsbury, Pittsgrove (earlier Pilesgrove), Fairton, and Cold Spring became a part of the presbytery during its first twelve years. Though founded originally by New Englanders, these congregations were now very mixed. Scots, Scotch-Irish, Dutch, Huguenots, Welsh, and English settlers were being freely received by all these Puritan churches.

Settlement of the Scotch-Irish in Pennsylvania had begun to gather momentum.[44] The first mass immigration did not come until in 1720, but along the upper and lower branches of the Octorara, Scotch-Irish were moving in. Along the Elk River, the Brandywine, and other streams, small bands of settlers were working their way. Shortly after 1720 congregations were in existence at Pequea, Lower West Nottingham, Derry, New London, Pencader, and the Forks of the Brandywine. Delaware also received a great many Scotch-Irish. As in Pennsylvania, these settlers moved into the wilderness along the river valleys. At Apoquinimy (Drawyers) a church was founded of Dutch, Huguenot, and other nationalities.

Maryland Presbyterianism continued to grow for a few years, but soon failed, as did the Virginia congregations which were more or less adjuncts of the Maryland churches. Only Cecil and Somerset counties were able to maintain their early churches. After the Anglican Church became established, immigrants who were Presbyterians tended to avoid the colony. Few ministers came to it and gradually most of the Presbyterians conformed to the Church of England.

By 1716, Presbyterian churches had so multiplied that a synod was formed to comprise four presbyteries — Philadelphia, New Castle, Long Island, and Snow Hill — though the last named was never erected. This synod was given no specific constitutional powers or charter. Rather, it continued as it had before, and was in fact the presbytery of the whole while the three newly formed presbyteries functioned as local or regional courts. This ambiguous character of the synod's jurisdiction over against that of the presbyteries was to cause difficulties in the future, yet little else could have been done at this period in the Church's growth. Seventeen additional ministers had joined the Church since its founding. Five had come from New England, three from Wales, six from Scotland, two from Ireland, and one was of uncertain origin. He also was probably a New Englander. Of the eight Scottish and Scotch-Irish clergymen, three had been sent out by the Presbyterian ministers of London. The total number of ministers in active service was now twenty-five: eight Scotsmen, seven Scotch-Irishmen, seven New Englanders, and three Welshmen.[45]

Among the new ministers were two of the most eminent men in American Presbyterianism, Jonathan Dickinson and William Tennent, Sr. The early life of the latter has, until recently, been quite obscure.[46]

William Tennent was born about 1673, perhaps in Scotland, rather than in Ireland as the usual tradition goes. On his mother's side he was related to James Logan, of Pennsylvania. He was educated at the University of Edinburgh, receiving his M.A. on July 11, 1693. Sometime later he was licensed by one of the Scottish presbyteries, from which he presented credentials to the General Synod of Ulster, at Antrim, in 1701.[47] He was received by the synod as a probationer, but seems to have taken no charge. The following year he married Katherine Kennedy, the daughter of a famous Presbyterian minister, Gilbert Kennedy, for whom was named the first son, Gilbert Tennent, born February 5, 1703.

For some now unknown reason, Tennent took orders in the Anglican Church, July 1, 1704. In 1703 the Irish Parliament had passed severe laws against the Roman Catholics and the Presbyterians.[48] Some of Tennent's relatives had conformed to the Anglican Church,[49] perhaps during this period of extreme intolerance. Tennent at one time, just when is not certain, was chaplain to a nobleman in northern Ireland who may have been an Anglican. Some one, or all, of these circumstances may have been the cause of Tennent's going into the Anglican Church.

Quite a few years later with his wife and a family of four sons and one daughter, Tennent landed in Philadelphia and was "courteouslie entertained by Mr. James Logan, Agent and Secretarie of all Pensilvania." Ten days later, September 16, 1718, he applied for admission to the synod then in session at Philadelphia. His credentials "and the testimony of some brethren here present"[50] were sufficient to gain him admission. Evidently some members of the presbytery had known Tennent when he was in Scotland or Ireland. The synod then asked for a written statement of his reasons for "dissenting from the established Church in Ireland." His seven reasons, six referring to episcopal polity and one to Arminianism, were inserted in the book of synod "ad futuram rei memoriam," and the moderator was ordered to "give him a serious exhortation to continue steadfast in his now holy profession." Tennent had fallen from Presbyterianism once, a fact that may account, in part, for the manner in which the main Scotch-Irish faction treated him and his sons. He settled among the Puritan Presbyterians, first at

East Chester, New York, and later, 1720, at Bedford, New York.

The conditions under which the Presbyterians labored were quite adverse. They had few strong congregations, except in the areas settled some time earlier by New Englanders. Out on the frontier the members of each struggling congregation were scattered over a wide area. The small meetinghouses were often far away from the homes of the people. Roads were very bad. Frequently the meetings had to be held in barns. The people were poor, and unable to support a pastor in any adequate manner. Preachers were hard to secure, especially for the frontier charges. More than one minister or candidate who came from Ireland was found to be a renegade who had forged his credentials.

The settlers to whom these Presbyterian churches ministered had come to these new frontier settlements with little vital and practical godliness. The religious life of Scotland at this time was falling more and more under control of the so-called Moderate party. The Presbyterianism of Ulster, while intensely and polemically orthodox, was especially devoid of deep or fervent piety during this period. New England Puritanism also had lost its early zeal and spirit. On the frontier, poverty, hardship, suffering, disease, bereavements, Indian wars, sudden death all bred callousness, resentment, and cynicism. Coarseness and indecency were only too prevalent. Extreme individualism stifled brotherly kindness and mercy. The race for land and business opportunities, competition between the old and the new settlers, or between settlers from different homelands, created tensions in public and private life. Litigiosity abounded, promoted by much slander and talebearing, and accentuated by the very excessive use of liquor. The lack of educational institutions and common social activities hindered progress within the various groups, and delayed their fusion. The fact that many of these immigrants had fled persecution at home, had come to the colonies as indentured servants, or had been deported from the homelands, only increased these antisocial attitudes.

When all the old traditions, mores, conventions, and customs of the homeland which made for a formal adherence to religion and morality were sloughed off at the frontier, indifference to the Church and even to common morals, became everywhere evident. The Church was weak in all these immigrant groups, and even weaker in the community at large, because of the great number of opposing Churches or sects. Franklin said of Andrews, the Presbyterian minister in Philadelphia, that he spent most of his time in polemical preaching against other Churches or in defense of his own. Much of the religious work was of this order. The social effects of irreligion, natural religion and dead polemical orthodoxies of many varieties were more apparent on the frontier, where no traditional restraints made for at least superficial morality, than they were in the old, stable communities of Europe and Great Britain.

Under such circumstances the ministry of any Church would be severely tested. The favorable lot of an established Church and ministry was not to be found by the clergy of these Presbyterian churches. Such prestige and influence as they were to have must be won by each minister individually. Whatever he was to accomplish in the way of spiritual, moral, educational, or benevolent advances depended in large measure upon his own influence and ability. He could look for no help from other local organizations or from Church boards. The situation demanded a ministry endowed with the resources of deep piety and great personal zeal and initiative.

Such men, unfortunately, were not to be found in large numbers in the early synod. Among the New Englanders there were a few like Jonathan Dickinson and John Pierson. Among the Scotch-Irish and Scots there were William Tennent, Sr., and George Gillespie. On the whole preaching was of an order not calculated to arouse or quicken the Church. Even of the better ministers, the greater number were very slow to grasp the meaning of the American situation. They continued to live, think, and act as though they were still a part of their homelands. They made no move to found local schools, or local institutions such as had sprung up so quickly in the New England colonies. The homeland remained the only conceivable source of all education, culture, and standards. In colonies such as the Middle Atlantic colonies, where the population was so mixed, each was but one of many groups which felt much the same about their own homelands. The frontier conditions were soon to break down all these old orders, leaving some men to continue living in an unreal world of yesterday while impelling others to attempt the creation of new forms and new orders adequate for preaching the Gospel in the frontier situation.

2

THE EMERGENCE OF A PATTERN

Not long after the growing Church had become a synod embracing three presbyteries, factions began to appear within its membership. As time wore on, certain trends and events made these groups more and more distinct. Within a decade after the first open clash of opinion in the synod, the Church was broken into three well-defined and self-perpetuating parties. The synod's laxity in disciplining unworthy and scandalous ministers caused the first rupture.[1] Robert Cross, a young Scotch-Irish pastor, was charged with a serious moral offense. His presbytery, New Castle, referred his case to synod without a hearing. In synod he was found guilty of fornication. Thereupon he confessed his guilt with great show of repentance, and the synod let him go with no greater penalty than that he should not occupy his pulpit for the next four Sundays. He was allowed also to retain his membership on the controlling committee of the synod. After four Sundays out of his pulpit, he might resume his work if the people would consent. (The following year Cross reported to the synod that his people were paying him so poorly that he would have to look for a new congregation. Evidently he had remained in charge of the church.)

To this decision and sentence George Gillespie, a minister of New Castle Presbytery, entered a formal protest. The following year, 1721, he tried twice to have the affair reconsidered, but lost.[2] He then introduced an overture which caused considerable discussion. It was finally passed as follows: " As we have been for many years in the exercise of Presbyterian government and church discipline, as exercised by the Presbyterians in the best reformed Churches, as far as the nature and constitution of this country will allow, our opinion is, that if any brother have any overture to offer to be formed into an act by the Synod, for the better carrying on in matters of our government and discipline, that he may bring it in against next Synod." Though a majority of the twenty-one ministers and nine elders present approved this overture, six ministers — four New Englanders and two Welshmen — entered a written protest. Synod appointed two Scotsmen to draw up an answer to this protest.[3]

Just what lay back of all this has often been disputed. Some things, however, can be said with certainty. The argument of the overture is that, since for many years these Presbyterians have been using the general forms and procedures of the European Presbyterian Churches, there would be nothing against carrying European Presbyterian usage farther by allowing any member who wished to present overtures looking forward to the passage of such acts as would improve the government and discipline of the Church. The wording of the overture indicates that previous to that time no such acts or laws had been made, and that some agreement was necessary before such acts or laws could be of any binding authority. Whatever constitution they then had did not allow such measures.

Moreover, it is fairly certain that Gillespie was looking forward to introducing at the next synod some measures that would make for better government and discipline. What were these measures? Ashbel Green was no doubt right in seeing in this move the first skirmish on the American scene of the great " subscription controversy " then raging in the Presbyterian Churches of Scotland, Ireland, and England.[4] Gillespie may well have had in mind an act to establish a more highly organized Presbyterianism, with definite standards to which subscription would be required. Stricter discipline would thus be made legally possible.

Required subscription to a doctrinal creed and to articles of Church government was not new to eighteenth century Presbyterians. The Solemn League and Covenant of Scotland had demanded all this and more. At the Revolution Settlement of 1690 in Scotland, when the Presbyterian Church was established by law, the Westminster Confession of Faith was ratified by Parliament as the Confession of the Establishment.[5] The judicatories of the Church of Scotland were then allowed to use subscription to this Confession as a test of ministerial communion. Ministers who had served under the former episcopal establishment, or Roman Catholic priests, were to be excluded if they would not subscribe to the Confession. A few years later, 1696, any minister or lay member of the Church was forbidden by the General Assembly to speak, write, preach, teach, or print anything whatsoever that would be contrary to, or even inconsistent with, any view contained in the Confession.[6]

As a bulwark against heterodoxy in the Scottish Church subscription was soon found insufficient. Professor John Simson professed subscription and so did all his many supporters and students. He was defended by saying that he had but rephrased in more modern terminology the truths of the subscribed Confession. For over a decade his case was before the General Assembly. Finally he was found guilty of expressing "himself in such terms, as are subversive to these blessed truths," though the Assembly acknowledged him personally as orthodox.[7]

So much dissatisfaction was felt over the conduct of the Simson trials that some presbyteries adopted more stringent tests of orthodoxy. Candidates were asked to answer "Yes" or "No" to hypothetical explanations of certain doctrines. A candidate, in Auchterarder Presbytery, upon being rejected as "unsound" after such a test, appealed to the General Assembly in 1717. General Assembly ruled that no further tests of a candidate's orthodoxy could be used than those laid down by itself. Moreover, it pronounced the "Auchterarder Creed" heretical in no uncertain terms.[8]

The Auchterarder statement was at worst a clumsy overstatement born of excessive zeal. But partisan spirit made of it a growing controversy. Gradually the supporters of the Auchterarder policies began to spread their views more widely by circulating reprints of an old book entitled *The Marrow of Modern Divinity*. The book soon became extremely popular. The General Assembly's Commission in 1721 extracted from this book numerous sentences and passages. These were chosen without due regard for their context, however. The General Assembly then pronounced these and the *Marrow* to be heretical.[9] The Assembly was led by men who were so intent upon certain political objectives that they fell into error themselves. The defenders of the book, the "Marrow Men," were able to show that the Assembly had condemned statements in the book that were quoted from Luther and other famous divines. Furthermore they had made certain statements in their act condemning the *Marrow* that were contrary to the Westminster Confession of Faith. The General Assembly's Commission now began a finish fight against the "Marrow Men."[10]

Thus far had the controversy over subscription and orthodoxy gone in Scotland by 1722. It is amply clear that the American Presbyterians were quite cognizant of it all. Some of the American ministers had come from Scotland after the struggle began. Others had friends and relatives in the homeland.

The Presbyterians of England had also passed through a controversy over subscribing to the Westminster symbols.[11] For some time they had been united with the Congregationalists as the United Brethren, under the Heads of Agreement formulated in 1690-1691. The growing anxiety over the spread of Arianism led many to feel that every Dissenting minister, Presbyterian or Congregationalist, ought to be asked to declare his views on the doctrine of the Trinity. He was offered his choice of doing so by using Article I of the Church of England's XXXIX Articles, the answers to Questions V and VI of the Westminster Assembly's Shorter Catechism, or words of his own choosing. Whatever words he chose, declare himself he must.

Some ministers complied readily; others, though they subscribed, were accused of using ambiguous language; and some refused to subscribe at all. In 1719 at Salters Hall, the assembly of Dissenting ministers was split on this issue. The nonsubscribers professed their belief in the doctrine of the Trinity, but asserted that " humane compositions " could never be used as tests of orthodoxy. The Bible alone could so be used. The subscribers replied by saying that the issue was plain enough. The doctrine of the Trinity was so essential and so well known that there was little room for doubt or hesitancy. To this the nonsubscribers replied by saying that there would always be controversy over any manmade explanations of the Biblical truths. Hence it was better to subscribe to the Bible than to someone's explanation of it. No explanation could satisfy all. Moreover, if they were forced to subscribe to what someone considered the correct doctrine of the Trinity, they would soon be compelled to subscribe to other authentic interpretations and no one knew where the process would end.

Since there was no binding constitutional organization behind the United Brethren's Assembly, the two contending groups merely met apart after 1719. No regular act of procedure separated them. Some of the leading men, such as Edmund Calamy and Isaac Watts, had nothing to do with either side. Calamy felt that there were elements other than religion involved. Gradually many of the nonsubscribing party conformed to the Church of England. A few others became avowed Arians. This brief controversy and its results soon became for many the classical illustration of what opposition to constitutionally imposed creeds really meant. Those who rejected subscription were thereafter not infrequently considered secret heretics or hypocrites. Rigidly enforced subscription seemed essential to the preservation of the Church.

Those members of the new synod in America who had come from Ireland were aware, also, of the subscription controversy that had been raging for some time in the General Synod of Ulster. This body was at first quite loosely organized. Frequent reference was made to the Acts of the General Assembly of the Church of Scotland, yet the General Synod was conscious of being a wholly separate body. In 1698 it was voted " That Young men, when licensed to preach, be obliged to Subscribe the Confession of Faith, in all the Articles thereof, as the Confession of their Faith." [12] This was made more exact and binding in 1705. Moreover, subscription was now required to the worship, discipline, and government of the synod, [13] although an official Directory of Discipline was not as yet in existence. A year later a check was made to see whether or not the various presbyteries were requiring subscription. They were. [14]

In 1697 the synod had appointed a committee to draw up a set of questions to be asked of young men at their trials for ordination. [15] Twenty years later no body of questions had been agreed upon. In 1716 a committee was appointed to draw up a scheme of discipline for the synod. [16] The following year this committee was ordered to incorporate into its work the questions to be propounded at ordinations. [17] The Committee on the Discipline never finished its work. Quite evidently the committees were unwilling to act.

The reasons for all these delaying tactics were chiefly two: first, a great difference of opinion regarding the rights of a presbytery over against the rights of the synod, [18] and, secondly, a growing tension over the matter of subscription.

The controversy over subscription was occasioned by fears and suspicions. An informal organization of the more influential and able ministers, known as the Belfast Society, had dominated the affairs of the synod for years. Some of the Belfast Society were friends and students of Professor John Simson, of Scotland. The entire society were against compulsory subscription to the creeds. They were, moreover, keenly interested in contemporary religious thought and literature. No heterodoxy was ever proved against them, yet many suspected them of secret heresy and evil designs. [19]

In 1719 a long, hard fight for unconditional subscription to the Westminster Confession and Catechisms, and to the partially defined worship, government, and discipline of the Church, was inaugurated by a group of ministers opposed to the Belfast Society. They called the Belfast group "New Lights." After four years of exceedingly bitter controversy a group of more moderate men, led by Robert Craighead, brought about a compromise. This compromise, called the Pacific Act, reasserted the loyalty of the Church to the Westminster Confession and Catechisms and required subscription to them by all, " which is thus to be understood as now is practis'd by the Presbyteries, that if any person call'd upon to subscribe shall scruple any phrase or phrases in the Confession, he shall have leave to use his own expressions, which the Presbytry (sic) shall accept of, Providing they judge such a person sound in the Faith, and that such expressions are consistent with the substance of the doctrine." [20] This Pacific Act did not produce peace. The following year, 1721, the strife was more virulent than before.

When, therefore, Gillespie's rather vague overture was brought into the synod at Philadelphia in the fall of 1721, the New England group seem to have connected it at once with the subscription controversies in Great Britain. Accordingly they opposed Gillespie's overture, and protested when it was passed over their opposition. Gradually, in civic and religious affairs, there had been a growing tension between the over-enterprising Scotch-Irish and the older settlers of New England, Welsh, Quaker, and Dutch stocks. A bitter squabble had been raging for some time in the New York Presbyterian congregation, between the Scotch-Irish newcomers and the older Puritan group. Andrews, in a letter to Benjamin Colman, a Congregational minister of Boston who was very friendly with the New England Presbyterians in the middle colonies, traces Gillespie's move and the opposition to it to this strife in New York and to the Irish subscription controversy. [21] Two parties were beginning to form, one led by Dickinson and comprising the more cosmopolitan elements of the infant synod, and the other embracing most of the Scotch-Irish. If the Scotch-Irish were able to secure subscription to the Westminster doctrinal symbols and Directory, they would be in a fair way to control the Church. Therefore the four New Englanders and the two Welshmen protested. Gillespie's move seems to have been without party spirit and made in the interests of moral decency among the clergy. It soon became a party issue, controlled by a group among whom none other than Robert Cross was a leader.

When the synod met in 1722, Jonathan Dickinson preached the opening sermon. He argued that the Bible was a sufficient rule on all the major issues of crucial importance. He developed the same argument that was used by all Dissenters against the Church of England and the Roman Catholic Church. He declared that to make extra-Biblical laws was to say that the Bible is not sufficient, whereas against the Romanists and the Anglicans the stock Presbyterian argument was that the Bible, and the Bible only, is all-sufficient for all necessary doctrines and rules. He further argued that if it be said that an official interpretation of the Bible is necessary, because men interpret it differently, that is not a new argument, but merely the argument of the authoritarianism of Rome and the Anglicans. In fact, Romanists, Anglicans, Presbyterians, and all the rest, each advancing a creedal interpretation of Scripture, prove that human interpretations are too fallible to be made into official binding statements of what is, and what is not, Biblical truth. When this is done, he asserted, the official interpretation, and not the Bible itself, becomes the rule of faith and life. This would mean also that there no longer existed any standard by which the orthodox creed could be tested or revised. It would in the end supersede the Bible as the authority over men's consciences. Moreover, in his opinion, the creedal statements and the Biblical truth may, by virtue of theological controversy, actually cease to be rules of faith and life and become things in and for themselves. When a Church judicature undertakes such legislative power, it usurps a power which Christ never gave to it. This is, he continued, exactly what the Church of Rome and the Church of England and others have done in the name of tradition, order, necessity, suppression of heresy, etc. Against such usurpations the fathers of Presbyterianism had taken their stand on the all-sufficiency of sacred Scripture.[22]

A compromise was then reached whereby four points were agreed upon: the "keys of church discipline" grant "executive power of church government" to presbyteries and synods; the "mere circumstantials of church discipline, such as the time, place, and mode of carrying on in the government of the church" may be regulated as the judicatory sees fit, conformable to the Word of God, but these acts may not be imposed on conscientious objectors; synods may compose directories of government and "recommend" them to the lower judicatories, which may "decline from such directories when they conscientiously think they have just reason so to do"; appeals may be made from lower to superior judicatories which have "authority to consider and determine such appeals." Any signer either of the Massachusetts Proposals of 1705 or of the Connecticut Saybrook Platform could have concurred in this compromise.

This same year, 1722, a threat in the Presbytery of New Castle by Gillespie to publish in pamphlet form the details of the Cross case was met with official action forbidding him to do so without the approval of synod.[23] The same presbytery a year later so unmercifully handled a minister who bathed himself in a creek on Sunday as finally to depose him from the sacred office. Synod repealed the action of presbytery, however.[24]

New Castle seems to have been the first presbytery in America to demand subscription. There is no record in the minutes of this presbytery as to when subscription to the Westminster Confession and Directory was formally adopted. The first instance of its requirement is found at the licensure of William McMillan: " I do own the Westminster Confession of faith as the Confession of my faith. Sic subscribitur. Will: McMillan. Sept. 22, 1724." Two years later, in this same presbytery, subscription was again required at the licensure of two young men.[25] It is interesting to note that in all these controversies over subscription, acceptance of the Bible as an "infallible rule of faith and life" does not enter into the discussion. The issue in controversy was not whether or not the Bible was true, but rather which interpretation of the Bible was true. When, at a later date, subscription to the Bible as the only rule of faith and life that could be considered infallible was adopted, it was done in order to reject the views of the extreme subscriptionists, who desired only a pledge to the creed. Had they gained their point, the creed, as in Roman Catholic usage, would have become the final authoritative statement of the meaning of the Bible.

During the years just elapsed, the controversies in the Scottish and Irish Churches had been reaching a more violent pitch. By 1725 it was quite apparent that the ruling clique in Scotland were going to carry things on until they had secured a complete victory. Their victory, however, was to be a schism in the Church. In Ireland the subscription party exscinded the nonsubscribers in 1726 by a very highhanded and unconstitutional exclusion act.[26]

These British controversies had their repercussions in the American synod. In 1727, John Thomson, of the Presbytery of New Castle, introduced an overture calling for official adoption of, and subscription to, the Westminster symbols.[27] It was referred to the presbyteries. Only New Castle Presbytery's action is known. Having discussed it at several meetings, they unanimously voted to lay the measure before synod.[28] In 1728 synod postponed action until their next meeting. Opposition was developing to the overture. It was therefore enacted that the synod of 1729 should be a full synod rather than a delegated body as it had been for the past few years. Never again did it meet as a delegated body. It resumed, and retained, its original character of the presbytery of the whole.

When the synod met in 1729, the controversy had been carried on for some time in print. Thomson's overture had been printed, and Jonathan Dickinson had printed an answer to it. The argument advanced by Thomson ran about as follows: He had "proposed an expedient for preventing the ingress and spreading of dangerous errors." The "unquestionable duty of every Christian" and especially of ministers, and every organized church, is the "vindication and defense of the truths we profess." Since the synod was utterly independent of all other judicatories upon earth, "it is not in the power of any superior ecclesiastical judicature to call us in question for our neglect, or for our errors or heresies should we be corrupted with them. . . . We are in no small way of being corrupted in doctrinals. . . . It is true, as I take it, we all generally acknowledge and look upon the Westminster Confession and Catechisms to be our confession . . . but the most that can be said is, that . . . [they are] the confession of faith of the generality of our members, ministers and people; but that it is our confession, as we are a united body politic, I cannot see . . . we have no confession which is ours by synodical act." Therefore he urges that the synod " publicly and authoritatively adopt the Westminster Confession of Faith, Catechisms, etc, for the confession of our faith, as we are a particular organized church." Moreover, " to oblige every candidate for the ministry [and actual minister], to subscribe, or otherwise acknowledge, *coram presbyteris,* the said confession of theirs, etc. and to promise not to preach or teach contrary to it." Present members of the synod would be censured if they preached anything contrary to these symbols without first submitting these views to synod's examination. These measures, Thomson believed, " may, through the divine blessing, prevent in a great measure, if not altogether, our being deluded with the damnable errors of our times." Thomson spoke freely of the possibility of a schism in the Church because of his overture, but expressed his hopes for a subsequent reunion.

This overture, which runs for several pages, is very important for an understanding of the founding of the presbytery in 1706, and for the general character of the early synod. It is clearly stated by a leader of the Scotch-Irish group that the Church was totally independent of any and all of the Scotch, Irish, or English Presbyterian Churches. Also, he says that they have never officially adopted any confessional statements. By common consent alone they have been following the Westminster Standards. He asks that the synod adopt these Standards officially, and demand an unqualified subscription to them of all entering the synod, and impose them upon all present members of the synod under a threat of censure. Moreover, whereas Gillespie had thought of a reform in conduct and discipline, Thomson is concerned only with doctrinal errors.

Dickinson's argument was the same as in 1722. He argued that " a joint acknowledgment of our Lord Jesus Christ for our common head, of the sacred Scriptures for our common standard both in faith and practice, with a joint agreement in the same essential and necessary articles of Christianity, and the same methods of worship and discipline, are a sufficient bond of union for the being or well-being of any church under heaven." Subscription must be, he said, to the Word of God, not to a human interpretation of it. " We all of us know that the subscription under debate, has been scrupled by many godly, learned and faithful ministers of Christ, that it has made horrible divisions and confusions in other churches, and that it is like to have the same sad effects among ourselves. . . . But how do you know that the Assemblies

Confession etc. is contain'd in the Word of God?" he demanded. "You indeed, and we that agree with you in the same Creed do thus interpret the word of God. But I challenge you to bring one Word to evince your Certainty; that our Interpretations are agreeable to the Meaning of the Holy Ghost; and have the Divine approbation that any Sect under Heaven may'n't bring in the same Cause.". . ." If all qualified Candidates can well understand the whole of that large Confession, it's a just Matter of shame to me, who have be'n a Minister between twenty and thirty Years; and yet don't understand several Things in it. . . . I'm afraid therefore, that most of our Candidates must subscribe blindfold, or be kept out of the Ministry from invincible Necessity."

Instead of subscription, Dickinson urged that the purity of the Church would be preserved far better by strict examination not only of a candidate's belief but of his experience; "strict discipline in the church, especially with reference to scandalous ministers"; "that the ministers of the gospel be most diligent, faithful and painful in the discharge of their awful trust."[29] To Dickinson the granting of more authority to the synod which had so signally failed in the Cross case would be more likely to bring forth further evils than to bring forth reforms.

Dickinson clearly connected Thomson's move with the subscription controversies abroad. In 1726 the Irish subscriptionists had illegally exscinded the nonsubscribers, and in Scotland the ruling clique were at this time hurrying on to a Pyrrhic victory which was to reach its climax in the Erskine secession movement. Andrews wrote to Colman that the whole cosmopolitan group had the feeling that the growing Scotch-Irish group would just as soon be rid of all but their own party. In some ways, Andrews felt, separation might be better, "for the different countrymen seem to be most delighted with each other, and to do best when they are by themselves."[30] The more cosmopolitan group in the Church, whose attitudes were shaped by English Puritan backgrounds and ideals as embodied in such combinations of Congregationalism and Presbyterianism as the Heads of Agreement and the Saybrook Platform, feared that they would suffer the same fate that had befallen the minority groups of Scotland and Ireland, once the Scotch-Irish group gained the weapon of compulsory subscription.

Already a large part of the pattern of American Presbyterianism had been determined by this tension between the New England and Scotch-Irish segments of its membership. No doubt backgrounds played a great part in the attitudes of the two groups. The hatred that the Scots and Scotch-Irish had for the old England no doubt colored their attitude toward the "new" England, with its growing wealth, its aristocratic established Churches, its proud colleges, its cultured people, and its assurance of its own power and importance. Was this but another form or branch of the old England? The few Scots and Scotch-Irish who settled in New England knew well the scorn and dislike of the New Englanders. They were despised as uncouth and untutored. Even as late as 1738 this feeling was violent enough to cause definite outbreaks. In that year the Presbyterian church at Worcester, Massachusetts, was burned to the ground by townspeople who wished to be rid of the Scotch-Irish.

At this time, 1729, there was as yet no thought of an independent United States of America. Moreover, outside of New England the various religious bodies in the colonies were under the control of European judicatories. The Bishop of London was over the colonial Anglicans. The Dutch Reformed Church in the colonies was governed by the Classis of Amsterdam. The Roman Catholics also were controlled from abroad. If the Scotch-Irish group were to gain complete control, there would be nothing to prevent them from placing themselves under some superior judicature in the homeland. Thomson had called it a disadvantage that there was no superior judicature to bring the synod to account if it went into error and heresy. Would the Scotch-Irish group later argue that the General Assembly of Scotland, or the Irish Synod, ought to be asked to assume responsibility for keeping the synod free from heresy? The opponents of the subscription measure may well have had many nondoctrinal reasons also for not wishing to grant such a weapon to the Scotch-Irish. At any rate Dickinson's work was not " a hasty and ill-considered production, the doctrines of which he soon and entirely abandoned." [31] Both parties were decided in their views, yet both feared a schism.

The Adopting Act of 1729 was therefore a compromise. The first part was a preamble or general agreement as to what was to be understood by subscription. All legislative power in the Church was renounced; only administrative power was claimed. The need of a standard of doctrine and practice was admitted. A distinction was made between the essential and necessary articles of the standards, and those not essential and necessary. If any minister or candidate had any scruples about any articles, he should state them at the time of making subscription. " Synod or Presbytery shall judge . . . [whether or not] his scruple or mistake [be] only about articles not essential and necessary in doctrine, worship or government." If his scruple or mistake could be resolved, he was to be accepted as a minister, and the members " solemnly agree, that none of us will traduce or use any opprobrious terms of those that differ from us in these extra-essential and not necessary points of doctrine." This action occupied the morning session.

At the afternoon session each of the members who had any scruples presented them to the synod. All were found capable of solution save some regarding the civil magistrate and his relation to the Church. The Confession and Catechisms were therefore adopted with certain exceptions in regard to those points upon which no common ground could be found. Four days later the synod declared that they judged the Westminster Directory to be " agreeable in substance to the Word of God " and " do earnestly recommend the same to all their members." Thus the Directory was " recommended " rather than " adopted." [32] This meant that the presbyteries were given complete autonomy regarding their own affairs, and that the synod regarded the Directory as a guide or pattern rather than as basic law. The synod, therefore, adopted for themselves no form of government, and made no attempt to set up any rules for the presbyteries.

The compromise in this Adopting Act involved several points. For one thing, the meaning of subscription to the Confession was stated carefully and at great length. The Church claimed no more than administrative power. The need for a standard was confessed, but two concessions were made. First, that in these Westminster Standards there were some doctrines that were necessary and essential to the whole, and others that were not. Secondly, it was granted that these essentials might be understood and stated differently by some. The judicature asking subscription was therefore to hear patiently the scruples of the entering brother. If his trouble was due to a misunderstanding, or involved a view of doctrine, worship, or government that was not incompatible with a fair interpretation of these symbols, he was to be admitted to the judicature without official censure or social ostracism. Upon these bases Dickinson and the cosmopolitan group accepted the Scotch-Irish subscription plan. Present at the meeting were three New Englanders, one Welshman, and fourteen Scotch-Irish. Absent were four New Englanders and three Scotch-Irish. The actual strength of the two parties was thus about one to two in favor of the subscriptionists. The compromise was due to moderates within both parties. The act itself was modeled in great part after the Irish Pacific Articles of 1720 and the ideas of Jonathan Dickinson.[33]

The extreme subscriptionists were by no means satisfied with this compromise. Some few left the synod and joined with Scottish secessionist groups that were about in the area.[34] Others attempted a ruse that was widely used in the nineteenth century by the Old School group. These ardent subscriptionists began to distinguish between what synod had done on the morning of the day of the Adopting Act, and what was done in the afternoon. The morning was called a " preliminary act," and the afternoon part " the Adopting Act." In this manner adoption by unqualified subscription was proved. The only permissible scruples were those concerning the civil magistrate. This was, however, a breach of faith. Any impartial reading of the minutes must reveal that the morning's session was devoted to reaching a basis for the agreement that followed in the afternoon. To cut between the basis of the agreement and the agreement itself, in order to obviate the basis, was a breach of faith.[35] Furthermore, the fact that the eighteen men present found that they could harmonize their views on all but the matter of the civil magistrate's authority over the Church (in Scotland, Presbyterianism was supported by the civil authority) did not mean that for the future other ministers might not scruple other points and be sustained in their scruples.

Moreover, even a cursory reading of the minutes of the Assembly that wrote these Westminster Standards will convince one that the Westminster divines disagreed in no small manner on some points, and that the Standards as finally issued represented the best possible compromise between these men.[36] To demand an unqualified subscription to these Standards was not only to demand what their own authors refused,[37] but to demand an implicit submission to ecclesiastical authority, in other words, to deny the whole basis of the Reformation, Lutheran and Calvinistic. Only the blindest kind of dogmatism could refuse to leave open at all times the possibility, pointed out by Dickinson, that a creed written under such circumstances as was the Westminster Confession might not be in every detail a transcript of the fullness of the divine revelation. Subscription to the " system of doctrine " was the only reasonable mode of subscription. This was the compromise of the Adopting Act which the extreme subscriptionists tried to obviate by cutting the first part, with its concessions, out of the Adopting Act, and by enacting stricter measures in those presbyteries that they were able to control.

In 1730 the New Castle Presbytery, and in 1732 the Donegal Presbytery, both controlled by extreme subscriptionists, adopted resolutions demanding unqualified subscription. Moreover, whereas the synod had " recommended " the Westminster Directory, New Castle Presbytery required unqualified subscription to it in the same terms as the Confession. These measures were a violation of the Adopting Act, and ushered in a long, grinding fight for supreme power over the presbyteries by the synod.

Beyond the party issues involved lay two different understandings of all that which they had discussed. Neither group was found to differ from the other on any vital point in the statement of doctrine, when they had talked things over. Both parties were intent on keeping out unworthy ministers. But, as to the function of doctrinal statements, and as to what made a minister unworthy, these two groups clashed repeatedly and violently.

The subscriptionist party thought that authoritative and correct creeds would lead men to the truth, in the sense of rational truth about God, and so would lead to correct concepts about God and man. Dickinson, on the other hand, thought of creeds as being fair statements of the general beliefs of a given Church body. The only purpose of these creeds was to point beyond themselves to Scripture. Whereas the subscriptionist party looked upon the creed as a final condensation of the truths contained in Scripture, Dickinson said a creed was but one of the many helps available for the study of the Bible. The creed could not be made the only help, nor the authoritative help. The Bible, and the uninterpreted Bible, was the only standard of truth. When authoritative interpretations are imposed, "religion itself, with all its blessed and peaceable Doctrines, is become a subject of Debate, instead of a Rule of Faith and Life." For Dickinson, truth was that which leads men by a right rule of faith and life to conversion and holy living. Such truth was so apparent in Scripture that not only were binding creeds unnecessary, but they generally led to dissensions in churches, and to making rational truth about God the purpose of religion. Dickinson was thus advancing against the subscriptionist party the old stock argument that all Reformed theologians had used against the Romanists and the Anglicans.

An unworthy minister in the eyes of the subscriptionists was one whose ideas were out of harmony with the authoritatively established creed. To Dickinson, an unworthy minister was one who was unregenerate, unethical, and careless in his holy calling, whatever his creedal notions were. When, accordingly, these two groups joined in confessing that their infant Church was in danger from unworthy ministers, in danger of straying from the true Gospel, and that urgent measures were needed, it is not remarkable that their plans for reform proved wellnigh irreconcilable. As long as Dickinson and some of the moderate Scotch-Irish ministers could keep the compromise symbolized in the Adopting Act alive and in force, there was hope of co-operation and success.

Among the Scotch-Irish, about this time, besides the extreme subscriptionists and the moderates, a third group were forming around William Tennent. In due time their activities destroyed the delicate balance of power in the synod. It was they who inaugurated the reform movement that saved both the doctrines and the ethics of their Church.

Though they began their reformation under rather tumultuous circumstances, the aid of George Whitefield and the timely co-operation of the New England group made of it the first and the most lasting of all the reforming movements in American Presbyterianism — the Great Awakening.

THE GREAT AWAKENING COMES

After spending several years, 1720–1727, as pastor at Bedford, New York, William Tennent, Sr., moved to Neshaminy, Bucks County, Pennsylvania. While at Bedford he seems to have become somewhat acquainted in Connecticut, and to have entertained some hopes of succeeding Timothy Cutler as president of Yale, when the latter defected to the Anglicans and was removed.[1] His oldest son, Gilbert, had received the degree of A.M. from Yale in 1725, and had been licensed the same year by the Presbytery of Philadelphia.[2] As a scholar and teacher, William Tennent, Sr., was unique and without an equal in the synod. He himself educated his four sons, three of whom were to become men of great force and influence. Very early the need for a better ministry seems to have called forth in him the desire to prepare a group of such men in his home, in much the same way as he was teaching his own sons. When vast areas were without a minister, when few men could be found in New England or Great Britain for service in the middle colonies, and, when of the few who did come, some were quite undesirable as pastors, none could help feeling that something must be done. By 1733, four young ministers had entered the synod after having studied under William Tennent, Sr. These were his three sons, Gilbert, John, and William, Jr., and Samuel Blair.

Thus a third group began to exert an influence in the synod. They were all Scotch-Irish and seem to have had no special connection at this early time with the group led by Dickinson. In the subscription controversy none of the Tennents had taken any active part. William Tennent, Sr., and Gilbert Tennent had signed the Adopting Act at synod in 1729. John Tennent signed an unqualified subscription in New Castle Presbytery to Confession, Catechisms, and Directory late in 1729. Hence, if they were not opposed to the generality of the Scotch-Irish on this point, in other ways their outlook was much like that of Dickinson. The Tennents as a group were definitely English Puritans in spirit.

Very early the actual leadership of the Tennent group passed into the hands of Gilbert Tennent. As a preacher he has well been called second only to Whitefield in power and success. He had, during his late teens, passed through a conversion experience such as was well known in Presbyterianism since Puritan times.[3] The intensity and richness of his experience and zeal, and his unusual native endowments, were not quickly harmonized. He began his regular ministry in 1726 in the Presbytery of New Castle, where both he and his brother John rashly failed to keep some of the rules of the presbytery.[4] No doubt these foolish acts were to be remembered by the leaders of the New Castle Presbytery, John Thomson, Robert Cross, Thomas Craighead, and George Gillespie. Perhaps, too, the Tennent brothers and these men had formed opinions of each other in that short period of time that had influenced the young Tennents to seek other fields. Little by little, in one fashion or another, it was becoming evident that the Tennent group and the generality of the Scotch-Irish were not compatible. But these differences were to become shattering when accentuated by the Great Awakening which entered Presbyterianism about this time under these two Tennent brothers in their new locations at New Brunswick and Freehold, New Jersey.

At New Brunswick, Gilbert Tennent became acquainted with Dominie Theodorus Jacobus Frelinghuysen, a Dutch Reformed minister who had been a storm center in the colonial Dutch Church since his arrival in 1719. When he came to New Jersey, Frelinghuysen found the churches spiritually dead and contented with a most perfunctory orthodoxy. He began a vigorous reform based on evangelistic preaching, strict enforcement of the discipline of the Reformed Church, and zealous visitations. A considerable revival followed, which spread to other churches about, both Dutch and English.[5] As far as the Great Awakening in general was concerned, Whitefield could say that Frelinghuysen "was the beginner of the great work" in that area.[6]

Frelinghuysen is generally called a German Pietist by modern historians, though it is admitted that no clear evidence can be found to connect him with German Pietism.[7] It is notable that his Dutch opponents, who knew Dutch ecclesiastical affairs well, never call him a Pietist, but rather a Koelmanite and a Labadist.[8] The Presbyterians and the Germans, who were not so familiar with the Church in Holland, called him a Pietist. He himself lists the name "Pietist" as being one of the "opprobrious epithets . . . by which [he and his friends] are shamefully aspersed by unfaithful ministers."[9] Koelman and Labadie had been denounced as false teachers by the Dutch Church; hence in

Dutch circles the names " Koelmanite" and " Labadist " hurt.[10] Moreover, there was some reason for the name "Koelmanite." Before leaving Holland, Frelinghuysen had written a catechism, in the preface of
which he had spoken highly of Koelman.[11] The specific accusations
brought against Frelinghuysen are much more meaningful when
viewed in the light of the contemporary conflicts in the Church of Holland than in the light of some supposed, though untraceable, connection on his part with German Pietism.

In the light of this background it will be instructive to note the authors whom Frelinghuysen cited in his defenses and recommends in
his sermons. No German Pietists were ever mentioned. He used, besides the Church Fathers and Calvin and Beza, largely Dutch authors.
These were such well-known Dutch evangelicals as Witsius, Brákel,
D'Outrein, and Verschuir. Brákel's book *Reasonable Service,* on the
practice of piety, which also included a section " against Pietists, Qui-
etists and their like," was quoted by name. Verschuir was highly
praised. Frelinghuysen seems to have known him personally. Besides
these Dutch authors, Frelinghuysen quoted William Ames, and William Guthrie's *The Christian's Great Interest,* which Koelman had
translated into Dutch. Most frequently, however, he quoted the Heidel-
berg Catechism, upon which he preached regularly in due Dutch fashion. He was never at a loss for a Scripture verse, a famous Dutch author,
a Catechism answer, or an official pronouncement of the Dutch Church,
with which to prove his views. A collection of ten typical sermons by
Frelinghuysen, published in Holland in 1736, drew a highly commenda-
tory statement from the faculty of the University of Groningen.[12] Another smaller collection was later issued in Holland. Evidently his person and his views were neither foreign nor unusual in the homeland.

The usual manner of connecting Frelinghuysen with German Pietism is to argue that since he was a German, and not a Hollander, by
birth he must have been educated in some one of the current German
schools of religious thought and practice. His native city, Lingen, was
under Dutch control from 1597 to 1702. Frelinghuysen, who was born
in 1691, grew up and was educated in Lingen during the last phase of
Dutch control and the early period of Prussian control. A Dutch professor in the University of Lingen first interested him in a study of the
Dutch language. Frelinghuysen was ordained by a Dutch minister at
Emden in 1717.[13] Emden was under Dutch control from 1595 to 1744.
As the province passed from Dutch to German hands, Frelinghuysen
was induced by his Dutch professor to cast his lot in with the Dutch
and the Dutch Church under which he had been reared. There is accordingly no evidence for, and no reason for, connecting him with

German Pietism.[14] He had never been associated with any German religious group.

.It is not remarkable that Gilbert Tennent and Frelinghuysen recognized in each other a kindred spirit. Their common Calvinism, their common Puritan heritage, and their common religious outlook would naturally draw them together. Moreover, it is quite likely that Gilbert Kennedy, an Irish Presbyterian minister who had been forced to take shelter in Holland because of his religious views, and who there became very influential, was either Tennent's uncle or grandfather. William Tennent, Sr., had married a Katherine Kennedy, whose father and brother both bore the name Gilbert and were well-known Presbyterian ministers in Ireland. A Gilbert Kennedy, who published Edwards' *Narrative* in a Dutch translation, was well known in the Tennent party.[15] Hence the situation in the Dutch Church may have been fairly well known among the Tennents, through sources other than Frelinghuysen. This too might well have made them quick to see in Frelinghuysen a man of like mind and heart with themselves.

When Gilbert Tennent came to settle in the Presbyterian congregation in New Brunswick, situated among many of Frelinghuysen's converts, he was impressed by their soundness and godliness. His own ministry at New Brunswick was not very successful, and he found his zeal flagging. The success of Frelinghuysen, however, had given him a sense of the possibility of doing something far more significant. Also, Frelinghuysen wrote him a kindly letter of exhortation which impressed him deeply. Frelinghuysen's work and his letter, Tennent later said, " excited me to greater earnestness in ministerial labors. I began to be very much distressed about my want of success; for I knew not for half a year or more after I came to New Brunswick, that any one was converted by my labors, although several persons were at times affected transiently.

" It pleased God to afflict me about that time with sickness, by which I had affecting views of eternity. I was then exceedingly grieved that I had done so little for God, and was very desirous to live one half year more, if it was his will, that I might stand upon the stage of the world, as it were, and plead more faithfully for his cause, and take more earnest pains for the conversion of souls. The secure state of the world appeared to me in a very affecting light; and one thing among others pressed me sore; viz. that I had spent much time in conversing about trifles, which might have been spent in examining people's states towards God, and persuading them to turn unto him. I therefore prayed to God that he would be pleased to give me one half year more, and I was determined to endeavour to promote his kingdom with all my might at all adventures. The petition God was pleased to grant manifold, and to enable me to keep my resolution in some measure." [16]

Frelinghuysen's influence upon Tennent, therefore, was twofold. His successful ministry was both a rebuke and an inspiration to Tennent. In theological ways he added little or nothing to Tennent. The sermons of William Tennent, Sr., John Tennent, William Tennent, Jr., and Gilbert Tennent all cite and recommend the same literature, and all follow the one pattern, namely, evangelical Puritanism. The entire group of William Tennent's later students also followed this pattern, though only Gilbert Tennent had any close connection with Frelinghuysen. The theological and evangelistic basis of the Tennent group came from William Tennent, Sr. While Gilbert Tennent hesitated over putting it into practice, Frelinghausen's influence proved decisive. Through Frelinghuysen he was moved to practice what he had learned from his father.

Gilbert Tennent had determined to exercise " greater earnestness in ministerial labours." There are available rather clear testimonials as to what this " greater earnestness " meant. One of his first printed sermons was " A Solemn Warning to the Secure World." In the preface to this sermon he defends both his unpleasant subject and his harsh method as being " of the most suitable, necessary and profitable; considering the general and lamentable Security that prevails so exceedingly among the children of this generation." People took God and heaven for granted and went on their way feeling perfectly secure for time and eternity. Tennent considered this a static and presumptuous " religion," and an affront to God. In another of his early sermons he made the same emphases. " Being thoroughly convinced, by Scripture, Reason, Experience, and the universal consent of the most godly, eminent, and useful divines of the Protestant Church, as well as by the suffrage of the antient Fathers; of the great necessity of a work of humiliation, or conviction, in order to a sound conversion from sin and Satan, to God and holiness . . . and perceiving . . . the gross Ignorance of this important truth . . . and thereby a presumptuous Security fatally introduc'd . . . for hereby they are induc'd to content themselves with a dead form of Piety, resulting from a religious Education, and historical Faith; instead of seeking after the Power and Life of Christianity . . . I say, Perceiving and considering the aforesaid Particulars, I have thought it my Duty, to insist frequently upon this Subject in the Course of my Ministry." [17]

The great problem, as Tennent came to see it, was the " presumptuous Security " of his parishioners. They professed belief in the Bible and orthodox doctrine, they had been regularly baptized, somewhat catechized, and considered themselves good Presbyterians. Their belief in the Bible and in orthodox doctrine was to them the same as saving faith. This perversion of faith gave rise to a further disintegration. They were saved, according to their concept of orthodoxy, by faith and not by works. It became quite possible for many of them to dispense with most of the Christian graces, and at times even of common morals, while thus eschewing salvation by works and resting wholly upon their "faith" in orthodox ideas. Tennent, therefore, developed the preaching of "convictions" which he, and his colleagues also, took over from the English Puritans. By preaching that no one ever became a Christian without first passing through the terror of realizing that he was not a Christian, Tennent sought to break up the "presumptuous Security" which he found all about him. Also, he held out the possibility of a true believer's coming to know for himself that he was a Christian.

After some years of this kind of preaching and work among his people, Thomas Prince, of Boston, said of him: "I found him a man of considerable parts and learning; free, gentle, condescending: and from his own various experiences, reading the most noted writers on experimental divinity, as well the Scriptures, and conversing with many who had been awakened by his ministry in New Jersey, where he then lived, he seemed to have as deep an acquaintance with the experimental part of religion as any person I ever conversed with; and his preaching was as searching and rousing as any I ever heard. He . . . [aimed] directly [at] their hearts and consciences, to lay open their ruinous delusions and shew them their numerous secret, hypocritical shifts in religion, and drive them out of every deceitful refuge wherein they made themselves easy, with the form of Godliness without the power." [18] The anguish of coming to the conviction that one was not a Christian, and the subsequent joy of coming to know that one had become a Christian indeed, were the two foci about which the preaching of all the Tennent group swung. Under such preaching, among rough and ready frontier folk who were accustomed to giving free vent to their feelings in all social, political, or religious matters, whether by way of opposition or support, the reactions of the congregations were unexpectedly violent. Strong men wept; some groaned and cried out. By 1729, Tennent's scattered congregations between New Brunswick and Staten Island began to thrill with new life. The Great Awakening had begun in the Presbyterian churches.

Though the Great Awakening in a sense began with Gilbert Tennent's rousing preaching, the Tennent group usually regarded John Tennent as having had the first actual revival. John Tennent had settled in a badly divided and torn congregation at Freehold, New Jersey.

Though he preached essentially the same views and doctrines as all the Tennents, he stressed more the love of God, and was less vehement than his brother Gilbert. His congregations were also less demonstrative. A rather considerable revival resulted from his labors, although death brought his pastorate to a close in two brief years. Jonathan Dickinson composed an elegy in his memory which was later inscribed upon his tombstone.[19] John Tennent was succeeded by his older brother, William, Jr., who, of the four sons, seems to have been the most like his father. Of the father little is heard in all the controversies. In these Gilbert took the lead, while William, Sr., and William, Jr., supported him. Charles, the fourth son, was never very prominent. While William, Jr., held and ardently preached his father's views, and enjoyed much success in evangelistic work, he was more retiring and exercised more of a devotional and teaching ministry. Under his pastorate the revival begun by John Tennent reached its climax. From the very start of his ministry, William, Jr., disapproved of all crying out and fainting in his services.[20] His preaching was not contentious, though searching and thorough. The revival produced great and permanent results.

The Tennents' determined effort to break down the smug complacency of the Church did not go unopposed. Moreover, their preaching that a believer might receive the assurance of his being a Christian aroused deep resentment. Their opponents decried the Tennents' preaching of assurance, not because they did not themselves believe that one could have the assurance that he was a Christian, but because if the kind of assurance that the Tennents preached was genuine, then it was wholly unlikely that their opponents were Christians.[21] The Tennents' preaching of convictions and assurance was a challenge to the whole religious life of the Church. For people who had more or less taken it for granted that they were Christians, and had been assured of it by their own appraisal of their faith and life, the Tennent preaching came as a terrible shock. Some sought and found a living Christian faith; others fought back with bitter animosity.

Instead of the generalized preaching and pastoral work of the day, the Tennents began a method of close, personal preaching coupled with intensive and searching counseling with their people. Gilbert Tennent described his methods to Whitefield a few years later by saying: " Since you was here, I have been among my people dealing with them plainly about their souls' state in their houses; examining them one by one as to their experiences, and telling natural people the danger of their state; and exhorting them that were totally secure, to seek convictions; and those that were convinced, to seek Jesus; and reproved pious people for their faults; and blessed be God, I have seen hopeful appearances of concern amongst a pretty many in the places I belong to." [22] Hitherto it had been customary to preach general principles, abstract doctrines, or polemics against other denominations, with little or no specific application to one's hearers. The Tennents' war cry became, " *Generalia non pungent.*" They denounced this generalized preaching, for by it ministers " carelessly offer a common Mess to their People, and leave it to them to divide it among themselves as they see fit." [23] Such " general preaching," the Tennent party insisted, left the sincere seeker at a loss as to how to find God, and allowed the hypocrite to cover his sin with theological acumen. As they saw it, men fell roughly into four groups:

1. Those who were genuinely converted and who had " a comfortable assurance " of being God's children.
2. Those who were earnestly seeking conversion, but who were not in all respects satisfied with their progress.
3. A great group of people who needed help, who were still not awakened to their need, asleep and unconcerned spiritually, but who could be reached.
4. Rebellious, headstrong sinners, definitely opposed to all that was good and godly.

It was worse than useless to preach the Gospel " in general " when men were of such diverse states. A way of preaching and counseling had to be used that would apply the Gospel threatenings or promises to each man and woman according to his or her condition. Only by such means would every parishioner be brought to make a personal choice for or against the service of God. As Samuel Finley, a younger member of the Tennent group, stated the issue, " A minister may live long, may preach Truth, and nothing but Truth, as long as he Lives, and yet do no real Service to the Souls of men; because he Preaches not those Truths which have a Tendency to answer the End of God's Glory, and Sinners Salvation." [24]

Their opponents accused the Tennents of belittling morality, decrying doctrine, and destroying the very foundations of all rational religion by their preaching of convictions and by their views of assurance. They charged them with heresy and malice. The Tennents' ideas and practices, they asserted, were without precedent in all Christendom. In their defense the Tennents declared that what they were preaching and doing was but a carry-over from such divines as Alleine, Baxter, Shepherd, Guthrie, Flavel, and other earlier Puritan " experimental " preachers. [25]

During the height of William Tennent, Jr.'s revival at Freehold, while Gilbert Tennent was laboring zealously around New Brunswick and Frelinghuysen was still active among the Dutch in the same general area, the New Awakening produced some reactions in the Synod

of Philadelphia. An overture was passed during the sessions of 1733:
" To use some proper means to revive the declining power of godliness,
the Synod do earnestly recommend it to all our ministers and members,
to take particular care about ministerial visiting of families, and press
family and secret worship, according to the Westminster Directory,
and that they also recommend it to every Presbytery, at proper seasons
to inquire concerning the diligence of their members in such particulars." [26] Since Dickinson was absent, the impulse behind this overture
no doubt came from Gilbert Tennent. The extremely cautious wording
was given it by a committee of six, composed of five men who soon
fought the revival vigorously, and one man who took no great part for
or against the Tennents. No mention was made of the " revival of godliness " then going on not far from synod's meeting place.

On the records of synod the year following, the signs of the times
can be read quite clearly in three very important entries, each of which
drew the party lines more sharply: " Inquiry being made with respect
to the overture made last Synod, in order to revive the decaying power
of godliness; and it being found that it has not yet been fully put into
execution, the Synod do not only renew the said order, but earnestly
obtest every one of our brethren of the ministry, conscientiously and
diligently to pursue the good designs thereof." [27]

There were in the synod members who would have nothing to do
with any form of revival effort. A long period of controversy was thus
ushered in. During its opening phases, each of the various parties
within the synod strove for certain objectives in legal and orderly ways.
But it soon became evident that the regular and lawful adoption of an
overture was not sufficient. Some refused to obey the synod's orders. As
overture followed counteroverture, disregard for the synod's authority
became more apparent. In view of the fact that the Tennent party have
been generally accused of rejecting the legal and proper authority of
the synod, it is instructive to note that the first refusal to obey the regularly adopted rulings of synod came from a group who were opposed to
the revival.

The subscriptionist party, which now emerged as the antirevival
party, moved at this same session of the synod, 1734, to secure that an
annual check should be made by the synod of the books of each presbytery, in order to learn whether or not subscription was being rigorously
enforced in each of these lower courts. This move, as later events
proved, was but the first in a drive by this party for an all-powerful
synod controlled by themselves through the weapon of subscription.[28]

The other party countered with a motion even stronger. Gilbert Tennent introduced an overture that called to synod's attention that the

Westminster symbols, which were so ardently being pressed upon all, contained some provisions that were not being followed by the presbyteries. The directions for ordination, which had been drawn up by Puritans and Scottish Covenanting Presbyterians, who were very zealous for a converted and sincerely pious ministry, required an examination of candidates for the ministry which included, not only their proficiency in the arts and doctrines, but a careful inquiry as to whether or not they had any experimental knowledge of the salvation that they were to preach to others.[29] He who was to urge men to yield up their lives wholly to God must himself have led the way. Dickinson, who had urged similar measures in 1722 and 1729, at the beginnings of the subscription controversy, had now found ardent support among the Tennent group. The synod thereupon passed two overtures, one urging that great care be taken in admitting men to the ministry, and a second ordering that all ministers were to be most diligent and faithful in their duties. The order was an expansion of the order of 1733. Taking a cue from the overture on subscription, synod required further that the above minute be recorded in each presbytery's book, that it be read at the opening of each session of presbytery, and that a written record of the reading be made each time in the presbytery's books. Those who did not carry out this order were to be subject to censure.[30]

When synod convened a year later, 1735, it was found that subscription had been faithfully required of several new members. But the order of synod on the examination of candidates and on the means of reviving religion had not been fulfilled by all. Synod once more ordered that it should be done hereafter. The subscriptionist party's activity in the Church at large was no doubt reflected in another synodical order that the " whole adopting act be inserted in [each] presbytery book." [31] Some presbyteries, evidently, were already using the " shorter " form which was to be forced through the synod in 1736.

At this same synod a trial was held which not only revealed the futility of subscription as a means of keeping out heresy, but was also the occasion of enabling the subscriptionist party to gain new ground in 1736. A Scotch-Irishman by the name of Samuel Hemphill had been made assistant to Andrews in Philadelphia. Andrews had never been a capable preacher. Hemphill, however, soon created a stir by his eloquent delivery of unusually fine sermons. Before long those who were well-read began to hear from Hemphill sermons that they recognized as those of famous worthies. Even worse, those who were concerned for orthodoxy found that he preached the sermons of bad theologians. Hemphill had twice made subscription to the Westminster symbols, in Ireland and in America. When he was tried for heresy by a commission of the synod, he was supported by freethinkers, deists, and the like, among them Benjamin Franklin, more out of spite for Andrews than from persuasion of Hemphill's honesty. His sermons proved to have been stolen from well-known Arian and other heretical preachers. He was ejected and soon disappeared.[32]

Hemphill had tried to plead in his defense that he understood subscription to the Confession to mean subscription to the essential articles thereof. To this, Dickinson answered that when Hemphill made subscription he had registered no scruples, and that his sermons, being Arian and stolen also, were not in accord with what synod, the sole judge in such matters, considered to be the essential articles of the Confession. No individual had the right silently and privately to decide what was, and what was not, an essential of the Confession. The subscriptionist party took the matter to heart. Subscription must be ironclad, with none of those distinctions between essentials and nonessentials that let heretics in between the bars. No doubt Andrews' painful experience accounts for his joining of the subscriptionist party by the next year.[33]

In 1720 George Gillespie had proposed the strengthening of the synod's authority in order to bring about some much-needed reforms. Dickinson had answered that conflict, not reform, would come from such measures. During the ensuing years (1721–1736), the truth of his predictions had been well borne out. Robert Cross, whose facile shriving of his immoralities by his friends in the synod had led Gillespie to move for the strengthening of that body's authority, was now rapidly becoming the dominant figure in the subscriptionist party, which party was also now the antirevival party. Dickinson had pleaded that only spiritual renewal, thorough discipline of scandalous ministers, and deeper devotion on the part of all to their holy calling could protect the Church from those " damnable errors " and " soul-destroying errors " that the subscriptionists professed to fear so much. However, subscription had come, and had been made more rigorous year by year. Nevertheless, in those presbyteries where the subscriptionist party was the strongest, ministerial discipline was the most lax and conditions generally were the worst.

Meanwhile, in an obscure backwoods settlement, and almost unobserved, the most important event in colonial Presbyterianism had taken place, the founding of William Tennent, Sr.'s "Log College." Although by this time he had trained and sent into the ministry four young men, and no doubt had others under his care, Tennent seems not to have built the school until late in 1735. Earlier that year he had purchased the land on which it was to stand.[34] The building, " a log cabin eighteen by twenty feet in size, perhaps two stories high," was probably erected that same fall. This erection of a school building marks the beginning of a definite move on the part of William Tennent, Sr. He resigned one of his two churches, and gave himself wholly to the Neshaminy congregation and to the school. During the next five years seven very capable young ministers joined the synod. Before his work was done, Tennent had trained possibly twenty-one men,[35] many of whom were of unique usefulness in the American Presbyterian Church.

The main body of the Scotch-Irish clergy, who were the subscriptionist-antirevival party, and for whom Scotland and Ulster were the sources of all norms and standards, refused to consider anyone an educated minister if he were not from a Scottish university. Tennent's school soon received the scornful title of " Log College." Scottish university work in this period was in a deplorable state, and little improvement was to come for some time. At Edinburgh graduation fees were no longer being paid to the professors, and students were therefore not being required by the faculty to study any particular course. Graduations fell steadily until they reached the total of three for the year 1745, and the next year no one took a degree. At that same university the six-year theological course then worked out in actual practice for most students to six years of lectures in Latin by one professor on a single Latin textbook of secondary importance, Pictet's *Compend,* during which total time the professor would cover only one half of the text. The lectures of the other two professors were optional, and frequently both the professors and the students omitted them.[36]

The Scotch-Irish ministers were not ignorant of how their fathers had faced and were still facing their own educational problem. The Irish universities were closed to all Presbyterians. Those who could find the means went therefore to Scottish universities to study for the ministry. Since not enough men could go to Scotland, the Irish Presbyterians founded " private schools " at various places from time to time, at Antrim, Newtownards, Comber, Killileagh, and Dublin. Poverty and prelacy made these private schools ephemeral and weak. Some of the most famous ministers in the Irish Presbyterianism of that day, such as Joseph Boyse, d. 1728, Francis Iredell, d. 1739, and John Leland, d. 1766, had been " privately educated." [37] Francis Alison, who was shortly to become Tennent's most inveterate enemy, and vice-provost of the College of Philadelphia, was a devoted disciple of Francis Hutcheson, who before going to a chair at Glasgow had conducted one such private school at Dublin.[38]

The English Puritans had had many excellent private academies. When they were driven out of the English universities, the Puritans had founded a number of these academies and the movement had not yet spent its force. These Dissenting schools, often conducted by only one or two men, had made a lasting contribution to British higher education, influencing even the quality of university teaching.[39]

In the light of what was being done in the universities of Scotland, and what had been accomplished and was still being accomplished by the small private Presbyterian academies of Ireland, and the Dissenting academies of England, it was not wholly unlikely that Tennent would be able to produce " graduates " fully as competent as his Scottish-educated opponents. As time went on, his students as a group proved themselves much better equipped intellectually than the Scotch-Irish subscriptionist group who so greatly scorned the " Log College." Religiously and morally they surpassed their detractors even more. Educationally they founded more schools and colleges on the American frontier than the Scottish-trained group dreamed possible. Tennent had not only a vision of what could and must be done, but also the ability to carry it out.

No opposition whatever had been raised against the licensure and ordination of the first four men trained by Tennent. In fact, on the records that remain of the examinations of three of them the examiners reported themselves well pleased. The Tennent group, however, were definitely " different " in their views of Presbyterianism, were the source of the revival that had begun to spread abroad, were co-operating with Frelinghuysen whom many Presbyterians disliked, were drawing closer and closer to the New England group who opposed strict subscription, and had sponsored in synod an overture requiring all candidates to be examined as to their piety. " That such an act of Synod [requiring examination of candidates' experiences] should have been needed, and, because needed, hated by many, is a fact painfully suggestive. It accounts for the attempt to break down the Log College." [40] When, therefore, William Tennent, Sr., erected a school building, and began laying plans for extending the revival by a new type of ministry, the opposition began to organize.

The influence of the revival was being greatly increased by Gilbert Tennent's preaching in such places as New York and Perth Amboy. Also, in 1735, he published three of his sermons in New York [41] and one in Boston.[42] These, together with two sermons by John Tennent and an account of the revival at Freehold, published at Boston,[43] made the entire movement well known just at the time when a similar awakening was beginning in New England under Jonathan Edwards. The Great Awakening was gaining in power and scope.

Since 1729, the membership of the synod had increased by seventeen ministers. Five had come from New England, nine were from Ulster, and three were from Tennent's private school. The New England group who followed Dickinson's leadership (Andrews no longer did) now numbered fourteen. The Tennent group had four dependable members, and could count three other men to stand midway between them and the main group of Scotch-Irish, which now numbered six-teen plus Andrews. Besides these, there were two Welshmen and an Englishman. Since it was already evident that the Tennents' views were much like those of Dickinson, the synod as a whole was about evenly divided.

The opportunity for which the subscriptionist party had been seeking came at last in the synod of 1736. Eleven New England men (Dickin-son and every other influential man), Gilbert Tennent and Samuel Blair (the two leaders of the Tennent group), three Scotch-Irish mem-bers generally friendly to the Tennents, Evans and Orme (Welsh and English ministers), and three other Scotch-Irishmen — twenty-one members all told — were absent. Twenty members assembled, sixteen of whom were of the subscriptionist party. Such wholesale absences were not fortuitous. The New England group, in all likelihood, deliberately stayed away, anticipating a controversial session. (They admittedly did such a thing a few years later.) Gilbert Tennent and Samuel Blair were no doubt on one of the evangelizing tours that were to cause trouble in the following synod.

With full control of the synod, the Scotch-Irish party turned their attention to the Adopting Act. The so-called first or preliminary part, which stated the agreement upon which the Adopting Act rested, was eliminated. The new preliminary statement read: " That in order to re-move said offence [complaints of loose-ness by the subscription party] and all jealousies that have arisen or may arise in any of our people's minds on occasion of said distinctions and expressions [i.e., the distinc-tions between essential and non-essential articles of the Confession, and the right to present scruples], the Synod doth declare, that the Synod have adopted and still do adhere to the Westminster Confession, Cate-chisms, and Directory, without the least variation or alteration, and without any regard to said distinctions. And we do further declare, that this was our meaning and true intent in our first adopting of said Con-fession, as may particularly appear by our adopting act which is as fol-loweth [here follows the second section only of the Adopting Act of 1729]." [44] The overture passed unanimously. The stronger men of the New England party were absent, and those of the Tennent group pres-ent were not opposed to strict subscription.

In this manner the Adopting Act, which the New England group and a part of the Tennent group looked upon as a sort of basic document or constitutional agreement, was set aside. They charged in a later manifesto that such acts made " the terms of communion as variable as any weathercock, so that a man is in continual danger of being cast out of communion." [45] An ironclad, unqualified *ipsissima verba* subscription was now required of all as a condition of membership.[46] The subscriptionist party had won. But they had won too much. The Dickinson group and the Tennent group were drawn closer together by this revision of the Adopting Act, and by two other moves that the subscriptionist-antirevival party now carried out.

The first of these two moves came in Philadelphia. The congregation in that city was rather badly shaken up by the Hemphill affair. Part of the members now asked to have Robert Cross as their pastor, while another part asked to have Dickinson. After much debate during the sessions of 1735, in which synod reversed themselves several times, they created a distinct congregation for each of the groups, rescinded this order, declared that a new congregation *could* be erected for Cross if the people desired, and finally appointed a committee to attempt a reunion of the two factions of the church. The committee failed, and supplies were ordered sent to a new congregation made up of the more radical Scotch-Irish faction in Andrews' old congregation. Dickinson and several other New England men did not approve of these measures.[47] The synod of 1736 had given the Scotch-Irish party a complete majority and a free hand. Cross became stated supply of the new congregation, and Andrews was left in charge of the remainder of the congregation, largely those who had asked for Dickinson. Since Andrews had now become a member of the subscriptionist party, this group maintained control of the Philadelphia situation even while creating two churches to quiet matters down. Dickinson was left in Elizabethtown.[48] (In 1738 the two congregations were united, with Andrews and Cross as senior and junior pastors, and the coup was complete.)

The second incident came up as an antirevival faction in William Tennent's church sought to have him put out of their pastorate.[49] The Log College had now become quite active, with several students pursuing their work under Tennent. The revival was also gaining momentum. If Tennent could be ousted from his pastorate, his movement could be hampered. The ground of the ouster appeal was that Tennent had never been officially installed by presbytery or synod. Synod ruled that since he had been there for ten years, and since not all were against him, his own presbytery's action in upholding his right to remain pastor was to be sustained.[50]

These two moves made much clearer the basic issue behind all these maneuvers: the Scotch-Irish party were driving for an all-powerful synod through which they would be able to root out the growing revival. When the first presbytery was founded, it had little authority over the congregations that adhered to it.[51] Moreover, though the presbytery seems from the first to have conducted licensures and ordinations after the order of the English and Scottish Presbyterians, even this authority rested upon mutual consent. This lack of clear-cut authority is seen also in the fact that in this early period few, if any, men were formally installed by the presbytery. The congregations seem to have acknowledged the presbytery as empowered to ordain, but seem not to have regarded installation by the presbytery as either necessary or desirable. The ministers assumed charge of the pastorate solely by action of the local church. Boyd at Freehold, Tennent at Neshaminy, McNish at Manokin, Anderson at New York, and others apparently were never installed by the presbytery.

Beginning with the Act of 1722, and especially after the Adopting Act of 1729, the synod and the presbyteries steadily increased their authority over both the clergy and the congregations. Nevertheless, as late as 1727, Ebenezer Pemberton (for New York City) and Daniel Elmer (for Fairfield, New Jersey) were ordained in New England by Congregationalist councils for service in churches then adhering to the synod. Each man took charge of his pastorate without installation by the presbytery involved. Pemberton's admission to the synod was delayed because of this irregularity, but in the end the synod accepted him without ordering any installation.

It was the Scotch-Irish party's desire to carry through rigid subscription, and to eliminate the revival, which impelled them to seek further authority for the Church judicatories. Another factor may also have had an influence upon them. For some years several of their number had been involved in disputes with their congregations. A year after his exoneration by the synod, Cross had reported that his congregation was supporting him so poorly that he would have to look for a new charge.[52] Several members of Donegal Presbytery also had been in difficulties with their people. Most of the wrangling in this presbytery at this time stemmed directly or indirectly from arrears in ministers' salaries. Finally, in desperation, the presbytery had issued a general appeal to all churches for financial succor for John Thomson,[53] and had passed a drastic law sponsored by James Anderson. This law provided that any person who was in arrears on his pledge to the minister was to be excluded, with his entire family, from the Lord's Supper, and was to be refused baptism for his children. In presenting the overture, Anderson confessed that " if ministers were more faithful God would accompany

and follow a preached Gos [sic] with more efficacy, in ye conversion
and regeneration of Souls, there would not be great cause of complaint
of peoples paying honour to, and mentaining of us, as there is." [54] Force-
ful steps also were taken to eradicate the criticism of the clergy by the
laity of Donegal Presbytery. This threat failed, however, to quell the
tide of resentment that was welling up against several of the Donegal
ministers. Greater and greater power for the Church courts was the
only solution of the difficulty sought by these clergymen.[55] The synod
of 1737 witnessed another concerted effort in that direction by these
men.

Just why it is hard to say, but in 1737 once again synod met with all
but one of Dickinson's party absent. Richard Treat, never a strong man,
was present. The Scotch-Irish party had sixteen members to three Log
College men. Two other ministers were present, both of whom were of
a mediating turn of mind. Another attempt to oust William Tennent,
Sr., was defeated.[56] A more significant measure was passed, whereby no
minister or probationer could preach in any vacant congregation without the consent of his own presbytery and of the presbytery under
which the congregation was placed. Moreover, no vacant congregation
could invite a minister or probationer to preach, even for one service,
without the consent of presbytery, and, before accepting, this man must
await the next meeting of that presbytery, then appear before it in person, preach before it, and have his fitness to preach the supply sermon in
the vacant congregation determined by the presbytery. Since few men
could give so much time and travel to such enterprises, the rule was but
a ruse to keep vacant congregations vacant until men whom the antirevival group approved of could be found. The welfare of the congregation was not taken into account. Furthermore, no minister in any presbytery could invite any minister or probationer to preach in any vacant
congregation without permission from his presbytery.[57]

While this act seems to have been aimed against the evangelistic efforts of the Tennent group, no evidence remains as to whom the synod
had in mind.[58] Probably some were quietly preparing for the day when
the " graduates " of Tennent's Log College would be looking for place-
ment. If the activities of these young men could be " controlled "
through this synodical order, Tennent's plans for spreading the revival
in the Presbyterian Church would collapse. No complaints had been
made as yet against the Tennents' revival activities. The opposition remained under cover, working through control of the synod, and of all
but one of the presbyteries. The East Jersey, or New York Presbytery,
in which nearly all the Dickinson group were located, was the exception. The Long Island Presbytery had practically ceased to exist as an

organization. Donegal, Lewes, New Castle, and Philadelphia Presbyteries were controlled by the main Scotch-Irish party. The Tennent group were scattered here and there all through the synod.

Feeling in the synod was now intensified by another affair. Richard Zancky (or Sanckey) (then, or later that same year, the son-in-law of John Thomson) had come up for ordination in Donegal Presbytery. It was discovered that his ordination sermon was plagiarized. Moreover, he had chosen heretical writers from which to plagiarize. To a friend, Henry Hunter, in the neighboring Presbytery of New Castle he had furnished the same materials for the same purpose. Zancky, however, was merely rebuked and his ordination delayed for a time.[59] The same synod found Joseph Morgan, one of its older members who had long been a bitter opponent of Frelinghuysen, under suspension for drunkenness.[60] By 1737, therefore, it was evident that the future was to bring " not . . . peace, but a sword " to the American Presbyterians.

4

THE DEFEAT OF THE LOG COLLEGE MEN

Though the schism that finally occurred did not come until 1741, the die was actually cast by the synod of 1738. From the beginnings of the Church in 1706 until 1738, over eighty ministers had labored under its jurisdiction. Thirty-one had come from Ireland, twelve from Scotland, twenty-one from New England, ten from England and Wales, six were from Tennent's Log College, and the backgrounds of the remaining six are uncertain.[1] As the parties generally aligned themselves, the Scotch-Irish subscriptionists had contributed forty-three men during these thirty-two years; the New England, old England men, thirty-one; the Tennent group, six; and no one can now say which party held the loyalties of the six whose origins are obscure. The Scotch-Irish party had maintained a precarious plurality for some years. In 1738, of the synod's forty-seven listed members only twenty-eight were present: Dickinson and four of his friends, five of the Tennent group, fifteen of the Scotch-Irish subscriptionist-antirevival party, and three Scotch-Irish members who stood alternately with the main party and with the Tennent group. Eight of the Scotch-Irish group, eleven of Dickinson's followers, and William Tennent, Sr., were absent. The Scotch-Irish party, who were now a bare half of the synod's total enrolled membership, took advantage of their majority at this session and cast the die. Several most significant measures were passed which led irrevocably to the schism of 1741.

The first move was regarding vacant congregations and itinerant ministers. Everywhere in the presbyteries on the frontier, and in Donegal Presbytery especially, there were a large number of communities without any regular preaching. Donegal Presbytery was the storm center on the matter of intrusions, though trouble was reported two years later in a lesser degree in New Castle Presbytery, and one year later in Philadelphia Presbytery.

When one considers what a " congregation " meant at this time, the vacancy and itinerancy problem becomes easier to understand. The boundaries of one single parish, for instance, might extend for more than twenty miles from the meetinghouse in any direction. Whatever territory had been assigned to a certain presbytery was assumed to be wholly under their control whether or not they were doing anything to provide it with a ministry. Not all these parishes had meetinghouses, and when one did have a building, it was often practically inaccessible to many of the persons whom the presbytery had assigned as belonging to that "congregation." Dozens of severe struggles were held over the tendency of presbyteries to be too conservative in permitting new communities to have a place of worship of their own. Roads and transportation were such that real hardships arose from presbyteries' reluctance to act when meetinghouses were too far apart. Presbyteries' reluctances usually arose through the local minister's plea that a dividing of the congregation would hurt him financially. On the frontier, ministers frequently found it hard to collect their salaries. This was especially true when the minister was unpopular with his people. The demand for dividing a congregation usually meant less support for the local minister. Consequently he would oppose the division, and the resulting tension between him and his people would make his salary payments even smaller, and the situation increasingly bitter.

An intrusion, therefore, could occur in any one of several very understandable ways. Frequently presbyteries were unable to fill all the requests for ministers that came to them. Yet, if a congregation that its presbytery could not supply wished to call in some Presbyterian probationer, or a minister from another presbytery, it ran grave risks. It was ordered first to ask its own presbytery to approve the man, even though he was an active Presbyterian minister. Since presbyteries seldom met more than once a quarter, it was very hard for a vacant frontier church to plan so far ahead. Moreover, when the request was made at a meeting of presbytery, any one minister could have the petition denied without stating his reasons.

When long-vacant congregations and earnest ministers rebelled against such rules, the congregation committed a "censurable offense," and the minister was guilty of an "intrusion." A preaching service held, upon invitation, in a barn belonging to one of the people was counted an "intrusion," if a minister in another congregation, even a hundred miles away yet in that same presbytery, did not like (for reasons which he did not have to state) the visiting minister from another presbytery who had preached. The preferences and desires of the members of these vacant churches were never recognized in any of these rules against "intrusions." The clergy of the Scotch-Irish group were trying to take all power into their own hands. Too many of the lay people were interested in the revival movement. If left to themselves, they would call Log College men. The Maidenhead-Hopewell congregation had to defend their right (1738) to hear a second candidate before accepting the man whom the antirevival presbytery was seeking to force upon them in defiance of all Presbyterian law.[2] Similar instances of presbyterial highhandedness occurred in other presbyteries.

Going uninvited into a church that was under a regular pastor, trying to preach in his pulpit, or setting up a rival congregation, was not done by the Tennent group. After the schism of 1741, rival churches did spring up, but not before. The only culpable offenses came from two temporary hangers-on of the Log College group.[3] Gilbert Tennent did, however, consistently maintain that people who were under ministers opposing the revival had every right to use an " extra-ordinary method " by calling in an occasional itinerating evangelist to preach. No minister " owned " his congregation. Samuel Blair declared, " But they could never charge either of us [himself and Gilbert Tennent], and that I know of, with any Irruptions, as they call them, into their proper Congregations, that they could judicially censure."[4] The Scotch-Irish party themselves stated a few years later that the intrusion issue had arisen over " sending missionaries into vacancies in the bounds of other presbyteries without their invitation, and against their judgment, without so much as hearing their reasons or striving to satisfy their conscientious scruples in the matter."

The Tennent group secured action at this synod erecting a new presbytery, called the New Brunswick Presbytery, made up of Gilbert Tennent, William Tennent, Jr., Samuel Blair, Eleazar Wales (a New Englander), and John Cross (a Scotsman who had been quite successful in the revival).[5] The two other Tennents, William, Sr., and Charles, remained in the Philadelphia and New Castle Presbyteries respectively. The object of securing the erection of this presbytery, as the Tennents told Whitefield the following year, was to enable them to license and ordain a group of godly and well-qualified men for the ministry.[6] The territory for which they asked was very large. It included the present presbyteries of New Brunswick, Monmouth, Elizabeth, Newton, and Lehigh. Here then would be ample opportunity for evangelism and expansion. Then too, since the right of licensure and ordination had always belonged to presbyteries, they could now train, license, ordain, and use a native ministry for the frontier Church. During the first three years of the existence of this presbytery, 1738-1741, it had an average of six ordained ministers. Undaunted, however, these ministers preached with more or less regularity in fifty different stations scattered from the Delaware Water Gap to Cape May, endeavoring to provide at least some kind of Christian ministry in these tiny frontier communities of New Jersey.[7]

The opposition party could not let matters rest thus. Unless something were done quickly, the Church of the future would be shaped by ideals other than their own. They determined, accordingly, to root out the Tennent group entirely. Someone from Lewes Presbytery brought in an overture which proposed that in order to make sure that all who entered the ministry were duly qualified, all who had not a degree from some New England or European college should be examined by a committee of synod. This committee would then issue, if the applicant seemed fitted, a certificate which synod would accept in lieu of a university degree. Moreover, all who came before the synod for licensure, whatever school they came from, should also be examined. Since most of the candidates from Ireland were licensed before emigrating, this rule would not apply to them. The bill was passed by a majority, though not unanimously.[8]

The overture as such was very reasonable and good. It was, however, not wholly fair. No mention is made of William Tennent, Sr., and his excellent work, nor was he given a place on the committee of examiners for his area. The supposition of the overture was that locally trained men were coming into the synod who were not properly qualified. This was quite untrue.[9] The Log College men then in the synod were the three surviving sons of Tennent — Gilbert, William, Jr., and Charles — Samuel Blair, and, in the view of some, David Alexander. That this last-named man was trained in the Log College is very doubtful.[10] As for the regular Log College group, their subsequent record in the Church shows them to have been men of unusual ability, and of passionate zeal in providing educational facilities for others. The Scotch-Irish party's record, on the contrary, shows very little accomplished in educational work, and not a single man, save Alison, to compare with the Tennents, the Blairs, Davies, Smith, and the others who came from the Log College group. The bill was passed, though Gilbert Tennent charged during the debate that it was intended to wreck his father's attempts to train a godly ministry.

The Tennent group undoubtedly were confirmed in their analysis of the act on the education of ministers by another action of the synod. Gillespie presented to synod a protest against Donegal Presbytery's failure to discipline John Thomson's son-in-law, Zancky, for plagiarizing his ordination sermon. Moreover, the presbytery had omitted from their minutes any word about Zancky's plagiarism. The ruling party in the synod, however, passed a resolution stating that Zancky had given signs of deep repentance, etc., and that he might now be ordained.[11] The manner in which the antirevival party thus overrode all objections in order to spare Thomson's son-in-law, together with the manner in which they were shortly to ordain John Hindman, and Thomson's own son, is clear evidence of how little sincerity or moral earnestness lay behind this professed concern over the educational weaknesses of the Log College.[12]

The synod of 1738 was a victory for the subscriptionist-antirevival party, who had made the utmost use of the opportunity granted them in having a majority present at the sessions. The die was cast, but they had not foreseen the events that were to follow. By the year 1739 the three parties, the Scotch-Irish party, the Log College men, and the group from New England, had become quite clearly defined.

As the Church had expanded, some very significant patterns had emerged. New York and New Brunswick Presbyteries were now made up largely of second and third generation descendants of the New England Puritan settlers. Mingled in these congregations were descendants of other early settlers — Scots, Dutch, and Huguenots. Intermarriage had begun to blend all these Presbyterians into a homogeneous Church. Here the Church was stable, ministerial discipline was strict, and the congregational life was regular and wholesome. The subscriptionist party was almost nonexistent in these presbyteries, and Jonathan Dickinson and Gilbert Tennent were the two most influential leaders. Here also the revival had had its greatest influence.

The presbyteries of Philadelphia, New Castle, and Lewes also were located in areas where the population was very mixed. The earlier Puritan stock had been balanced in most of these Presbyterian congregations by the large influx of Scotch-Irish. The small Dutch and Huguenot elements were mingled largely with the older stock. For the most part the older settlers stood over against the Scotch-Irish immigrants, and there was as yet little intermingling. In these presbyteries the subscriptionist party, who included most of the Scotch-Irish and were bitterly opposed to the revival, were now fairly well entrenched. An earnest and sincere minority led by such men as Gillespie, of New Castle Presbytery, and William Tennent, Sr., of Philadelphia Presbytery, were at times able to maintain the integrity of these presbyteries and were at other times overruled by the majority.

The Scotch-Irish on the outer frontier labored under less favorable circumstances. The scattered settlements, with poor means of communication, often without a meetinghouse or any regular preaching, with no schools, with every opportunity for vice and scarcely none for virtue, needed bitterly a ministry of the strongest type. The loneliness of the frontier only intensified the individualism of the Scotch-Irish. Since their homeland was not in a flourishing state of spiritual life when they left it, they had come to America not a deeply religious people. Their formal piety was soon dropped off, and in their isolation and lack, degeneration set in. Worst of all, a great portion of the clergy were not fitted for their tasks. That many were spiritually and morally delinquent is only too obvious. Yet even such men as Thomson and Alison, who were moral men personally, seem to have been unable to meet the situation. They were still living in the Old World, with its traditions and hereditary ways and outlooks. Nevertheless these traditions had lost their real meaning. They had become abstract and impersonal, the marks of a party rather than the expressions of a living Christian faith.

When, therefore, the Log College wing of the Scotch-Irish looked back over their traditions and saw how, in other days, great declensions in spiritual and moral life had been overcome by their forefathers, they took steps toward revitalizing their inheritance from Puritanism and Scottish Presbyterianism. They attempted to restore to the Church the preaching message of such English Puritans as William Perkins, John Preston, or Richard Sibbes; or such New England Puritans as John Norton, Thomas Hooker, Thomas Shepherd, or John Cotton; or such Scottish and Scotch-Irish revivalists and reformers as David Dickson, Robert Blair, John Livingstone, and Andrew Stewart. The piety they inculcated was that which had been made well known by such writers as Richard Baxter, Joseph Alleine, John Flavell, Samuel Rutherford, William Guthrie, James Durham, and John Bunyan.[13] References to these and similar authors are frequent in the Tennent literature.

The Log College men used few of the methods and means that were commonly associated with the later revivalism. The " protracted meeting," a concerted effort exerted over a period of weeks, was unknown. Revival preaching was largely confined to the stated services of the week — Sunday morning and afternoon and one weekday afternoon. Evening services were impractical on the frontier. The "mourners' bench," the "inquirers' room," the "anxious seat," and other methods for bringing about an immediate conversion during the service, were not used. These were first introduced in the nineteenth century, and raised the celebrated " New Measures " controversy. Those affected by the preaching of the Log College men generally sought spiritual counsel in private, after they had left the meetinghouse. Although it was felt that the sinner would be better off if he made his own pilgrim journey into the Kingdom, personal counseling played a great part. Many of those who were convicted of their sin because of the preaching they had heard would call upon the minister during the week. The ministers themselves gave much of their time and tireless energies to systematic home visitation. Often persons convicted of their sin would find peace and assurance through the help of members of their families or other lay people. The Christian home as a teaching and nurturing cell, or unit, of the Church was an essential part of the theory and strategy of the Tennents. Sudden conversions were rare. Long periods of conviction and struggle were more common. Lay activity was an important factor in the Great Awakening.

The Log College revivals were not sudden outbursts. Such momentary movements were called " stirrings," or some such name, to indicate that they had not developed into a real revival. A true revival was one that carried on for several months, or even as long as two consecutive years. As the Log College men saw it, this was a revival in contrast to a passing emotional stir that had no real constructive and lasting results.

One of the best contemporary descriptions of a revival in this period is that by Samuel Blair of the revival that he saw in his congregation at Fagg's Manor, Pennsylvania, in 1740. The account reveals clearly the outlook and methods of a typical Log College revivalist. When Blair came to the church as pastor, he wrote, he found many good religious people in it who performed their religious obligations rather well. Yet they were, he felt, formal and rather light about it all.

" If they performed these duties pretty punctually in their seasons, and, as they thought, with a good meaning, out of conscience, and not just to obtain a name for religion among men, then they were ready to conclude that they were truly and sincerely religious. A very lamentable ignorance of the main essentials of true practical religion, and the doctrines nearly relating thereunto, very generally prevailed. The nature and necessity of the *new birth* was but little known or thought of, the necessity of a conviction of sin and misery, by the Holy Spirit's opening and applying the law to the conscience, in order to a saving closure with Christ, was hardly known at all to the most. It was thought, that if there was any need of a heart-distressing sight of the soul's danger, and fear of divine wrath, it was only needful for the grosser sort of sinners; and for any others to be deeply exercised this way (as there might be some rare instances observable), this was generally looked upon to be a great evil and temptation that had befallen those persons. The common names for such soul-concern were, *melancholy, trouble of mind, or despair*. These terms were in common, so far as I have been acquainted, indifferently used as synonymous; and *trouble of mind* was looked upon as a great evil, which all persons that made any sober profession and practice of religion, ought carefully to avoid. . . . There was scarcely any suspicion at all, in general, of any danger of depending upon self-righteousness, and not upon the righteousness of Christ alone for salvation. Papists and Quakers would be readily acknowledged guilty of this crime, but hardly any professed Presbyterian. The necessity of being first in Christ by a vital union, and in a justified state, before our religious services can be well pleasing and acceptable to God, was very little understood or thought of; but the common notion seemed to be, that if people were aiming to be in the way of duty as well as they could, as they imagined, there was no reason to be much afraid."

Blair's people were mostly Scotch-Irish immigrants, traditionally Presbyterian. The revival began after he (and another unnamed minister who aided him for a few weeks) had been preaching "awakening" sermons for about six months. As the revival came on, Blair wrote, he observed that concern grew on the people, and weeping occurred during his preaching. "While I was speaking . . . , they could no longer contain, but burst out in the most bitter mourning. I desired them, as much as possible, to restrain themselves from making a noise that would hinder themselves or others from hearing what was spoken: and often afterwards I had occasion to repeat the same counsel. I still advised people to endeavour to moderate their passions, but not so as to resist or stifle their convictions. The number of the awakened increased very fast, frequently under sermons there were some newly convicted, and brought into deep distress of soul about their perishing estate. Our sabbath assemblies soon became vastly large: many people from almost all parts around inclining very much to come where there was such appearance of the divine power and presence. I think there was scarcely a sermon or lecture preached here through that whole summer [the revival began in the spring after a whole winter of awakening preaching], but there was manifest evidences of impressions on the hearers; and many times the impressions were very great and general: several would be overcome and fainting; others deeply sobbing, hardly able to contain, others crying in a most dolorous manner, many others more silently weeping; and a solemn concern appearing in the countenance of many others. And sometimes the soul exercises of some, though comparatively but very few, would so far affect their bodies, as to occasion some strange, unusual bodily motions. I had opportunities of speaking particularly with a great many of those who afforded such outward tokens of inward soul concern in the time of public worship and hearing of the word; indeed many came to me of themselves in their distress for private instruction and counsel; and I found, so far as I can remember, that, with by far the greater part, their apparent concern in public was not just a transient qualm of conscience, or merely a floating commotion of the affections; but a rational fixed conviction of their dangerous perishing state. . . . They saw that they had been contenting themselves with the form, without the life and power of Godliness; and that they had been taking peace to their consciences from, and depending upon, their own righteousness, and not the righteousness of Jesus Christ. In a word, they saw that true practical religion was quite another thing than they had conceived it to be, or had any true experience of.

"The main scope of my preaching through that summer, was, laying open the deplorable state of man by nature since the fall, our ruined, exposed case by the breach of the first covenant, and the awful condition of such as were not in Christ, giving the marks and characters of such as were in that condition: and moreover, laying open the way of recovery in the new covenant, through a Mediator, with the nature and necessity of faith in Christ, the Mediator, etc. I laboured much on the last mentioned heads, that people might have right apprehensions of the gospel method of life and salvation. I treated much on the way of a sinner's closing with Christ by faith, and obtaining a right peace to an awakened wounded conscience; shewing, that persons were not to take peace to themselves on account of their repentings, sorrows, prayers, and reformations, nor to make these things the ground of their adventuring themselves upon Christ and His righteousness, and of their expectations of life by Him: and, that neither were they to obtain or seek peace in extraordinary ways, by visions, dreams, or immediate inspirations; but by an understanding view and believing persuasion of the way of life as revealed in the Gospel, through the suretyship, obedience, and sufferings of Jesus Christ, with a view of the suitableness and suffering of that mediatory righteousness of Christ for the justification and life of law-condemned sinners; and thereupon freely accepting Him for their Saviour, heartily consenting to, and being well-pleased with, that way of salvation; and venturing their all upon His mediation, from the warrant and encouragement afforded of God thereunto in His Word, by His free offer, authoritative command, and sure promise to those that so believe. I endeavoured to show the fruits and evidences of a true faith."

Blair made it a practice to talk things over privately with each convert until he was certain that the latter understood what conversion was and could see in himself the corresponding evidences of such a change. He found, he records, that the professed converts fell roughly into four classes: (1) Those who really knew what conversion meant, whose experiences seemed genuine, and who had a well-grounded assurance of their salvation. (2) Those who had passed through vivid experiences of conviction, who had valid conceptions of Christian experience, but who could hardly believe that they were truly saved. These Blair encouraged to trust in God both for salvation and for its assurance. (3) Those whose understanding of conversion was obscure, whose general education was poor, but whose Christian experiences seemed genuine, and whose assurance of salvation was clear. These he worked with, instructing them, and striving to bring them into a knowledge of the ways of salvation that would enable them to grow properly. (4) Those whose ideas of conversion were false, or who were wholly ignorant on the matter, but who had worked themselves up emotionally and had gone through what they thought was a conversion experience. These Blair taught the meaning of conversion and sought to bring them into it.[14]

Those who fought the revival made much of the "excesses" that they saw in it.[15] Yet many of the laity of all classes were able to overlook these things. William Tennent, Jr., and Jonathan Dickinson opposed the faintings and the outcries from the very beginning. Gilbert Tennent never encouraged them, nor did he ever regard them as in any way necessary, or indicative of more than terror and remorse. Moreover, there is good reason to believe there was much less uncontrolled emotionalism than the exaggerated reports and subsequent accounts would indicate.[16] Long before such unusual outbursts as at Rowland's revival at Maidenhead and Hopewell, or before Davenport's unhappy affair in New England, the opposition had framed its case. Yet even so, most of the lay people, knowing full well the facts about these excesses, continued to make their choice between the two groups of clergymen. They knew the Tennents, and they knew their opponents. That the greater part of the Church chose to follow the Log College men rather than their opponents cannot be overlooked in forming an estimate of the movement.

Thus there were pitted against each other two rather unevenly matched groups. The Log College party numbered but five men, supported at times by three sympathizers. Their opponents numbered around twenty. Yet the Tennent party were men of unusual force and ability, and, with the laity turning more and more in their favor, the situation was becoming critical. The opposition were a group of small men who knew of no means adequate to reach the public. Their patterns of action were the highhanded policies of the ruling cliques in the Presbyterian Churches of Scotland and Ireland at that time. The Log College men came to the conclusion that the opposition were against every form of real revival, reform, and discipline. Not realizing the consequences, and depending upon their own growing strength and popularity, they loosed so devastating an attack upon the opponents of the revival that these in turn were driven to their last resort, namely, the illegal expulsion of the Tennents.

Another critical year had come in 1739. Synod met, with the Scotch-Irish group again holding a clear majority because of the absence of most of the New England party. In rapid succession four measures were passed against the Log College party. The Presbytery of New Brunswick, controlled by the Tennent party, protested against two acts passed by synod the previous year, the act against the Log College and the act against itinerating. Both protests were overridden, changes being inserted that left the meaning and application of the acts still definitely against the revival and its supporters. In the eyes of the main Scotch-Irish faction the Log College group had violated each of these acts in the past year.

In accordance with the usual procedure, synod appointed committees to check the records of the various presbyteries. To examine New Brunswick Presbytery's books synod chose two men, Henry Hook, who had been suspended some years earlier on the gravest of charges and then lightly shrived,[17] and Richard Zancky, newly made a member of synod. These good gentlemen reported to synod that the New Brunswick Presbytery had examined and licensed John Rowland, in violation of synod's act requiring a prior examination before one of its commissions. This presbytery had written: " Presbytery came to this unanimous conclusion, viz.: That they were not in point of conscience, restrained by said act from using the liberty and power which presbyteries have all along hitherto enjoyed; but that it was their duty to take the said Mr. Rowland upon trial, for which conclusion they conceive they have several weighty and sufficient reasons." [18] The presbytery here was harking back to two things: first, the right of a minority to protest in a point of conscience. This had been posited by Jonathan Dickinson and several others as far back as 1722 and accepted by the synod. Secondly, the presbytery pointed out that the rights of licensure and ordination have always belonged to a presbytery. On this right of licensure, granted by the Directory for which the Scotch-Irish party were so zealous, the Log College men professed to stand.

An issue was thus raised as to whether the real seat of authority in Presbyterianism lay in presbytery or in the higher judicature. The Tennents claimed it for the presbytery and their opponents claimed it for the synod.[19] No form of government had, of course, as yet been adopted by the synod; everything, therefore, depended upon arguments based on English and Scottish precedents, or upon majority votes in a given session of the synod. Gilbert Tennent argued that to grant such power to synod was contrary to the Presbyterian system, a reflection upon the presbyteries, and in the end reared a system so much like the legislative powers of the Church of England as to make wrong the Presbyterian protests against the Anglicans. A synod able to legislate as it pleased would soon equal the Church of England in bigotry and intolerance.[20] As a compromise, the New Brunswick Presbytery offered to allow synod to send two official representatives, with power to vote, to sit with them each time they were examining a candidate for the ministry. The Scotch-Irish group countered with a demand for enough representatives to constitute a clear majority.[21] Quite evidently they were not interested in any compromise that would result in the ordinations of Log College men.

The issue was not over whether or not Rowland was fitted for the ministry. His subsequent record, like the records of other Log College men, shows him to have been equal to most of his opponents, and far superior to many of them.[22] Those who opposed his ordination argued that he was inadequately trained in philosophy and metaphysics.[23] The most common charge against the Log College was that it was weak in what were then called " physicks, ethicks, metaphysicks and pnewmaticks." The Tennents, to a man, opposed the ordination of untrained ministers, and the use of lay exhorters, from the very beginning of their work through to the end.[24] Among the " several weighty and sufficient reasons " they claimed to have had for licensing Rowland, one may well have been the fact that Donegal Presbytery had ordained Richard Zancky, John Thomson's son-in-law, on August 31, 1738. It seems that he had a sermon of his own on that occasion. New Brunswick Presbytery licensed Rowland a week later, September 7, 1738. John Thomson, Jr., the son of the leader of the opposition, was ordained about that same time in Lewes Presbytery.[25] He was evidently a man of no promise, for after supplying here and there for a few months, he ceased to exercise his ministerial office and departed with his father to Virginia. The ordinations of Zancky and Thomson, Jr., no doubt played a part in the New Brunswick Presbytery's attitude toward their licensure of Rowland.

How much of a party issue Rowland's case was is seen in the demand of the antirevival group that Rowland make up his supposed educational deficiencies by studying further under an ardent member of their party, Alison.[26] This was a direct insult to William Tennent, Sr., and though he would have submitted for the sake of peace, his sons and former pupils would not. Ashbel Green is perhaps right in saying that part of the reason for this struggle for a synodical examination lay in Alison's jealousy of William Tennent, Sr.[27]

Not only had Rowland's licensure given the antirevival party offense, but so had his pastoral activity and the considerable revival that accompanied his labors. Following the suspension for drunkenness of Joseph Morgan, an opponent of the revival, the Presbytery of Philadelphia had divided his old congregation, the Maidenhead-Hopewell-Amwell charge. One of the newly formed congregations was made up almost wholly of people in sympathy with the revival. In an effort to quell this interest, the presbytery attempted to force upon the church the settlement of John Guild, a young opponent of the revival. However, a considerable number of the congregation stood upon their Presbyterian right to hear another candidate as well, and the presbytery had been compelled to grant them this their constitutional right. Fearing, however, that their interest in the revival would lead the congregation to seek to hear a Log College man, the presbytery granted them leave to call any *regularly* licensed or ordained man. The church invited John Rowland, and almost at once experienced a revival of unusual proportions.[28] The antirevival party then charged that Rowland was not a *regularly* licensed man. The congregation, therefore, was guilty of acting "disorderly," and Rowland was guilty of "intrusion." A month after Rowland began preaching at the Hopewell church, the presbytery moved to regain control of the situation by restoring Morgan to his ministerial office, and asking the congregation to receive him again as their pastor. The move was more than a failure, for not only did the people refuse to receive Morgan, but they also demanded that they be permitted to leave the jurisdiction of the Philadelphia Presbytery and be placed under New Brunswick Presbytery, on whose borders they were located.[29] A long and exceedingly bitter fight ensued.

A short while later the Presbytery of Philadelphia, controlled by antirevival ministers, censured William Tennent, Sr., for allowing Rowland to preach as a guest in his pulpit. The congregation also were rebuked for tolerating Rowland's presence in the pulpit.[30] The presbytery had met on that occasion at Tennent's church for the purpose of installing there, as copastor with Tennent, Francis McHenry, a young member of the Scotch-Irish party. Tennent had protested against McHenry's settlement for some months, but had finally agreed to it. After having been rebuked by the presbytery for allowing Rowland to preach in his pulpit, Tennent had denied their right to interfere and had left the meeting. His defiance of the presbytery had made the issue regarding Rowland all the more intense. It was against such a background that the synod of 1739 found Rowland's licensure illegal, and the New Brunswick Presbytery guilty of violating the laws of the Church. That characters such as Zancky and Hook were appointed to bring in the report on Rowland's licensure, of which everyone already knew in detail, was doubly hard for the Log College men to endure.[31]

Once synod had disposed of Rowland's case, they proceeded to lay plans for erecting a school or seminary. No mention was made of Tennent's school, nor was Tennent asked to co-operate. Yet William Tennent, Sr., his three sons, and Samuel Blair all voted for the new school. So did Dickinson and Pemberton, the two New York Presbytery members present. The committee appointed on the matter was to be synod's general commission and certain correspondents from each of the presbyteries. Three months later the commission met. To a man, Dickinson's party and the Log College men, those on the general commission and those appointed as correspondents, were absent. Just why all these were absent can only be conjectured. The committee was composed of ten of the Scotch-Irish party, one of the Log College party, three of the Dickinson group, and two men who took a middle course. Those of the committee who did meet sensed a stalemate. After deciding to write to Pemberton, asking that he forward their appeal for money to New England, they adjourned, having accomplished nothing.[32]

That fall the New England group centering in the Presbytery of New York met at the church of John Pierson, one of Dickinson's closest friends, and an influential member of the presbytery in his own right. Pierson was under attack, it seems, from a group within his congregation who felt that he was not sufficiently zealous, and that he was cool toward the revival. Dickinson preached before the presbytery and the congregation a stern and pointed rebuke to the critics of Pierson, declaring that " when our Consciences are imposed upon by sinful Terms of Communion, or what we esteem to be such; when our Minister is openly vicious or immoral; or his Doctrines heterodox and subversive of the Fundamentals of Christianity, and vital Piety; when the Ordinances of the Gospel are neglected, or corruptly administered; and the great Duties of the Ministry sloathfully omitted, or triflingly and carelessly performed; and when there can be no Redress of such Grievances from the Discipline Christ has appointed in his Church; I think a Man may then have a Call to peacefully withdraw from such a Ministry, and list himself under another." But, Dickinson continued, none of these conditions exists in this congregation. In no uncertain terms he reprimanded Pierson's critics.[33]

Turbulent and undisciplined feelings were everywhere being stirred up by the heated controversy over the revival. A crisis in the life of the Church had come. In principle Dickinson and the Tennents were in agreement as to when a people might criticize and leave a minister. But would the preaching of such things produce reform or mere chaos? The Tennents had never criticized Pierson, but those aroused by the revival had. For the New England men the problem had become severe. Was the Tennents' picture of the declension within the Church's ministry true? If so, then the New Englanders were on record as being against such a ministry. Or was the antirevival party correct in saying that the revival movement was a fanatical thing which struck at all but its own adherents blindly, indiscriminately, and perversely? If so, then any minister, however godly and useful, might well suffer what had befallen Pierson unless this ugly frenzy were rooted out speedily. Upon the spiritual insight and moral integrity of the New Englanders had come to rest the future of American Presbyterianism.

As the year drew to a close, it was apparent that the Log College group had been decisively defeated within the Church courts. The outlook for them in the Church at large also was bleak. The entire scene was changed, however, by the sudden and unexpected appearance of George Whitefield.

WHITEFIELD TURNS THE TIDE

The fame of the great English evangelist George Whitefield had reached the American colonies before his unannounced arrival at Philadelphia, November 2, 1739. His only purpose in stopping there was to take on a few supplies which would enable him to complete his journey to Georgia. There he intended to carry forward the work of an orphanage that he had founded on his first trip to Georgia. An evangelistic tour of the middle colonies was far removed from any of his thoughts.[1] Notwithstanding Whitefield's plans, events took a very different course. Upon his arrival in Philadelphia he could not be silent, but preached in the Anglican Church, and from the courthouse steps, to large audiences. On November 10, William Tennent, Sr., hitherto unknown to Whitefield, called upon him. It has been suggested, and in view of subsequent events it is not at all unlikely, that Tennent came to ask Whitefield to stay in the area for a season and assist in the revival begun by the Log College men.[2]

Immediately after this meeting with the elder Tennent, Whitefield began an evangelistic tour of the strongholds of the Log College men, and of the New England group headed by Dickinson. On November 13 he preached for Gilbert Tennent, November 15 for Pemberton, November 19 for Dickinson, back to Gilbert Tennent on the 20th, for Rowland at Maidenhead on the 21st, at the Log College in Neshaminy the 22d, and in Philadelphia from the 23d to the 29th. After three days with William Tennent, Jr., and others in New Castle Presbytery, he passed out of the bounds of the synod. He had been in the area of the synod an even month.[3] During this short period of time the young evangelist, just twenty-four years of age, had preached to thousands of hearers, of all classes. Even men like Franklin had been impressed. Morals were reformed, and the spiritual life of the churches, especially the Presbyterian, was much revived. How much his success was the harvest of the labors of the Tennents is seen in that once he left the borders of the synod he found himself preaching to tiny congregations in a spiritual desert.[4] Short though his stay was, Whitefield aroused a good deal of opposition. In such journals as the *Pennsylvania Gazette*,[5] and the *Boston Weekly News Letter*,[6] the evangelist was attacked and defended. At times he openly courted opposition by his attacks on the clergy.

For the Log College men Whitefield had turned the tide of battle in a critical hour. Not only had the evangelist spread their localized revival all through the synod, but he had definitely won the large and influential New York Presbytery, led by Dickinson, to the revival cause. The troubles of Pierson at Woodbridge, which had so aroused Dickinson, were not to be identified with the revival as such. These New Englanders had been prepared for the coming of Whitefield by the news of Edwards' great revival in New England, and by a considerable revival in their own midst. Aaron Burr, a recent graduate of Yale, had been converted during the Edwardean revival in Connecticut. After about a year and a half of earnest labor in Newark, he started a considerable revival in his congregation during August of 1739.[7] Accordingly, when Whitefield came among them, he found the New Englanders eager to receive him. The Tennents were now no more five lone men in the midst of the hostile Scotch-Irish majority who opposed the revival. An intense interest in a form of Christianity that meant something to ordinary folk had been aroused among the laity of the entire synod by Whitefield. The entrance of lay people into the movement in large numbers effectively altered the balance of power in favor of the Tennents. But for Whitefield, the opponents of the revival might have stamped it out. After Whitefield's tour the opposition fought on, but theirs was a losing fight.

The revival had been spread throughout all the colonies, not only by Whitefield, but by the colonial press. Periodicals in Philadelphia, New York, Boston, and Charlestown (South Carolina), had carried glowing accounts of Whitefield's evangelistic preaching and its wonderful results. During that same year, Gilbert Tennent had published in Boston and New York seven items, William Tennent, Jr., one, and Samuel Blair one; and the Tennent group had issued jointly a book of four sacramental sermons. By the end of 1739, sixteen different publications by the Log College men were being sold by booksellers from Boston to Philadelphia. An earlier year, 1737, had witnessed also the first American edition of Jonathan Edwards' *Faithful Narrative of the Surprising Work of God*. The London edition of 1736 was likely circulated in some measure in the colonies even before that time. In 1738 a reissue of the *Narrative* was published, together with several of Edwards' revival sermons.

Whitefield was definitely an Anglican when he first arrived in Philadelphia. He preached in the Anglican Church, or in the open air, as an Anglican, using the rituals and liturgies of the Establishment. When he preached in Gilbert Tennent's meetinghouse, he used the Anglican ritual. Upon being excluded from the Anglican pulpit in New York, he was greatly distressed. Only after learning that Commissary Vesey had once preached in the Dutch church did he accept Pemberton's invitation to preach in the Presbyterian church. Gilbert Tennent had a great influence on the young English evangelist. Tennent's passion, zeal, and preaching made a deep impression on him. Moreover, due to the Log College men, Whitefield's theological views underwent a great change. Before coming to Philadelphia, Whitefield was more or less a follower of the Moravians and German Pietists. Under the influence of the Tennents, Whitefield gradually turned from the theology of the Moravians, Wesley, and German Pietism, to a type of Calvinism which finally won for him Toplady's praise, and cost him the friendship of the Moravians and the Methodists.[8]

By the spring of 1740 the revival had spread over a very wide area. Aaron Burr's congregation was at the zenith of its awakening. Jonathan Dickinson was aiding young Burr in the work. Another church in that presbytery, Goshen, New York, was having a great revival under its pastor, Silas Leonard, a recent graduate of Yale. William Tennent, Jr., was his counselor and helper. Rowland's revival at Maidenhead was in a most fruitful stage. The most remarkable revival of this year was under Samuel Blair at New Londonderry, or Fagg's Manor, Pennsylvania.[9]

Over in the neighboring Presbytery of Donegal, twenty miles from Blair's church, was a vacant charge, the Nottingham Church. As interest in the revival grew in Blair's congregation, many from the nearby church at Nottingham began to attend his services. Donegal Presbytery had made only a feeble effort at supplying this vacancy. They had assigned supply preachers for only two Sundays between October, 1739, and May, 1740. Of these two preachers one, John Thomson, failed to obey the presbytery's appointment.[10] When, therefore, some of the congregation asked Blair to preach in their church, he complied. According to the synod's rule on itinerants, the people had no right to ask Blair in to preach. They ought first to have waited until the next meeting of their presbytery, Donegal, and then to have asked permission. If when this request for Blair's preaching was presented, any one minister in the presbytery had objected (his reasons need not have been given), the request would have been thereby vetoed. The Nottingham people had long been orderly, and their church had long been vacant.

Moreover, all knew that Donegal Presbytery would never allow Blair in any of its pulpits. Both the Nottingham people and Blair, therefore, ignored the presbytery, and violated synod's rule on " intrusions." Even worse, the people later invited Gilbert Tennent to come and preach. Donegal Presbytery demanded that Blair's presbytery (New Castle) discipline him for " intruding." New Castle Presbytery had in it few friends of the revival, and there was little doubt that the disciplinary censure would be forthcoming as soon as that body should meet.

When Tennent came, therefore, to preach at Nottingham on March 8, 1740, he cast all reserve and discretion to the winds. The sermon, " The Danger of an Unconverted Ministry," on the text Mark 6:34, was no mere tirade, but a carefully wrought polemic of such devastating efficiency that it accomplished too much. It was directed squarely against the opponents of the revival, who were well known to all in the area of Donegal Presbytery. Their opposition to the revival, Tennent said, proved that they were themselves unregenerate. Though they had all the training, orthodoxy, party zeal, bigotry in small matters, yet they were dead in heart, and were making of the ministry no more than another trade or profession. They cared not for the sheep. Just as in Jesus' day he had felt that the people were without shepherds, though there were myriads of well-trained priests, lawyers, scribes, and Pharisees, so, Tennent said, today we have university-trained, legally ordained, orthodox preachers, but no shepherds to seek the lost. He urged his hearers to pray for those under the ministry of unconverted preachers and to apply, in a regular way, for permission to hear occasional sermons by converted preachers, if they felt that their preacher was not helping them to find a true conversion experience. No pastor, he said, had a right to bind other men fast to himself as the only preacher whom they could ever hear under any and all circumstances. That would be a " yoke worse than Rome."

The situation in the Church, and the situation in the Nottingham congregation, had set the stage for a more or less definitive statement by Gilbert Tennent, the acknowledged leader of the Log College group. That he selected the topic " The Danger of an Unconverted Ministry " indicates that he had chosen to make such a statement. By preaching on the nature of the ministry, Tennent caught the antirevival group on their weakest side, and also gave himself the opportunity of stating fully what the entire Log College group had often declared, in briefer form, was the real issue in the controversy over the revival. Unregenerate men, Tennent declared, have no call of God to the ministry. " Our Lord will not make men ministers, 'till they follow him. . . . Pharisee-teachers, having no experience of a special work of the Holy Ghost, upon their own souls, are therefore neither inclined to, nor fitted for, discoursing frequently, clearly, and pathetically, upon such important subjects." Unconverted ministers preach mostly on law, and on duty, thereby actually preaching salvation by works. Since they themselves know nothing of the struggle of soul through which earnest seekers after God must go, they are but little help to those who are seeking God. Their ministry is therefore generally unprofitable, as the Bible, reason, and experience prove. Moreover, their ministry endangers both doctrine and piety in the Church, for in effect they teach self-salvation through education, and deplore any real struggle of soul.[11]

By saying that unregenerate men had no call from God to the ministry, as all the Log College men repeatedly did, Tennent knew that he was reiterating a hated point. This theme of a divine call to the ministry had aroused the antirevival party to their depths. It was bad enough to call them unconverted ministers, but worse yet to add, or rather to premise, that only converted men were ever called by God into the ministry. The issue of a divine call to the ministry had figured largely in the controversy over the examination of candidates for the ministry as well.

" If it be inquir'd," wrote Samuel Finley, one of the more fiery of the younger Log College men, " What is this Call? And how may a Candidate be satisfy'd concerning it? I answer in brief, the ordinary Call of God is to be gather'd from the sincere and ardent desires of serving him in the Ministry of the Gospel, which he puts in the Hearts of those he Calls; from the Qualifications, and Dispositions which he gives, fitting them for the Work; from the secret Strength wherewith he supports, and supporting encourages them to undertake it, notwithstanding the known Difficulties that attend it, and the Sense of their own insufficiency for it; and his opening, in the Course of his Providence, a Door of entrance into the Office agreeable to the Order of his Church." [12]

To the antirevival party, however, the issue seemed very different. They denounced the Log College men for " their industriously persuading people to believe that the call of God whereby he calls men to the ministry, does not consist in their being regularly ordained and set apart to that work, according to the institution and rules of the word; but in some invisible motions and workings of the Spirit, which none can be conscious or sensible of but the person himself, and with respect to which he is liable to be deceived, or play the hypocrite; that the gospel preached in truth by unconverted ministers, can be of no saving benefit to souls." [13]

Gilbert Tennent specifically answered the charge by saying: " In Answer to the aforesaid Charge, we declare our Opinion as follows,

namely, we believe that there is a Necessity of previous Tryals and Ordination in order to the Ministry; and that such who are regularly set
apart, being sound in Doctrine, and blameless in Life, however their
inward State may be, are true Ministers in the Sight of the Church, and
that their Ministrations are valid. But in the mean time, we think that
none should undertake the ministerial Work but those that are truly
gracious; those that intend therein chiefly the Glory of God and Good
of Mankind; those that are inclined of God thereto: For we know not
how a graceless Man can be faithful in the Ministry.

"As to what is farther alledged in this Paragraph, *namely,* that the
Gospel preached by unconverted Ministers in Truth can be of no saving Benefit to Souls, according to our Opinion. This Charge we deny
as slanderous. God, as an absolute Sovreign, may use what Means he
pleases to accomplish his Work by. We only assert this, that Success by
unconverted Ministers Preaching is very improbable, and very seldom
happens, so far as we can gather." [14] The New Englanders, led by Pemberton and Burr, were shortly to express themselves no less decisively.
"A Minister of Jesus, that has never experienced a regenerating
Change; that has not received Christ the Lord; that does not walk in
the Steps of his humble and self-denying Life, is one of the greatest
Solecisms in Nature, a perpetual Contradiction of his Character, and
often proves an extensive Mischief to the Church of Christ." [15]

The revival party were not agitating themselves and their people
about the possibility that this or that minister who seemed all right
might be a secret hypocrite. "That some have judged some Ministers
to be carnal, I own; but that this was done without just Ground, I deny.
I have no Hesitation to say, that the Ministers whom they judged carnal, discover'd themselves too plainly to be so, in the Course of their
Lives; some by Ignorance of the Things of God, and Errors about
them, bantering and ridiculing of them; some by vicious Practices,
some both Ways, all by a furious Opposition to the Work of God in
the Land; and what need have we of further Witnesses?" [16]

The Log College men stood with classical Protestantism in making
the efficacy of a minister's labors depend, not upon his personal holiness, but upon his "calling." They contended, however, that there was
a distinction to be made between God's call of a man into His ministry
and the presbytery's ordination of a man. This the antirevival party denied. John Thomson granted that a distinction could be drawn between
the so-called inward and outward calls to the ministry. But, he said, the
inward call had only to do with the man's call to his personal salvation.
The outward call alone had anything to do with the call to the ministry. God is properly said to do whatever is done by the duly consti-

tuted officers of his Church. Therefore every man duly set apart by the Church is truly *called of God,* and he and his people are to look upon him as such, be he converted or a secret hypocrite.[17] Thomson, forsaking the entire Reformation tradition, declared that whatever a sinful, erring group of men calling themselves a presbytery might do had to be accepted by all men as the voice and act of God.[18]

The Log College men saw the issue clearly. " This is the Point at which Mr. Th . . . n and I [Finley] do part asunder, viz. That the Call of God to the Office of the Ministry, is distinguished from, tho' not opposed unto, the Presbytery's Trying and Ordaining a Person to that Office. This he denies, and we affirm." [19] Finley goes on to show the absurdity of Thomson's identification of the acts of Donegal Presbytery with the acts of God, by pointing to follies which that body had committed in ordaining men whom they knew were unworthy. " If Mr. Th . . . n say this is impossible for a Presbytery to do, to try a Man, and not approve of him, and yet set him apart by Ordination; then I will prove, that it is possible, because Mr. Th . . . n and his Brethren of Donegal Presbytery have actually done it; and if they please, may call upon me to prove it: They know I was present, when they examined and appointed to ordain a certain Man, and also did ordain him, and how little able they were to approve of him." [20]

By demanding that the acts of a Church judicature be recognized as the acts of God, the opponents of the revival revealed that beneath their entire policy lay an ugly form of clericalism. Not only did they assert their right to ordain whom they would and when, in defiance of the moral and religious sensibilities of their fellow ministers and the lay people of the Church in general, but they also demanded that such acts be looked upon as the acts of God, and therefore beyond question. It was this clericalism that also enabled the antirevival group to connive at the exoneration of immoral ministers and still demand that other ministers and the laity accept these dubious products of presbyterial and synodical trickery without protest.

Moreover, this same clericalism allowed them to assert, in defiance of the Presbyterian form of government, that, once installed in a congregation, by whatever scheming, the minister's position was like that of a husband, the divinely appointed head of the family and the household, and that the congregation was like the wife, the dutiful and submissive spouse, who must submit to her husband's authority in all things or be found guilty of adultery. Under such an interpretation of the minister's prerogatives, the session as the representatives of the people could have but little of the authority with which Presbyterianism had always clothed them. It was this same clericalism that gave birth to the arrogance and aloofness toward their people with which Gillespie charged the antirevival group as a whole.[21] Samuel Davies' words at the ordination of two young products of the revival would have seemed to these upholders of the rights of the ministry as perverse fanaticism. In the presence of the assembled presbytery and the two candidates for ordination, Davies told the congregation: "Look upon us [the clergy] as the friends, the lovers of your souls. If you can discover that we are not worthy of that character in some suitable degree, then it is your right as men, as Christians, and I may add, as Presbyterians, to reject us, and not own us as your ministers." [22] For the revival party the rights of the Church were greater than the rights of the clergy.

Gilbert Tennent's sermon on "The Dangers of an Unconverted Ministry" was aimed, therefore, at the basis of the entire position of the antirevival party — the qualifications and authority of the ministry. The opponents of the revival were driving for a "high-Presbyterianism," beyond all precedent and constitutional right, in an effort to kill the revival by ecclesiastical pressure. The "Nottingham sermon" technically contained nothing contrary to the Westminster theology, or to Puritan piety and ethics. Yet seldom, if ever, were these things stated in such a scathing denunciation. No names were mentioned. That was not necessary. Tennent preached the sermon with a deliberate plan in mind. The opposition were in control of the Church judicatories, where they could control the entrance of all new members, thus maintaining their majority forever, though the Church might meanwhile die for lack of an adequate clergy.

The Log College men, defeated by this controlled Church organization, appealed to the laity. They stated the issue as being for or against any real revival of spiritual and ethical life in the Presbyterian Church. They struck so hard, and loosed such a force in turning a spiritually aroused, but not spiritually disciplined, laity against an apathetic and in some instances morally corrupt clergy, that they well-nigh lost control of the situation. Prompt recognition of the error by Gilbert Tennent, the stability of William Tennent, Jr., the moral earnestness of several young men who were just then coming into the ministry, plus a timely coalition with the New York Presbytery, saved the Great Awakening in the Presbyterian churches from becoming lost in a riot of internecine strife.

Once the Nottingham sermon had been preached, the center of the strife was to be found in the Church at large, not in the Church judicatories. Moreover, the war was in the open now, no longer behind the shelter of Church laws, educational requirements, and the like. At this juncture Whitefield came again. On April 13, 1740, Whitefield landed at New Castle, and the following day he was in Philadelphia. He was as popular as before, if not even more so. Moreover, he aligned himself more openly with the Log College men. He remarks in his *Journal* that he had met with little opposition from Presbyterian sources as yet. Yet his comments reveal that he had accepted the Tennents' opinions and views regarding the majority of the Scotch-Irish Presbyterian preachers. When Whitefield joined with the Tennents in a campaign against these preachers, they in turn looked upon Whitefield no longer as an Anglican cleric, but as a cohort of the Log College men. Hence, one day when Whitefield preached in Samuel Blair's church, James Anderson, an ardent minister of the opposition party, publicly attacked him as soon as he had finished his sermon.[23] A finish fight had begun, some phases of which were no credit to either side.

There is now no need to justify or condemn the violence of these two contending parties. Their subsequent stagnation left the Scotch-Irish party self-condemned. The Log College men themselves later confessed their own rashness. The traditional accounts of the ensuing squabble of 1740 to 1741 have charged the Log College men with great disorderliness in professional conduct, in ecclesiastical polity, and in doctrinal emphasis.[24] In fact, they were more orderly and legal in ecclesiastical matters than were the opposition during the whole period. As for doctrinal matters, they were never guilty of error according to the then acknowledged creeds and standard authors.

Among the Dickinson group, Whitefield made new friends this year. In so doing he drew these members of the New York Presbytery closer to the Tennents. On May 5, 1740, Jonathan Dickinson preached his famous sermon on "The Witness of the Spirit." Clearly and passionately he preached the same traditional Puritan-Presbyterian doctrine that the Tennents had so warmly espoused. Even more important than showing his concord with the Tennents was the fact that he had chosen to show his agreement with them on one of the most frequently and violently attacked tenets of the revival group — the assurance of salvation. Dickinson had gone out of his way to align himself with the revival, and against its opponents. The die had been cast, and the future character of American Presbyterianism had been determined.[25]

The "intrusion" issue had now become a hopeless tangle. There was no possibility of keeping Whitefield out of any community. Thousands flocked to hear him wherever he preached. To the opponents of the revival, and even to some later churchmen,[26] Whitefield was the worst of all intruders. So jealous had some of the opposition party become in the matter of their rights that John Elder refused to allow Presbyterian preaching in Harrisburg, Pennsylvania, for some time after the town was incorporated. He demanded that the Presbyterians of the town come to him at his church in a nearby town.[27] Such ministers were demanding the sole right to control the Church, without any regard for the interests, needs, or desires of the lay people. They were introducing clericalism under the guise of a due regard for proper order and government. A group of them later declared that the people of a congregation were free to choose their pastor, but that when they had once chosen "the charge of the Work and Flock devolved upon him, so Also the Rule and Authority over his Flock, to command their Attendance upon his orderly and timeous Administrations." [28]

The real issue in the intrusion controversy was not raised by the Tennents' intruding into their opponents' occupied churches. The thing now fought for by each side was the dominance of the Church. It was a struggle for control of the new areas as yet unoccupied, the vacant congregations on the frontier. The Tennents were training a group of young ministers who were able to man these places. In the competition for new churches, which could give additional ecclesiastical influence and power, the Log College group had in their college and their locally trained ministry an advantage which their opponents could not meet. Too few young men were coming from Ireland and Scotland. The only way to defeat the Tennents was to eliminate the Log College, and to confine the main Tennent party to New Brunswick Presbytery. Even though the opponents of the Tennents could not succeed in all of this, they could at least maintain a majority in their own presbyteries by excluding Log College men in the future. Then, lest they should lose their majority in synod, they demanded the right to control entrance to the synod by a new set of rules.

Whitefield closed a triumphant campaign in the middle colonies on May 13, 1740. His followers had begun to erect a nondenominational tabernacle in Philadelphia for him and all other preachers who were in sympathy with him. This meant the Tennents and friendly preachers from the Baptist, Moravian, and other denominations. Moreover, it definitely connected the whole Tennent program with the whole Whitefield movement. The spring campaign by the Tennents and Whitefield had been intense. The opposition had also grown in vigor and virulence. The tide, however, had been turned. Strong lay support had come to the Log College men. Moreover, the New England group in the synod had become their close friends and co-workers in the revival. On this fast-flowing tide of popular support the Tennents proved to be only fair navigators, and although Whitefield had saved them from shipwreck, he could not pilot them.

When synod met at Philadelphia on May 28, 1740, both sides in the revival controversy had ceased to exercise discretion. Dickinson and six other members of the New England group were present. One of them, Pierson, was chosen moderator. This group seem to have striven for peace and harmony throughout the sessions of synod. Running concurrently with the synodical meetings was a campaign of evangelistic preaching in Whitefield's tabernacle. Here the Tennents, Samuel Blair, Rowland, and James Davenport (who had not yet begun his career of madness) preached to throngs from Philadelphia and nearby towns.[29] Many of those who were highly aroused by the revival attended synod's meetings as visitors. The Tennent plan of pitting an awakened laity against the ruling clique within the Church judicatories was now becoming very open and telling.

In synod it was reported that the breaking out of war between England and Spain had made it impossible to carry out any plan for a synodical school. Money would be too hard to secure from British donors.[30] The matter of the protests by the Tennents the previous year was discussed next. The first had to do with the examination by synod of candidates who had not had university training. All agreed that " Synod are proper judges of the qualifications of their own members." [31] This the opponents of the Log College felt was an admission that their whole case was just. The Tennents did not.

Their argument, as printed a short while later by Samuel Blair, presented the Log College case thus: Whenever differences of opinion arise in Churches, " there is just as much Reason why the minor Part should be always bound in Conscience not to submit to any Thing they judge inexpedient, as why the major Part should be always bound in Conscience to enjoin what they judge to be expedient: So that if the Argument here be just, then it will follow, that Church-Judicatures must split and separate so often as ever they differ about any Thing." [32]

Blair denied that John Thomson, the leader of the opposition, cited a valid example when he stated that all organized bodies have the right to determine their membership rules. The Church, Blair said, is not an ordinary man-made organization. It is based wholly on the " Laws and Constitutions of Jesus Christ." All Church judicatories are bound by constitutions and laws given in Scripture. He brought forward the regular stock arguments of divine-right Presbyterianism, which both sides held to rigorously when opposing the Anglicans and Romanists. The opposition had demanded the right to pass binding laws for which there was no Biblical warrant. They justified their case by saying that their laws were not anti-Biblical, and were expedient, therefore all must obey them or leave the Church. This, Blair contended, was the old argument for image worship, sign of the cross in baptism, stated liturgies, and the like. It was " an extravagant claim of power." Legislative power never belonged to the Church.

Synod could, therefore, judge the qualifications of its members, but the criteria were to be drawn from a Biblically grounded constitution. Such a Biblically grounded Presbyterianism had in the past given the rights in question to each presbytery.[33] The synod rejected the Log College protest, nonetheless, and renewed the requirement for a synodical examination of all who had had " a private education." The situation was further complicated as four additional ministers, and several elders, joined with the Tennents in a fresh protest.[34]

The itinerancy law, which had been passed unanimously the year before, was repealed entirely. It had proved useless. The synodical examination would be more effective. This issue was pushed farther by granting that such men as were ordained by presbyteries without synodical examination would be recognized as Gospel ministers, but not as members of synod.[35] This left the Log College' preachers as an extralegal, though tolerated, form of clergy, lower in rank than a Presbyterian minister. They could be ministers of Jesus Christ, but not of the synod. They would have been free-lance evangelists permitted to operate in restricted areas. No matter how many of such the Presbytery of New Brunswick might ordain, they could never challenge the majority of the Scotch-Irish party in synod. (New Brunswick Presbytery had ordained only one man, John Rowland, during all this controversy, and had licensed two others.)

At this juncture two plans for healing the sores caused by this act on examinations were proposed.[36] Dickinson proposed arbitration by the ecclesiastical bodies of Scotland or Ireland, or else by sympathetic ministers of London or Boston. Tennent refused, saying it would be impossible to agree on the statement of the issue. No doubt one side would have said the issue was the revival controversy, and the other would have said it was concerning an educated ministry. Moreover, Tennent said that the " majority of church judicatures almost everywhere are dead formalists." [37] Evidently Tennent had formed an adverse opinion regarding the ruling bodies of the Churches of Great Britain due to their handling of the recent subscription controversies. Gillespie proposed that each presbytery be allowed to ordain men, but that synod should be allowed to check over each new minister's examinations. If they judged necessary, they could re-examine these men. This would leave synod in full control; hence it was also rejected by Gilbert Tennent.[38] Gillespie in no wise approved of the synod's rule, but he was trying to make peace. Of the rule, he later said that its real intent had to do, not with the examination of candidates, but with the synod's quest

for power: " I answer, here is a fair Speech, but there is Poison here.
. . . The Pope of Rome arose by such like of Reasonings. . . . This
Act of Synod was afterwards turned into another Shape; but still is
wrong." [39]

Tennent stuck hard by the position from which the Log College men
never retreated, and which thereby became normative for American
Presbyterianism in contrast to Scottish Presbyterianism, namely, that
the presbytery and not the higher judicature was the fundamental unit
of Church organization. Therefore, the presbytery had the sole and inviolate right of ordination. A synod could censure a presbytery for
abuse or neglect of its office and prerogatives, but it could not by passing
a few rules alter these offices and prerogatives, for they were inherent in
the nature of a presbytery.[40] " And to make it farther appear, that this
Act is an Encroachment upon them [i.e., the due rights of presbyteries],
let it be observed, that by the same Method of Proceeding, all the Power
of Presbyteries may be taken away; and so our Constitution of Government in its present Plan thereof, entirely unhing'd: For, if the Synod
can take away, at its Pleasure, one Privilege and proper Business of
Presbyteries, What hinders but that by the same Power they may take
away another, and another, 'til they take away the Whole, by the same
Rule that this Act is made? " [41]

Healing measures could hardly be effectual in the face of such deep
differences. As the debate hurried on to some inevitable final clash,
Samuel Blair asked for an *interloquitur* in closed session. The place
was crowded with spectators at the time. The synod replied that whatever he had to offer might just as well be done in open session. Nothing
daunted, Blair presented a paper denouncing the opponents of the revival, and calling attention to some of the grievous ills existent in the
Church. Gilbert Tennent, without prearrangement, then read a most
scathing protest against the doctrinal and spiritual declension of the
Church, and against a section of its ministry.[42] Blair and Tennent intended to give general rebukes in a closed session. When read in public,
by order of synod, these papers became tirades. In the debates that followed in synod, and later in some presbyteries, Tennent and Blair were
urged to bring specific charges against specific persons. When they
asked for time and for a regular trial, the opposition made counterproposals. Both groups were sparring and neither desired a trial.[43] Synod
closed by exhorting their ministers to be more faithful, etc. Dickinson,
according to Gillespie, " owned the great decay of vital religion " in the
synod.[44]

During the month of June, the revival for which Dickinson had been
working in his congregation broke out. He had waited long, while aid-

ing Burr just a few miles away.[45] The Log College men began an intensive campaign in the colony of Virginia this same summer.[46] Gilbert
Tennent spent two hard months in evangelistic work in southern New
Jersey. His preaching in Philadelphia in June had drawn enormous
crowds. A newspaper reported that eight thousand people attended one
open-air meeting.[47]

In other ways the ensuing summer was a very difficult time for the
antirevival party. Though they had challenged Tennent and Blair to
prefer formal charges against any of their members whom the Log College men thought delinquent, the prestige of the Scotch-Irish group
was badly diminished by their mishandling of some charges that were
laid that summer against certain of their clergy by persons from their
own congregations. The solidly Scotch-Irish Presbytery of Donegal was
the scene of all these debacles. Over in the adjoining Presbytery of New
Castle a layman told Gillespie about some " gross immoralities " among
the Donegal clergy. The Presbytery of Donegal appointed a committee
to secure information on the subject. Also a day of fasting and prayer
was ordered and a statement lamenting " these unhappy divisions " was
to be read to the people assembled. John Thomson was ordered to secure copies of Blair's and Tennent's papers read in the previous synod,
together with Tennent's *Apology* [for the acts of New Brunswick Pres-
bytery], "in order to make Some animadversions on those papers, and
Sd Apoly to vindicate our Characters, and give ye world a Just representation of ye things charged on us in Sd papers." [48]

In the September meeting of presbytery a very ugly situation began
to develop. Samuel Black's congregation preferred serious charges
against him, and asked that his pastor relation with them be dissolved.
Moreover, they asked that when Donegal Presbytery sat to hear the
case, Blair and Gilbert Tennent be present. Presbytery thought this
looked " a little partial as if they wanted to choose their own judges,"
and voted to ask New Castle Presbytery to select any two correspondents except Blair and Tennent. At the same meeting, charges were preferred also against Samuel Caven.[49] Francis Alison, of Philadelphia,
was the corresponding member sent to the trial by New Castle Presbytery. Black was charged with drunkenness, indifference to his ministerial duties (he openly called the ministry his " trade "), and opposition
to the revival. Presbytery refused to take cognizance of the last charge,
and let Black off on the other two counts with a rebuke. His people appealed the case to the next synod. Caven was exonerated entirely. Presbytery then received charges from Alison and Thomson against three
of the revival preachers, Alexander Craighead, David Alexander, and
Samuel Blair. Each man was charged with " intrusions." Trial for

Craighead and Alexander was set in the following month.[50] Blair belonged to another presbytery, hence trial could not be appointed for him.

Perhaps no ecclesiastical trial in colonial history was more thoroughly burlesqued than that of Alexander Craighead and David Alexander. The trial took place at Craighead's church. He had made every provision for it. Alongside the church he had available a large shelter (called a "tent," though made of wood) in which open-air assemblies and Communion services were usually held. A crowd of people had been gathered, so large that both the church and the tent were filled. Alexander defied the presbytery outright, and roasted them for the delinquencies of their members, mentioning some by name. During Alexander's hearing, Craighead harangued a large crowd in the tent adjacent to the church. Here again the moral failures of the Donegal clergy was the theme, and names were freely mentioned. The next day when Craighead was tried, he excoriated his prosecutors and judges while Alexander held forth in the tent, aided by Samuel Finley, then a young licentiate. The climax came when the lay people in the church broke up the Craighead trial by "railing" at the presbytery. Samuel Caven, who had been under fire, asked to be released from his pastorate. Finally, presbytery, lamenting such disorderly proceedings, and such contempt of the judicatories of Christ's Church, suspended Craighead, cited Alexander to stand trial at their next meeting, and adjourned.[51] Samuel Black added to the burdens of the presbytery by becoming notoriously drunk on his way home from this trial, in which he had served as a member of the court.[52]

On September 9, 1740, some members of New Castle Presbytery presented to that body a list of questions regarding Whitefield's doctrines, demanding that presbytery either answer them or allow them to be printed.[53] They were printed under the title of *The Querists, or an extract. . . .* The tone of the first part of the pamphlet was moderate, yet the latter part was bitter, even to accusing Whitefield of being a Papist in disguise, and suggesting that the whole revival was a fake. The doctrinal errors charged against Whitefield were some of his unguarded statements, and some overly vivid and too literal applications of Biblical passages. Whitefield had revealed no intention of teaching false doctrines. All these alleged errors could have been ignored without harm to the Church. When the questions were presented in presbytery, Samuel Blair was present. He attempted to show that Whitefield's remarks had been lifted out of their context and that they involved no real errors. His defense was rejected with a demand that the bare expressions, and words in themselves, be considered, without regard to Whitefield's general views and the context of these excerpts.[54] The entire issue was wholly partisan.

At the same meeting Blair and Tennent were again challenged to present formal charges based on their two papers read in synod. They refused. Presbytery then demanded a " Yes " or " No " answer on whether or not Blair and Tennent had aimed at any of their members in the papers. Presbytery stated that if Tennent and Blair answered, " No," the matter would be dropped. If they answered, " Yes," the presbytery would proceed to a trial. Both Tennent and Blair refused to be stampeded into a trial for which they were not prepared.[55]

Charles Tennent defended Whitefield against the Querists in a letter to the editor of the *Pennsylvania Gazette,* and thereby caused himself some controversy.[56] When Whitefield arrived in New York from New England late in October, he published at once a pamphlet embodying a very moderate, yet reasonable, retraction of the " unguarded expressions," as he called them.[57] Later the Querists published a letter, taking caviling " exceptions " to some parts of Whitefield's reply.[58] Samuel Blair wrote a severe reply to the Querists' first pamphlet.[59] Franklin printed the original *Querists,* Tennent's letter, and Whitefield's letter, in one binding for circulation. The Querists issued a third piece, made up largely of selections from Gilbert Tennent's Nottingham sermon.[60] These Querist pamphlets ground into the souls of the Log College men and Whitefield. And their authors had intended that they should. These were the antirevival party's answers to the Nottingham sermon by Tennent.

Whitefield preached in the New York and Philadelphia areas until the first of December. His new tabernacle was not quite finished, yet it was regularly used. Before leaving, he persuaded Gilbert Tennent to undertake an evangelistic tour of New England. Tennent hesitated, but finally went. He campaigned from December 13 until March 2 in the Massachusetts and Connecticut colonies. Uncommon interest and success greeted his labors. In Boston phenomenal crowds greeted him. At New Haven over half the students of Yale College were converted under his preaching. Many of them were soon to find their way into the ministry of the Presbyterian Church in and around the presbyteries led by Dickinson, Pemberton, and the other older New Englanders.

A large part of the New England clergy received Tennent with open arms. Men like Thomas Prince, Thomas Foxcroft, and Benjamin Colman heartily approved of him.[61] Others, like President Clap of Yale, Timothy Cutler, Charles Chauncy, (and) the anonymous author of *The State of Religion in New England . . . ,* detested him. Clap asserted that Jonathan Edwards had revealed to him a scheme arranged by the revivalists whereby Whitefield was to bring over from England "godly" young men to be trained at the Log College for service in New England. These men were then to follow in the wake of Tennent and Whitefield with the express purpose of supplanting the whole New England clergy. Edwards denied ever having said any such thing. Clap finally admitted he might have surmised "some of the details" of the "plot." [62] The entire story was a fabrication by Clap.

The press had featured largely in the revival and its controversies during the year. Dickinson had published two sermons. Samuel Finley had printed a defense of Whitefield. Gillespie had also issued a defense of the Tennent group. *The Querists* had enjoyed three editions or re-prints, one of which was put out from a Boston press. Several other attacks on Whitefield were issued by Baptists and Anglicans. Gilbert Tennent's Nottingham sermon had gone into a second edition, and into a German translation. (The Germans, both Pietists and Moravians, were much influenced by Whitefield's work.) Besides the Nottingham sermon, Tennent issued but one other piece this year. Whitefield gave to the press eighteen titles, which appeared in twenty-seven editions or reprints during the year. The periodicals of the colonies, from South Carolina to New England, had followed the revival and its opponents. [63]

During the early part of 1741, while Tennent was in New England and Whitefield in Georgia, the revival controversy had been forced to a new low by the opposition. An exceedingly scurrilous attack on Whitefield was inserted into the February issue of Franklin's *The General Magazine* with the title "A Wonderful Wandering Spirit." The same issue printed a letter against Tennent together with his defense. A month later Blair's rejoinder to the Querists' first pamphlet, *A Particular Consideration . . . ,* appeared. It was unusually bitter. Finley's *Christ Triumphing and Satan Raging . . .* followed late in April. Its title adequately sums up its contents and spirit.

Donegal Presbytery met again in April of 1741. It was not a very auspicious meeting. Laymen were present to offer charges against four members of the presbytery: Samuel Black, Samuel Caven, James Lyon, and David Alexander. Black's case, which had become notorious since the Craighead-Alexander trial of the previous winter, was temporarily delayed, pending arrangement of a trial. Among other charges lodged against Caven was that "when Mr. Caven is abroad a bad story invariably comes back after him." Lyon and Alexander were both accused of drunkenness. Caven's and Alexander's cases were put over until May. Lyon was tried at once, acquitted (though adjudged guilty of misconduct in the excessive use of liquor), and thereupon officially given a call to the badly divided congregation of Nottingham, where so much of recent history was still fresh in the minds of laymen at least![64]

This presbytery's odd ability to create impossible situations for itself appeared in another incident. John Hindman, a man of no ability and less prudence, was then in the process of going through his trials. Gillespie, in the neighboring Presbytery of New Castle, protested that Hindman was unfit for the ministry. Presbytery thereupon ruled that " he has always Since he came among us discovered so much imprudence and childish Simplicity that we look on it as dangerous to admit him into Such a weighty and difficult office." No action more definite was taken, and a few months later pressure was brought to bear on certain persons, and the man was both licensed and ordained in less time than any other candidate had been thus far in the presbytery's history! Synod, ever watchful lest poorly educated men find their way into the ministry, ignored the case. The man had a brief and inglorious ministry.[65]

John Thomson now came forward with a long overture which, after a preamble lamenting the sad state of affairs in the Church, made several drastic proposals for strengthening the authority of the Church's government. He asserted that only by such an increase of authority could " order " be restored. He urged: (1) That presbytery adopt some rule to which local church sessions could point for authority in disciplining their members. (2) That all lay persons before being admitted to the privileges of either sacrament be obliged to subscribe to the Westminster Confession of Faith and the Larger and Shorter Catechisms, and promise to submit to the government of the Presbyterian Church. (3) That all who are to be admitted to either sacrament promise first never to go to hear " disorderly preachers " [meaning any one of the Log College men]. (4) That no minister of the presbytery allow any of these revival preachers in his pulpit or go to hear one of them. Contempt of Church rules, Thomson declared, is contempt of Christ, and is worthy of the same censures as " adultery, fornication, drunkenness, etc.," because these are only against the second table of the law. The overture was " carried by a great majority." [66] When presbytery met in May, Black's case was heard, and when further charges, including that of suppressing evidence by threats of violence, were preferred, further action was postponed. Alexander next came up for trial. He took the pulpit in defiance of presbytery, read a prepared statement admitting the charge that at a funeral he had drunk too much, and again defied presbytery. For the drunkenness and for contempt of the presbytery, he was ejected. Caven's case was not brought up until June.[67]

The Synod of Philadelphia convened on May 27, 1741, with barely one half of its members present. The Scotch-Irish faction had sixteen members in attendance, and the Log College group seven. Gillespie, Craighead, and Alexander were the other ministers who answered the roll. The entire New England group were absent. Andrews was made moderator. The right of Alexander and Craighead to sit in the synod was challenged at once. Their controversy with Donegal Presbytery was then brought before the synod. Alison forced the issue of Craighead into first place on the docket, in spite of protests that the prior place belonged always to other stated items. The Log College men then urged that a committee of synod take over the matter, and study the whole case.[68] For three days synod argued the issue without success. John Thomson protested " against some Brethren in the Synod (who he said were of a different opinion from the rest) being concerned in the committee." This led Tennent to think that a solution was not desired, but that an excuse for splitting the Church was being sought. His suspicions of such a coup were further aroused when synod deferred action on the appointment of the standing committees (usually one of the first items on the docket) until a later time.[69] After three days, during which little was accomplished, the synod adjourned on Saturday to resume on Monday afternoon.

Monday morning Gillespie had a private talk with Tennent. He accused him of trying to split the Church. Tennent fully convinced Gillespie that he by no means desired a schism, though he was determined to see some reforms brought about. Gillespie departed satisfied.[70] When synod met that afternoon, they were presented with a written protestation. Robert Cross, who brought the paper in, read it and laid it before the moderator. Briefly, the *Protestation* made five categorical demands and protests, levied seven accusations against the revivalists, and declared that unless the New Brunswick group gave " suitable satisfaction to the Synod, and particularly to us, who now enter this protestation," those who presented this paper would not consider themselves bound by any future act of the synod made by and with the New Brunswick men. They concluded by saying that the revival group had " no right to be acknowledged as members of this judicatory of Christ, whose principles and practices are so diametrically opposite to our doctrine, and principles of government and order." Continued union with them was therefore " most absurd and inconsistent." The protesters confessed their great sins, etc., which were, they said " the meritorious cause of our present doleful distractions," but asserted that they were confident that the first requisite to a real reformation must be their faithfulness in restoring discipline and government to the Church.

The five demands were: the maintenance of ironclad subscription to the Confession, Catechisms, and Directory as of synod's Act of 1736;

that no minister or elder be allowed to sit and vote in synod if he has violated or been accused of violating this or any other present or future rule or order of synod; that the New Brunswick group have forfeited their right to membership in the synod; that unless complete satisfaction be given, they will not be bound by orders drawn by a synod in which the Log College men sit; that unless the revivalists give such complete satisfaction, and change their ways, those signing the petition shall declare themselves to be the true Presbyterian Church and the others to be schismatics.

The accusations were: the principles of Church government elaborated by the New Brunswick group in their *Protest* and *Apology* of the previous year were heterodox and anarchical; New Brunswick's protest against synod's rule on the examination of ministerial candidates rendered them unfit to sit in synod; the revivalists intruded into other congregations; they rashly judged and condemned their brethren in the ministry; their conception of God's call to the ministry was wrong, as also were their views on the terrors of the law and on the assurance of salvation.[71]

The Cross *Protestation* demanded complete capitulation or schism. At the same time it was asserted that the New Brunswick group had already forfeited all right to membership in the synod. In a disorderly rush forward to sign the *Protest,* it was found that more were in favor of it than were against it. The majority thereupon declared themselves to be the synod. There was no actual vote and none was recorded. In any poll the ministerial vote would probably have been 12 to 10, with some elders on each side.[72] Synod's total ministerial membership at the time was 47.

Two accounts were afterward given of the scene that followed the signing of this *Protest.* On their minutes the protesters entered their account as follows:

" Upon this it was canvassed by the former protesting brethren [the Log College men], whether they or we are to be looked upon as the Synod. We maintained that they had no right to sit whether they were the major or minor number. Then they motioned that we should examine this point, and that the major number was the Synod. They were found to be the minor party, and upon this they withdrew. After this the Synod proceeded to business." [73] The Log College men charged:

" The Narrative our Brethren give of what happened after the Protest was signed, is a strange Misrepresentation of the Affair. ' After the Protest was entered and subscribed . . . they thought it expedient to withdraw.' As to the *Brunswick*-Party's (as they are pleased to call us) insisting that they should be cast out of the Synod, it is what I know nothing of; such a Thought did not enter into my Heart. . . . But how can our Brethren assert, what it was not possible for them at that Time to know, without our Declaration, which they had not? *namely,* That we concluded that all these Members, who had not signed their Protest, would join with us? What we concluded upon, was this, That those who had not signed the Protest, had not rejected us; and therefore were so far upon our Side of the Question that they could join with us in Judicatories.

"Our Brethren call themselves a great Number; the Truth is, there was but a small Difference between them and us as to Number, which will appear thus; The Persons they protested against, were these, *viz.*

"Ministers.
"William Tennent, Senior,
"Richard Treat,
"Samuel Blair,
"Charles Tennent,
"James Alexander,
"Alexander Craighead,
"William Tennent,
"Eleazar Wales,
"John Rowland,
"Gilbert Tennent.

"All the rest of the Ministers in Synod (besides these now mentioned, and the Protesters) were only Four in Number, *namely,*

"Messrs. George Gillespy,
"Alexander Hutchison,
"Jedidiah Andrews,
"—— M" Henery.

"The Two first of those last mentioned, seemed inclinable to join with us; which put us on a Par as to Number with our Opponents: And Mr. M" Henery was also dissatisfy'd with the Protest. But the Number of the Elders, on each Side of the Question, I cannot tell; not having the Synod's Minutes by me. It is evident from what has been said, that there was a Majority of Non-protesting Ministers. . . .

"It is alledg'd by our protesting Brethren, 'That when some who did not sign the Protest, convinced us, that they would not be of our Party; that upon this, we thought it expedient to withdraw.' This is a gross Mistake; for some of the Non-protesting Members convinced us of no such Thing. Neither was any Thing like this, the Occasion of our Withdrawing; we stay'd 'till the Moderator commanded Silence. Our protesting Brethren say, 'That our Withdrawing put the House into a little Confusion.' Here is another strange Misrepresentation; for the

Confusion the House was in, was neither after, nor occasioned by our Withdrawing; it was before we came away, and was occasioned by the Reading and Signing of the Protest; we did not come away 'til our protesting Brethren came with us; and that was after the Session was concluded, with Prayer, as usual. The Roll indeed was counted, but not with the View mention'd by our Opponents, but to see whether in respect of Number, our protesting Brethren could cast us out, according to the Tenor of their Protest.

"The Truth is, the Reading and hasty Signing of the Protest, put the Assembly into Disorder; we were surprized with the extraordinary Method of Proceeding, and knew not well what to do; we were loath to be cast out so hastily, without speaking any Thing in our own Defence; but our Attempts to speak were repulsed, the House being confus'd, one spoke one Thing, and another another, and sometimes two or more at once; so that it's hard to tell what was said. Mr. Blair, I remember, offer'd more than once, to read a Paper; but the Motion was rejected, and Silence enjoin'd by the Moderator; and thus the Assembly, after Prayer, broke up." [74]

Just how the schism should be regarded has often been debated. There is, however, no room for caviling. The Tennents were illegally put out of the synod. The Scotch-Irish group, who now became known as the "Old Side," repeatedly stated that they had "rejected," "ejected," or "cast out" the "Brunswick brethren," [75] and that they "excluded some of our members from our communion, on account of irregularity and misconduct in the following of Rev. George Whitefield, one of the English Methodists." [76] The synod in a letter to President Clap, of Yale College, on May 30, 1746, said that "divisive practices, obliged the Synod to exclude him [Tennent] and others of his stamp, from their communion". . . ."But we can assure you, that Mr. Gilbert Tennent, and his adherents, were disowned as members, and excluded communion, before his famous tour through the churches of New England." [77] This letter, drafted by Cross, Alison, Evans, and Griffith, the first three of whom were the leaders of the antirevival movement the signers of the *Protestation* of 1741, thus assures Clap that before Tennent went to New England (he was there from Dec. 13, 1740, to March 2, 1741) the whole revival group had been disowned and excluded by the synod. This would indicate that the schism was planned by Cross, Thomson, Alison, and others, after the heated synod of 1740. What happened on June 1, 1741, had been agreed upon before December of the year previous. Clap then was told the "practical truth," although the statement was actually false. Large sections of the preamble of the *Protestation* were taken from the overture that John Thomson had presented in Donegal Presbytery two months earlier.

The twelve ministers who signed the *Protestation* and ejected the revivalists were in themselves a rather motley group. Cross, whom Gillespie had once sought to bring to justice before synod, was now the leader of the Old Side. John Thomson, the implacable advocate of unqualified subscription, was their ablest pamphleteer. Francis Alison was the only man of the group who could compare intellectually with William Tennent, Sr., Samuel Blair, Samuel Davies, or Samuel Finley. Though much opposed to the Log College and the revival, he signed the *Protestation,* but questioned the legality of the exclusion of the New Brunswick men. John Craig, who had just been received into the synod that year, and Adam Boyd signed only after some thought.[78] Robert Cathcart, James Martin, and Robert Jamison were men of very indifferent careers in the ministry.[79] John Elder had been active against the revival in Donegal Presbytery. The other signers, Richard Zancky, Samuel Caven, and Samuel Thomson have left behind them records of moral failure and laxity. Of these twelve ministerial signers, seven were from the undisciplined and bitterly antirevival Presbytery of Donegal: J. Thomson, Craig, Boyd, Elder, Zancky, Caven, and S. Thomson.

The two groups in the Church had come to the parting of the ways, not over dogmas, Church government, or educational standards, but because of " a determined resolution to endeavour to awaken the Presbyterian Church from a state of great declension in vital piety." [80]

6

THE BROKEN BODY

When once the heat of the controversy had passed, and the Log College men were no longer a minority group struggling for their existence, the formless character of their whole movement became quite apparent. They were now faced with the problem of organizing and carrying forward a Church of their own. While their churches had followed Presbyterian patterns in general, several factors had operated powerfully to the breaking down and discrediting of all form and order. More and more emphasis had been upon spontaneity, freedom, and individualism. The fact that the antirevival group had controlled the Church judicatories, used them against the revival, and degraded them by their lax discipline of immoral clergy, had made all Church courts suspect for many lay people. Moreover, in their defense of themselves, the Log College men had again and again set their " individual " or " minority " conscientious scruples over against the high-riding acts aimed at their extermination by the synod and the presbyteries. The support of thousands of lay people had been back of their defiances of these Church courts. Whitefield, by his guileless following of visions, his earnest but confused theological convictions, and his emotional and formless manner of preaching, had done much to make the laymen impatient with due form and order. To them it seemed that more was done for the salvation of men by those who defied all forms than by " the old formalists."

Great numbers of people had been brought into the churches by the revival.[1] Many of these people were second-generation colonists who had little or no religious background. A large percentage of them were without previous knowledge of Presbyterianism. Most of them were from humbler walks of life with few cultural advantages. The task of fitting them into some stable form of Presbyterian Church order would have been difficult under any circumstances. In places where these new converts were mingled in a strong older Presbyterian congregation the process of assimilation was going on rather well. However, in new churches, or in older churches where the new element predominated, or was largely of another social stratum, the problem of spontaneity and freedom over against form and order was intense. New immigrants were also coming into the colonies in large numbers during the period of the Great Awakening. Their part in the difficulty of creating a new order was significant, in that they naturally were much more deeply attached to the old orders of their homelands than were the second-generation colonists. The desperate shortage of ministers which left many of the travailing congregations vacant for months, or even several years, with a supply preacher once a month or less, made the rebirth of American Presbyterianism very difficult. Only the founding of the College of New Jersey, providing as it did a large number of native-born ministers, met this need.

The revival had indeed crushed the old order of the Scotch-Irish party. Also, it had discovered and released a new spiritual life all through the colonies, which was now pouring out unguided, unrestrained, and wholly spontaneous. It was, therefore, essentially even without a clear and ordered goal or purpose. It was rapidly becoming individualistic and subjective, and, accordingly, in danger of becoming inwardly selfish. Excess and folly had appeared in some places as the new life rushed out in confused and individualistic forms. As long as they had remained a part of the synod, and had, therefore, the support of a traditional even though corrupt form, the Log College men had not been compelled to struggle with these problems. Now that they were, by virtue of their ejection from synod, a tiny new denomination, the task of creating a form adequate to their needs, and true to their newly won spiritual vitality, fell upon them overnight. Though they quickly grasped the meaning of their situation, and strove mightily to bring a new order to the birth, the task was to prove too great for them. The new order was not to be born until the Dickinson group joined forces with them a few years later. Their painful struggles while still alone were made more bitter by the taunts of the antirevival party, who saw in their hopeless travail a vindication of their own formalism and the revivalists' due reward for breaking the old forms.[2]

The old synod, now controlled by the Scotch-Irish subscriptionists and opponents of the revival, took to themselves the name of the Synod of Philadelphia. Until the late 1730's the synod had usually been called merely "the Synod." Popularly the old synod became known as the "Old Side," and the Log College men as the "New Side." The day after their ejection from the synod, the Log College men and their adherents organized themselves into the "Conjunct

Presbyteries of New Brunswick and Londonderry." In organizing they passed several resolutions, among them one stating that " we do adhere as closely and fully to the Westminster Confession, Catechisms, and Directory, as ever the Synod of Philadelphia did in any of their public acts and agreements about them." [3] It has been supposed by some that by this resolution the Tennent group approved of the synod's Act of 1736 which demanded unqualified subscription, and that the Log College men only retreated from this position when uniting with the Dickinson group in 1745.[4] Some other factors throw a better light upon the true meaning of this resolution.

In the Cross *Protestation,* which was directed against the Log College men by name, and not against the Dickinson group, the first two demands were that the ironclad subscription Act of 1736 be acknowledged and obeyed. Some months after this, Samuel Blair, in his *Vindication of the Brethren . . . ,* published in defense of the ejected group, specifically attacked the Act of 1736.[5] Were the revivalists then falsifying their position? In 1729 none in the synod were found to be at variance with the doctrines of the Westminster symbols. The point involved was the authority of synod to lay down the terms of ministerial communion in a rule, or rules, resting for their validity upon no more than the will of a majority of the synod. The compromise Adopting Act of 1729 had conceded that synod possessed no such " legislative power." The synod must demand in matters of doctrine and polity no more than "the essentials." These " essentials " could not be legislated by synod, but were to be found in the Bible, which was the only final rule. The Act of 1736 overrode this concession and asserted the right of the synod to enact such rules as they saw fit. The Cross *Protestation* reiterated this assertion clearly and forcefully, and demanded that it be conceded by the Tennents. The Conjunct Presbyteries stood, however, where Dickinson had stood in 1722 and 1729. They were as orthodox doctrinally and as Presbyterian ecclesiastically as the Adopting Act of 1729 required. But they did not recognize the legality or validity of the acts of 1732 and 1736, and the Scotch-Irish group knew it. For that matter, neither did the Dickinson group ever acknowledge these acts as binding. If synod had authority to enact one rule on their own authority, then they could enforce their will in all things: the act against the Log College, the acts against itinerant evangelistic preaching, etc. The revival group were fully aware that the Adopting Act of 1729 was utterly essential to their whole case.

Once organized, the new Conjunct Presbyteries issued *The Declaration of the Conjunct Presbyteries . . . ,* which had been prepared at their order by Samuel Blair. This pamphlet set forth their views on the revival and on the late controversies in the synod. A literary war now ensued. The June issue of *The General Magazine* carried a " Supplement to the History of a Wandering Spirit," and, even more scurrilous, "An Infallible Receipt to Make a New Kind of Convert." Robert Cross published the June 1, 1741, *Protestation* with a polemical preface. Tennent compiled a pamphlet containing *Remarks upon a [Cross] Protestation,* and the *Protest* which he and others had presented to the synod of 1739, together with an *Apology* in its defense. In answer to this the Old Side synod published *An Examination and Refutation.* . . . John Thomson issued *The Government of the Church* that same year. Three years later, 1744, Blair answered with *A Vindication of the Brethren.* . . . Nothing really new was brought out in these publications.

Peace did not descend very quickly upon the Conjunct Presbyteries. Alexander Craighead demanded that the new group adopt the Solemn League and Covenant. They refused, saying that such acts belonged properly to national bodies and not to Church courts. Craighead severed relations with them, and began a violent campaign against both the synod and the Conjunct Presbyteries. He charged them with abandoning the Westminster Standards, and renouncing their heritage. A small Cameronian group gathered around him.[6] More serious was the case of John Cross, at one time highly thought of by Whitefield and the Tennents because of his evangelistic labors. He was not at the synod of 1741, since he was under citation to appear for trial by order of the Presbytery of New Brunswick. That body now assumed jurisdiction over him, and deposed him from the ministry for an act of "unclean speech and carriage" committed six years previously.[7] In 1746 he sought restoration, but was refused. The revival group intended to have in its membership no Gospel-happy antinomians.

The hardest blow caught by the two struggling presbyteries was struck by a devoted friend, James Davenport. From the early days of Whitefield's ministry in the colonies, Davenport had been known as one of the saintliest and ablest of the young Congregationalist evangelists. He was well known and beloved by the Presbyterian revivalists, though he had never become a member of their fold. In July, 1741, he went from his Long Island congregation on a preaching tour of Connecticut. Reports soon began to come back about his " excesses." However, the campaign was a success, and Davenport returned to Long Island for the winter. The following winter, Aaron Burr wrote to his friend, Joseph Bellamy (also a friend of Davenport's), that he was "disquieted" by some of Davenport's actions.[8] That summer Davenport embarked on a fanatical career in Connecticut and Massachusetts.

Davenport's mad evangelizing threw his friends into consternation. Seemingly his wild ways proved every charge that had been levied against the revival. The opposition, both in the middle colonies and in New England, were hardly sorry for the opportunity thus afforded them and made full use of it — though suffering severely from the fanatical followers whom Davenport drew out of their churches. Only after much labor and heartache did Davenport's friends bring him to see his errors. Gilbert Tennent disowned several of Davenport's acts and practices in a letter published in a number of newspapers.[9] Other friends labored with him also, but without much immediate success. During the winter he seems to have had somewhat of a change of attitude, and the following year he asked New Brunswick Presbytery for permission to accept a call to the Maidenhead-Hopewell Church. Presbytery refused, demanding that he first recant of some of his past actions. He did recant on several counts, but he and the presbytery continued to differ about some of his past acts. At length he was given a temporary permission to supply the congregation until the next meeting of the Conjunct Presbyteries. When they met several months later, Davenport's case was not brought up. The Maidenhead-Hopewell Church asked for supply preaching. Evidently Davenport had not stayed to wait for the hearing. The following year, two New England preachers brought him to his senses. He published his *Retractions,* which were reprinted several times and widely distributed by the friends of the revival.[10] Two years later New Brunswick Presbytery received him into the Presbyterian ministry.[11]

Other troubles also greeted the new Log College presbyteries. One of their ministers, John Rowland, was made the victim of a plot early in 1742, and was charged with horse-stealing. William Tennent, Jr., and two others testified in court that Rowland had been in another part of the colony evangelizing at the time when the horse was stolen. Rowland was acquitted, but popular feeling was whipped up against him to such an extent that he was forced to move from New Jersey to Pennsylvania. Tennent and the other two witnesses were later charged with perjury, the Chief Justice of New Jersey, Robert Hunter Morris, being one of the leading instigators. Several of the most prominent lawyers of the middle colonies volunteered to defend Tennent and he was finally acquitted.[12]

George Gillespie, a Scotsman, had found himself unable to go with either party when the schism was made. Returning to his church in Delaware, he wrote a long letter to Dickinson. Later the letter appeared in pamphlet form. The difficulties that beset the Church had their origins, in large part, in ministerial failures, he said. Men who train for the ministry are too early separated from the lay people. The evil effects of this lack of contact with laymen are that ministers are aloof, cold, and indifferent toward their people. The ministry is looked upon as an aristocratic calling. Moreover, the clergy resist allowing the elders any real part in the life of the Church. The people easily come to feel that the ministers have no interest in their souls. The situation is made even worse when presbyteries ignore the indignation of the lay members of the Church toward scandalous ministers, and assume that if they as a presbytery have exonerated a man, the laymen should acquiesce. The fact that the ministers of presbytery clique together to exonerate these men only convinces the people that they are themselves indifferent to morals. The people conclude that they are clerical adventurers and ministerial tradesmen.

Gillespie asserted that the synod of 1741, which the New York Presbytery had failed to attend, had illegally ejected the Log College men in order to stop the revival. He defended the revival, though confessing some blemishes. It was opposed, he said, " by vile sinners, formalists, lovers of smooth things, sellers of strong drink, storekeepers, gracious persons who were in great decays spiritually, by some ministers and by Satan." Especially reprehensible to his mind were the " scandalous and scoffing papers" written against the revival, the "History of a Wandering Spirit," and the "Receipt to Make a New Kind of Convert."

The real cause of the trouble, as Gillespie saw it, was the Act of 1738 " depriving the Presbyteries of their essential Rights" in the matter of examining candidates. Ordination is a right conferred by Christ upon presbyteries. Examination is a part of ordination. The claim that the act aimed only at a learned ministry is false. It aimed at rule by the synod. If synod took away one right, they could take away all on the same grounds. Whereas he had once thought that Tennent was intent upon dividing the Church, Tennent had cleared himself satisfactorily enough. The Cross *Protestation,* Gillespie said, opened his eyes. " The divisive Protest aforesaid being entered at our Synod, opened my Eyes, so that now it plainly appeareth who were hottest for a Division, to wit, the Protesters." [13] Gillespie's letter throws much interesting light upon the controversy. He was not a member of either party.

In the latter part of 1741, the whole Presbyterian group were much troubled by the vigorous activities of the Moravian Count Zinzendorf and his followers. Tennent, Dickinson, Pemberton, and Finley all wrote against them in severe terms. To them Moravianism meant antinomianism and separatism in their worst forms. The Old Side accused the New Side of denouncing in the Moravians that which they themselves had always stood for. Gilbert Tennent denied this, saying, " The passages referred to in the Moravian sermon were occasioned by reports of a separating disposition in New England; I was informed that some were separating from the ministry of such as were sound in principle, regular in life, and approvers of God's work; and that some staid at home, rather than they would hear such, merely because they judged them to be unconverted." [14] It was one thing, Tennent felt, to call a Samuel Black or a Samuel Caven unconverted, but it was another thing to call unconverted an upright minister who, though sympathetic with the revival, did not appear demonstrably " spiritual " or " on fire," or " converted." Finley had a talk with Zinzendorf, and found that the Count believed and taught that sin was only in the flesh, and that " the best remedy against the Infection of the sinful matter is the Body's Fermentation in the Grave "; that Christ made a satisfaction or ransom to the devil, which was " the Fiend's deserved Fee "; and that " some Charitable People who did not get their Sins pardoned here, would be pardoned hereafter, and that by means of others to whom they had done Good, interceding for them." [15] Dickinson looked upon these early Moravians as antinomians.[16] Whitefield remonstrated with Tennent for writing against the Moravians, but he also, a few years later, wrote against them.[17] A layman, William Livingston, of New York, a trustee of Pemberton's church though not a member, and later one of the leaders of a politico-religious " Presbyterian party " in New York, attacked in his *Independent Reflector* these criticisms of the Moravians by the Presbyterian clergy. He was against all creeds as such.[18]

The load of controversy multiplied, and unruly and turbulent spirits on every hand finally broke Tennent's spirit. In great dejection he wrote a letter to Dickinson in February of 1742. He confessed that he had " mismanaged " in doing what he did, that he could not justify the " excessive heat of temper " that he had sometimes shown, and that he felt it his duty to " acknowledge it in the openest manner." In a time of " great spiritual desertion " he had been given, he said, " a greater discovery of myself than I think I ever had before." The Moravians had awakened him to the dangers of enthusiasm and separation. Moreover, at a time when the Presbyterians were torn by strife, the heretics were consolidating and growing. Davenport's excesses had been a grievous burden to him.[19]

The form of this letter, containing as it does specific rejections of certain carefully stated views of Davenport and a number of formal statements on various matters, together with a line in its closing paragraph: " I wish you success, dear sir, in your journey. . . . May your labours be blessed to that [the checking of " such enthusiastical fool-eries "] end," raises an interesting question. How did Tennent know that Dickinson was about to go on a journey in the interests of peace and quiet? Dickinson was about to go to Boston for counsel, and must have asked Tennent for some sort of statement to carry with him. Was Gillespie's long letter — delineating so many things that the " Reverend Brethren of the Presbytery of New York " had known as well and as long as he himself — written for the eyes of Boston ministers also?

In New England, Dickinson counseled with Edwards and others in Connecticut and with some of the Boston ministers. The decision seems to have been that the withdrawal of the Cross *Protestation* by the Old Side synod was to be demanded as essential to the New York Pres-bytery's continuing in relation with them. After that was achieved, the New Brunswick group were to present a recantation of certain errors.[20]

In May of 1742 the synod met as usual in Philadelphia. The New York Presbytery met with them. In the city at the same time were gathered most of the New Side clergy. Twenty-four ministers were in attendance at the synod. Of the New England group, seven were pres-ent. Dickinson was chosen moderator, and Alison clerk. Upon Dickin-son's motion a committee was named to meet with the New Side " and try all methods consistent with gospel truth, to prepare the way for healing the said breach." The committee were Dickinson, Pemberton, and Pierson from the New York Presbytery, together with Thomson, Cathcart, Alison, Evans, and Andrews.[21]

This committee met with the New Side group, and found that Ten-nent seemed willing to make as full a retraction as was necessary to satisfy the Old Side.[22] Thereupon the synod's committee secured a closed meeting of the entire synod and the entire New Side delegation. This *interloquitur* accomplished nothing. The Cross *Protestation* would not be withdrawn by the Old Side. The New Side proposed that the entire matter be arbitrated by a panel composed of all those in synod who had not signed the *Protestation* or who had not been excluded by it. The Old Side asserted that they " were the Synod, and had acted as such in the rejection, and in so doing they only cast out such members as they judged had rendered themselves unworthy of membership, . . . and therefore would not be called to account by absent members, or by any judicature on earth." They were, of course, willing to give to any and all a statement of their reasons for ejecting the New Side. How-ever, there could be no thought of reopening the case. The final judg-ment had already been given. The case was closed.

In the face of this intransigence, the New England group, led by Dickinson, Pierson, and Pemberton, laid a formal written protest before the synod. This document asserted that the New Side had been excluded from the synod by a protest, without trial, in "an illegal and unprecedented procedure, contrary to the rules of the gospel and subversive of our excellent constitution." Moreover, Dickinson and his nine adherents protested against the Old Side's refusal to allow the synod of 1742 to try the legality of the Exclusion Act of 1741. Going farther, they asserted that the New Side must be considered as members in good standing of the synod until they had been given a fair trial as prescribed by the Scriptures and by Presbyterian law. They further protested against some of the scurrilous pamphlets that had lampooned the revival. Finally, they protested against all irregular and divisive practices that destroy the peace of the Church. Of the Old Side only Alison was willing to have the legality of the exclusion tried. The synod, however, adjourned as he presented a written statement of his views.

In July, Thomas Clap published Tennent's letter of February, 1742, in the *Boston Evening Post*. Early in August it appeared also in the *Pennsylvania Gazette*. No doubt many an eyebrow was raised by both friend and foe when this rather unusual letter was made public! So much was made of this letter by his enemies that Tennent published an explanation of it in the newspapers. The essence of his explanation was: "As to my Confession of Mismanagement in the Affair of the Debate with the Synod, it respected only the Defect which I conceived attended my Manner of Performing, what I did then and do still look upon to be Duty. I was not, then, nor have not been since, convinced that the Matter or Substance of what I contended for was wrong; and the Words of the Letter considered in their Connection will easily bear this Sense." Tennent asserted that he had no idea that the letter would be printed, and that it was published without his consent.[23] Dickinson could perhaps have echoed this last statement.

About that same time Andrews wrote to Pierson complaining that the protest of the New York men had been needless, unseasonable, and unkind.[24] He asserted that the Dickinson group had acted only to clear their own names and reputations from any implication with the ejection of the New Side men. They had, therefore, purely selfish motives. Moreover, by this needless and selfish act they had rendered the Cross group less open to reunion. The Cross group had, up until that act, been thinking about plans for reunion. Now they were not, because "an inclination not be undervalued or despised more or less obtains with all men." The unkindness of the New Englanders' *Protest* appeared in that they had given aid and comfort to the enemies of the Old Side. Finally, he asserted that "it was chiefly the transaction of one man, who in an ostentatious, noisy manner" had managed the matter.

Dickinson, of course, who had been the leader in making the protest, was the "one man" meant.

Not content with a protest in synod, Dickinson issued a carefully prepared pamphlet in defense of the revival. Bearing the title *A Display of God's Special Grace* . . . , it appeared anonymously in Boston, with a preface signed by Benjamin Colman, Joseph Sewall, Thomas Prince, John Webb, William Cooper, Thomas Foxcroft, and Joshua Gee. This preface, bearing a date line of August 10, 1742, posed the issue thus: "The grand Question is . . . Whether it [the revival] be a Work of God, and how far is it so?" Both the author and the prefacers asserted that in spite of some human frailties and blemishes the revival was definitely "A Display of God's Special Grace." From that stand the Dickinson group never faltered. It accounts for their final withdrawal from the synod and their union with the Log College men. In that union the genius of an American Presbyterianism was to be shaped.

Now that reunion was hopeless, the struggle became more embittered and the breach wider and wider. Each side began to send ministers into the areas of the other group. Feelings ran higher and higher. The Old Side attacked the revivalists with a virulence not hitherto used in even such things as the "History of a Wandering Spirit." The New Side, though censorious and cutting, remained sober and dignified in comparison with the lampoonery of the Old Side. The general public followed hard after the New Side.

Far more important, however, than their combats with the Old Side was the amazing missionary and evangelistic work of the Tennent group. New recruits had come to them from the Log College. From the outer frontier of Pennsylvania, to the "spiritual desert" of southern New Jersey, and to the "Great Valley" of Virginia, these new recruits and the intrepid older New Side men rode their preaching circuits. Some of these circuits were as long as two hundred miles through the forests. Everywhere the cry came for a minister to preach the reviving Gospel. A very disturbing call, however, came from Milford, Connecticut. There a group had split off from the established Congregational Church, and had formed a new congregation. They wished to become a Presbyterian church and to join New Brunswick Presbytery. The presbytery found that the new congregation had been legally formed under Connecticut law, but still they hesitated to invade Connecticut. They urged the congregation to make one more regular effort, through a duly called council of Congregational churches, at healing their differences with the old congregation. If such an effort were made and failed, the presbytery would accept their petition for membership.[25]

Once again, as synod convened in May, 1743, the New York Presbytery moved to have the excluded men received back and recognized as members. Proposals and counterproposals were made, but the real issue remained unchanged. What was to be done with the *Prostestation* of 1741 and the ejection of the Log College men? The Old Side men were adamant. The New York Presbytery gave notice that they would consider forming a new Synod of New York.[26] Dickinson's feelings as he left the synod of 1743 on the last day of May are best revealed by a very significant move. Whereas he had undertaken the previous year vigorously to defend the revival in his *A Display of God's Special Grace,* he had done so anonymously. Seven prominent New England divines had signed a preface, but the author had remained unknown. He now consented to allow Gilbert Tennent to reissue the work and to place the author's name upon it. Moreover, Tennent and five New Side men were permitted to attach an additional preface which connected the pamphlet definitely with their cause. This second preface bore the date June 1, 1743.

Two months later, at New Brunswick, three presbyteries met in joint session, the two Conjunct Presbyteries and the New York Presbytery. Two principal items were on the docket: (1) Should the Milford, Connecticut, church be received by New Brunswick Presbytery and a minister sent to them? (2) Should Gilbert Tennent accept a call to become the pastor of a proposed New Side Presbyterian church in Whitefield's tabernacle in Philadelphia? Both issues were grave indeed. If the Conjunct Presbyteries made these two moves, it would be invading the home territories of two of the greatest enemies of the revival, the Old Side Synod of Philadelphia, and the established Congregational Church of Connecticut. Once embarked on such adventures, the Log College men would be more than occupied. After much deliberation the three presbyteries came to the conclusion that both moves should be taken. Finley was sent to Milford, where the colonial authorities promptly arrested him. Tennent made arrangements to leave New Brunswick, where his usefulness seemed now past.[27] Dickinson, who was present at the meeting, must have given the Log College men some assurances as to the future relations of his group to the Conjunct Presbyteries.

Early the next year Gilbert Tennent became pastor of a New Side Presbyterian congregation which worshiped in the Whitefield tabernacle. Since this building had been erected for Whitefield's followers of all denominations, the other groups, especially the Moravians, protested against its being used to house the new Second Presbyterian Church. Later Tennent's congregation erected a building of their own. For some time the Old Side maintained a steady stream of criticism against

Tennent. His dress, pulpit mannerisms, and the like drew comment. Gradually he became much more polished in dress and much more literary in his sermonic style. He withdrew more and more from polemics and devoted his energies to building up the new Conjunct Presbyteries. Not all of Tennent's old followers, however, approved of his emphasis on the teaching of doctrine and on Presbyterian order. He seems to have striven especially to counteract the " deflated " spirits of the new converts, who felt that the new emphasis was but "backsliding." One of his erstwhile converts, Herman Husbands, who was later to become prominent in the Regulator Movement in North Carolina, wrote: " The Presbyterians [i.e., Gilbert Tennent] gave out from the Pulpit, ' That the Power of God had left them,' and said, it ' was from the great Opposition it met with by the World,' meaning those that oppos'd the New Lights. I thought for my own Part, the Opposition in myself was the most material. But I remember the minister took much Pains from the Pulpit, to encourage his Hearers to depend on their former Experiences, and not throw away their Confidence, assuring them there was no Possibility of falling from Grace . . . All this Shuffling would not do with me . . . they were turning back to Old Presbyterianism, and a State of dead Forms. Thus I left them. . . ." [28] Others of Tennent's converts went off with the Baptists, some — James Carmen, Benjamin Miller, and Isaac Bonnell — becoming preachers.[29] Still others followed Husbands into the pure freedom of the Quaker fold. Nevertheless, the new congregation grew and prospered.

Tennent was quite aware of the problems inherent in his situation. He remarks that, of the converts in this new congregation, those who had had good Christian upbringing and education usually remained stable Christians. It was not to be wondered at, he said, that some of those others, who were largely ignorant of Christian things, soon fell into erroneous ideas or into their old manner of living. Not all of this latter group were lost, but such losses as did occur took place almost wholly from this group. Also, " though there was a considerable falling off in the liveliness of the religious feeling of the people, yet they were growing more humble and merciful, and that their whole conversation made it evident that the bent of their hearts was towards God." [30]

In 1745 the Synod of New York was formed by a union of the Conjunct Presbyteries and the Presbytery of New York. To this new synod most of the New Side men adhered. Gillespie, however, made his peace with the Old Side and issued a pamphlet *Remarks upon Mr. George Whitefield, Proving Him a Man under Delusion*. He criticized Whitefield for calling the Wesleys good men, and for praying for them. Also Whitefield had defended the Moravians against Gilbert Tennent. The

Erskines of Scotland had disowned Whitefield, and so ought all others. This appeal to the example of the Seceders is perhaps a clue to the whole of Gillespie's career. About this same time, he also repudiated his letter to the Presbytery of New York. With great thankfulness, the Old Side published his recantation in the newspapers. For them it was a notable victory.

The articles that served " as the plan and foundation of their synodi-cal union " were agreed upon by the Synod of New York as follows: The Westminster Confession and Catechisms were adopted " in such manner as was agreed unto by the Synod of Philadelphia, in the year 1729." The Directory received " approbation . . . as the general plan of worship and discipline." On matters of discipline any person who could not in conscience submit to the decision of the majority would "peaceably withdraw from the body." Moral failures, doctrinal errors, etc., were to be handled judicially by the proper bodies. Ministers were to be admitted if they " have a competent degree of ministerial knowl-edge, are orthodox in their doctrine, regular in their lives, diligent in . . . designs of vital godliness, and . . . will submit to their discipline." To " avoid all divisive methods " the new synod would from the start maintain correspondence with the Synod of Philadelphia. Moreover, they would not meddle in the strifes of any other Presbyterian or Con-gregational body. A special testimony to the revival as a " work of God's glorious grace" was officially adopted.[31] The new synod, there-fore, retained the original Adopting Act of 1729, provided for strict discipline and a loose adherence to the general pattern of Presbyterian government, made no educational requirements of candidates for the ministry that would militate against the Log College, stressed minis-terial life and conduct equally with orthodoxy in doctrine, definitely strove for irenic relations with Philadelphia and New England, and acknowledged the revival as a work of God. The New York Presby-tery contributed nine ministers to the new synod and the Tennents brought in thirteen. With the founding of the Synod of New York, the destiny of American Presbyterianism was determined, and the creation of a new order became possible.

7

THE BIRTH OF A NEW ORDER

In the welding together of the Log College presbyteries and the New York Presbytery the genius of an American Presbyterianism had been forged. It was a union of second- and third-generation New England Puritan Presbyterians and a group of the younger Scotch-Irish Presbyterians who, through William Tennent, Sr., had been thoroughly imbued with the piety and views of English Puritanism. They were as orthodox as their opponents, yet they so defined orthodoxy as to make it include practical piety. Doctrine, therefore, apart from piety was false doctrine, in that it attempted to claim for a part that which could be true only of the whole. Their outlook on the Church was colonial-American. The ministry was not an aristocratic calling. For the most part the clergy of the New York Synod were colonial in origin, not born in manses, educated under humble circumstances, and close to their people in thought and work. Intensely missionary-minded, they, by their unparalleled zeal and efforts, far outstripped the Old World Presbyterianism that had been transplanted into the colonies, and gave birth to a new order of Presbyterianism, an American Church.

The task of creating a new order out of the chaos following upon the crushing of the old order was not to be an easy task for the Synod of New York. Since they were wholeheartedly committed to the revival, they inherited all the problems that had followed in its wake. That they sought by every means at their disposal to continue the Great Awakening, even while wrestling with its eccentrics and its enemies, indicates the depth of their conviction that it was " a work of God." Their geographical position, and their deep roots in New England, placed them in the center of the bitter controversy which still raged about the revival in New England and in the middle colonies. The vigorous and constructive part that the new synod took in this controversy brought two very important results. It brought to their support a host of New Englanders like Jonathan Edwards, Benjamin Colman, and Thomas Prince, and gave to them a large percentage of the young men of New England whom the revival had turned toward the ministry.

Gradually the excesses of the revival were brought under control. In 1743, David Brainerd, writing to Joseph Bellamy of their tribulations, notes that their worst difficulties were then coming from two situations in New England, and from the strife over the Moravians.[1] Troubles of their own persisted, however, for Samuel Finley wrote Bellamy over two years later saying, " We have some yt treat us in ye same manner as your Eastern Exhorters, & equally pervert ye Scriptures. . . ." [2] Before the close of the decade the situation was well in hand in all but a few congregations — so much so that Eleazer Wheelock, in writing to Bellamy in 1749, sought to prove his arguments for a presbyterian form of government by saying, " You know how God has overruled things in ye Jersies." [3] By a wise use of the authority of presbytery over both the clergy and the congregations, by patient and thorough doctrinal exposition, by honest and even severe ministerial discipline, and by an unsurpassed evangelistic zeal, the dross had been purged from the Great Awakening movement in the New York Synod. The new synod were then able to reap from the revival a very large harvest. Numerically and spiritually this harvest of the revival was the strength of the synod.

Meanwhile the Log College had ceased to function. William Tennent, Sr., had resigned his pastorate in 1742, and in 1744 had offered his property for sale. On May 6, 1746, his pilgrimage was ended. Just when the Log College as such closed its unique career is unknown. It was probably about the time when Tennent disposed of the property upon which the " college " stood. From the Log College had come some of the most influential and useful men in colonial Presbyterianism.[4]

The new synod came into being, therefore, without a place to train their ministry. The two New England colleges, Harvard and Yale, were in the hands of men bitterly opposed to the revival. In spite of this hostility to the Great Awakening at both Harvard and Yale, a number of men who had been converted during the revival were entering the ministry from these schools. Gilbert Tennent's preaching at Yale had led many students to conversion and to the ministry. Among these was David Brainerd. In the controversy between students and faculty at Yale over the revival, Brainerd made some rash comments to a fellow student on the religion of certain of the faculty. These comments came to the ears of the faculty, and Brainerd was denied his degree only a few weeks before he was to have graduated. He turned to his friends, Dickinson and Burr, for counsel and advice. When Dickinson went to New England in 1742, he interceded at Yale for Brainerd but without success. Brainerd was willing to apologize and make amends, but

President Clap and his associates, who were determined to stamp out the whole revival movement, refused to relent. Apparently it was during this plea for Brainerd that Dickinson gave to Clap the letter that Gilbert Tennent had written.

In spite of the opposition of the faculty, a number of students at Yale continued their interest in the revival. Several of these — Samuel Buell, David Youngs, David Bostwick, Thomas Arthur, John Grant, Job Prudden, Thomas Lewis, and Caleb Smith — had come into the Synod of New York by 1747. Four Harvard men had come also — Eliab Byram, Jacob Green, Nathaniel Tucker, and Timothy Symmes. These recruits, however welcome, were not adequate for the crying needs of the new synod. Another college, dedicated to the same interests as the revival and located in the middle colonies, was needed. To the founding of such a college a number of the New York Presbytery's leaders turned their thoughts. Anglican opposition to the chartering of any institution, local churches, or colleges for the Dissenters was pronounced. As early as March, 1745, before the actual founding of the Synod of New York in September of that year, Dickinson, Burr, Pemberton, and Pierson, all ministers in New York Presbytery, and three laymen, Peter V. B. Livingston, William Smith, and William P. Smith, all of New York City, had formed the nucleus of a board of trustees and had begun to raise funds for a college. Their first request for a charter was rejected by Governor Lewis Morris because of Anglican hostility and Quaker disinterest. For the governor, who was himself an Anglican, the granting of such a charter was both personally distasteful and politically inexpedient.

It was not until the death of Governor Morris, May 21, 1746, that Dickinson and his friends were able to proceed farther with their plans. The interim governor, John Hamilton, the president of the Council of the Province, was prevailed upon by his advisers, who were friendly to Dickinson and his colleagues, to sign a charter for the College of New Jersey on October 22, 1746. In spite of Anglican outcries that the charter had been secured " suddenly " and " privately " from an interim governor who was too old and ill to know what he was doing, Dickinson and his six associates became the board of trustees, and pressed vigorously on in the founding of their school. Within six months they had added to their board four of the most prominent Log College alumni and one of their oldest and closest collaborators. Gilbert and William Tennent, Jr., Samuel Blair, and Samuel Finley were the Log College men. Richard Treat, a Yale man who for years had been a supporter of the Tennents, was the fifth new trustee. The College of New Jersey thus became representative of the whole Synod of New

York, and also placed itself in position to inherit the traditions of the
Log College. Jonathan Dickinson was now elected president of the
college, and Caleb Smith tutor.[5]

In May, 1747, classes opened in Dickinson's home at Elizabethtown.
The first students, numbering eight or ten, were probably men whom
Dickinson had previously been tutoring in the small classical school
that he had conducted for some years. Since February a few announce-
ments of the school had been appearing. One of these notices in a New
York paper promised that " equal Liberties and Privileges are secured
to every Denomination of Christians, any different religious Sentiments notwithstanding." [6] The school was founded on a broad liberal
arts foundation, and, though it was solidly in control of Presbyterians,
it was wholly independent of any Church judicature and open to students of all denominations on equal terms. Sorrow and distress came
early to the new college as its chief founder and first president, Jonathan Dickinson, died October 7, 1747. He had conducted the school
less than six months. Burr assumed charge of the college, which was
now moved to his parsonage, though he may not have been formally
elected president until the following year under the second charter.[7]

In 1748, Jonathan Belcher, a deeply religious man, born a New England Congregationalist, became governor of New Jersey. He was
quickly added to the Board of Trustees of the college and made its
president. Very soon a new charter was granted which placed the college beyond the attacks to which the first charter was so vulnerable.
Under this charter an enlarged Board of Trustees was named, including four members of the Council of New Jersey, several prominent
Pennsylvania laymen, and twelve ministers, all but three of whom,
Gilbert and William Tennent, Jr., and Samuel Blair, were graduates
of Yale and Harvard. Samuel Finley was dropped, due to Belcher's
desire to secure a large number of politically and financially prominent
laymen. A number of these laymen had no great interest in the revival, and some, Gilbert Tennent especially, resisted strenuously the
bringing in of men from the governor's council. However, the clerical
group, together with several of the laymen who were strongly devoted to the Church, constituted a majority, and no changes in policy
took place. The college was now moved to Princeton, New Jersey.

Money was desperately needed. In addition to the solicitation of gifts
in the colonies, several lotteries were run off in the interests of the college. Lotteries had become almost a craze in the colonies at that time.
They were used for the building of churches, bridges, town improve-
ments, the disposal of lands, and innumerable other private and public
ventures. As yet there had been little opposition to them from any

quarter, and none from the Churches. In 1748, however, the legislature of New Jersey had prohibited them. The College of New Jersey set up lotteries in Pennsylvania and Connecticut in order to avoid a clash with the New Jersey laws. In Pennsylvania the Old Side Presbyterians tried to stop the college's lottery, and by a lawsuit materially reduced the net proceeds to the college.[8] The Old Side had no religious scruples about lotteries, but they did have deep, conscientious scruples about the prospect of a strong college under the control of the New Side.

At length the trustees determined to send an emissary to Great Britain in quest of funds. Pemberton and, later, Burr were requested to go, but without success. The trustees then turned to Gilbert Tennent and Samuel Davies. After some hesitation the two men agreed to go. In November of 1753, they set sail, and reached London on Christmas Day. During nearly a year of ceaseless endeavor in England, Scotland, and Ireland, they were able to raise over £4,000 for the college and some additional special funds for scholarships.[9] Wherever Tennent and Davies went in Great Britain, they found the way prepared for them by the Old Side Presbyterians. Copies of Tennent's sermon *On the Dangers of an Unconverted Ministry* had been industriously circulated, and Robert Cross had written a number of letters seeking to frustrate their mission. President Burr wrote to David Cowell, who though still an Old Side Presbyterian had become a trustee and zealous promoter of the college: "Our good friend Mr, Cross has endeavored to prepare ye way for them [Tennent and Davies] in Scotland. I think he is in a fair way to lose the little remains of credit he has left." [10]

Tennent had frequently to explain the circumstances under which his "famous" sermon had been preached, and to assure his British benefactors that it was a rash act done in the heat of a terrible conflict, rather than a statement of the New Side's conception of Presbyterianism. Both emissaries had frequently also to explain their Church's laws regarding doctrinal subscription. Few of the clergy from whom they solicited money and support were friendly to creedal subscription. On one occasion Davies explained the Synod of New York's attitude thus: "I replied that we allowed the candidate to mention his objections against any article in the Confession, and the judicature judged whether the articles objected against were essential to Christianity; and if they judged they were not, they would admit the candidate, notwithstanding his objections." [11] Very significant in this explanation are the words "essential to Christianity." This is far broader than "essential to the Westminster Confession." Yet Davies

was continually oppressed by the doctrinal looseness of the Churches of
both England and Scotland. Even so, he could not accept some of the
extremes of English orthodoxy. He notes in his diary, " In the evening
visited Mr. Winter, a Congregational minister; but his dry orthodoxy,
and severe reflections upon those that deviated from rigid Calvinism,
were disagreeable to me." [12] In Scotland the great power of the General
Assembly over the lower judicatures and the clergy oppressed him
greatly. "I find a great number of the clergy and laity have of late
carried church-power to an extravagant height, deny to individuals
the right of judging for themselves, and insist upon absolute universal
obedience to all the determinations of the General Assembly." [13] Davies'
acts and comments provide an excellent unposed picture of a typical
New Side Presbyterian.

While it was true that the College of New Jersey was not part of the
Synod of New York, there was a sense in which each of these institutions was a part of one great enterprise, the Christianizing of the American colonies. The leadership of the college was the same as the leadership of the synod. It is not at all surprising, therefore, that as early as
1753 collections were ordered taken in all the churches of the synod.
Regular checkups were made by each presbytery in order to make certain that a collection had been made in every congregation under their
care. These collections were ordered almost annually throughout the
colonial period, though the aggregate receipts seem never to have been
very large.

Second only in importance for the future of American Presbyterianism to the founding of the College of New Jersey was the growing interchange of men and ideas between the Synod of New York and the
leaders of the revival in New England. Jonathan Edwards, Joseph
Bellamy, and other New Englanders became frequent correspondents
of the New Side men. Their books and sermons wielded a great influence, not only upon the New Side clergy, but upon the students of
the college. Students from New England began to come to Princeton
because the school was friendly to the revival. In 1746, Yale graduated
only twelve students. This decline in enrollment had been blamed
upon Whitefield, Tennent, and the other revivalists.[14] At length, in
1755, Yale appointed a New Side Presbyterian minister, one of their
own graduates, Naphthali Dagget, as college pastor and professor of
divinity. A revival shortly followed. Thereafter a considerable interchange of students took place between the churches of Connecticut and
the churches of the Synod of New York.

Men from the synod frequently studied at Yale and returned to
" read divinity" with a Presbyterian minister. Men from New Eng-

land often studied at Princeton and then completed their theological work in New England. Of the synod's ministers, Robert Smith and Samuel Finley seem to have been most active in preparing men in theology. Joseph Bellamy, Jonathan Edwards, and Samuel Hopkins in New England were the theological instructors most sought for by young Presbyterians from the synod. The influence of this cross-fertilization in the development of the new order of Presbyterianism that was the New Side can hardly be overestimated. Two unusual incidents were prophetic of the future of this interchange. In 1751, Samuel Davies failed in a great effort to locate Jonathan Edwards in a Presbyterian church in Virginia.[15] Only the slowness of the colonial mails caused the plan to collapse. Three years later strenuous efforts were made to bring Joseph Bellamy to New York as pastor of the Presbyterian Church. The effort failed though it greatly increased Bellamy's influence in the synod.[16]

With the ministerial recruits gained from both the College of New Jersey and from New England, the Synod of New York was in position to evangelize a great part of the settled area in the middle colonies. The revival had so strengthened the Long Island churches that a new presbytery had been formed in 1747 for the eastern part of the island. The churches adhering to this presbytery, called the Presbytery of Suffolk, were all served by graduates of the New England colleges. Vigorous evangelization work was thus being carried on all through Long Island. The churches of western Long Island belonging to the Presbytery of New York became part of Suffolk Presbytery when the latter body joined the synod in 1748. The New York Presbytery now began expanding up the "corridor" between Connecticut and the Hudson River, and in northwestern Jersey. Few settlers had gone to the great manors which covered most of the land along the western bank of the Hudson. Accordingly the Church did little in this area.

New Brunswick Presbytery had for its territory the larger part of New Jersey, and northeastern Pennsylvania. Few settlers had as yet, however, come into that section of Pennsylvania, and the presbytery's endeavors far overleaped their own borders. In addition to planting numerous new churches in New Jersey, and some in Pennsylvania, the presbytery began sending missionaries to Virginia and the Carolinas. After the College of New Jersey became established within the presbytery's borders, the majority of the young graduates turned to New Brunswick Presbytery for ordination. The presbytery soon stopped this procedure by ruling that they would henceforth accept no graduate for ordination who was not previously a member of one of their churches, or else a member of a church outside the bounds of the entire synod, i.e., a New Englander who wished to become Presbyterian, or a man from abroad. All through the colonial period the Presbytery of New York and the Presbytery of New Brunswick led all the other presbyteries (New Side and Old Side) in the number of men brought into the ministry. The revival interested men in the ministry, and the two presbyteries that took the lead in promoting the revival received the greatest number of these recruits.

Both the Synod of New York and the Synod of Philadelphia had a Presbytery of New Castle, commonly differentiated as New Side and Old Side respectively. New Castle Presbytery, New Side, was sprawled out over a large area, roughly the same as that occupied by two presbyteries belonging to the Synod of Philadelphia, namely, New Castle, Old Side, and Donegal. This large area included parts of Delaware and Maryland (where the older churches were of mixed backgrounds and the newer ones were Scotch-Irish) and the southern part of Pennsylvania, plus an undefined region to the southward. Here the bitterest phases of the Old Side, New Side controversy had been fought before the schism of 1741. Resentments continued to smolder in these areas long after " peace and union " officially brought the two " Sides " together again in 1758. The second, and the largest, wave of Scotch-Irish immigrants to the colonies had settled in these regions. For some reason hardly any ministers came to America with this massive migration, which occupied a space of nearly two decades. Most of these new settlers went to the frontier beyond Lancaster, Pennsylvania, and from thence they moved down into the Valley of Virginia and into the western parts of the Carolinas. New Castle Presbytery, New Side, with what aid it could get from New Brunswick Presbytery, and from Lewes Presbytery just to the south, did what they could to provide the new immigrants with ministers. On one occasion alone they appealed to New Brunswick for help, saying that they had vacant congregations in Pennsylvania, Maryland, Virginia, and in North Carolina. No less than fourteen vacant congregations were asking them for ministers in North Carolina. Unfortunately New Brunswick's situation was not much better, and only one man could be given to New Castle.[17] This constant shortage of clergymen was a serious problem to the rapidly expanding Church all through the colonial period.

The rise of New Side Presbyterianism in Virginia is one of the most thrilling episodes in colonial Church history.[18] The movement began wholly unsponsored among a few lay people belonging to an Anglican church in Hanover County. Stories of the great revival had aroused the interest of Samuel Morris and several laymen. They began meeting in 1740 at Morris' home for the purpose of reading together such books as Boston's *Fourfold State,* Luther's *Commentary on Galatians,* and some of Whitefield's sermons. Gradually the movement grew un til Morris erected a "reading house" in order better to accommodate the numbers who came. The established Anglican Church became aroused, and fines and other means were used to suppress the movement. Morris and his associates persisted, however, and finally secured a limited toleration for themselves, first as "Lutherans" and later as Presbyterians. In 1743 they heard of William Robinson, a Log College trained minister who was on a preaching tour by order of the Conjunct Presbyteries. They invited him to preach in their "reading house" and later called him as pastor. Another Log College man, John Roan, also came to preach. He so freely exposed the failures of the Anglican clergy in Virgina that a considerable uproar took place. Roan had to leave the colony, and Morris and his associates with difficulty satisfied the authorities as to their good behavior. The Old Side Presbyterians who had been trying to establish themselves in the Valley of Virginia, hearing of the New Side's difficulties, hastened to write to the Virginia governor, assuring him that these disturbers were not of their synod, and incidentally assuring him also that the New Side men were a group of professional troublemakers whom they had been compelled to cast out some years previous.[19] Later Gilbert Tennent and Samuel Finley were sent by the Synod of New York to visit Virginia. They made a favorable impression on the governor, and the Church was allowed to go on with its work. Samuel Davies came to the congregation as pastor in 1747, and under him the work began to spread rapidly. He fought a long, hard battle for full religious toleration in the colony, which issued victoriously only when he was able to press his case personally in London while there in behalf of the College of New Jersey.

Another mission that the New Side Presbyterians sought to carry out was that of evangelizing the Indians. In 1730, the Society in Scotland for Propagating Christian Knowledge had turned to several Boston ministers as the proper persons to direct, on their behalf, an Indian mission. Some work was done, but by 1738 the venture was an acknowledged failure, and came to an end. At that time Dickinson and Pemberton, who had been deeply concerned for the Indians, asked the S.S.P.C.K. to grant them funds for Indian missions. A Board of Correspondents was organized in 1741, consisting of ministers and laymen from the New York Presbytery and the Log College. This board sent out John Sargent in 1741, Azariah Horton the next year, and David Brainerd in 1743. These three missionaries met with such success that the synod instituted annual collections in their churches in order to expand the work. For over a decade these missions continued, until finally the dwindling of the tribes, migrations of the Indians westward, and other factors brought most of this endeavor to a close. In 1757, the board decided to purchase 3,000 acres of land in order to provide a fixed home for the Indians. Eventually the New Jersey government gave a large tract of land in southern Jersey as an Indian home, and John Brainerd became their minister. Gradually this venture also came to an end as the Indians became fewer and fewer.[20]

The character of the Presbyterian order of the New Side was revealed also in a number of lesser incidents during the years of its formation. During the colonial period attendance upon presbytery and synod by elders was never good. For several years, 1752–1754, the Synod of New York made a strenuous effort to increase the attendance of elders on the sessions of Church judicatures. Improvement was shown, but it was only temporary. From 1748–1756, New Brunswick Presbytery tried several means to bring their congregations to prompt and full payment of their ministers' salaries. Persuasion only was used, and presbytery was at length forced to leave the matter with the local churches. The problem of arrears in ministers' salaries baffled both Old and New Side groups throughout the colonial era. Presbytery did not have either the means or the power to force congregations to pay. Even denying a congregation the right to call another minister often failed to compel them to pay the arrears due the former pastor or his widow.

In their relations with other denominations, certain views of the Synod of New York were highlighted. During the Great Awakening the hard, narrow spirit of denominationalism which most of the colonial immigrants had brought with them was cracked in large sections of the Presbyterian Church. To the Log College men more than to any others must go the credit for this achievement.

It is quite significant that in the earliest published work of any of the Tennents, a treatise on regeneration written by John Tennent (who died in 1732), denominationalism is specifically condemned as a failure in Christian love.[21] The wholehearted reception given to Whitefield by the Log College men had a profound effect upon the entire Church. Quotations from Anglican scholars and even from Anglican bishops were quite common in the sermons of the Log College men. No New Side Presbyterian could easily have felt, therefore, that the Anglican Church as such was not in all respects a true Church. When William Tennent, Sr., was asked to list his reasons for leaving it to rejoin the Presbyterian Church, he stated that he objected to episcopal government and to the contemporary dominance of Arminian doctrines in the Anglican Church. Samuel Davies could quite honestly contend as a New Side Presbyterian minister for freedom to establish Presbyterian congregations in the midst of Anglican congregations even while writing to the vigorously evangelistic and Congregationalist New England leader, Joseph Bellamy, that it mattered little to him which party was uppermost. What mattered, he declared, was " living religion." [22] While in England, he noted with great aversion the narrow denominationalism and party spirit of some of the Dissenters. Upon leaving his congregation to take up the presidency of the College of New Jersey he urged his people to maintain good relations with their Anglican brethren, and to attend the Anglican churches occasionally until they found a successor to himself.[23]

The New Side Presbyterians had founded a new congregation in Philadelphia after the schism of 1741. When dedicating the first building which this congregation erected, Gilbert Tennent, the pastor, spoke what had been the consistent attitude of his party from the beginning: " All Societies, who profess Christianity, and retain the Foundation-Principles thereof, notwithstanding their different Denominations and Diversity of Sentiments in smaller Things, are in Reality, but One Church of Christ, but several Branches (more or less pure in Minuter Points) of one visible Kingdom of the Messiah; whose Honour and Interest rightly understood, is one and the same." [24] Therefore, although William McClenachan had once been a Presbyterian and then had become reordained as an Anglican, the New Side Presbyterians saw nothing wrong in attempting to aid him in securing an Anglican charge in Philadelphia. The furor raised over their act revealed clearly that whatever the personal views of the Old Side clergy may have been, they were willing both to arouse and to utilize denominational spirit as an instrument of ecclesiastical policy.

The Seceders of Scotland became more and more active in the middle colonies after 1741. One of these, Alexander Gellatly, made a favorable impression on the New York Presbyterians at first. Later, however, he and John Cuthbertson came into controversy with a number of the former Log College men of the Presbytery of New Castle. To the Log College men the Seceders' insistence upon the Solemn League and Covenant, upon separation from all others, their doctrinal rigidity, and other items, were both objectionable in themselves and a vain attempt to fix in the New World something that had meaning only in the past history of the Old World.[25] On the opposite extreme, the views of the early Moravian missionaries seemed to the New Side men as positively dangerous. Some of the Moravians themselves were soon to demand reforms on some of the points objected to by Gilbert Tennent, Jonathan Dickinson, and others. Therefore, although the first Moravians were well received by the Presbyterians in New York, it was not long before the New Side strongly opposed the Moravians, and eventually led even Whitefield to take sides against them.[26]

The activity of the Baptists during the revival began to bear fruit, and a number of New Side men took up the cudgels in defense of infant baptism. Samuel Finley had a public debate with the Baptist minister Abel Morgan, after which a pamphlet war between the two men took place.[27] Before long, however, Baptist students were at the College of New Jersey, and no attack upon the Baptist Church itself was ever made. Jonathan Dickinson wrote a number of treatises on infant baptism, some of which drew much attention in New England, and some were controverted in print, even in London.[28] Samuel Harker also debated with Abel Morgan.[29]

While, therefore, the New Side Presbyterians were active in defending their liberties and freedoms as a denomination, or in defending and propagating their own doctrinal views, they were the earliest pioneers in the New World in both confessing and recognizing the existence of a true Church in each of the many evangelical Protestant denominations about them. Moreover, whenever any group did raise the standard of exclusive claims, as the Seceders, or the cry of separation, as the Separates of New England, the New Side Presbyterians opposed them. Denominationalism as such was for them evil. This spirit was to remain among Presbyterians throughout the colonial era. It was to find numerous expressions during that time, and to come within reach of constitutional expression at the founding of the General Assembly.[30] Though excluded from such official affirmation, this spirit was to create close working arrangements with the Congregationalists under the Plan of Union established in 1801.

The growing boldness and hostility of the French gave rise in 1747 to an Association for Defence. The organization was started at a rally in Gilbert Tennent's church at which he preached a sermon on the justness of defensive warfare. The sermon was attacked at once by certain of the Quakers, and Tennent published several replies to their criticisms.[31] Throughout the following troubled years, leading up to and during the French and Indian War, New Side Presbyterians strove both to explain the incidence of the terrible war and to encourage their people to quit themselves as men and defend their homes and country. At the College of New Jersey graduation theses affirmed that it was "lawful, by Force and Arms, to resist those who are gradually invading our Rights." [32] Special days of prayer and fasting were observed throughout the churches belonging to the synod. Many of the clergy published sermons on various aspects of the issue. Two of these sermons are typical of all. Chauncey Graham preached February 12, 1756, on *Some few reasons suggested, why the heathen are at present permitted to rage in the British Colonies in North America:* . . . Samuel Davies, in preaching on *The Curse of Cowardice,* after General Braddock's defeat in 1758, cried: "Something must be done! must be done by you! Therefore, instead of assuming the State of Patriots and Heroes at home, to arms! and away to the Field, and prove your Pretensions sincere." But he also added, that the troublous times were an indication of God's displeasure and of the need of personal and national reformation. "Therefore in the Name of Jesus, the Captain of your Salvation, I invite you all to enlist in the spiritual Warfare. . . . The mean, sneaking Wretch, that can desert the Cause of his Country in such an Exigency; his Country, in the blessings of which he shared, while in Peace and Prosperity; and which is therefore intitled to his Sympathy and Assistance in the Day of its Distress; that cowardly ungrateful Wretch sins against God and his Country, and deserves the Curse of both. [Such conduct] . . . exposes the Wretch to the heavy Curse of God both in this and the eternal World." [33]

As the year 1758 drew to a close, seventeen years after the ejection of the Log College men from the Synod of Philadelphia, the new order of Presbyterianism which was the New Side had been firmly established. The Synod of New York was the strongest Church in the middle colonies, made up of many congregations scattered from the Hudson Valley to North Carolina, from Southampton on eastern Long Island to regions in the wilderness near Fort Pitt, Pennsylvania. It was possessed of a thriving college and numerous classical schools, which were giving back to it an ever-increasing number of able and zealous pioneer ministers. Its clergy were among the finest on the American continent. The new order, a truly American Presbyterianism, was distinguished by its tone, discipline, and spiritual vitality.

8

THE WITHERED BRANCH

Just what the Scotch-Irish party had planned and hoped to accomplish after the ejection of the Log College men is difficult to determine. Those who signed the *Protest* of 1741 and made the schism were a small minority in the synod, twelve out of the forty-seven ministers. Barely one half of the ministerial members of the synod, twenty-six out of forty-seven, were in attendance at the 1741 sessions. The ejection of the Log College men without trial by a vote of twelve to ten, with four men not voting, constituted a grave political risk. Since eleven of the twelve signers of the *Protest,* and quite probably the twelfth, Samuel Thomson, as well, were Scotch-Irish, they no doubt had as the pattern of their deed the Irish synod's ouster of the Presbytery of Antrim in 1726. At any rate, when defending their deed in 1744, the protesters declared, "And were it needful to produce them, there are not wanting precedents of this method of procedure in Presbyterian churches, yea and in civil judicatures. . . ." [1] After 1726 the antisubscriptionist cause in the Irish Presbyterian Church had dwindled. Its chief support had been the Presbytery of Antrim.

No doubt this pattern of success greatly influenced Cross, Thomson, and the other Scotch-Irish leaders. What they overlooked, however, was that whereas the main issue in the Synod of Ulster had been creedal subscription, the real issue in the American Presbyterian Church was the Great Awakening. It was this difference that was to bring defeat to the Scotch-Irish party. It cost them the support of the Presbytery of New York and of the greater proportion of the lay people throughout the synod. Moreover, the very serious disciplinary problem within their own ranks is hardly to be separated from their inveterate enmity toward the Great Awakening. Alison and Thomson seem in themselves to have been upright men. But many of their followers found, all too easily, in the frontal attack which they maintained against the " excesses " of the revival a convenient cover for immoralities of the grossest kinds in their own lives. The withering of the schismatic Scotch-Irish party was accordingly inevitable.

No doubt his own hopes greatly colored the report on Philadelphia Presbyterianism that Robert Jenney, of the Anglican Church in the city, sent to the Bishop of London in 1743. " The Presbyterians are almost broken to pieces; one of their Preachers told me that he hath scarce a Dozen Hearers, when any of these Vagrant Preachers (as he calls them), holds forth at Whitefield's Building." [2] However much Jenney may have exaggerated the plight of this man (Robert Cross is meant, it seems), the Scotch-Irish group did suffer severely at the hands of the entire revival group, ministers and laymen, after the schism of 1741. Following the synod of 1742, the Log College men began to take over as many of the older congregations as would follow them, and to set up rival congregations wherever they had failed to capture the whole flock. From this double threat few if any of the antirevivalists escaped unscathed. Some had to seek new congregations; others were faced with rival churches very near their own. This " unsettling " of the " former pastors " was to become a major issue in all future discussions of reunion.

The future of the Old Side schism grew darker as it became more and more evident that not only had they failed to carry the majority of the lay people with them, but that the Presbytery of New York, in entirety, was going over to the Log College side. Two bright stars appeared, however, in 1744, which seemed to promise much. George Gillespie, an honored senior minister whom all respected highly, and who had initially been almost persuaded to take the Log College path, dramatically recanted at a meeting of the New Castle Presbytery. Undoubtedly Gillespie's return to their fold did aid the Old Side, especially in certain Scotch-Irish congregations. It did not, however, swerve the New York Presbytery from announcing one month later that they were about to form a new synod together with the Log College men.[3]

The other bright star that for a while shone upon the Old Side was the wholly unexpected offer of a merger with the German Reformed Churches of Pennsylvania. Many thousands of Germans from the Palatinate had settled in Pennsylvania. They had very few ministers and only a few organized churches. The Reformed Church in the Netherlands had become interested in these Germans and had given them some aid. Later they came to the conclusion that these German Reformed people should join with the American Presbyterians and made this proposal to the Synod of Philadelphia in 1744. The synod received the proposal with joy, but the Germans refused the merger. In 1751, a second attempt was made by certain leaders of the Dutch Church.

The Germans were now more approachable. Suddenly, however, opposition developed in Holland, and the entire matter was dropped.[4]

The Scotch-Irish group had become known as the Old Side, the bearers of the old tradition. Their ministers and churches were made up largely of Scotch-Irish immigrants. Andrews and the old Philadelphia church, David Evans and his Welsh congregation, and some of the mixed congregations of New Jersey and Delaware were exceptions. The great strength of the Old Side was in Pennsylvania and Maryland. In 1746, at the first meeting of the Synod of Philadelphia as an exclusively Old Side institution, they had on their rolls twenty-two ministers — sixteen Scotch-Irish, four New Englanders, and two Welshmen. The areas open to them for expansion were largely to the west and to the south. Northward, through New Brunswick and New York Presbyteries, they had no reason to hope that they were welcome. Eastward, along the Jersey, Delaware, and Maryland shores, they managed to hold their own, but gained little except in the Baltimore area. The great mass of Scotch-Irish who entered during the years 1740–1760 had settled largely in Pennsylvania, west of Lancaster, and in the Shenandoah Valley of Virginia. These immigrants had been accompanied by almost no ministers. They became the Old Side's greatest missionary field. A grievous shortage of clergy prevented the Synod of Philadelphia from accomplishing very much among them. By the time of the reunion in 1758, " the Old Side had not settled one minister in Virginia in ten years."[5] Itinerating missionaries were being maintained in Virginia and the Carolinas, but seldom had new congregations been established. The principal gains of the Old Side in new congregations were made in western Pennsylvania.

In spite of the withdrawal of the Presbytery of New York and the loss of the great popular support, the Old Side might have been able to overcome their early losses and make great strides in the evangelization of western Pennsylvania, Virginia, and the Carolinas. By failing, however, to secure an adequate ministry the Old Side lost all their hopes of growth. The inability of the Synod of Philadelphia to found a school for training their ministry, and to achieve any real discipline among their clergy, sealed their fate.

As early as 1739, during the height of the Scotch-Irish party's attack upon the Log College, John Thomson had asked Donegal Presbytery to overture the synod, asking for the establishment of a " publick school or Seminary of learning." Though New Castle Presbytery concurred, and the synod appointed a committee, the project was not undertaken.[6] After the schism of 1741 the matter was again brought up. In 1743 the Synod of Philadelphia established a school at New

London, Pennsylvania, under the care of Francis Alison. In every way Alison was the best of the Old Side men, and he seems to have made all possible efforts to establish a worthy school. Through the synod an approach was made to President Clap, of Yale College, asking that close working relations be set up between the two schools. The synod proposed that they send the graduates of their school to Yale for degrees. They hoped that perhaps Yale would ask no more than one year's additional study of these men: " As learning is not in the same esteem in this government [i.e., colony] as in New England, we beg all the indulgance your constitution can allow us, lest parents grudge expenses if they run high. We heartily agree that our scholars be examined by the President and Fellows, and be treated only according to their proficiency." [7] For some reason this plan failed to go through.

Alison next turned to Scotland for counsel. Some correspondence was had with Francis Hutcheson, of Glasgow University, but to what effect is unknown.[8] Financially the school had great difficulties. The synod ordered collections taken on its behalf, but not nearly enough was ever secured. Finally, after nine years of service, Alison left, without being duly dismissed, in order to accept a position at the newly organized College of Philadelphia. The synod's school was thereupon moved to Newark, in Delaware, and placed under the care of one of Alison's former pupils, Alexander McDowell.

Alison had left the synod's school because it was a failure. Through nine years he had labored well, for he was a competent man. Yet in excusing his irregular and abrupt departure, synod admitted that he had acted aright, and expressed the hope that in his new position he might be able to promote their cause. Accordingly, though the Newark school was continued in a small way, the Old Side's hopes were now set on the College of Philadelphia. Alison added to his teaching duties the office of assistant to Robert Cross in First Church, and shortly emerged as the leader of the Old Side.

Even before Alison had come to Philadelphia, the College of New Jersey had gotten well under way. The trustees of the college were at that time seeking someone to go to Great Britain in quest of financial aid. A year after Alison began his work in Philadelphia, Samuel Davies and Gilbert Tennent sailed for London. The prospect of success on their journey was too much for the Old Side to bear. Cross, aging, but still their leader, wrote a number of letters to Great Britain in an attempt to turn certain influential people against Tennent and Davies. Through some means, also, a number of copies of Tennent's sermon, *On the Dangers of an Unconverted Ministry,* were dispatched to Great Britain.[9] When, then, Davies and Tennent succeeded in their mission, the Old Side felt compelled to make a new start in their own behalf. Alison approached Provost William Smith, of the College of Philadelphia, with a proposition. The Old Side Presbyterians wished to have Smith establish an arrangement whereby their students could study divinity with Robert Cross while regularly enrolled in the College of Philadelphia. In this manner they could at last have a school for the training of their clergy. This scheme also failed, but since William Smith's description of it to Samuel Chandler, an English Presbyterian, affords so excellent a picture of Old Side thinking at this time, it is worthy of special note. There was a good deal of Smith's own spleen in the letter, but, nonetheless, it was basically an Old Side interpretation of the current situation. Smith had been brought up in Scotland, and knew Presbyterianism well.

Rev. Dear Sir: I had your several Favors by M^r. Barton, . . .

I have rambled from the main Purport of this Letter, which was . . . to make known to you the State of the Old Presbyterian Congregation in this City; the members of which have lately addressed you, to provide them with a Minister. . . .

It would be needless to give you a minute Account of the Occasion of the late Separation among the Presbyterians in these Colonies. When M^r. Whitefield first came to these Parts, among several of his Doctrines, many run away with that of an instantaneous sort of Conversion or *new Light,* the Signs of which were Falling into Fits, Faintings, &c., &c. . . .

Hence, I presume, arose the original Distinction between New Light, & Old Light Presbyterians, by which the two Parties are now vulgarly denominated. The former followed Whitfield; and he & they did not fail to " deal Damnation round " on the other side, as well as on all Persuasions different from theirs. But tho' this began the Difference, it was widened & continued by Matters relating to Church Government, as will appear in the Sequel.

With the same Degree of Extravagance with which Whitfield condemned his Adversaries, he extolled his Adherents, tho' they had nothing to recommend them but their blind Attachment to his Doctrines. Among others, he proposed the two Tennents & some others to his Followers in this City as the only Gospel Ministers. One of them is a Man completely accomplished in all the Degrees of Ignorance & Weakness. The other I need not tell you of. He is the same you saw in the Character of a *Sturdy Beggar,* & who came recommended to you (as you told me) under the uncommon Name of *Hellfire T——nt.*

Upon the Strength of Whitfield's Recommendation this Man left his little Congregation in New Jersey & came to this Town an itinerant, as it was thought, on his Master's Plan. He was sure to have the greater Part of Whitfield's Mob after him; and of Course more than one-half of the Presbyterian Congregation follow'd, & stuck by him, as he professed himself a

Presbyterian. Several others of the lower Sort did the same from other Congregations. . . .

As this settlement was a Manifest Intrusion into M^r. Cross's Congregation, in Contempt of all Order & Right, M^r. Tennent had no way to justify it but to pretend that himself & several others of his Kidney who made the like Intrusions & Settlements in other Places, being a Majority, were the Synod, & those who adhered to the old Doctrines were Separatists. In Consequence of this the New Lights associated themselves into a kind of independent Synod, protests were entered, pamphlets published, & the Difference widened without any probability of a Reunion, but by the entire Submission of the Tennents, &c., who are certainly the Separating or Seceding party, which is not very like to happen, as they think themselves by far the strongest, & hope soon to swallow up the other Side by their Numbers.

To accomplish this, their first Method was to take Men from the Plough to the Pulpit in a few Months, by which Means they deluged the Country with their Teachers, having no higher Idea of the sacred Function than to think any person qualified for it who could *cant* out a few unintelligible sounds concerning Conversion, Saving Grace, Reprobation, Election, &c.; without ever striving to adorn the Heart with the Christian Virtues of Meekness, Peace, Charity, Long-suffering, Kindness, and Forgiveness. . . .

Tho' the Party were thus continually encreasing in Numbers & Biggotry, yet they soon began to think that they never could establish themselves in the Opinion of the world without consulting at least the Appearance of human Learning, which at first they thought unnecessary to the Character of a Gospel-Preacher. To complete their Scheme, therefore, they founded a Seminary, called the Jersey College, & have even got the Dissenters in England & Scotland, as you know, to contribute to the support of it, though a Nursery of Separation from themselves. You knew the design, but did not oppose it, being pleased, as I myself was, to see Learning encouraged in America, in any Stands whatever; for true Learning, if they have Recourse to it, will in process of Time bring them to see that the Essentials of Religion do not consist in any of those little party-Tenets about which they contend so warmly.

But in the mean Time the old Presbyterians are in a difficult Situation. It would be giving up the Justice of their Cause should they accept of Ministers from a Seminary set up against them, & they would in a few years be entirely lost among the New Party, & so fall into the Trap laid for them. On the other hand, they have no Seminary of their own nearer than New-haven, in Connecticut, & with the small Livings (made yet smaller by their Divisions) they find it impossible to answer the growing Calls of Congregations, by sending to G. Britain or Ireland for Ministers.

To redress these inconveniences, some of them have spoke to me about a project for ingrafting a Seminary upon our Philadelphia-College, which is erected upon the most extensive & catholic Bottom. The Scheme is this. They propose to collect about 12, or £1400, not to be laid out in raising superb Edifices like their Jersey-Brethren, but to the more humane & useful Purposes of maintaining yearly 6 or 7 poor Students of Genius & Piety to learn the

Sciences & receive their Degrees under the Professors of our College, and to read Divinity at the same time under the eldest Minister of the Oldest Presbyterian Congregation, who is to have a small Salary for his pains out of the Fund. . . .

In the mean Time the Congregation in this City can see no Way so good as applying to you for a Minister. M^r. Cross, the present worthy Minister, is very infirm, & his valuable Assistant, M^r. Alison, is not only engaged in one of the most important Offices in our College, but also so subject to pleuritic Disorders that it is feared his Life will be but of a short Date. At the Time I am writing this he is so ill, that his physicians think him in imminent Danger, & if he recovers I think they will advise him against frequent Preaching for the future. Both he & M^r. Cross are willing to see the Congregation supplied in their Life-Time with an able Laborer, who may animate & support their just Cause, when they are laid in Dust. This they think the more necessary, as the new Party have even had the Assurance to think of putting one of their Number into that Congregation.

To defeat this Design at present was not difficult, as they are capable to encourage an able Man to come over to be at the Head of the affairs of the Old Party, & to superintend the Students in Divinity, should the foregoing plan take Effect. Since M^r. Tennent purged M^r. Cross's Congregation, the Remainder are some of the most substantial & sensible People of this place, & still a large Body. A Minister among them will be admitted into the genteelest Company in Town; & what they have promised they will overpay. . . . They have put great Confidence in you; but they know the Character to which they have confided." [10]

The main intent of Smith's letter to Chandler had been to second a plea that the Old Side had already made to Chandler. The First Church in Philadelphia was the Old Side's stronghold. Cross was aging and Alison was ill. A man was needed not only to take over the Church but also " to be at the Head of the affairs of the Old Party." The Old Side had no younger men capable of leadership.[11] In the letter which the committee of First Church wrote to Chandler, they asked that in speaking to any prospective candidate he should " let him know that the Congregation will Accept of a Minister, who will openly declare his belief of the Essential Articles of his faith, Contained in the Westminster Confession of faith." [12] The Church preferred a man from England, " purely on acc't of the Language in the Publick Exercises." Quite evidently Cross and Alison, both of whom were present when these letters were approved by the committee, were not expecting to require their own synod's Adopting Act of 1736 to be enforced upon the new pastor of their leading congregation.

The fact that the Old Side sought from Samuel Chandler a new leader for their party indicates clearly that the real motive behind the long drive in the synod for an ironclad subscriptionism had been political, and not doctrinal or religious. Chandler was well known as one of the strongest and most influential of the opponents of subscriptionism among the United Brethren during their tussle with that issue. He was, moreover, popularly looked upon as leaning toward Arianism, though he of set purpose avoided all theological preaching and discussion. From the group of which he was a leader sprang, even in his time, a vigorous Arian movement.[13] That they turned to the leader of the Arian party within English Presbyterianism for a young minister to succeed Alison and Cross as head of the ultraorthodox, subscriptionist, antirevival party, which stood for the policy of making all things in colonial Presbyterianism according to the patterns of Scotland and Ulster, is a very clear, good commentary on the true character of the Old Side.

For that matter, though Alison led the subscriptionist Old Side party for many years, he himself taught all his students the systems of Francis Hutcheson, whose avowed determination to put a "new face" upon the Scottish Church gave birth to the "Moderate Party."[14] Chandler succeeded in persuading Andrew Bennett to come to Philadelphia. He arrived after the reunion of 1758, refused ordination according to the terms of the reunion, and made his way to the southward.[15]

The supreme tragedy of the Old Side was the moral failure of its clergy. The twelve men who forced the schism of 1741 had as their colleagues in the formation, so to speak, of the Old Side, six other ministers and several licentiates and students. Of the twelve, four had records unworthy of their calling even in 1741.[16] During the years between the schism and the reunion four more of these original Old Side men were found guilty of serious offenses, and two who were in disgrace in 1741 sank even deeper. Worse even than this great percentage of unfit ministers was the vacillation of the Old Side presbyteries in their disciplining of these men. Black's case became notorious before he was at length deposed, yet he was soon restored and sent to Virginia.[17] Hamilton Bell, a student at the time of the schism,[18] carried on relations with a married woman in a most public manner. His various trials and hearings were dragged out for twenty-three months to the day.[19] Andrews was found in bed with a public woman, deposed, and restored in a few months, though the story was well known in Philadelphia.[20] James Lyon, whom Donegal Presbytery tried to settle at Nottingham (the scene of Tennent's On the Dangers of an Unconverted Ministry) in April of 1741, after his first exoneration on charges of drunkenness, was before presbytery on further charges that same year. He was not finally disciplined until some members of the neighboring Presbytery of New Castle preferred charges of immorality against him over a year later.[21] Samuel Caven, of whom many of his people said that he never went abroad but what an evil report about him came back, was before presbytery several times, but never received a sentence more serious than to be rebuked.[22] Samuel Thomson was suspended for immorality in 1749 but restored.[23] Samuel Evans was also dropped from the ministry. His activities against the revival were significant enough to earn for him some undeserved blame perhaps, yet by 1751 the Old Side were at length compelled to drop him from their ministry.[24]

It is difficult indeed to evaluate the career of the Old Side as a separate synod. Despite their arrogant pretensions to superiority over the Log College men, the clergy of the Old Side left behind them little or no lasting contribution to the Church. Alison alone is the exception. From the Old Side party prior to the Revolutionary War there are to be found less than a dozen publications of any kind, and few manuscripts. Cold, aloof, and without a deep sense of mission, they could not give themselves to the Church, and struck no roots within it. They are the contrast by which is measured the greatness of those whom they sought to cut off. Though their cause had been hopelessly lost, they maintained a defiant, proud stand during all the negotiations for the reunion. To them were all the proposals made, and for a long time they conducted their replies as though the issue were whether or not they would receive again the New Side into "our Synod." Yet only the reunion saved them from extinction.

9

UNION WITHOUT LOVE

Throughout the period of the schism in colonial Presbyterianism, 1741–1758, the initiative toward reunion was taken by the New Side. Until his death in 1747, Jonathan Dickinson had led all the attempts at reunion. When the Synod of New York had been formed in 1745, he had insisted that correspondents from each synod attend the meetings of the other synod. Also, he had proposed that once every three years the two synods meet together, " to order public affairs for the glory of God, and the good of the church." The Old Side conceded that "the proposals seem fair," but answered, " Till these dividers of our churches, and who chiefly make up that body [the Synod of New York], declare against the late divisive, uncharitable practices; till they show us in what way they intend to have their youth educated for the ministry, and be as ready to discourage all such methods of bringing good learning into contempt as the shepherd's tent, we shall be shy to comply with their proposals." [1] The rupture thus became complete and in a measure fixed.

This rebuff by the Old Side, and the untimely death of Dickinson, brought to an end all efforts at reunion until 1749. That year negotiations were reopened by the Synod of New York. A generous set of proposals was sent to Philadelphia, and a joint commission of the two synods held a two-day meeting in Trenton. Three issues proved insoluble: The Old Side would not discountenance the *Protest* of 1741; nor would they return to the Adopting Act of 1729. The third issue was the Old Side's insistence that all presbyteries (and therefore later the congregations) be merged, and be reconstituted as before the schism. This would have left the older Old Side men in control of most of the congregations in existence before 1741 and would have ousted many of the younger New Side men. Usually the New Side's congregations were far stronger than the Old Side's in each locality. On these three points the New York commissioners refused to grant the desires of the Old Side. [2]

That same year Gilbert Tennent published a long plea for reunion under the title, "Irenicum Ecclesiasticum, or a Humble Impartial Essay upon the Peace of Jerusalem." In these sermons, which he had preached earlier in his own congregation, he made many retractions and conciliatory approaches to the Old Side. Nothing was said by Tennent of the very touchy issue of ministerial discipline. For that matter, this issue was evaded all through the period of reunion, only to burst out with vengeful fury less than two years after the reunion. In spite of Tennent's generous concessions and politic tact, no great enthusiasm from either side greeted his efforts. Reunion was still far away. These sermons did, however, reveal that Gilbert Tennent was now the New York Synod's leading advocate of reunion.

Once again, the following year, a commission of the New York Synod elaborated a set of proposals for reunion. The proposal on creedal subscription was rewritten to make it more acceptable to the Old Side; several concessions formerly acceptable to the Synod of Philadelphia were reaffirmed; intrusions were to be forbidden, but pulpit exchanges were not to be refused when requested; presbyteries were not to be remodeled; the *Protest* of 1741 was to be declared void; and a statement favorable to the revival was requested. The Synod of Philadelphia, in response to the New York Synod's request of 1749, now came forward with a statement of proposals. On doctrinal subscription they asked that the Westminster symbols be adopted " according to the plan agreed on in our Synod," i.e., the Act of 1736. The New York Synod had proposed a return to the Act of 1729. The only concession made by the Old Side was " that no acts should be made, but concerning what appears to the body plain duty, or concerning opinions that we believe relate to the great truths of religion." This concession did not obviate the fact that the Old Side was still insisting on an all-powerful synod. Further, the Old Side demanded " that all public and fundamental acts of this [their own] Synod stand safe." Synodical examinations of candidates for the ministry were likewise demanded. Presbyteries were to be merged, and wherever New Side congregations had arisen " to the disadvantage of former standing congregations, the ministers supplying them shall be removed, and all proper methods taken to heal the breach." Wherever such splits had not hurt the Old Side congregations, both were to continue, and wherever both Old Side and New Side congregations were vacant, they were to be united. On other points the Old Side closely paralleled the New Side. No mention was made of the *Protest* of 1741, or of the revival.[3] To these demands the New York Synod replied that if a synod alone were judge of what was " plain duty " or " the great truths of religion," then these were very insufficient guarantees against usurpation of power by the synod. The New Side refused to make acceptance of all the Old Side's acts and rules since 1741 a term of reunion. Forced reuniting of congregations was also rejected. " Seeing by the goodness of Divine Providence we have now a college erected, we see no necessity for the alternative of the Synod or their commission examining candidates before they be admitted to Presbyterial trials." For further details the New Side referred the Synod of Philadelphia to their proposals of 1750. An impossible set of demands had been given a deservedly cool answer by the Synod of New York.[4]

A letter revealing wounded and angry feelings was sent to the Synod of New York by the Old Side when this cool answer of 1751 was taken up in 1752. They charged the New Side with hypocrisy in proposing to bury in perpetual oblivion all the old differences, and then constantly bringing up the *Protest* of 1741. The Old Side were willing to act toward the New Side, upon reunion, as though the *Protest* " had never been made, looking upon the design of the protestation answered by reasonable terms of union; and if any thing further be intended by your insisting that said protestation be declared void and of no effect, we assure you we are well satisfied that said protestation was made on sufficient and justifiable grounds, and we are not in the least convinced that the Synod acted wrong in said step." The Old Side declared that they felt they had been given reason to believe that the New Side would consent to reuniting presbyteries and congregations. Had not this been true, they would have considered all negotiations useless. A testimony favorable to the revival they would not give. The Old Side were willing for the sake of peace to accept all the ministers and congregations of the New Side upon reunion, but felt that some " salve " should be found for the injuries they had received at the hands of some of these. Their proposal of an all-powerful synod was both Presbyterian and right. They were glad that the New Side now favored a college-trained ministry, although they noted that not all the New Side had previously thought this. Furthermore, they called the New Side's attention to the fact that there had been colleges available before the College of New Jersey had been erected. The Old Side had among their members men as capable of examining students " as either the tutors, trustees, or rectors of your college, so that we think the approbation of our Synod, or committee, a good alternative, and yet will give it up if you oblige all your candidates to bring college certificates, unless in extraordinary cases, and these shall be settled to prevent such disorders as we have seen and felt in time past."[5]

The intent of the Old Side in the discussion of reunion is here made quite plain. They put the New Side in the position of asking for readmission to " our Synod." The design of the *Protest* of 1741 was to be secured through the terms on which the New Side would be readmitted. The *Protest* was right, and its purpose was to be gained or there would be no reunion. Unless the old congregations were to be restored as before, and the New Side men who were now " supplying " them (this denied the legality in church law of the pastoral relationship in each of these congregations) were to be dismissed, all negotiations were useless. Men ordained by the New Side since the schism of 1741 would be admitted by the Old Side, but only if some suitable " salve " were provided by the New Side that would make their admission " consistent with the rights of gospel ministers [i.e., the Old Side]."

It is not surprising that the New York Synod found themselves too busy to answer the proposal of a reunion until 1753. They then made it plain that the Old Side's determination to achieve the ends of the *Protest* of 1741 through the terms of reunion would not work. In fact, simply because that was the Old Side's plan, the New Side would continue to demand that it be declared void. There would be no forced merging of presbyteries and congregations, nor any all-powerful synod. The revival was not an unmixed good, but its abuses had been eliminated, and the Old Side's reflections on it were wrong. As for the intrusion issue which the Old Side had raised again, if that issue was to be reopened, the New Side had not only a defense to make, but some charges to place. It were better, however, to drop the whole matter. "We do not presume to treat you as criminals on the present footing, and we expect to be treated as a judicature on equal ground." [6]

Neither side took any particular action the following year, but the Synod of Philadelphia noted that since " a very pacific temper seems to prevail in the members of both Synods," a joint committee ought again to be appointed. At the meeting of this joint committee the entire matter was deliberated at some length, but no agreements were made. In 1756, the New York Synod, on the basis of their committee's report, noted that only the issue of the *Protest* of 1741 now seemed insoluble. They therefore proposed reunion on the basis of a number of points in previous proposals that seemed agreeable to all, and asked that upon reunion the reunited body " hear and determine the differences between the protesters, and those protested against, if needful." [7] The Synod of Philadelphia evaded this proposal by suggesting that the basis of reunion be that of the *status quo ante* June 1, 1741; that all presbyteries be united; and that the *Protest* of 1741 be allowed as " the private judgment " of those who made it, but that the Synod of Philadelphia disavow it as a synodical term of communion.[8] The Synod of New York demurred, but appointed a committee to meet with the Old Side's committee. The College of New Jersey also granted to Francis Alison an honorary degree. No doubt this act had a healing effect. The joint committee was successful in working out a plan of reunion, and the two synods agreed to meet in a common place at a common time for their 1758 sessions. If then each synod accepted the committee's plan, reunion would be consummated.[9]

With some slight amendments and changes by both synods, the committee's report was adopted in each synod. David Bostwick, moderator of the Synod of New York, had preached a sermon on " Christ Exalted and Self Disclaimed," which typified the New Side's attitude. Francis Alison, preaching before both groups on " Peace and Union Recommended," stated that " Gilbert Tennent . . . has written more and suffered more for his writings, to promote peace and union, than any member of this divided church." [10] In the name of the Old Side he quoted " that eminent saying of one of the fathers: ' We must maintain union in essentials, forbearance in lesser matters, and charity in all things.' " Further he adds, " We must also unite to promote external purity and holiness of life, for, without this, ' No man shall see the Lord.' 'Tis necessary to the conversion of sinners, and the reformation of mankind. . . . In promoting and preserving peace and unity among Christians, we are carefully to follow the commands and example of Christ and his apostles; and not the expedients of our own devising. . . . We should remember, that no two men are all agreed in all points; and that where they are agreed, they generally differ in their ways of explaining and defending them. . . . In a church like ours in America, collected from different churches of Christ in Europe, who have followed different modes and ways of obeying the ' great and general command of the gospel,' there is a peculiar call for charity and forbearance." [11]

On May 29, 1758, the reunited Church met, with Gilbert Tennent as moderator, and Alexander McDowell as clerk. The sessions were held in Tennent's church in Philadelphia. The terms of reunion as adopted were both broad and generous.[12]

No reference was made to the controversial " essential-non-essential " phrases of the 1729 Adopting Act. Neither was any repetition made of the unqualified demands of the Act of 1736. The section on the adoption of the Westminster symbols was definitely a compromise statement. Alison's sermon revealed very well the mood of the majority of the Old Side. They had known since the schism of 1741 that the abandonment of the Act of 1736 would be a part of the price of reunion. The New Side's view of this opening statement may be judged from Davies' application of it in an ordination service for two young men six weeks after the reunion. He put questions to them thus: "Do you receive the Westminster Confession of Faith as the Confession of *your faith;* that is, do you believe it contains an excellent summary of the pure doctrines of Christianity as taught in the Scriptures? . . . And do you propose to explain the Scriptures according to the *substance* of it? " (Italics are Davies'.) [13] The " systematic " form of subscription embodied in the Act of 1729 was, therefore, restored in spite of avoidance of all reference to the past controversies.

Gilbert Tennent, in preaching before the entire synod the following year, clearly expressed the underlying attitude of the New Side toward subscriptionism: " Why should a perfection in knowledge (or principles) more than in practice be insisted on in order to communion, seeing both are unattainable in this life? Is any branch of the visible church infallible in its decisions about small and comparatively doubtful points? if not, then why should any express such a zeal and confidence about them, as seem to suppose it? " [14] Five years later, writing in the name of, and at the order of, the synod, John Blair wrote, " That, therefore, is an essential error in the synod's sense, which is of such malignity as to subvert or greatly injure the system of doctrine and mode of worship and government, contained in the Westminster Confession of Faith and Directory." [15] While in England, Davies recorded in his personal diary the reply that he gave to an English critic of subscriptionism, a reply that was by no means " subscriptionism." [16]

In any matter brought before a judicature, the minority was to acquiesce in that judgment which a majority decided to be " indispensable in doctrine or Presbyterian government " or peaceably withdraw from the body. Protests were to be allowed, but they must be accompanied by validating statements and proofs. Protests could not be made the means of exclusion acts. Moreover, such protests were allowable only on conscientious grounds, not on matters of mere opinio... or preference. Accusations against a fellow member of the synod were to be made only in an orderly and legal manner. Each presbytery was to control vacancy and supply work within its own borders. Itinerating in another presbytery was forbidden.

The *Protestation* of 1741 was declared to have been " the act of those only who subscribed it. . . . The said Synod declare, that they never judicially adopted the said protestation, nor do account it a Synodical act." Examination and licensure of candidates for the ministry were made the prerogatives of presbyteries. The requirements were adequate learning, " experimental acquaintance with religion, and skill in divinity and cases of conscience," acceptance of the Westminster symbols, and a promise of subjection to Presbyterian government. No synodical examination was required.

The closing article of the Plan of Union owned the revival as a definite work of God, although some blemishes were confessed. Several of the major errors or evils were explicitly defined and abjured. This article is notable in that it alone, of the eight articles, distinguishes parties in the New York Synod: " The members of the New York Synod . . . declare . . . their approbation of the revival. . . . This united Synod agree in declaring . . ." a more guarded approval and a rather long discussion of good and evil effects of the revival.

Most notable in the statements about the revival are these: " The late religious appearances "; " A blessed work of God's Holy Spirit in the conversion of numbers was then carried on "; " Since the time of the aforesaid religious appearances." The Great Awakening was past. True, there had been small local revivals — one at the College of New Jersey in late 1757, for instance — and others were to follow soon, but as a widespread intercolonial mass movement the Great Awakening had come to a close. The movement in the Presbyterian Church had begun late in 1729 or early in 1730 and had reached the height of its intensity during 1739-1741. In the years immediately following, 1741-1746, the movement was more widespread, due to the intensive missionary activities of the Log College men, the return of George Whitefield, and the almost spontaneous revival in Virginia into which the New Side poured so much aid. Thereafter sporadic local awakenings recurred here and there until the new Great Revival of 1800 again spread over the entire new republic.

By 1758 the Old Side Synod of Philadelphia, who had begun their separate existence in 1741 with twenty-seven ministers, had dwindled down to twenty-three ministers. Their churches were not thriving, and their one effort at founding a college had failed. Alison had begun their synodical school, but upon his resignation it had been dying a lingering death. From abroad only two or three ministerial recruits had come to the Old Side, and but one or two had come from New England during the entire period.[17] They had received five ministers, had ordained an average of one per year,[18] and had lost eleven by death over the seventeen years.[19] They had " few men of distinguished promise, with congregations mostly in obscure places and not remarkable for size, liberality or zeal." [20] The Old Side had been unable to reproduce.

The Synod of New York had begun with thirteen ministers from the Conjunct Presbyteries, and nine from the Presbytery of New York.

In 1758 the ministers on the synod's roll numbered seventy-three. New recruits had come from the Log College alumni, the College of New Jersey, and the New England colleges, from the newer small private schools, and from abroad. In addition to the College of New Jersey and its predecessors, Dickinson's classical academy and the Log College, the New York Synod leaders had founded Fagg's Manor Classical School (1740, by Samuel Blair), Nottingham Academy (1744, by Samuel Finley), and Pequea Academy (by Robert Smith in 1750). From these schools, which were copied after the Log College, had come some of the strongest clerical and lay leaders of the synod. None of these schools were under the synod. All were private enterprises. A rather striking commentary upon the spiritual tone of the two synods is furnished by these statistics. In seventeen years the Old Side had a net loss of five ministers, and the New Side a net gain of fifty. The contrast in the growth of congregations was even greater. The assumption, therefore, by the reunited Church of the name "the Synod of New York and Philadelphia" was a clear indication of the relative prestige of the two former synods.

Following the formalities of reunion, the first action taken by the synod was the "modelling of the several Presbyteries." The presbyteries of Suffolk and New York were to continue as they were. They had within their bounds no former Old Side men. New Brunswick Presbytery, New Side, had within its bounds only two Old Side men — Cowell, of Trenton, and Guild, of Hopewell. This presbytery was ordered to "continue as it is, only that Messrs. Cowel and Guild are added to it." A Presbytery of Philadelphia was formed. It consisted of three former Old Side men, and nine former New Side men, all that were in the area of the former Old Side Presbytery of Philadelphia, and the former New Side Presbytery of Abington. A Presbytery of Lewestown was erected in the Maryland, southern Delaware area, consisting of two former Old Side men and three former New Side men. In these areas the Old Side were so hopelessly in the minority that merging of the presbyteries, in accordance with the Old Side's insistence, caused no great problem. However, the two former presbyteries of New Castle, Old Side and New Side, were left intact until the following year. Donegal Presbytery, Old Side, was also left unchanged. Its territory was therefore shared with New Castle, New Side, as before. (A year later a merger was carried out.) In Virginia, the former New Side Presbytery of Hanover, consisting of seven ministers, was now augmented by the addition of three former Old Side men.[21]

A study of the numerical strength of the various presbyteries is most illuminating. The largest presbytery by far was the New York Presbytery, which was twice as large as any of the three standing next in line, and comprised one fourth of the entire synod. Most of its men were from Yale. New Brunswick, Philadelphia, and New Castle (New Side), each had twelve ministers, drawn from very mixed backgrounds, as were the churches they served. Hanover and Lewes also were staffed by men from various places. Suffolk, on Long Island, was wholly made up of New-England-trained men. Donegal and New Castle (Old Side) were solidly Scotch-Irish. Over one fourth of all the ministers of the

The Clergy of the Reunited Church

Presbytery	Total Clergy	EDUCATION						
		Yale	College of N.J.	Scotland and Ireland	Misc. Private American	Log College	Harvard	Unknown
New York	23	16	4	—	1	—	2	—
New Brunswick	12	2	4	—	—	3	2	1
Philadelphia	12	2	3	3	—	3	—	1
New Castle (N.S.)	12	—	3	—	3	4	—	2
Hanover	10	—	4	2	4	—	—	—
Suffolk	9	7	—	—	1	—	1	—
New Castle (O.S.)	7	—	—	4	3	—	—	—
Donegal	6	—	—	6	—	—	—	—
Lewes	5	1	2	—	2	—	—	—
Totals [22]	96	28	20	15	14	10	5	4

synod were from Yale College. These, together with the graduates of the College of New Jersey, were exactly one half of the synod. Fifteen men had come from Ulster and Scotland, all but one probably trained in Scottish universities. Both the New Side and the Old Side had ordained a number of men who had been trained in small colonial academies. Ten Log College graduates were still active in the ministry. Harvard had furnished five ministers. The place of education of four ministers is in doubt. One of these was probably educated somewhere in Germany.

It is not surprising that, in spite of the many professions of forgiveness and reconciliation recorded in the formula of reunion, trouble soon broke out anew. As early as the second assembling (1759) of the reunited synod, serious strife was resumed. At this meeting Cross had been elected moderator, but had declined the chair because of age and infirmity. A former New Side man, Richard Treat, was chosen instead. An attempt was made by the three former Old Side men who were in the Valley of Virginia, Black, Craig, and Alexander Miller, to have themselves and two former New Side men, Brown and Hoge, consti-

tute a presbytery distinct from Hanover Presbytery. They argued that
they were at a great disadvantage in having to travel to Hanover
County for meetings of the presbytery. The synod denied the request,
saying that Hanover Presbytery was too small to be divided. They did,
however, order that the meetings of Hanover Presbytery be held alternately in the Valley and in Hanover County. They promised also that,
if no reason then unknown should later emerge, the Valley might be
organized into a separate presbytery as soon as it had six or seven regular ministers.[23]

Offense was taken at this decision, for Hanover Presbytery was predominantly New Side, whereas the proposed presbytery would have
left the Old Side in control of the Valley. Moreover, the synod's argument against a presbytery of only five members was weak, since, in
the reunion, Lewes Presbytery had been erected with only five members. In principle the synod may have been correct, but a precedent had
been set. The issue was complicated by a number of other factors. The
three former Old Side men, Black, Craig, and Miller, had belonged
to Donegal Presbytery before the reunion and had refused categorically
to leave that body and join Hanover Presbytery. Also, Donegal Presbytery, through Black, was trying to assert its authority in the Valley in
spite of the synod's orders. Black's congregation, moreover, was seeking to be rid of him because of "his confessed immoralities."[24] Later
Black was again suspended from the ministry for misconduct, and
Miller was deposed from the sacred office for immoralities.[25] The characters of these Old Side men may, therefore, have had something to
do with the synod's refusal to erect them into a presbytery that would
control so important an area as the Valley of Virginia.

New York, Suffolk, New Brunswick, and Lewes Presbyteries had no
difficulties. Philadelphia Presbytery, however, found little peace in the
reunion. Cross resigned his pastorate at the presbytery's first meeting,
pleading advanced age and ill-health. Kinkead, another former Old
Side man, was already in disgrace and never actually became a member of the new synod. Alison, the third Old Side man, was Cross's associate at the old First Church, but devoted his major interests to his
important position at the College of Philadelphia. Thus by their first
meeting after reunion, Philadelphia Presbytery had only one former
Old Side man in the active ministry. This weakness of the Old Side
in their own former capital was the occasion of very serious trouble
almost at once. Alison and Cross strove desperately to keep the First
Church in the hands of men favorable to their viewpoint.

The most outbroken evidences of the smoldering of the former animosities came in the Scotch-Irish area. The two New Castle Presby-

teries and Donegal had been merged a year after the reunion. One of the Old Side's avowed objectives in demanding, during the reunion negotiations, that the presbyteries be merged was that thereafter the congregations also should be merged. These merged, or "reunited," congregations should then be given to those men who had held them before 1741, and the ministers "supplying" the New Side "separations" should be dismissed. The terms of reunion in 1758 had ruled out any forced merging of congregations, and had left other matters to be worked out. As these former Old Side or New Side congregations fell vacant, it was hoped that they would unite with the neighboring congregations.

When Donegal Presbytery was reconstituted, it had a minority of former New Side men. One of these ministers was George Duffield. Upon the first meeting of the new presbytery, the usual order of business was set aside, and the moderator, a former Old Side man, placed in the hands of John Steel, another Old Side man, a call to a church in Duffield's own town. The entire matter had been arranged beforehand, and, in spite of the New Side men's protests, the call was voted and Steel accepted it. After the meeting Duffield wrote an angry letter to a friend, but Steel succeeded in intercepting the letter. Thereupon, Steel charged Duffield, before a later meeting of the presbytery, with defamation of character and the like. (Finally in 1761 the issue was settled. Steel was compelled to return the stolen letter, and each man retained his pastorate as before the reunion.[26]) This incident, together with the tense situation in Philadelphia, ripped open the too lightly healed divisions between the two groups, and soon began to poison the entire reconstituted body. Philadelphia and Donegal Presbyteries had proved to be festering sores that the reunion had not healed.

The synod of 1760 found that the situation had deteriorated even more. A very rigorous contest had taken place in Philadelphia Presbytery over the admission of three young men — Samuel Magaw, Hugh Williamson, and John Beard. Former New Side men had been very dissatisfied with the answers given by both Beard and Magaw to questions "on the work of grace in his soul." Williamson had been a member of New Castle Presbytery. For some reason, no doubt seeking to avoid such an examination as held up Beard and Magaw, he had irregularly gone off to New England and there been licensed. Then he had appeared before Philadelphia Presbytery seeking admittance as a licentiate. The former New Side men of New Castle and of Philadelphia Presbyteries argued that all this was illegal. The vote in Philadelphia Presbytery had thereupon been tied on the question of receiving him.[27] All this controversy was brought up in the synod, whose sessions followed those of the presbytery in less than a week.

One of the early items on the synod's order of business was the report of a committee that had been appointed to converse with Samuel Harker, a former New Side man, who had been accused of preaching sentiments contrary to the received doctrine of predestination. The trouble had begun as early as 1757, but the former New Side synod had been trying to bring Harker back into line quietly by private discussions. The committee now reported that it believed Harker's "sentiments" were not so far wrong as to preclude hope of his continuing usefulness. It had therefore cautioned and admonished him, and was satisfied that the synod should drop the matter. The committee had been made up wholly of former New Side men. Upon hearing the committee's report, the synod refused to drop the matter and appointed two new committees to hear Harker, both with Old Side representatives.[28]

Hugh Williamson was received by the synod, though they refused to rule on the issue of principle involved in his case.[29] This move was definitely an attempt at easing the tension within the Church. Williamson, however, never went on to ordination.

During the sessions of this synod another occasion for strife appeared. William McClenachan,[30] an Irish Presbyterian minister who had served various New England Presbyterian churches since 1734, took orders in the Anglican Church in 1755. After some service with the Anglicans in New England, he had set out for Virginia with a view to settling there. While en route, he had passed through Philadelphia. Finding there many Anglican admirers of Whitefield who were much dissatisfied with the Anglican clergy of the city, he decided to go no farther. Dr. Robert Jenney, rector of Christ Church, was not at all well and allowed McClenachan the use of the pulpit rather freely for nearly a year. Then trouble broke out, and Jenney and his friends sought to get McClenachan out of the city. When denied the use of Jenney's pulpit any longer, McClenachan began to preach at the Statehouse, with considerable success. About this time a number of former New Side men in the Presbyterian synod wrote (without McClenachan's knowledge, they later insisted) a letter to Archbishop Secker of Canterbury asking him to have McClenachan "inducted" into Philadelphia.[31] The letter was signed by eighteen of the most prominent former New Side men.

In some way news of the writing of this letter got out almost at once. The letter was dated May 24 (1760), in the midst of the synod's sessions. Two days later, William Smith, the Provost of the College of Philadelphia and a prominent Anglican, asked his colleague at the college, Alison, to take the matter up with the synod. The synod answered that the letter was no synodical act, had never been before them, and that they could not be responsible for the private acts of their members.[32] A pamphlet controversy shortly broke out over this letter. No real principle was at stake in the letter, and the fact that it provided an opportunity for the unleashing of so many ungoverned passions was a further indication that all was not well with the synod.

To the problems of 1760 the sessions of the synod of the following year only added. Harker had become confirmed in his heretical notions, the McClenachan case was still being bitterly fought over in the Presbyterian household, and in unhappy Donegal Presbytery preparations were under way to lay charges of drunkenness against Sampson Smith, who had been moderator of the Old Side synod at the time of the reunion.

A year of strife followed the adjournment of the synod of 1761. William Hannah, a former New Side student who had fallen into disrepute with his old friends in New Castle Presbytery, had become a center of strife in the synod. Following his rejection by New Castle Presbytery, he had gone to New England and had there been licensed. Returning to Philadelphia, he tried to do as Williamson had done, namely, enter Philadelphia Presbytery without having anything further to do with New Castle. The Presbytery of Philadelphia ruled that he belonged properly to the New England association that had licensed him, but did allow him to do supply work. Soon he fell into trouble, and the presbytery had refused to recognize him as one of their regular members just one month before the sessions of the synod of 1761.[33] He had, however, gained some friends among the former Old Side ministers. When, therefore, a petition for a minister to go to Albany, New York, had been presented to the synod of 1761, and the synod had arranged for the usual supplies to be sent, the Old Side saw an opportunity. After the synod had adjourned, several former Old Side ministers dispatched Hannah to Albany as though in answer to the church's request to the synod. Hannah was received as from the synod, and at once was ordained in Albany by a picked group of Congregational ministers who were fully aware of what had been and was being done. The trick was hotly resented by all the former New Side men.[34] It came oddly from the Old Side men, who had so long professed to be the upholders of Presbyterian law and order.

The trial of Sampson Smith before Donegal Presbytery a month after the synod of 1761 only intensified the crisis. Seated in the presbytery among his judges were two of his brothers-in-law. Also, his father-in-law had been invited to come in from a neighboring presbytery and join as one of the judges. The result was that he was acquitted, and that three former New Side men appealed the case to the synod of 1762.[35]

It was at this juncture that Nathaniel Hazard had written to his friend Joseph Bellamy: " There has been warm work, I understand this time at our Synod about the examination of candidates for the ministry; one part for and one part against any enquiry being made respecting the Candidates religion. I expect they will split again by and by. Some of ye infallibility of some of yr [i.e., their] infallible brethren has been most shockingly laid open in a pamphlet,[36] printed a few days ago at Philadelphia." [37] His prediction of another split in the Church was no doubt rather widely believed among the scarcely reunited Presbyterians. Warmer works were, however, yet to come.

Whatever may be said about the admirable tone and stability of the presbyteries of New York and Suffolk — and they were the brightest ornaments, in all probability, of the Church at that time — their lack of a sense of responsibility for the welfare of the whole Church was marked. Suffolk Presbytery had not had one member at synod from 1758 to 1762. As the synod opened in 1762, everyone knew that the stage was set for trouble if not for tragedy. Once again New York Presbytery, by far the largest presbytery of all, by deliberate plan was absent almost to a man. The exasperation that the Scotch-Irish party had manifested in 1742 toward the New York Presbytery's desire to review the actions of the previous sessions of the synod was at least partially justifiable. When the largest presbytery stayed away en masse from a synod because they feared controversy, and allowed the two irreconcilables to stage a finish fight, it was difficult to see why they should all be on hand the following year to insist that the *status quo ante* must be restored. The mediating and balancing force of the two New England presbyteries might have made the synod of 1762 less acrimonious. As it was, the two opposing sides met head on.

For more than five days the synod debated a query that had been presented the previous year: " Whether a candidate's declaration of his own exercises and experiences in religion, given in the way of a narration of these, or in answer to questions put to him concerning them, should be required by a judicature as one appointed, warrantable and useful mean of forming a judgment of his experimental acquaintance with religion, according to which judgment they are to admit or reject him." [38] Every member of the synod was asked to state fully his views on the question, each man speaking in order as his name appeared on the roll. Three former Old Side men entered dissents to this order, but were overruled. When at length the last had spoken, three full days had been devoted to the speeches. A roll-call vote was then taken on the question. A majority voted to answer the question in the affirmative. Each party thereupon appealed to Article VI of the terms of reunion as the justification for their stand.

Thereupon, two members of the Presbytery of New York, in the name and by the appointment of that presbytery, who, fearing a breach in the synod on this question, chose to be absent, presented a set of proposals to maintain peace and harmony.[39]

A committee was appointed to study them and all other means of accommodation, and bring in overtures. After much deliberation on the committee's report, a compromise was offered:

"The Synod earnestly desiring that all due liberty of conscience be preserved inviolate, and that peace and harmony be maintained and promoted, do agree that, when any person shall offer himself as a candidate for the ministry to any of our Presbyteries, every member of the Presbytery may use that way which he in conscience looks upon proper, to obtain a competent satisfaction of the person's experimental acquaintance with religion, and that then the Presbytery, as a Presbytery, shall determine whether they will take him on further trials." This agreement did not satisfy a number of the members of the synod.[40]

At length the synod yielded to a request, several times made during its sessions, for the erection of a new presbytery for the adherents of the Old Side party in the Philadelphia area. Though synod cautiously ruled that this presbytery be set up "for one year at least," it had a long career. The Second Presbytery of Philadelphia was to be made up of Cross, Alison, Ewing, Simonton, and Latta.[41] Cross had been out of the active ministry since 1758; Alison and Ewing had as their main interests their positions in the College of Philadelphia. This presbytery, and their part-time pastorates, gave to these men a political position of great strength in the Church. Their secular employments gave them a freedom and an independence that enabled them to challenge the synod with withdrawal whenever they were dissatisfied. Moreover, their presbytery was essentially a political bloc and not a true presbytery. When, as later happened, the presbytery became a catchall for malcontent Old Side sympathizers, an evil situation was made worse.

The objection most frequently made by the Old Side to the questioning of ministerial candidates about their "soul exercises" was that this was an unwarranted invasion of the person's spiritual life. As such, the objection had some merit. In the absence of any dependable data as to how such examinations were conducted by those who believed in their usefulness, somewhat of the merits of the New Side, Old Side controversy may perhaps be judged by the records of the men over whose examinations these contests took place. It is a singular fact that of the men who failed to satisfy the New Side party regarding their "soul exercises," not one ever continued in the Presbyterian ministry or did it any credit.[42] Whatever these invasions of the candidates' spiritual lives were as to their form and manner of conduct, they seem to have operated with at least some degree of insight.

Behind all this bitter struggle lay two stubborn facts, not often mentioned in synod, perhaps, but none the less determinative. For the Old Side the fact that dogged their pathway was that a truly alarming percentage of their young students were going over to the Anglican Church even while students. When, then, those whom they had managed to save from the enticements of London were brought up before presbyteries on charges of this or that, or were found answering unsatisfactorily to questions regarding their "soul exercises," the Old Side party were seriously tempted to think only in terms of their dwindling numbers. So many of their men had gone to the Anglican Church in one way or another that Alison twice came to the verge of resigning his position at the College of Philadelphia because of it. The New Side taunted the Old Side with their Anglican "converts," [43] and an Anglican minister once wrote to London: "Pray send them [a certain vacant parish] an affable, kind and courtious English Clergyman; such a one will add weight and do real and essential service to the Church; as most who are sent from here for ordination are generally young Presbyterians who cannot be supposed will make much effort for the advancement of, or likely to make many converts to our Churches." [44]

In the eyes of the New Side party the stubborn fact about the matter of examinations that could not be overlooked was that there were altogether too many instances of ministerial delinquencies, few of which were handled with anything approaching the necessary discipline. The Old Side clung desperately to the thesis that formal questions alone were valid in these examinations, yet most of the moral failures among the clergy came within their ranks, as did likewise nearly all the miscarriages of justice. The New Side, accordingly, vigorously rejected the Old Side's formal examinations. Since their own questionings into the religious experiences of candidates had proved successful in spotting some unworthy candidates, the New Side believed that so useful a system should be made standard. The ministry had to be made above reproach, and this was the best known method.

The New Side party's insistence on strict discipline of scandalous ministers was soon given a severe test. In rapid succession several of their own clergy were brought up to trial.

Samuel Harker's case had now become serious, since he had published his views and was advertising his book in the colonial newspapers.[45] The synod "disqualified" him from any further exercise of the ministry in their jurisdiction. A question was raised as to what this meant, and the synod were divided as to its meaning. Finally, a majority voted that it meant he was disqualified from any exercise of the Christian ministry. Evidently a number of the synod were unwilling to suspend or depose a man for such doctrinal aberrations, and the term "disqualify" had been used as a compromise. Harker soon published *An Appeal to the Christian World*, in which he defended himself by leaning upon the distinction between "essential" and "nonessential" doctrines in the Confession of Faith—a distinction, he asserted, allowed by the Adopting Act of 1729: "I take the Essence of the Christian Religion to consist in Communion with Jesus Christ; i.e. in believing his Doctrines, and conforming the Heart and Life to them; therefore no error can be essential, which is not of such malignity as to exclude the Advocate or Maintainer of it from Communion with Jesus Christ." [46]

John Blair, a New Side party man, was appointed by synod to answer this appeal. Blair answered by saying that the issue was not whether or no certain doctrines were "essential to individual salvation." Persons can be saved, he said, who hold some errors. But, he goes on, "guides and pastors" must be on a different basis. As individuals, they have their rights of private judgment, but as ministers, responsible for the salvation of others, and exercising that ministry through the Presbyterian Church, they must preach and teach in accordance with what that Church as a whole believes is proper in order to lead men aright. Faith, as saving faith, is the same for a minister or a layman, but each does not have the same responsibility.[47]

Andrew Bay,[48] Daniel Thane,[49] Andrew Sterling,[50] and Charles Tennent[51] came up at various times during the period 1760–1765 on charges of drunkenness or immorality. Each had been a New Side minister before the reunion. In all three instances the presbyteries involved were predominantly New Side in their sympathies. Yet in each instance trial was speedy, and justice was even sternly measured out. In Sterling's trial two Old Side leaders, Alison and Ewing, were invited in as correspondents though they did not belong to the presbytery concerned.

Perhaps no man did the whole cause of colonial Presbyterianism more harm than John Murray. When he appeared on the scene in 1764, the Second Church of Philadelphia had been in trouble for some time. In 1762 the pastor, Gilbert Tennent, needed assistance because of his age. Duffield, a strong New Side party man, was called, over the opposition of Tennent and the trustees, who were seeking to make the calling of an assistant pastor the occasion for bringing the congregation into agreement with them on certain other matters. The Presbytery of Philadelphia ruled, however, that the call was valid. Duffield's own presbytery, Donegal, refused to allow him to accept the call, and Second Church began to look for another man. Shortly thereafter Tennent died. The church buried him with so much pomp and ostentation that years later it was still struggling to pay off the accumulated debt.

Word then came down from New York that a wondrously gifted Irishman, John Murray, had just arrived from Ulster. His piety, talents, and zeal, it was asserted, equaled those of Whitefield and Tennent. He was sought at once, and sought on bended knees. At length a special committee of the presbytery was requested by the congregation in the hopes that they might be able to overcome Murray's diffidence. When Murray asked them to decide for him, they refused, saying they possessed no such power. More meetings were held, and Murray charged, before a full presbytery, that the committee had not properly encouraged him. Eventually, after more than a year in which the tortured congregation had prayed, pleaded, and exhorted both heaven and Murray, the great day came and Murray accepted the call.

Two months later, letters came from Ireland indicating that there was much about Murray that had yet to be learned. At a special meeting of the presbytery, requested by Murray, he assured his brethren that all was well and that these charges against him were but a part of the sufferings that all true ministers had to bear. Presbytery advised him to go at once to Ireland and return with the proofs of his innocence. In the meantime he was to retain his church and salary. Murray set out on his journey accompanied by the tears and prayers of his people. In October he reappeared, having traveled only as far as Boston. He was, of course, still intending to sail for Great Britain. Soon he requested a dismissal from the congregation, but both church and presbytery were firm that he should retain the call and prove his innocence. He went again to Boston, from which place he sent the presbytery a " formal dismission of himself from the congregation and resignation thereof." From Ireland then came an official record of Murray's career in Ulster. Through unbounded conceit and vanity he had forged a number of papers in order to gain a victory over an Irish presbytery who, he felt, had not properly appreciated his gifts. On the heels of these very damning papers came another group of letters to the presbytery that proved Murray's innocence. Somewhat perplexed by these two sets of papers, the presbytery made an investigation, and learned that the papers proving Murray's innocence had been sent, not from Ireland as they purported to be, but from Boston! Murray was thereupon suspended and ordered to return to Philadelphia for trial. He ignored the presbytery, for he was then busily engaged in shepherding a Boston congregation of Presbyterians who knew nothing of his background. Presbytery struck his name from their roll, and sent a full report to the Presbytery of Boston, who had no official connection with them and little intercourse. The New England Presbyterians proved unable to bring Murray to justice, and his subsequent career among them was one of the principal causes of the breakdown of that once promising church.[52] Murray's case had been difficult for the New Side party because so many of the lay people considered him a transparently innocent man, eminently holy, and hounded to the death by the foes of spirituality.

In these cases of discipline four predominantly New Side presbyteries had been put to the test: New Brunswick, New Castle, Lewes, and Philadelphia. Their rulings indicate how strong was the determination of the New Side to maintain the standard of what they termed " a godly ministry." In language that New Brunswick Presbytery used in 1767 when disciplining Charles McKnight, a Log College alumnus, for suspending a church deacon without trial, " Tenderness to a Brother should not operate so as to patronize, countenance or Screen him when wrong." [53]

The controversy over the ministry broke into print in the year 1766. Patrick Allison, one of Francis Alison's abler pupils, published that year an anonymous pamphlet, *Thoughts on the Examination and Trials of Candidates for the Sacred Ministry*. Taking for his avowed standard the work of a famous Scottish worthy, James Durham's *The Dying Man's Testament to the Church of Scotland, or a Treatise Concerning Scandal,* Allison proceeds to prove that there are three qualifications for a minister: gifts, learning, and holiness. Still following Durham, he states that gifts and learning are *ad esse,* or of the very being of a minister, whereas holiness is but *ad bene esse,* or of the wellbeing of a minister. The first two qualifications allow of testing and examination; the third can never be tested. The hypocrite can give as good a narrative as the examiner requires, while a truly gracious but overly conscientious man will fail to do justice to his real experiences. That this judging of " secret spiritual states " is based on an entirely false premise, he argues, is shown by the whole past history of the Church. If due and regular ordination by a lawful church body does not make a man a true minister of Christ, how can his supposed "secret states" be the final standard? Baptism then becomes always of uncertain validity; the Lord's Supper is void even for good people; and so forth. Either due form and order are the sole guarantors of a true ministry or the Church becomes anarchic. Faithful trial, of course, must be made of a candidate's visible graces, but these are not the *essential* criterion.

To this pamphlet John Blair, of the New Side party, replied with *Animadversions on a pamphlet entitled "Thoughts on the Examination . . . of Candidates. . . ."* Blair argues that the inquiry that Allison advocated into the visible graces of a candidate did not go far enough. An examination of the latter's doctrinal ideas and his external life was inadequate. The real issue, according to Blair, was how were his ideas and his life related? If his theology was working in his own life, he ought to be able to give some account of it! If he could not, something very serious was wrong, either in his ideas or in his life.

"No valuable Ends," James Finley, of the New Side, wrote, "can be answered by bringing unqualified men into the Ministry. We may by this Means, it is true, increase the Number of Votes, in order to overbear Antagonists; gain livings to our Friends; and have Vacancies in the Church fill'd by these, in the Stead of Men we dislike. But are these Ends fit to be avowed by the Servants of Jesus Christ? surely no! Their Concern should doubtless, be to have the Church supplied with such as bid fair for propagating the Redeemer's Interest in the World, and for being Ornaments to their Profession. But are unqualified Persons; are those who are dissolute, conceited, and vain, at all likely to answer these Ends? . . . And have we any Reason to hope that their Practice will be much better than their Doctrines? or rather is there not too much Reason to fear such a Behaviour as will dishonour their function, and be a Stumbling-block to others? Ministers of this Sort have often turned out, some Drunkards, others Lewd, others worldly wise Men; who for the Sake of worldly Gain, have neglected their Office, and often shifted from one Denomination to another; Many Instances of which, even this infant Church has seen. It therefore appears plain, that instead of their answering any valuable end in the Ministry, they are most likely to be unprofitable, or rather hurtful to the Souls of Men, and a Disgrace to their Office.

"Nothing, therefore, should engage them to indulge their Brethren in their Impieties, nor deter them from dealing faithfully and impartially with them; not the fear of weakening a Party, irritating Brethren, and making them Enemies; nor any other Consideration. For if they tolerate or wink at the faults and extravagances of one another; if they appear backward to search thoroughly into Matters of

Complaint or Fame; if they conceal or labour to blacken and brow-beat Evidences; such conduct can be no Honour to their Function, but will rather bring themselves into Contempt, mar their Usefulness in the Ministry, prevent their dealing faithfully with and censuring the faults of their Hearers, and Wound the Consciences of the Godly." [54]

Involved in this same controversy was a struggle extending nearly a decade and a half over whether or not, and upon what conditions, further ministers, or candidates for the ministry, should be accepted from "foreign" Churches, especially from Ireland. The more radical New Side men were demanding that Scotch-Irishmen be virtually barred, since, they asserted, too many unworthy men from that quarter were coming over. True it was that it had been necessary to reject a number of these, and of the few who had been accepted since the re-union some had proved unworthy. The Old Side party who were pre-dominantly Scotch-Irish regarded this proposed ban as a slur upon themselves and upon the whole Presbyterian Church of Ulster.

Behind this long and bitter struggle over the ministry, and the nature of the reunited Church, was the rising sense of a new world and the dwindling power of the old world and its norms. For the Old Side, the source and fountain of all true Presbyterianism lay " at home," across the sea. Many of these men had left this " home " two, and even three and four, decades before. Consequently their concepts of Ulster and Scotland were often unfortunate and invalid. Yet by setting their standards and loyalties upon the Church "at home" rather than the Church " in the colonies," they in fact and in practice denied to the American Church the right to a genius and character of its own. The New Side, on the other hand, in their determination to build the Church according to what they conceived to be its own genius, born of the mingled bloods of its members and of the Great Awakening, may often have been unduly harsh in their generalizing of the bad character of a section of the Scotch-Irish clergy.

So sharp did the controversy become that the synod attempted to separate further the warring parties by the rearrangement of presby-teries. In 1765 the Old Side party of Donegal Presbytery asked that either their presbytery be divided or the New Side members added to it at the reunion be assigned elsewhere. The synod refused to grant this request. Rather they broke up both Donegal and New Castle Presbyteries, the two predominantly Scotch-Irish presbyteries from which, together with the Second Presbytery of Philadelphia, all this trouble came. A Presbytery of Lancaster and a Presbytery of Carlisle were formed by shifting the organizing basis of the two former pres-byteries. The synod hoped, it seemed, thus to break up the " parties " and "cliques," thereby eliminating certain personal clashes. The plan was an utter failure, and a year later matters were more bitter than ever. Synod then restored the two old presbyteries, but this solved nothing. Seven irreconcilable Old Side men from Donegal — Steel, Tate, Samuel Thomson, Sampson Smith, McMordie, Elder, and Beard — renounced the reunion of 1758 entirely, constituted themselves the true Presbytery of Donegal, and withdrew from the jurisdiction of the synod. Had the synod allowed them to go their way, their absence might have been for both the cleansing and the healing of the synod. Morally and personally they were of the worst of the synod's clergy.[55] So devoted were the synod, however, to holding the Church together that these seven men were allowed in 1768 to state their own terms of reunion with the synod. Steel, Tate, Elder, and McMordie asked to be joined to the Second Presbytery of Philadelphia, although all four of them were in churches far away from the bounds of that judicature. The synod relented and received them on these grounds. Beard, Smith, and Thomson also chose their own presbyteries and returned.[56]

The New Side party were a great majority in the synod, and most of them seem to have been determined to avoid at any price another schism. A minority of the New Side party did protest, however, that all this was a denial of all Presbyterian order, and that the creation of party-controlled presbyteries was only laying the foundations for endless future quarrels. Though the future course of the Church was to vindicate their warnings, the desire for unity alone was heard.

Each side now settled down to the " task " of increasing their clergies in accordance with their own criterion as to what constituted a worthy ministry. Some restraints were placed upon this race for political strength by a synodical ruling that no man could be ordained by any presbytery *sine titulo*, i.e., unless he was being ordained to a particular call. In other words, if a presbytery were not growing in the number of congregations, they could not increase the number of clergy. The only exceptions allowed were that men who were to go to the people on the frontiers might be ordained as missionaries.[57] It was on the frontier, accordingly, that the contest for new strength took place. The union begun without love and maintained without harmony was bringing forth the seeds of strife for generations yet unborn.

PART II

The Shaping of the Future

10

THE NEW LIGHT

The driving force that shaped American Presbyterianism in its formative years, and thereby determined also its later course, was the reinterpretation of the Christian life which inspired the Great Awakening. This conception of the Christian life was introduced by the Log College men, who in turn had heard it preached and taught by William Tennent. Against it one group in the Church had united in what came to be known as the Old Side. Toward it the New England group were drawn and they, together with the Log College men, eventually became the New Side group. The rapid growth and superior character of this New Side group soon brought them, and their views, to the forefront. After 1745, when the Synod of New York was founded, this conception of the Christian life became normative for most of American Presbyterianism. Around it and its propagation centered most of the history of the Church in the colonial era.

The opponents of the Log College men declared that the Tennent views and ways were not Presbyterian or Calvinistic. In fact, some of the Old Side men asserted that they were without counterpart in all Christendom. In calculating derision the Old Side men called the Tennents the "New Lights." In Ireland the antisubscription party, centering in the Presbytery of Antrim and in the Belfast Society, had been dubbed the "New Lights." After their expulsion from the synod a number of this group became Arians, and brought the term "New Light" into even greater odium. By calling the Tennents "New Lights," the Old Side sought to attach to them the name of heresy, and the reputation of being opposed to any true Presbyterianism. An examination of the literature left by the Log College men indicates clearly that their outlook was essentially that of English Puritanism. Their sermons and other writings are full of references to and recommendations of the works on "experimental" religion by Joseph

Alleine, Philip Doddridge, Richard Baxter, John Flavel, Matthew Henry, Thomas Halyburton, and numerous others in this same tradition.

Scotland too had often heard preaching like that of the Log College men. David Dickson, the revivalist of Stewarton and Irvine, divinity professor at Glasgow and Edinburgh and coauthor of *The Sum of Saving Knowledge,* had been an awakening preacher of great fame in seventeenth century Scotland. The " Stewarton sickness," so similar to the emotional outbreaks under the preaching of the Log College men, had occurred under his rousing preaching at Stewarton.[1] George Hutchison and Alexander Nisbet were men of like passions.

Northern Ireland had been Presbyterianized by preaching of the same order. One illustration from the memoirs of John Livingston, a revivalist of great power, will suffice. " Robert Blair . . . was indeed a chief instrument in that great work of God that broke out afterwards in Six-mile-water, and other parts of the county of Antrim and Down, and elsewhere in the North of Ireland; and this not only by his own ministry, wherein he was both diligent and faithful, but especially by stirring up other ministers . . . One time, hearing Mr. James Glendinning, he drew him aside, and dealt with him to follow another way of preaching, and deal with people's consciences, to waken them, which so prevailed with the man that he fell upon a thundering way of preaching, and exceedingly terrified his hearers." [2]

The views and practices of the Log College men were, accordingly, nothing new or unusual in either Scottish Presbyterianism or English Puritanism.[3] The ever-recurring attempt to find the source of the Tennents' views in Pietism, or in " Methodism," is difficult to understand.[4] Just as the subscription controversy in colonial Presbyterianism had been only the reverberation of similar struggles in Great Britain, so also the Great Awakening movement, and the controversy over it, are to be explained in terms of identical movements and struggles within English Puritanism and Scottish Presbyterianism. To the Federal theology which was Puritanism's legacy to all Presbyterianisms, whether of the Old World or of the New, are traceable all the views of the Log College men, those of the Dickinson group, and those of the Old Side. To turn elsewhere for their origins is to reject the obvious in favor of the imagined.

The Federal theology was in itself an uneasy blend of incompatible elements. Side by side in it lay insights drawn from Calvin, rationalistic and legalistic elements contributed by scholastic Protestant orthodoxy, and other components. The Federal system was in part a result of the introduction of scholastic rationalism into Protestant theology, and in part a protest against it. The most basic change that this rationalism had brought into Protestant theology was the establishment within it of the medieval notions that reason was completed by revelation, nature by grace, and man's efforts by God's assistance. Lest, then, this reorientation lead inescapably to the Arminian conclusion that man, though a sinner, had a great deal to do with his salvation, further changes had to be made. Predestination became the beginning point of theology. From the so-called "eternal decrees" of God the whole system of doctrine was logically deduced stage by stage. The doctrines of the primacy of grace and the impotence of sinful man to save himself were preserved by positing the doctrine that reason was actually completed by revelation, nature by grace, and man's efforts by God's assistance only for those few whom God had predestined to receive these aids.

While rationally satisfying to many "Calvinists," this scholastic orthodoxy had appalling practical effects. Everything in human life and destiny had been predetermined in the eternal decrees of God. Human life and human history were but the playing out of a drama in which the actors were carried forward irresistibly in fixed roles. Against this glittering product of scholastic logic some kind of revolt was inevitable. Into the Biblical concept of "covenant" or "testament" were read the current political notions of mutual compact. The harsh character of rigid predestinarianism was moderated by the assertion that, whereas God could indeed rule by arbitrary fixed decrees, yet he had not done so. Rather, he laid aside his full prerogatives and ruled over men through entering into covenants, *foedera,* with them.

The Federal theology, based on this scheme of covenants, shortly sprang into being.[5] Even before the close of the sixteenth century, its main tenets had taken form in English Puritanism, and also, in a measure, in Scottish Presbyterianism. It was never fully systematized until the Westminster Assembly of Divines gave it classic creedal statement. Though typically Puritan, and carried to its clearest development by Puritanism, the Federal, or Covenant, theology was to take its deepest roots in Scottish Presbyterianism. The "Covenanter" movement in Scotland, together with the adoption of the Westminster symbols by the Scottish Church, settled this theology deep in the hearts of the Scottish people.

The Federal theology took form and developed so gradually within Puritanism that its incompatibility with Calvin's thought was seldom noticed. Calvinistic orthodoxy had already blurred men's perception of the Reformer's real views, and many Federalists were not at all backward about preferring their own "completely reasonable" system to that of Calvin. Yet the Federal theology owed many of its insights to the Genevan Reformer, and these fitted oddly into the " Covenant theology." A further eccentricity was introduced into this theology because of the fact that Puritan piety and preaching had inherited through Lollardry the medieval imagery of the Christian life as a pilgrimage.

As long as Puritanism remained essentially a reforming movement within the Church of England, devoting itself to preaching and to the fostering of the Christian life, the blended character of its theology caused no great problem. However, as Puritanism made its great bid for power in the English Church and began to write new creeds and new forms of ecclesiastical polity, various schools or groups of Federalists arose, each stressing some part or parts of Federalism's mingled theology.

According to the Federal theology, when Adam was created, God had entered into a covenant with him. This compact was called the covenant of works. The terms of this agreement were that Adam was to obey God's law and thereby achieve for both himself and his posterity the blessings of felicity in this life, and immortality. Adam entered upon this covenant, not as an individual, but as the federal head of the human race. Moreover, the law that he was to obey was the eternal law of God, which was the same as natural law. This law was part of Adam's own nature. Adam's sin of disobedience broke this covenant, and made it henceforth impossible for man to achieve salvation by his own or Adam's works of obedience. Nevertheless, the covenant of works remained God's basic relationship to mankind. The law to which it required obedience was the eternal law of God. It was, moreover, the natural law of man's own reason and conscience. Abrogation of this law was impossible.

Another, subsidiary, covenant, therefore, came into effect between God the Father and Jesus Christ, whereby Christ was to become man and achieve by his obedience that which Adam had failed to earn. This covenant of grace, or the covenant of redemption, was so drawn between the Father and the Son that the Son became the federal head of only a part of mankind, that is, of the elect. The rest of mankind were " passed over " in the drafting of the agreement. This agreement was termed a covenant of grace because God in his mercy thus allowed to some men a second probation. By his life and death Jesus Christ stood probation in the covenant of works on behalf of the elect, and earned their salvation by his works. In his grace God then " imputed," or " reckoned," the works of Christ as being the works of the elect, and declared that the elect were just. Thus by the works of obedience to the eternal, natural law the elect were justified and redeemed from sin.

In all this God had dealt wholly with two federal, or representative, heads, and not with men themselves. The punishment of Adam's sin of disobedience had been that henceforth all men were born with an innate "habit" (the medieval *habitus*) or "principle" of sin. This habit or principle inevitably gave rise to acts of sin, for the dominant element in a man was his habit or principle. No individual man or woman had ever had any part in bringing upon himself or herself this punishment. All those arrangements had been made between God and Adam, who represented mankind. Likewise, the elect for whom Christ had earned salvation had taken no part in the transactions relating to the covenant of grace. If, therefore, the rigid logic that explained the presence of original sin in the world by the notion of the imputation of Adam's sin to his posterity as a just punishment on all whom he represented were followed out, impossible consequences would ensue. Those for whom Christ had earned salvation ought logically to come into the world justified. Some few Federalists, especially certain later Dutch Federalists, did assert that the elect were justified in and from eternity, but few Puritans could follow logic quite that far. The problem of Federal-Puritan thought became: How are the elect actually redeemed?

So deeply ingrained in Puritan thinking was the notion of the "principle," or "habit," of a man as the controlling factor in him that it shaped not only the doctrine of sin but also the doctrine of redemption. The elect must somehow be given a new *habitus,* or principle. This principle must be man's natural or original principle. When Adam was created, he was intended to serve God in obedience to God's eternal law and in conformity with his own reason and conscience. Here, then, was the pattern of the new principle, which went under many terms: a principle (or habit) of grace, of faith, of obedience, of love; a spiritual principle; etc. To the elect sinner was to be given a habit or principle such that he would obey that natural law of his own reason and conscience which in turn was essentially one with God's eternal law. This principle of grace was to be "infused" into man, because it had to come from outside himself and without his activity or co-operation. This infusion was regeneration.

Thus far, most Puritan Federalists were in agreement, for all this was but the abstract statement of theological ideas. When, however, it was asked, How did the Holy Spirit go about infusing the principle of grace into a sinner? the Puritan household had always found its peace disturbed. At this point the question became a practical matter. The more rationalistic group usually replied that God always acted as he saw fit. In his own time and way, the Holy Spirit working immediately would infuse the principle of grace into the elect sinner. Ministers accordingly were to preach sound doctrine and the faithful observance of the moral law, leaving to God himself the matter of infusion or regeneration. Church members were to be faithful in their obligations to the Church, and to live sober, moral lives, waiting patiently and hopefully for God to give them a new principle. Even a sinner knew the moral law and could obey it in some measure. Moreover, whenever he was regenerated, if he was of the elect, he would still find the meaning of his life in that obedience. Therefore, regenerate or not, this was his great business.

To the more evangelical, or the experimental, Puritans this extreme rationalistic attitude was unacceptable. God did not work immediately and wholly unpredictably. He worked rather through the means of grace that he had himself instituted — preaching, the sacraments, Bible-reading, prayer, and Church discipline. The Holy Spirit working through these means of grace called men out of the city of destruction and sent them on a pilgrimage to the celestial city. This pilgrimage led through the "terrors of the law," under which the sinner saw his self-righteousness compared with the law of God and was driven to abandon all hope of being saved by his own goodness or efforts. When, then, he saw afar off the righteousness of Christ, which alone could save him, he was led on his journey by that sight. Passing through the gate of repentance, he found himself at the foot of the cross. There he laid down his burden of guilt and knew his sins forgiven. Looking up, he saw before him now the road that henceforth was to be his only home. Far down the years, at the end of the road, lay the Holy City. Along the road as a pilgrim-warrior he was to make his way, without regard to his comfort, welfare, or security. He was under orders, and that, and only that, mattered.

In the end, for the evangelical Puritan, the pilgrimage, the Christian life, was the essential. The theology was important, but it was only the rational explanation of the stages of the pilgrimage. Anyone might memorize all the theology but never become a pilgrim, whereas even a rather ignorant pilgrim could conceivably make it through to the Holy City somehow by God's good grace. Hence theology was always subservient to preaching and piety in evangelical Puritanism. Illogicalities in theology were not nearly so serious as self-righteousness, complacency, legalism, and coldness of heart. No heresy was so evil as a bad life.

For the rationalistic Puritan, theology was primary. Orthodox theology gave a true statement of God's relationship to man, and God would not take lightly any falsification of his glory, wisdom, power, or righteousness. Therefore it was utterly essential that men have and retain right ideas about God and themselves. Whenever, accordingly, the unpredictable spontaneity of the religious life clashed with the theology, the former must be laid aside. That alone could stand which was rational, logical, and according to the eternal natural law.

Real though these differences may have been in some regards, they were nevertheless differences within the Federal school. At times these differences were hardly more than emphases or stresses. The evangelical stream in Puritanism flowed beside the more rationalistic, frequently intermingling in a single individual. Some Puritans were intensely rationalistic when writing a theological treatise, for then the dogmatic interest was paramount, but warmly evangelical when preparing a practical or "experimental" work, since the concern for the Christian life was then uppermost. At other times the rationalistic group of Federalists completely separated from the evangelical. If the more evangelical group veered close to "enthusiasm," the rationalistic group represented the decadence of Puritanism.

In common with all Presbyterians and Congregationalists the American Presbyterians had inherited the Federal theology, problems and all. Jonathan Dickinson was a good example of a man in whom the two streams of Federalism intermingled freely. In his early controversial writings, defending the Presbyterian doctrines of baptism and the ministry, he stands within the rationalistic stream of Puritanism. However, in his controversy with the Presbyterian subscriptionists, he is in the evangelical stream. It is not surprising, therefore, to find Dickinson and the group about him later joining forces with the Log College men. Their deepest sympathies had always been with the evangelical approach to Federalism.

Yet, with the Log College men, this evangelical approach to Federalism was always in the nature of a "stress," or "approach," as it was with the "experimental" preachers and writers of Puritanism. The basic structure of Federalism was retained. It was for this reason that the Log College men accepted subscriptionism at first, and fought it only after it became extremist. Again, it is thus quite understandable how, when the reunion of the New Side, Old Side synods took place in 1758, both groups could say that in all the controversy there had been no doctrinal disagreements between them. The disagreements had been on the practical side, on the matter of the Christian life.

The ultrarationalistic interpretation of Federalism had borne within the Old Side its inevitable fruit of decadence. Legalism prevailed, but yet the law was not taken seriously. The number of the elect within the covenant of grace was irrevocably fixed, and for each of these the work of Christ had earned full and final salvation. Federalism had worked out into eudaemonism, the notion that all things work for the happiness and welfare of men. True, it was a eudaemonism only for the elect. But since faith for the Old Side men had become little more than belief in right doctrine, and all Old Side men were soundly orthodox, it was not too difficult for these men to number themselves among the elect.

While many of the Old Side men remained upright, moral, and sober men, others of them became libertines. He who had faith (i.e., believed orthodox doctrine) was of the elect. Hence he could not be lost. He might be a source of scandal to the name of God, but if he held sound doctrine he could not be called an unbeliever or an apostate. Therefore, the Tennents' ways were wholly illogical, and were mere "enthusiasm." If a man could believe the pure truths of right doctrine, with all their deprecation of man's sinful state, helplessness, unworthiness, vileness, etc., this was ample witness that into him God had indeed infused the principle of grace. No "natural" or "unregenerate" man would ever assent to doctrines that taught such things about himself. Unfortunate though these failures in conduct might be, the gradual ways of sanctification would care for these problems in due time, and do so far better than the Tennents' excoriations would.

Moreover, no elect lay people could be seriously harmed by any failures of the clergy, for the number and identity of these elect also had been fixed from eternity. They might not like what their pastor did, but it did them no real hurt. Therefore they should bear and forebear. Going to hear the Log College revival preachers, however, was a breach of faith with their pastor, and was as bad as adultery. Contempt of a presbytery was contempt of God, for God had himself ordained that presbyteries should govern his Church. Even when rationalistic Federalism did not work out into moral laxity, its eudaemonistic tendencies all too often produced complacency and smugness in the Church at large. Moralism was prevalent among many colonial Presbyterians.

It was against such a background as this that the Log College men had revived the evangelical Puritan interpretation of Federalism. The old Puritan doctrines of "convictions" and "assurance," and the pilgrimage motif, were the spear points of the Tennent evangelistic preaching, although even during the revival their sermons touched on the whole range of doctrine. Under such treatment the static character of the Federal doctrine had been broken up, but so had the peace of the Church. The Old Side rationalistic Federalists had reacted violently against the reintroduction of this evangelical interpretation of Federalism.

One of the striking aspects of the preaching of the Log College men was its heavy dogmatical approach and content. It might have been expected that at least during the revival their preaching would have been more popular and topical, and cast in terms of their hearers' interests, fears, hopes, and needs. Instead, these men faced the problems of their day and analyzed them dogmatically. In their preaching they erected before their auditors the heavy structure of the Federal theology, and then, so to speak, stood between it and their people to reason and plead. To their hearers they argued that this dogmatic structure gave a true picture of the relations between God, man, and the world. Though the picture was awesome and difficult to understand, yet, because it was true, all who entertained any thoughts of ever being saved of God must know these doctrines.

"I would here intreat your closest and most careful Attention to what may be spoken upon these Heads," ran a typical sermon from the Great Awakening, "because this great Doctrine of a Sinner's Justification, is something difficult to understand, and yet very necessary to be understood, as I have already shown you. . . . You ought to consider, that the Mysteries of Christianity are not so mean as that a thorough Knowledge of them should be so easily obtained, and therefore it concerns you to apply yourselves to them with the utmost Care and Diligence." [6]

The pilgrimage motif had been inherited by Puritanism from the medieval Church. In the course of its career in Puritanism it had become an allegorization of the *ordo salutis* of the Federal theology, the logical sequence of the several stages or steps in salvation. This pattern the Log College men laid hold on and used with telling vigor. Theologically these preachers would have agreed that salvation was not a matter of several strictly defined stages. Their practical desire to help seeking men and women find God, however, led them to do as had the evangelical Puritan Federalists, namely, to dramatize in temporal terms pattern experiences by which the seeker might both chart and check his course. Also, they thus set forth in this manner their conviction that it was by a series of plain, rational steps that God led men, neither magically nor immediately but mediately, into salvation. Although this dramatizing of the *ordo salutis* was to become theologically fixed during the nineteenth century revival movement, it remained a practical device in the Great Awakening. No better proof of this can be found than the fact that none of the leading figures in the Great Awakening was uniform in the pattern experiences which he presented.

Much less did they all adhere to a single pattern.[7] In a general way typical Puritan patterns were followed. These men themselves had not undergone identical experiences, and none expected that every seeker who followed this pilgrim journey would tread, lock step, in the footprints of his nearest predecessor.[8]

The divinely appointed way of salvation, accordingly, was seen from two aspects. From God's side repentance and faith were alone required, and these were God's own gifts. From man's side, if repentance and faith were to become real in experience, they would become so only through a severe struggle. " By nature we have blind Minds, and stony Hearts, neither discern the Things that be of God, nor are willing to be subject thereto. Eph. 2:1, 3. I Cor. 2:14. Rom. 8:7. Nature in its present fallen and corrupted State, fights against the Grace of God, as long as it can. And therefore the Citadel of Man's Heart, must be taken by Storm, if the King of Glory takes Possession of it. . . . The native Darkness of the Mind must be banished and the Light of Day introduced. The Obstinancy of the Will broken, and it made plyant to the Will of God; the Disorder of the Affections removed, and they fix'd in their free, general and supreme Bent, upon God and divine Objects." [9] In this contest between the Holy Spirit and unregenerate man the great change that gave man a regenerate habit or principle took place. In the beginning of this struggle man saw himself as pursued; in its later stages he saw himself as seeker. From God's side it had been the work of the Holy Spirit entirely. The length of time occupied by this struggle or pilgrimage was accounted as incidental, and a matter of individual characteristics, backgrounds, obstinacy, poor guidance, and the like. During the Great Awakening instantaneous conversions were both urged and reported with approval, and conversions drawn out over as long a period as two years were also reported. Each genuine conversion, it was felt, involved the essential elements common to all.

Since it was God who was saving men, and not men who were saving themselves, the pilgrim way which the evangelical Federalists presented was for them an appointed way. As Samuel Blair put it, there is but one way for a sinner's justification appointed by God, that is, the Gospel. God requires that sinners comply with that way which he has appointed, believe in it, and depend upon it; otherwise they cannot be justified by it. If man determined the way to God, then he and not God was the final authority.[10] God could, of course, act in any way that he saw fit on any given occasion. But he had chosen to act mediately in all usual circumstances, through the appointed means of grace. Men were not to expect that any other extraordinary means would be specially arranged for any of them. All were made subject to the ordinary, i.e., the ordained, means.[11]

These means were " Means, not of Instruction only, but of Grace: the Reason is, because it is in the Use of these Means, the Holy Spirit, ordinarily communicates or bestows Grace on Sinners, and builds up his Children in Holiness, until he brings them safe Home to Glory." [12] However, " the necessity of our so attending, doth not argue any desert in it, or that God is brought under any obligation; it only argues that God is sovereign in choosing the way of his bestowments, and even when we attend in that way he is sovereign in bestowing, or not bestowing, as he pleases." [13] All this was but typical Calvinism, Federalist and Nonfederalist.

The Old Side accused the New Side of teaching men to depend upon the means of grace, which they declared robbed God of his sovereignty and made the means of grace a means of putting God under obligation to men. While the New Side men did not teach men to depend upon the means as in themselves saving, they did insist that these means were given of God as actual means of grace, not mere religious duties or means of instruction. If God had chosen to act thus, it was no infringement on his sovereignty if men did what he had appointed for them to do. To those, then, who followed these God-given means of grace the strongest kind of encouragement was given to hope for the gift of grace. God had not instituted these means for nought.[14]

Two errors were to be avoided, the New Side men believed: the first, that of merely preaching that men should repent and seek salvation, and then not giving them any counsel or guidance as to how to do so; the second, that of teaching men to believe that if they will do their part, God will do his. The first error leads men to do nothing about repentance, and the second turns men to depending upon their own righteousness. Rather than these, men should be shown plainly the way of salvation that God has appointed, and urged to take it as the end and destruction of any and all dependence upon their own meritorious works in behalf of their salvation.[15] Through the means of grace men receive as a gift the salvation of God. Over and over again in the sermons of all the New Side men came the assertion that it was God who was at work in his own means, by his Holy Spirit. Therefore it was, and only therefore, that these means had any efficacy.[16]

The means of grace themselves were generally accepted as being the Bible; the Gospel ministry; the ordinances of worship, such as the two sacraments, Baptism and the Lord's Supper; praise; and prayer. These means of grace were to be found only in the Christian Church, and no true Church existed without them. Accordingly both New Side and

Old Side were much opposed to the views of the Quakers and the early Moravians. These bodies made little of the concept of stated means of grace.

Federalism had been unwilling to accept Calvin's doctrine of the universal, visible Church of history as the Body of Christ. Despite the distinctions that he made between his doctrine and that of the Roman Church, the Federal theologians felt that Calvin's views were too close to those of Romanism and Anglicanism. Accordingly the Presbyterian Federalists had elaborated the doctrine that the invisible Church was the Body of Christ, the true Church. Among the Presbyterians the visible Church had been seen largely as a governmental and disciplinary body, organized by men, though in obedience to God's command to do so. Generally speaking, a very strict distinction was maintained between the visible Church and the invisible. Some Federalists taught that it was through the visible Church in history that God called the invisible true Church. This position the New Side men shared.[17] The more rationalistic group, stressing the immediate secret agency of the Holy Spirit, declared that such views were Roman and Anglican. The visible Church was organized solely for governmental and disciplinary purposes.[18] Prominent among these purposes was the defense of right doctrine. Here the Old Side men took their stand.[19] Contrary, therefore, to much of what has been said, the New Side men strengthened rather than weakened the current Presbyterian doctrine of the Church, by a return to a view more nearly approaching that of Calvin.[20]

The ministry of the Church was divinely instituted, and no true Church could be without a Gospel ministry. Here again the New Side came closer to Calvin's doctrine of the ministry than did their Old Side brethren. Besides giving to the laity and to the elders greater rights and liberties over against the clergy than did the Old Side, the New Side men made the minister a direct personal agent of God in the salvation of men.[21] As Samuel Finley said: " The Word of God when preach'd with Power, appears with such Evidence, as to cast down Imaginations, ever so Towering, and baffle contrary carnal Reasonings. The Conscience is convinc'd, the Mouth stopped, and the Heart pierced as with a Sword, broken as with an Hammer, and melted as with Fire; over-aw'd with Majesty, and constraine'd by Love." [22] In Gilbert Tennent's words, men were to hear preaching " as the very Word of God, as a Message from Heaven to us." [23] No minister consciously acting as such a personal agent of God could ever be unconverted or careless or immoral. Hence there had arisen the long struggle over the nature of the ministry.

The Sacrament of the Lord's Supper occupied a most prominent

place among the means of grace in New Side thought and praxis. Their
heritage from the early Covenanting days of Scottish Presbyterianism
had endeared this sacrament to many of their people, and for those of
other origins it was no less a sacred and hallowed service. The Log
College men, especially, made of it an evangelistic medium of great
importance, following the older Scottish patterns. For them the Sacrament was a memorial of Christ's passion, a badge of Christian profession, a mutual seal of the mutual engagements of God and man in the
covenant, the communion of saints, and communion with God. As
such it was reserved as the great privilege of those who were true
Christians.[24] The Sacrament meant nothing without faith; therefore
those who were without faith had no right to it.[25] All this was traditional Presbyterianism, and hence had arisen the awesome "fencing
of the tables" by warning off and debarring all who were unfit to
partake.

The Log College men saw here an evangelistic opportunity, however.
Instead merely of debarring the unfit, they proclaimed vigorously that
while the unfit might not approach so holy a table, yet the table bore
witness to the fact that Christ had died for the unfit. They were even
more searching and consistent than their Old Side brethren in their
fencing of the tables. However, their concern was not with the fence,
but for the men and women who were found out beyond it. Consequently they did what the Old Side never would do, namely, strove to
bring every man and woman present at the service to communion with
God and each other in the Sacrament. The unconverted were asked:
"Do you, my dear brethren, heartily consent to this formula [sur-
render to God]? Then the contract is ready for sealing; therefore, let
us rise and crowd round the table of the Lord, and there annex our
solemn seals, and acknowledge it as our deed and act." Those who
did not come were rejecting God.[26]

However unworthy a professed struggling Christian might think
himself to be, Gilbert Tennent urged, the Sacrament was intended for
such as he. Even though he lacked the assurance of his salvation, he
was to come. The worthiness which God required of all was a confession of their unworthiness. Not to come to the Sacrament was "rebellion against God," "ingratitude towards Christ's dying love" and
"unkindness to God," "cruelty to our own souls."[27] The Lord's Supper, therefore, was made the occasion for an act of personal decision
for or against becoming a Christian. Except in the cases of the flagrantly
unworthy, the individual himself determined whether or not he was
fit to participate. No test of a communicant's conversion was ever required by the Log College men as a requisite for participation in the

Sacrament, nor was he taught that he needed the assurance of his conversion before he could come to the Lord's table.[28] The Supper was,
of course, not a converting ordinance, as had been urged by Stoddard
and others in New England at an earlier date.

In addition to seeking salvation through the means of grace in the
public service, men were urged to study the Scriptures, to read books
on experimental religion, and to observe morning prayer, private and
family.[29] The circulation of Puritan works on experimental piety
played a large part in the Great Awakening. The home was also of
great importance, and family worship was urged upon all. Those
fathers and mothers who could not pray were urged to use forms of
prayer, " as persons weak in their limbs do their crutches, till you can
lay them aside." To retain a meaningless prejudice against form
prayers was bigotry.[30]

In evangelical Puritan thought these " means of grace " were instituted of God, not merely as means of instruction, but as the actual
media by which he mediated to men his saving grace. How did they
mediate this grace? Here again the New Side accepted the answer of
their Puritan forebears. " God, in the bestowment of his grace or sancti-
fying the soul, treats man not as he would a stone, in the new modelling its form, but as a reasonable being; by his divine power making
use of motives and means in changing his disposition [i.e., habit]." [31]
God " uses the powers of moral suasion with us, and justly requires us
to exert our rational faculties in all the institutions of the gospel [i.e.,
the means of grace]." [32] Men were to " agonize " to enter the strait
gate, which " gate " was understood as meaning the terms or conditions of salvation, namely, repentance and faith. " To enter the strait
gate, then, means neither more nor less, than to begin to be a Christian: To submit to the terms of the gospel, or to enter a state of
grace." [33]

The stages or steps by which the struggle progressed, or by which
the seeker was led, were reducible to three major ones: conviction,
humiliation, and regeneration, within each of which, in individual
cases, few or many subsidiary steps would be required. The first major
stage was being convicted, or awakened, by the law to realize that one
was not a Christian. This awakening might be accomplished in a
moment, or it might occupy months, depending again upon individual
factors. In all instances, however, it came about through the presentation of the Law and the Gospel in the means of grace. It did not come
unmediated, or without the conscious, rational activity of the sinner's
own mind.

John Preston, one of the greatest of the Puritans, had said that there

were " three parts of the Apostles' Ambassage: to preach the Law first,
that it might be a schoole-master to bring us to Christ: and then to
preach Justification by Christ: Thirdly to preach Sanctification." [34] In
this, as in so much else, the New Side had been good disciples of the
" experimental " Puritans. The law as a schoolmaster played a prominent part in New Side evangelism. All who have ever been saved since
the Fall, said Samuel Davies, have been saved by the Gospel. Yet the
Law of Moses, as all law, was intended to drive men to Christ by making them sensible of their need.[35] " The Law and Faith open different
Ways to Heaven, the first by perfect Works, . . . the other by Faith
in a Mediator. . . . Now when we see the first Way shut up by our
Sins," said Gilbert Tennent, " we are constrained to fly to the second
for Relief." [36] From the roots of such views had arisen in all evangelical
Federalism's history the so-called " terrors of the law." These Preston
was himself a master in portraying, and Gilbert Tennent scarcely
less so.

The object of preaching the terrors of the law, however, was not to
frighten men into heaven, but that they might be " slain by the Law."
In evangelical Puritan literature the idea of " slain by the Law " had
played a prominent role, and so did it also among the New Side
preachers.[37] To be slain by the law meant to be compelled to abandon,
in the face of the law's requirements, any pretense of not needing salvation through grace, to have utterly destroyed any complacent or presumptuous self-righteousness, to be left alone before God as a confessed
sinner who could do nothing to clear himself, to cease from all efforts
at saving oneself — in Puritan terms, to be " humbled." Consequently,
Gilbert Tennent, whose heavy artillery outweighed that of any of the
other New Side preachers, points out again and again in a sermon full
of the terrors of the law that these terrors are directed solely and only
against the smug, the self-righteous, the secret hypocrite, and the presumptuous Church member who expects God to take him as he is and
for what he is. The terrors were not for the humble and confessed
sinner struggling with his doubts, fears, and sin. The law had slain in
him his hopes of salvation by works.[38] This preaching of the terrors
of the law was not, therefore, an emotional orgy, but a vehement attack on all forms of self-righteousness.

Just because, however, it overthrew the religious hopes or pretensions
of many, this preaching of the terrors of the law produced emotional
outbreaks on numerous occasions. The opposition party flatly declared
that these outbreaks were the objective of the preacher, and the religious experience sought for. The New Side men themselves were perplexed and troubled by these emotional displays. Gilbert Tennent,

Samuel Finley, and Robert Smith thought they were best explained as the "animal" reaction to, or indication of, the struggle of soul going on in the subjects. As such they were incidental to the main issue, and need cause no great concern one way or another. They ought, however, to be suppressed as much as possible. William Tennent, Jr., and Jonathan Dickinson practically forbade them in their congregations. Not one of the New Side men ever encouraged these outbreaks, or sought to arouse them.[39]

The Old Side opposed vigorously this preaching of the terrors of the law, not because in their judgment it was theologically wrong (Francis Alison again and again preached one sermon entitled "The Terrors of the Lord "),[40] but, they asserted, because the New Side only aroused men's passions.[41] The Old Side, as a group, laid all stress upon the doctrine that regeneration came immediately to men by the secret, inward working of the Spirit, whereby he implanted in them a new habit. This implantation of the new habit, then, was salvation. The whole New Side preaching of the terrors was, therefore, both unnecessary and wrong. The Old Side saw no reason for preaching so as to alarm men. It was quite possible to preach the whole of orthodox doctrine without disturbing men. In God's own time and secretly, new habits, or principles, would be infused into the elect by the Holy Spirit. Until then they were to live regular and sober religious lives.

Evangelical Federalists had always insisted that without this anguish of awakening, which produced the conviction that there was no hope of salvation in themselves, men would never be "humbled" to seek salvation through Christ. Instead, they would seek salvation through their own works or their own goodness. Consequently, the convictions produced by the law were utterly essential to any salvation through Christ. On this point the entire Tennent group, and the entire New England group led by Dickinson, were agreed.[42] The Log College men also were able to cite a host of English Puritan writers whose views were the same.[43] This insistence on the necessity of these convictions had two deep-seated roots in Puritan theology, their doctrine of God's way of working with men and their view of the nature of sin. God worked with men rationally, not magically. Addressing himself to the consciences of men, God by his Holy Spirit, working through the means of grace, convinced men that they could not save themselves.[44]

The function of these "preparatory" convictions was to reveal the true nature of sin as unbelief, a pride rooted in the assurance of one's own goodness and an enmity against the God who would not accept man at his own self-evaluation. "There is such Pride and Self-conceit in Sinners' Hearts that they are very unwilling to stoop to God's Way for this Justification." [45] Gilbert Tennent declared that all secure and carnal sinners were in fact enemies of Christ, though they did not realize it until they came face to face with God's law and gained some view of his holiness.[46] Being thus awakened, man's false security was threatened and he was both fearful and hostile toward that which threatened him, namely, God. Before God's holiness he was not righteous; before God's law he was rebellious; before God's demand upon him he was egocentric. Above all else man desired to be let alone to go his own way. Because God would not give him up man came to look upon God as his enemy.

As these Federalists saw it, what man sensed under these convictions was that he had come against, not an obstacle to the achievement of his own will, but the destroyer of his very egocentricity. Hence the " humiliation " which these convictions were to produce, in Federal thought, had a character wholly different from the humiliation of mystical piety. The purpose of this humiliation was the complete destruction of all egocentricity, whether the egocentricity of self-righteousness and merit or the egocentricity of looking upon God as the fulfiller of man's need of salvation. No particular degree of intensity or period of duration was insisted upon for these convictions. " It is enough," Gilbert Tennent declared, " [that] the End is answered, whether the Distress be more or less." [47]

With all evangelical Puritans, the New Side men asserted that God made use of motives as well as means in regenerating men. The problem of the proper motives to set before men in urging them either to seek or to serve God had, therefore, often been discussed in Federalism. Here again Old Side and New Side Presbyterians represented both traditional and current differences of opinion within Federalism. These differences came out sharply during the revival in a controversy between Gilbert Tennent and David Cowell, an Old Side minister from New England. The issue was over whether " the glory of God or our own happiness ought to be our ultimate principle of action." The issue was brought up in the synod of 1738, but put over until the following year. In 1739 the synod declared that there was no necessary clash between the two positions, and that the debate was meaningless. The " designs of the glory of God, and our own happiness, are so inseparably connected that they must never be placed in opposition to each other. For in all cases, he that actively glorifies God promotes his own happiness, and by a conformity to the Divine statutes and laws, which is the only way to happiness, we, in the best manner we are capable, glorify God." [48]

Tennent was later to call this doctrine " blasphemy," and its authors " rotten-hearted hypocrites," for it put " ourselves upon a level with

God." [49] Andrews wrote to Pierson that the Tennents "utterly disclaim all self-love, and make it a wrong mercenary thing, contrary to the spirit of the gospel, to have any eye to their own benefit in any thing they do, but only the glory of God, exclusive of their own good." [50] John Thomson criticized Tennent for drawing out the logical implications of his opponent's views on self-love as the basis of obedience. These consequences were not necessary, he asserted.[51] Samuel Blair well illustrated the Tennent party's views in one of his sermons: "Seeking yourselves, idolatrously setting yourselves up in the room of God, making yourselves your last End in all you do; and so living without God in the World, as if you were not Creatures made to serve." [52] The synod's ruling in the eyes of the Log College men was wrong in two regards: it definitely made man's happiness the basis or reason for his glorifying of God, and it assumed that man could glorify God by his own works of obedience to the law. By these his own works, then, he achieved, as a reward, happiness. This was salvation by works.

This anthropocentric and eudaemonistic notion of "happiness" as man's great good had always been associated with Federalism. It was part of the doctrine of man in that system. Adam had been created "not happy," with the promise of the reward of "happiness" if he stood his probation in obedience. By his fall he left all his posterity still in the position of not possessing "happiness." In early Federalism happiness meant little more than immortality. The word took on other connotations, however, in later Federalism, coming to mean "wellbeing" in a very broad sense. In Scotland men like Professors Simson, Hutcheson, Campbell, and Leechman, and the Moderate party generally, were frequently accused of combining this later meaning of happiness with the ethical views of Lord Shaftesbury.[53]

The sermons of Gilbert Tennent himself, and the Log College men generally, show that they used the term "happiness" in their own appeals to men. The entire Federal system, and Puritan literature generally, had been deeply dyed by the notion of happiness. At times the Log College men used the term in its older sense of immortality, at times in its later meanings, and at times they considered the notion itself wrong. In one long and labored discussion of the problem of the relation of God's glory to man's happiness, Gilbert Tennent examined twelve different possible solutions, and then propounded his own conclusion! The only way men may glorify God is in being saved by his grace. In that sense alone is man's happiness connected with God's glory. By yielding wholly to the will of God in faith and obedience for salvation through him alone, men glorify God in the only manner in which he desires to be glorified by them.[54]

The Federal theology as a system was based upon the view that man's reason or understanding was the point of contact for the Holy Spirit's regenerating influences. Once it was properly enlightened by grace it would guide aright the will and affections, although these latter might still remain too weak to act without divine aid. The problem of the Federal theology was man's obedience to the law. The objective, then, of regeneration was to bring about this obedience. Knowledge was, accordingly, the beginning point in any thought on, or moves toward, salvation. " Such is the Necessity of Knowledge in all religious Actions," Gilbert Tennent declared, " that without it the Mind cannot be good, or any service we perform accepted. . . . The three principal Things in the Christian religion are Knowledge, Faith and Practice, without which it cannot subsist." [55]

Religious knowledge, according to all Federalists, was of two kinds: speculative, doctrinal, or objective, and experimental, practical, or subjective. The former was the basis of the latter in all Federal thought, and, although some difference of opinion on the matter existed, the system demanded that the experimental knowledge be defined as quantitatively an advance upon the speculative knowledge. An accurate and competent knowledge of the fundamental doctrines of the Christian religion was utterly essential as the starting point in salvation. This doctrinal knowledge was not saving, and even the most wicked of the unregenerate might have it. But man was to be saved mediately, and this objective knowledge was an actual means used by the Holy Spirit. It was gained through hearing preaching, reading the Scriptures, and the other means of grace. Conscience, nature, and the Scriptures were all considered as contributing to this knowledge.[56] Credence in the validity or truth of this objective knowledge was known as historical faith, and as such fell short of that saving faith of which it was only the basis.

All this was bound up with Puritanism's concept of the relationship of the understanding, the will, and the affections in men. As created, man was governed by his understanding which had a natural knowledge of God's will. The understanding guided the will and thus the affections were kept in perfect harmony. After the Fall, man's will dominated his understanding, and his affections were thrown into utter chaos, each contending against the other. When, therefore, the Holy Spirit illuminated the mind, he broke past the usurping will and allowed the understanding once more to see aright the truths of the Gospel. The understanding then addressed itself to the will, with the Spirit's aid, showing it the wretchedness and danger of its position, and the supreme desirability of Christ and the Gospel. The will thereupon surrendered, since " a rational creature cannot Chuse evil

as evil, and therefore, the will must needs follow this practical judgment of the understanding." [57] The understanding once again came
to dominate the man's life, and the will and affections assumed their
proper natural subsidiary positions. [58] This then was the restoration of
the moral image of God which man lost in the Fall. It was also God's
act of regeneration.

Regeneration, accordingly, was seen as the reordering of man's faculties, a restoration of them to their proper functions. This was also
called the infusion of a new principle, or a principle of grace, or a new
habit, or a habit of grace. Just in what this principle or habit consisted
seems to have been somewhat of a problem to the New Side men, for
they defined it differently, and at least Robert Smith expressed concern
as to what it really did mean. Some thought the principle was the
" seed " from which holy actions sprang; others, that it was the divine
light which illuminated the sinner's mind; others, that it was a holy
affection; others, that it was a kind of new quality infused into the
soul which altered its tendencies, or a new temper or disposition of
the soul. All agreed, however, that it resulted from the understanding's
perception that Christ as he is seen in the Gospel was the highest and
greatest good. Since this perception remained, the will also remained
fixed, habitually, on Christ. [59] The perception remained because the
Spirit continued to illuminate the mind. [60] All this was essentially common Federal theology, and the Old Side differed with the New Side
regarding the infusion of a new principle or regenerate habit merely
in detail. [61]

Once the new principle was established, and the will fixed habitually on Jesus Christ, there sprang up, as the New Side men frequently
expressed it, a faith which justified, purified by leading to repentance,
and worked by love. This conception of faith as justifying, purifying,
and working obedience by love set the pattern for the doctrine of the
Christian life. [62] In itself faith was defined as consisting essentially in
assent, trust, and obedience. Assent involved historical faith — that is,
a belief in the truth of the Gospel — and also a willingness to be saved
by the merit of Christ alone. "The Lord will save none in any way
against their Wills; and none do consent and agree to this Way of Salvation through Christ, which God has appointed, until they embrace
Christ, and close with Him by Faith, but are still for being saved some
other Way." [63] Trust was a dependence upon Christ alone for justification, acceptance with God, and all blessings. [64] Obedience was understood as meaning " to resign ourselves to the Spirit," " a full and firm
Purpose of Heart to cleave to him, to deny [oneself], to take up [one's]
Cross and follow him," as subjecting " the Soul to the Scepter and

Yoke of Christ," and always as working by love to God and man.[65] Concisely put, the essence of faith was "receiving and resting."[66] So typically Federal was this understanding of the nature of faith that both John Thomson and Francis Alison defined it in terms scarcely differing.[67]

Faith having been so defined, it was impossible that it could involve essentially an assurance of salvation. Though the Old Side often accused the New Side of asserting that assurance was of the essence of saving faith, the New Side always denied both the charge and the idea itself.[68] In sermons published both before and after the controversy over the Great Awakening, the New Side separated assurance very strictly from faith. That all Christians might have the assurance of their salvation, and even that they ought to seek continually until they received it, Francis Alison declared no less plainly than did the New Side.[69] John Thomson and others of the Old Side granted that many Christians did receive this assurance, but felt that it was an exception rather than the rule.[70] The insistence of the New Side was that some degree of assurance was attainable by all true believers and that all should seek it. This was again traditional Calvinism, whether of the Lambeth Articles or of the Irish Articles, with their forthright assertion that *all* true believers had the assurance of their salvation, or the more cautious statement of the Westminster Confession that *many* received it. The issue between Old Side and New Side in this matter was that each group defined the nature of assurance in a different way, and had very different reasons for seeking it.

Since all Federalists agreed that no man could watch while God infused a new principle into him, all granted that no man could tell exactly when he had been regenerated. The illumination of the mind by the Holy Spirit was indeed in some measure empirically knowable. But since by definition this illumination was only an extension or heightening of man's natural knowledge, and since all agreed that even the nonelect were often given quite clear but nonsaving understandings of divine truths, no man could tell *infallibly* when in him the illumination was natural, and when it was from the Holy Spirit. Neither could he tell when the illumination which was from the Holy Spirit passed from nonsaving to saving, and when as saving it became so constant as to fix the will habitually on Jesus Christ.

In traditional Federalism, assurance was of two sorts: the ordinary, mediate, or common assurance which one gained from evident operations of the principle of grace in his life, and an immediate or extraordinary assurance which the Spirit gave directly.[71] The common assurance could be defined in several ways. John Thomson found it to mean, "When a Person by an impartial comparing of his Conduct with the Law of God, finds it agreeable thereunto [in the sense of sincere endeavor rather than of perfection of obedience]." [72] Dickinson found it to mean that the sinner knew he had been convicted of his sin, had been humbled so as to seek salvation only through Christ as offered in the Gospel, believed in Christ as his Saviour, loved God and his children, had victory over the world, and continued in a spirit of prayer.[73] The Old Side virtually rejected the extraordinary assurance in their assertion that it had been given only rarely in the whole of Christian history, and was not to be held out as a possibility for Christians in general.

When the reasons given for seeking any assurance, or for denying the necessity of seeking it, are examined, the real issue between Old Side and New Side becomes quite clear. For the Old Side, assurance was egocentric; for the New Side, it was theocentric. Francis Alison urged his auditors to seek assurance for three reasons: 1. "To secure Eternal happiness, to be Sure that we have an almighty and good father for our friend and that we shall never perish. . . . [2.] . . . without this [assurance] there can be little comfort in Religion, and little satisfaction in the ordinances [of worship]. . . ." 3. As a support in afflictions.[74] Assurance was to be sought for the comfort of man. The Old Side authors of the " Querist " pamphlets were also concerned for the comfort of men, and therefore rejected the idea that men ought to seek assurance. If assurance was insisted upon, men who did not have it would be distressed. The weak [those who did not have assurance], it was asserted, should be fed with milk if they were not able to endure meat.[75]

The New Side men were not concerned for men's comfort, but with men's presumptuousness. Men presumed upon God's mercy and supposed that they were Christians when they were not. Only those were sons of God whom God acknowledged as such. Therefore, the insistence of the New Side that all should seek for assurance was intended to destroy all self-righteousness. As Gilbert Tennent declared, our spiritual condition can be known, therefore God commands us to examine ourselves to see whether or not we are in the faith.[76] Jonathan Dickinson noted also that many had complete assurance that they were not regenerate.[77] Since the reason for seeking assurance then was that men might be led to seek salvation only in Christ, the New Side men could confess that assurance was not of the essence of faith, fluctuated in even the best of Christians, and had continually to be rewon by renewed self-examination and renewed appropriation of grace by faith. By its very nature assurance could never be achieved once for all. That some Christians maintained a steady faith, and thus enjoyed a steady assurance, was, however, asserted.[78] The unanimous and vigorous New Side polemic against both the Moravians and the Seceders for making assurance part of faith was, accordingly, wholly consistent.[79]

Sanctification, which began with regeneration, was the Spirit's work whereby he continued the work of illumination, regeneration, and justification in the believer.[80] This continuing work of the Spirit made faith, repentance, obedience, love, etc., to continue, in some measure, in the Christian. That holiness which sanctification produced was essentially obedience. " Obedience to God's law, from Love to God and regard to his commanding Authority, is the very Nature of Holiness." [81] " The most intelligent description of holiness, as it is inherent in us, may be this, ' It is a conformity in heart and practice to the revealed will of God.' " [82] The entire New Side could accordingly often use the terms " regeneration," " conversion," " justification," " sanctification," " holiness," " repentance," " saving faith," " renovation," " a principle of grace," and other related terms, interchangeably when urging men to seek God. In the end, what was to be sought under all these captions was an act of the Spirit that would result in making the sinner obedient to God.[83] Holiness was nothing else than obedience to the moral law, and holiness was the one great design of the entire plan of salvation.[84]

All this meant that the reason for the salvation of sinners was not to be found in their welfare, but in their restoration to the service of God. Few emphases were as uncompromisingly made in the New Side preaching as was this consistent and vigorous denial of any and all notions of eudaemonism. The nature of the Christian life was accordingly the service of God, not any form of religious experience psychologically interpreted. Neither did the notion of the value of one's religious experience for the individual play any role.[85] In the most blunt terms it was declared that man existed for God's purposes. Hence behind all this thought on regeneration stood at all times its unquestioned presuppositions, the doctrines of the sovereignty of God, and his predestination.

Good works were indeed required of the Christian, but not because they changed God's purposes and designs toward the doer, or excited his benevolence. Neither were they to be done because they in any way qualified one to receive Christ, nor because that by doing them sanctification would be furthered, nor in hopes that God would give further grace for further growth in grace. Good works were necessary because " they are one End of our Election," because they are part of sanctification itself, because they are done as an expression of obedience to

God, and, because they are an expression of gratitude to God, an evidence of reality of faith, and an aid to assurance.[86] He who does not have good works ought not to pretend to be converted. " An unjust, uncharitable Christian is as great a contradiction as a prayerless, or a swearing Christian. You can no more be a good man without loving your neighbor, than without loving your God. . . . No inward experience, no religious duties, no zeal in devotion can make you true Christians." [87] " Men seem to act as if they were entirely detached from one another, and had no connection, or were not at all concerned to promote each other's interest. Self-interest is their pursuit, and self-love their ruling passion." [88] The good as such, in God's sight, was possible only through grace. Christian morality differed from natural morality in that it was done in obedience to God's command, and done in the name of Christ.[89] Ethical good in general was " rectitude of a reasonable creature, or conformity to rule and law." [90] Christian morality was morality that conformed to Christian norms. Christian obedience was the obedience that God enabled man to perform.

The controlling note in the Federal theology, accordingly, had always been the concept of law. This note is regnant in all the Log College literature, and in the writings of all colonial Presbyterians. " The Moral Law, as to its Substance, is the same with the Law of Nature, which is immutable, and founded in the reasonable Nature of Man," Gilbert Tennent declared. " By the Law of Nature I understand the Light of Nature, or the practical Notions of the Difference between Moral Good and Evil, which we receive with our Nature; or a practical Rule of Moral Duties, which was originally impress'd on the human Mind when Man was first form'd to which Mankind are by Nature oblig'd. Altho' this Law of Nature was much broken by the Fall of Man, yet that there be some Remains of it in all, we have abundant Evidence from Scripture, Conscience, the Consent of Mankind, and the Voice of Reason." [91] This law is " co-natural " to man, and was engraven upon his heart at creation.[92] " Things that are Moral are commanded because they are intrinsically Good, and agreeable to that eternal Justice and Goodness that are in God Himself." [93]

The fall of man so far darkened man's understanding, will, and affections that a " second edition " of this moral law was needed. This second edition was given in the Ten Commandments.[94] The Decalogue was accordingly the best summary of this natural law, or moral law of love to God and neighbor. The Golden Rule itself fell into this same category. " This [i.e., the Golden Rule], says our Lord, is the Law and the Prophets, i.e., It is the Substance of the second Table of the Law, according to the Explication thereof by the Prophets: The

Law is just and reasonable, grounded upon the plainest Maxims of natural Equity and Right." The example of Jesus was the best possible explication of this law of love, but since, as the Bible records it, it is fragmentary and does not cover all circumstances of life, the law as summarized in the Decalogue is also needed for completeness' sake.[95]

During the most vigorous phase of the revival, and again during the controversy with the Moravians, this conviction that the law applied equally to Christian and non-Christian was forcefully asserted. "Christ is not exalted, but dishonour'd and the Interest of his Kingdom betray'd, while any that assume the Character of his Ambassadors neglect to inculcate the Moral Law." [96] That the Moravians denied that the law was any longer a rule for the Christian was denounced as one of their most serious errors.[97] An individualistic piety, or any notion that only Christians made for righteousness in society, was rejected. The assumption was that society was in some measure Christian, and that the function of the Church was to make it more so. This attitude was very plain in all New Side preaching. All their hearers were in some measure committed to be Christians, society in general was so committed, and so also were all the institutions of society — governments, courts, schools, and all others.[98]

The Christian, while obligated to obey this law of love, did so in a manner different from that of the non-Christian. The former obeyed it because of a sense of gratitude to God and without any thought of obtaining any merit or reward. The non-Christian obeyed through fear and with hopes of reward.[99] The Christian remained, however, both flesh and spirit, and, accordingly, never obeyed the law fully. Neither did he ever reach the stage of growth in which his obedience became natural, or could be assumed. In so far as he was aided by the Holy Spirit through grace, the spirit, or the new man, would triumph. In so far as sin prevailed, the flesh triumphed. The warfare between these two principles, the flesh and the spirit, or the old man and the new, continued throughout life, and determined the nature of man's obedience to God.[100] Though regenerated, justified, and living by faith, man remained both sinner and justified believer. "The more holy a Person is," Gilbert Tennent declared in the midst of the revival period, "the more they know of themselves. The Knowledge of God is that Glass in which they behold their own Blemishes, the secret Corruptions of their hearts, the Sins of their Practice, and the Defects of their Religious Service." [101] A continual renewal of repentance was therefore utterly essential.[102] "The evidences of pardon and the hope of salvation do not put an end to true repentance, but, on the other hand, promote it." [103] " Evangelical repentance does not consist in despairing agonies and hopeless horrors of conscience, but is attended with an humble hope of forgiveness and acceptance; and this hope is founded entirely upon the merits of Jesus, and not of our repentance and reformation." [104]

Against such a background it is not surprising to find that in discussion of the nature of communion with God, the element most stressed was obedience and not love, righteousness and not joy.[105] The emotional aspects of communion with God were not of the essence of true communion, but obedience was. Moreover, it was in the stated ordinances of worship that communion was best to be found.[106] The constant longing for the emotional aspects was a sign of immaturity.[107] An excellent illustration of this sense of obedience as the keynote of Christian living is to be found in a conversation between Whitefield and William Tennent, II, when the latter was an old man. Whitefield, whose soul was ravished at the thought of dying, asked Tennent if he did not feel the same joy. Tennent, generally reputed by his contemporaries to be the most " heavenly-minded " of all the Log College men, replied: " No, sir, it is no pleasure to me at all; and, if you knew your duty, it would be none to you. I have nothing to do with death. My business is to live as long as I can, and as well as I can. . . . I am God's servant, and have engaged to do His business as long as He pleases to continue me therein." [108]

This thrusting of obedience to the forefront of the Christian life had its influence upon the whole character of New Side preaching and teaching during the revival and subsequently. The Christian was not to flee the sinful society about him, but to lay hold of it and bring it into at least some degree of conformity to the will of God. In so doing he was to co-operate with whatever forces would work with him. No area of life fell outside the realms that God controlled and desired to use for his own purposes. Consequently wherever the Christian's work found him in that vocation he was to serve God. To be without " Publick Spirit " was to be without God. "Unless you conscientiously observe the duties of social life, you cannot enter the kingdom of heaven." [109] Such duties were those incident to the assumption of a responsible part in the normal functions of society. Out of this conviction came the interest of the New Side in education, in civil government, and in all public affairs. " Brethren, we were born not merely for ourselves, but the Publick Good! which as Members of Society we are obliged *pro virili* to promote." [110]

Both New Side and Old Side, evangelical and rationalist, emerged, therefore, at the same point — obedience to God's eternal law, the natural law of man's reason and conscience, was the essence of the Christian life. Federalism had always led to this conclusion. Moralism and complacency were inevitable, accordingly, whenever the rationalistic element dominated. Even license had then appeared. For a time the New Side had been able to combat this inherent weakness of the Federal system by reintroducing the Puritan pilgrimage motif, and the Puritan doctrines of convictions and assurance. In this context it had again become possible to bring the more evangelical aspects of the Puritan understanding of the Christian life to the fore. The Great Awakening within colonial Presbyterianism had been wholly shaped by this evangelical emphasis. Gradually, however, the rationalistic core of the Federal theology was to reassert itself, and come to virtually unchallenged supremacy as the century drew to a close. The New Light was snuffed out.

11

THE COLONIAL CHURCH

The Church of the later colonial period was both Presbyterian and American. As Presbyterian it had followed the patterns of English and Scottish Presbyterianism in large measure. As American it had felt from the beginning a sense of its own independence and its own destiny. Never conceding any authority over it to any non-American body, it had freely chosen, adopted, or rejected the older patterns of British and Continental Calvinism. To its heritage it had added from its own fertile genius. In the early period of its life the consciousness of its own destiny had not loomed large, and the memories of the older patterns had been very strong. Forces both within and without the Church had contributed to the fusing of these different immigrant Presbyterianisms and the re-forming of them into an American Presbyterian Church.

By the middle of the eighteenth century a distinctively colonial or provincial society had emerged in the American colonies. Nowhere was this development more marked than in the middle colonies, with their highly mixed populations and their greatly diversified society. The Presbyterian Church, largely confined to these colonies, and likewise in itself a blend of many backgrounds, had shared in this general colonial trend. In addition, even greater forces had been at work in its own midst. The form of the Presbyterian Church had given a new sense of unity extending far beyond the boundaries of any one colony. The members of Sylvanus White's congregation at Southampton, Long Island, were united in one church with the members of Henry Patillo's congregation in Wyliss Creek, Virginia. In the 1760's the people of the Newark, New Jersey, church might be disappointed but not unduly surprised if they were to hear their pastor, Alexander McWhorter, announce that, in accordance with an order from the synod, he was setting out that week to spend two months in North Carolina. During his absence the Presbytery of New York would send them supply preachers, some of whom might well be recent graduates of the College of New Jersey who had been brought up on the frontier of Pennsylvania. Moreover, when in 1754 the church in New York City was seeking an able pastor it sought earnestly to call John Rodgers from Drawyers Church in Maryland. Other preachers were called from as great distances. Once a year the clergy and some of their elders would meet at Philadelphia, or occasionally at New York, or at Elizabethtown, in the annual synod. Here the farmer elder, a Scotch-Irish immigrant from Tinkling Spring in Pennsylvania, could meet his brother elder, a New York merchant of mingled Dutch and English blood. The pastor of Conechocheague in Maryland, whose whole education had been received in Samuel Blair's small academy of Fagg's Manor, Pennsylvania, might have met his brother pastor of Smithtown, Long Island, the future president of Yale College, had the latter ever attended!

It was, however, the Great Awakening that first brought home forcefully to the average lay Presbyterian in the colonies a sense of the unity and common faith which he shared with so many other Americans. When Presbyterians of New England descent belonging to the Presbyterian Church of Newport, Long Island, heard the preaching of Gilbert Tennent, born in Ireland, educated by his father at Bedford, New York, and now pastor at New Brunswick in east Jersey, it gave them a new sense of oneness with thousands of other Presbyterians. Later, when they read in the weekly papers that he had recently preached in the Piscataqua area in Maine, and still later that he had preached at Hanover in Virginia, they would feel an even deeper sense of this unity. As Samuel Blair, Samuel Finley, and many others traveled from place to place in the evangelistic work, Presbyterians all through the middle colonies were drawn together. Within the individual congregations the revival had broadening results as converts from every background were brought in. The greatest unifying influence of the Great Awakening, however, was that it gave to nearly four fifths of the Church a common understanding of the Christian life and the Christian faith.

As fewer and fewer ministers came from abroad, and more and more of the clergy were American-born and educated at Yale or the College of New Jersey, the sense of belonging to an American Church increased. When in 1765 a minority group of Scotch-Irish or Scottish descent in one of the congregations of Lewes Presbytery complained that their pastor, John Miller, had introduced Watts's hymns into the worship of the church, they argued that his action was contrary to the rules of the Church of Scotland. The presbytery tartly replied that the Church of

Scotland had never addressed the American Presbyterian Church on the subject, and that if they had, their authority would not have been recognized.[1] Unassimilated groups such as this minority party did exist all over the Church, as certain people attempted to defend to the last some cherished nonessential from their past heritage. For the most part, however, the Church of 1765 was an American Church.

All through the colonial period strenuous efforts were made by the Church to evangelize the fast-spreading frontiers. In 1766 a collection for the " propagation and support of the gospel in such parts as cannot otherwise enjoy it " was required of every Presbyterian church.[2] Other collections also were taken, and in 1772 a collection was made to buy Bibles and books for the people on the frontiers. This was the beginning of the Church's official interest in Christian literature. While the far-flung missionary activities of the Church on the frontiers were always seriously hampered by a severe shortage of ministers, phenomenal growth was achieved in the colonial era.

In the colony of New York the Church was unable to expand west of the Hudson River, since that region was settling up very slowly. Few settlers cared to move on to the great semifeudal manors that occupied the land. The Church expanded, therefore, up the east bank of the Hudson, establishing congregations in the area between the river and the colonies of Connecticut and Massachusetts. Fishkill (or Rumbout), Poughkeepsie, Pleasant Valley, Washington Hollow (or Pittsburgh),[3] Schenectady,[4] and Albany [5] formed the Presbytery of Dutchess County in this region.[6] In 1766 in the city of New York Presbyterianism had grown strong enough to found a second church, collegiate with the old first congregation, called Brick Church. Significantly the New England element soon went largely to Brick Church and the Scottish group usually worshiped at the old building.[7] On Long Island the Church enjoyed a steady growth. New York had within its borders, in the late colonial period, three presbyteries, Dutchess, Suffolk (on Long Island), and New York (the city plus northern New Jersey to the region about Elizabeth). Throughout the colonial period New York Presbytery was the largest and strongest presbytery of the Church.

New Jersey was broken up into three presbyteries. The northern part belonged to New York Presbytery, the central region to New Brunswick Presbytery, and southern New Jersey belonged to Philadelphia Presbytery. Presbyterianism was strong in the colony. New Brunswick was second only to New York Presbytery in strength during the period when Philadelphia had both a First and a Second Presbytery. (Even after these two bodies were merged subsequent to the Revolutionary War, New Brunswick was about equal to the new Presbytery of Philadelphia.) The College of New Jersey was situated within its bounds, and the presbytery's great history gave it additional prestige in the Church. Its record for sending out missionaries to the frontier was scarcely equaled. Expansion within its own borders was going on steadily. Southern New Jersey was not being churched so rapidly since settlement was going forward more slowly.

By the latter part of the colonial era Pennsylvania was rapidly becoming a Presbyterian stronghold. Even though certain factors were still keeping the Church there weak, the basis for future strength was being laid. Presbyterianism in the colony was largely Scotch-Irish, the congregations at Philadelphia and a few places adjacent being more mixed. The Scotch-Irish during the period from 1760 to the close of the colonial era were very mobile. There was a great deal of settling and resettling among them, which kept their churches weak and often short-lived. In 1760, Francis Alison wrote an appeal to the Churches and people of Great Britain, asking for money for the Ministers' Fund. He dwelt at some length on the problem caused to the Church by the restlessness of the Scotch-Irish. "Another Circumstance which greatly discourages us, . . . arises from the Nature of the Country. The Inhabitants are inconstant and unsettled, and are always shifting their Habitations, either from a Love of variety, or from the fair Prospect of more commodious Settlements on the Frontiers of this, or the neighbouring Province; So that we can have no Certainty of any fixed number of Parishes, or Ministers in the Bounds of this or the neighbouring Provinces. When our People remove they are generally Suceeded by Strangers from Europe, . . . German Menomists, and Longbeards or Moravians. . . ." [8] The Scotch-Irish were very wasteful in their handling of their land, with the result that even good land soon failed under their methods.[9] As conquerors of the frontier, however, they played a most important role in breaking the way for others.

While the shifting about of the Scotch-Irish kept Pennsylvania Presbyterianism weak, and essentially a missionary area, it did spread the Church, however thinly, all through the colony at a very early date. As early as 1758, George Duffield, a Presbyterian chaplain during the French and Indian War, reached Pittsburgh, then Fort Duquesne. Patrick Allison also served as a chaplain in the region. Five years later Duffield and John Brainerd were ordered by the synod to make a preaching tour of the region, but were prevented from doing so by Pontiac's conspiracy. It was not until 1766 that Duffield, and Charles Beatty rather than Brainerd, made their famous journey.[10] Other men followed them on missionary journeys in the western regions across the Alleghenies, though no congregation felt strong enough to call a preacher before 1773. In that year Pittsburgh asked Donegal Presbytery for a minister, but it was not until 1785 that Samuel Barr settled there for a brief and troublous pastorate. Washington County had several missionaries permanently stationed in the region as early as 1776, among them John McMillan, founder of Jefferson College. After the Revolution, settled churches sprang up quickly under the care of Redstone Presbytery.[11]

Pennsylvania in later colonial times had within its boundaries four presbyteries. The First Presbytery of Philadelphia cared for two of the three churches in the city, a small area in Pennsylvania lying close to Philadelphia, and south Jersey. The Second Presbytery of Philadelphia had under its care one of the city churches, and a half dozen other rigorously Old Side congregations scattered about in the colony as far west as Harrisburg. Donegal Presbytery was situated in the Scotch-Irish area about Lancaster and extended westward without any strictly defined boundary. It included also a few churches in Virginia. New Castle Presbytery had a portion of southeastern Pennsylvania and part of Delaware as its territory.

Delaware and Maryland were under New Castle and Lewes Presbyteries, the former occupying the northern area and the latter the southern part of each colony. Lewes Presbytery was never large and just why it was never absorbed by New Castle seems odd. Delaware was a strong Presbyterian center, but the Church remained weak in Maryland.

Virginia was the territory of Hanover Presbytery, a strong, thriving group of churches. In the tidewater area where Davies had pioneered, the Church was barely holding its own. Here the Church was made up of mixed stock. In the Shenandoah Valley, Presbyterianism was largely Scotch-Irish. Many of the new immigrants from the wave of 1760 and onward had come down into the Valley from Pennsylvania, as had also many of the earlier settlers of that same origin who were now resettling.[12]

Hanover Presbytery had at one time cared for North Carolina also, but the rapid growth of the Church had necessitated the organization of Orange Presbytery (1770) to care for the two Carolinas. In 1765 the synod had sent Alexander McWhorter and Elihu Spencer into North Carolina for an extended stay in order to organize churches, and get them onto stable bases. Great efforts were made also to send missionaries into the area. Thomas Barton, an S.P.G. missionary, wrote in 1768, "True it is that there are Troops of Presbyterian ministers continually travelling thro' that country setting up meetings in every corner of it." [13] Most of Presbyterianism in the Carolinas at this period was situated in the mountainous area settled by the Scotch-Irish. Some few churches had been established in Georgia also by the Scotch-Irish.

This prodigious missionary venture was unequaled by any other colonial denomination. Moreover, it was now being carried on almost wholly by American funds and by a distinctly American clergy. The ministry of colonial Presbyterianism, though modeled largely on the patterns of British Presbyterianism, had been markedly influenced by factors operating in the American scene, especially the influence of the frontier and of the Great Awakening. Most of the native-born clergy were from humble lay homes. In large part they, or their families, owed their membership in the Church to the Great Awakening. Their early education was usually received in small schools conducted in the manses of their ministers. From these beginnings they went, some to larger, better academies such as those of Samuel Blair at Fagg's Manor, Pennsylvania, or Robert Smith's at Pequea, Pennsylvania, others to the College of New Jersey or Yale College. Youths from families not especially interested in the Great Awakening, and devoted more to the former Old Side views, would find their way to the academy at Newark, Delaware, or to the College of Philadelphia. Many young men were unable to bear the cost of going to college. For such students aid was provided either from a general fund administered by the synod or from funds granted by the applicant's home presbytery. Occasionally a presbytery would default on such aid. New Castle Presbytery noted in 1763 that two years earlier they had sent two men " to learning," but that the money for their support had not yet been fully raised. In 1777, New Brunswick Presbytery was still in debt to the College of New Jersey for the education of Joseph Rue, who had graduated the previous year. In spite of such difficulties, many students of very humble origins were enabled to attend college in preparation for the ministry. If they did not enter the ministry after completing college, it was expected that they would repay the money given them in aid.

By the 1770's a college education had become so fully within the reach of any prospective student for the ministry that presbyteries were reluctant longer to ordain men who had had only an academy education. New Castle Presbytery in 1775 asked the synod for ruling on whether or not they ought to ordain a graduate of Newark Academy who had applied to them. The synod were not made happy by the question and answered evasively. The presbytery must, the synod said, always be the judge, and while a college education was " highly expedient," the synod's reply was not to be understood by the presbytery as precluding men who had not had college opportunities.

The attempt, for such it had become, to require a college education of every candidate for the ministry did not go unopposed. Some who felt keenly the appalling conditions on the unchurched frontier protested. Jacob Green, himself a graduate of Harvard, wrote to Joseph Bellamy in 1775, " From a little above Albany to Georgia we want [i.e., lack] 300 preachers." This, he said, was evidence that their present system needed reconsideration. Sects of all kinds were going in everywhere, but the Presbyterians were unable to supply their churches with ministers. " These new parts of our land want men for preachers that will live with a small salary, men of self-denial, men that will take every prudent method to subsist in the world. The method we have been in, has been first to make men gentlemen and then make them preachers; and our candidates have no idea of being gospel ministers without living politely. This method is hurtful to religion for it will always leave great part of the Chhs destitute of ministers." Green proposed that men be trained to combine the frontier ministry with schoolteaching. This was no innovation, for a great many of the clergy were doing this already. But Green urged that an attempt should be made to recruit candidates for the ministry from among the schoolteachers in the colonies. Godly teachers could be trained for the frontier churches in a short time. Even in poor districts, a man could live if he both preached and taught school. Moreover, Green proposed that two new schools be founded, one in Connecticut and one in New Jersey, in which a two-year combined arts and divinity course would be given to large groups of young men destined for the frontier as preacher-teachers. Once out on the field, they would be given certain follow-up studies to complete. After a tour of duty on the frontier, Green hoped, many of these men would later return to some regular college. He was, however, impatient with the great amount of time spent by students in learning dead languages which they would soon forget. The apostles, he declared, ordained the best available men and sent them out.[14]

Green's plan was too radical for his brethren in the Presbyterian Church. The ideal of a highly trained clergy, the fear of heresy born of ignorance, and an intense dislike of shoddy preaching led the synod to strive constantly for higher standards. James Finley defended these requirements on one occasion, by saying: " Reason tells us, that he who is to teach others, should not himself be a Novice: He should apprehend things clearly, reason Solidly, and regularly Methodize his Arguments. Any one may easily see, that a little Smattering of human Literature, a superficial Acquaintance with Divinity, and experimental Religion, a Stock of uncouch [sic] Phrases, and useless Pedantries; or a Dexterity in amusing the Populace with empty high-sounding Harangues, will not do in a Gospel Minister; much less a prevailing Inclination to play the Plagiary: This is ' stealing the Word of the Lord from our Neighbours; 'tis strutting in borrowed feathers.' In order to be an able and useful Minister, guarded against Contempt, one should be thoroughly conversant in whatever is more directly necessary and subservient to the several Branches of the sacred Function; for Instance, the learned Languages, Rhetoric, Logic, History, Philosophy, etc. These are excellent Handmaids to Divinity." [15] Green's fears were, however, realized, and while the Presbyterian Church steadily raised its educational requirements for the ministry, its clergy, though expanding, increased more slowly than the needs. In 1759 the Presbyterian Church in New York, New Jersey, and Pennsylvania was stronger " than all other Christian Churches combined." [16] By 1775 it was still the largest group in these areas, but was losing its great lead.

An ordained minister was expected to attend every meeting of his presbytery and all meetings of the synod, unless he had an acceptable excuse. Also he was expected to serve as a supply preacher to vacant congregations whenever so ordered by his presbytery or the synod. Even men in their late fifties, from churches as influential as Second Church in Philadelphia, were ordered to ride great distances, and in all kinds of weather, on these missionary tours. If at any future time a better, or more preferable, church should seek to call him, the presbytery alone could decide whether or not he could leave his present church. If he grew dissatisfied with his congregation, or his people with him, no change was possible except after a hearing before, and a vote by, the presbytery. Even if the new offer was most attractive, and the relationship between the pastor and his present congregation most unhappy, it was not at all impossible that the presbytery would decide that the man should stay where he was. No one knew when the church would ever get another pastor if they allowed the man to leave. Hence it was often considered best to keep things as they were, and hope that gradually better conditions would develop within the church.

Ministers in some of the older city churches enjoyed good salaries and pleasant conditions. When James Sproat was called to Second Church, Philadelphia, in 1768, he was promised £250, plus a manse, plus £100 with which to purchase additional furniture for the manse, plus free firewood, and £30 toward his moving expenses. Many of his brethren were serving in the smaller churches for £100. Sproat fared no better than his brethren, however, in the matter of arrears on his salary. Presbyteries strove by all manner of means to bring churches around to paying their ministers regularly. Strict supervision of the promises made to a man was maintained. Rather " sharp " practices on the part of a congregation's committee were turned up at times. New Castle Presbytery once found, " By sd Proposals it appeared, that tho they [the Congregation's Committee] offer'd a subscription of £100, yet they would secure [guarantee] no more of this than they cou'd collect; the subscription was to be renew'd yearly, and if it decreased, he [the minister] was to lose what it fell; if it increas'd, the Increase was to go to lower their subscriptions. The Committee [of the presbytery] having consider'd all these Proposals concluded they cou'd not offer them to Mr. Alison [the minister being called] at all." [17] The Scotch-Irish had never been accustomed to paying their clergy a regular salary. Most of the Presbyterian ministers of Ulster lived almost entirely upon the Royal Bounty. On the American frontier the Scotch-Irish were accordingly often extremely reluctant to pay their minister any part of their desperately small incomes.

Church finances in the older congregations were still based largely upon pew rents. The task of collecting these rents was, however, becoming more and more difficult. Fines were assessed against delinquent renters, but without great beneficial results. Dispossession from pews brought some debtors to pay up their arrears, but others merely left the church. Collectors of the pew rents, usually members of the Committee of the Congregation or trustees, became so greatly discouraged that churches frequently hired collectors on a commission basis. Three to five per cent commission was paid. On the frontier subscription lists were most generally the means used to finance the church. Payment was often " in kind " rather than in money. Lotteries were used by many congregations for the raising of funds for church buildings. Some sentiment against this form of financing found expression, but for the most part lotteries were considered perfectly legitimate.

Many ministers were compelled to do secular work in order to live. Many farmed, a number practiced medicine or taught school, and a few had small trading businesses. Time and again these secular pursuits caused complaints as congregations felt themselves neglected. Frequently they alone were to blame for their minister's being thus occupied, although at other times a minister did become too deeply involved in these secular pursuits and continued them long after his congregation's generosity had made them unnecessary. Here and there a congregation made some provision for the care of an incapacitated aged minister, and a few instances of aid given to the widow and family of a deceased pastor occur. For the most part, however, the task of supporting a minister while he was in active service was too great to allow for any costly deeds of kindness to the aged and the bereft. Some of the ministers were able to provide a small income for their widows and orphans by maintaining memberships in the Ministers' Fund.[18]

In spite of hardships and handicaps, some heroic ministries were carried on by the colonial clergy. Some men, it is true, clung to the idea of an aristocratic ministry, stressed the duty of their people to " submit " to their " authority," arbitrarily used exclusion from the sacraments to enforce their authority and gain submission, and earned for themselves the reputation of having no true personal religious concern for their people. The greater part of the clergy proved by lives of astounding self-sacrifice, and by lives burned out before the age of forty, that they knew no higher call than that of the Gospel ministry among the frontier people.

In the first quarter of the eighteenth century no very uniform practice was followed in the matter of church officers. Some churches had elders organized into regular sessions. Other churches had boards of deacons. In the early records of the first presbytery elders were known as " assistants." Again, some churches had only committees of the congregation, who functioned very much as did the Congregationalist boards of deacons, or modern boards of trustees. This left the whole religious life of the congregation in the minister's hands. It was not unusual for a colonial church to exclude the minister from all participation in the financial affairs of the church. When a session of elders did exist in a local congregation, its ranks were replenished by nomination of the minister, election by the elders already in office, and approbation by the congregation. Some churches elected elders for a term of one year, others elected them for life.

By 1770 almost every congregation in the colonial Presbyterian Church had a session of elders. In that year the old First Church, the leading church of the Old Side party, at length formed a session.[19] The church in New York allowed its session to pass out of existence by failing to elect new elders, but it reconstituted the session in 1753 and maintained it steadily thereafter. Suffolk Presbytery in 1754 asked all their congregations to elect two or three elders.[20] By this time, also, the congregations were demanding a greater part in the choice of their elders. More and more they were asking, in contradistinction to the earlier practices inherited from the Old World, that the right of nomination of new elders be given to the session rather than to the minister, and that they, rather than the session, have the right of election. After their election the elders accepted their offices in the presence of the congregation and were installed. Ordination of elders was not uniformly practiced at this time. This is well indicated by a ruling in Donegal Presbytery in 1760, of which the synod approved, that election by the congregation without any further act could constitute a man an elder.[21] Lewes Presbytery records mention a " formal setting apart " of elders which may have been ordination in the sense of setting apart by prayer, though the evidence is not clear.[22] New Brunswick Presbytery disciplined a minister about this time for trying to create two elders without nomination by the session and without a vote by the congregation.[23] The session was the representative of the people, and election and formal installation in the presence of the congregation were means of keeping this relationship clearly before all. The session was not to be the creature of the minister. Elders were still being elected for only a term or for life, according to local desires, all during the colonial period. The session, moderated by the minister, cared for the ordering of the acts of public worship, the reception of new members, and the admission of persons to the sacraments; watched over the spiritual life of the people; and exercised the discipline of the church.

In many areas, especially in the only partially organized frontier regions, the church court or session was the only court before which redress of wrongs could be sought. These courts were begun originally in Calvinistic churches as a means of discipline. Since all needed discipline if they were to persevere in their pilgrimage in spite of their own waywardness and the temptations of this life, these courts were part of the churches' pastoral care of the souls intrusted to them. For the wicked, they could pronounce the sentence of excommunication. For the believer who had failed, these courts offered admonition, the opportunity of public repentance, and an exhortation to be henceforth more faithful. More and more, however, the pastoral element dwindled, and during the later colonial period such trials before church sessions disappeared in the older, more stable settlements. On the frontier they continued until well into the nineteenth century. One elder from each congregation was expected to attend the meetings of presbytery and synod, though defaults were more common than performances in this line of duty. Presbyteries sought to remedy this failure of the Presbyterian system, but without much success.

In the large churches a clear distinction between the duties of the session and the duties of trustees was struck by 1770. The office of deacon was recognized in many congregations, but not much was made of it. Smaller churches usually had all the business affairs of the church in the hands of the session. Wherever a congregation had no charter, and could not legally hold property in its own name, committees would be formed to hold the church property as their own personal property. Much trouble arose when members of these committees failed in business or died with the church's funds and theirs intermingled — though with no evil intent. The refusal by colonial governments to grant charters to local Presbyterian congregations was usually traceable to the pressure of the Anglican clergy.

The Great Awakening had brought into the New Side Presbyterian churches great numbers of the lower classes. Some of these had soon departed when the New Side began, after 1741, to create form and order for the guidance and direction of the free spirit of the mass revival. Even as late as 1763 this movement of the lower and even the middle classes away from the larger city churches was causing some concern. The Baptists drew many of these people away from the New York church,[24] and the Seceders called out many of the more rigidly inclined people from some rural churches. The inability of the Presbyterians to supply even a small part of the frontier communities who asked them for ministers meant inevitably that the churches that were better situated financially got the men, and the poorer places finally took ministers from other denominations. Gradually the Church came to serve the upper and upper middle classes by defaulting on its ministry to the weaker churches and by the growing scholasticism of its pulpit.[25] Since, however, only two or three per cent of the population of the colonies lived in towns or cities of over eight thousand population, the great part of the Church remained rural. The trend toward a ministry to the upper and upper middle classes had been established, but no more. It was only later, as America became urbanized, that this trend was to shape the growth of the Church.

Care for the needs of the poor and the unfortunate became more and more the concern of the Church. Local congregations raised money for local projects and the synod began to raise a large fund for "pious and public uses." In 1769 synod appointed a committee to cooperate with the Orphans' Court in the care of orphaned children.

It has been estimated that about one third of the people in the American colonies in 1763 were legally not free. Some of these unfree persons were white indentured servants, but most of them were Negro slaves. There was no great sense of the wrongness of slavery as such in colonial Presbyterianism. Some ministers, Samuel Davies pre-eminently, had shown a very great pastoral interest in the Negroes. In the city churches Negroes were seated in separate gallerys and received the Lord's Supper at "their own" tables. Negroes were, however, allowed to join the white churches as full members. There are no instances recorded of Negro Presbyterian ministers in the colonial period. Agitation for the freeing of slaves had begun to appear before the Revolutionary War. As early as 1768, Francis Alison wrote, "I am assured ye Common father of all men will severely plead a Controversy against these Colonies for Enslaving Negros, and keeping their children born British subjects, in perpetual slavery — and possibly for this wickedness God threatens us with slavery."[26] Alison freed his household slaves at his death (1779), though he seems never to have taken a public stand against slavery.

The first outspoken and clear denunciation of slavery as an institution by a Presbyterian was that of Benjamin Rush, an elder in the Second Church of Philadelphia and a prominent figure in colonial medical and scientific circles. In 1773 he published *An Address to the Inhabitants of the British Settlements in America, upon Slave-keeping.* This work met with an unusual response, going into at least five editions in Philadelphia, New York, and Boston that same year. Rush paid great tribute to the pioneer work of Anthony Benezet in the movement against slavery, and declared that as a result of that work three fourths of the province of Pennsylvania was now turned against slavery. To the typical defenses of slavery he gave blunt answers. To justify slavery because it brought the Negroes within reach of the Gospel, he said, was but to justify robbery because a part of the proceeds was given to religious purposes. The profit or income gained from the labor of slaves was but stolen from them. Being more humane to slaves was not the need; the system itself was a crime, and a breach of the Eighth Commandment. The Old Testament did not necessarily sanction slavery, and the New Testament was against it. If the Bible did not witness against so evil an institution as slavery, that would only prove that the Bible was not given of God. Rush carried his protest far beyond the theoretical stage, going so far as to accept a pew in a local Negro church, an act which cost him the loss of some of his medical practice.[27]

The following year Rush joined with Benjamin Franklin and others in founding the first abolition society in America, the Pennsylvania Society, for promoting the Abolition of Slavery; the Relief of free Negroes unlawfully held in Bondage, and for improving the Condition of the African Race.[28] When the Synod of New York and Philadelphia met that year, 1774, they found themselves face to face with the entire slavery issue. From New England had come a copy of a circular letter by Samuel Hopkins and Ezra Stiles. The letter asked for aid in educating, at the College of New Jersey, two free Negroes for missionary service in Africa. The synod began discussion of the proposal, "in consequence of which the subject of negro slavery came to be considered, and after much reasoning on the matter Dr. Rodgers, Messrs. John Miller, Caldwell, and Montgomery were appointed a committee to bring in an overture on this subject on Wednesday morning." In the end hearty concurrence was voted to the missionary project, but the synod was unable to reach a consensus on the issue of slavery itself.[29] Evidently antislavery sentiment had by that time become strong enough to balance forces with the traditional views. Further debate on the issue was put off until the next year. Unfortunately the year 1775 was to bring other issues so sharply to the fore that no further discussion of the problem of slavery was had in the synod until after the Revolutionary War.[30] Discussion of the problem within the Church at large, however, continued. By the close of the war a considerable body of opinion in the Church was to be abolitionist.

The attitudes of colonial Presbyterians toward the Indians varied. The synod still maintained the mission to the Indians begun by the two Brainerds under the former New York Synod, but the work had become very discouraging.[31] In the troublous times of the Paxton massacre John Brainerd defended the Indians under his care against the charge that they had collaborated with the Indians on the frontier in murdering settlers.[32] Sampson Occum, an Indian, was ordained for missionary work by Suffolk Presbytery on August 30, 1759, and for a long time worked on Long Island. He also made a trip to England on behalf of Eleazer Wheelock's school for Indians, Moor's Indian School, which later merged with Dartmouth College. Two alumni of Dartmouth, David McClure and Levi Frisbie, were sent to Ohio by the synod in 1772 to preach to the Indians.[33] They did not, however, meet with great success. Indian missionary work was carried on under great difficulties due to the constant wars, friction between the Indians and the settlers, forced removal of the Indians, or withdrawals of the Indians after selling their lands, the degraded living conditions of the Indians, and the rather inept approach of the missionaries. Such work was wholly pioneer work, and it took time to learn useful procedures. Presbyterian missions among the Indians were successful enough, however, to call forth from an Anglican, Colonel Babcock, the angry comment that they were " tucking and squeezing in every possible Crevice they can, their Missionarys amongst the Indians, who from their Solemnity, and ungraceful stiffness, and those recluse and unsociable dejected, Airs, which so remarkably distinguishes those splenatic and frightened Enthusiasts: for while these are continued; Piety is quite striped of its own proper Ornaments, and assumes the Habit of Craft Vice and Illnature. — And is enough to prejudice the Indians against the sublime Truths of the Gospel." [34]

Other Presbyterians who had suffered much from the forays of the Indians during the many wars and frontier raids felt much as did Joseph Montgomery, one of Alison's former students, who later took a very active part in the Revolutionary War. " The God of Heaven looks down with pleasure, whilst he views the laudable motives — and commands success. The Indian tribes, the natives of this land, Cruel in their natures, barbarous in their customs, numerous in their nations, potent and artful in their wars, either are prevailed on to sell their right to the soil or where they are refractory, are conquered * [footnote] (* The Indians, in the savage state, occupy much more land than is necessary, by the laws of Nature, for their support: It was, therefore, no violation of the law of Nature, in our Ancestors, to demand and acquire a share in those lands, which, when reoccupied were, from the impartial bounty of Heaven, alike the property of all.) and obliged to make room for our ancestors, who, thus purchase settlements in America at the expense of their lives and fortunes." [35] The typically Scotch-Irish Old Side, to which Montgomery belonged, never were able to bring themselves to an interest in Indian missions. Their situation on the frontier had instilled into them very different feelings. Their attitudes may also have aggravated the Indians' hostility.

As the colonial period drew to a close, the rising American spirit and the growing initiative of the American people in political, social, and economic areas began to assert themselves within the Church in the form of a demand for a greater participation by laymen in the life of the Church. Congregations began increasingly to seek the right to choose their elders rather than have them nominated by the minister and elected by the session. Church officers also began to assert a wider margin of rights and authority over against the ministry. As the Old World status of the ministry crumbled under the impact of the rising spirit of the New World, congregations became more and more assertive in their rights regarding the calling and the retention of their ministers. In the judicatures of the Church, however, lay participation was still limited largely to the local church courts. Few elders attended the sessions of either the presbyteries or the synod. No elder was ever moderator or clerk of any judicature during the entire colonial era. The growing sense of leadership among Americans generally, and the great prominence of lay leaders in secular fields of endeavor, however, began to balance the leadership of the clergy in American life, and gave to the laymen a very great, though unofficial, prestige and power in the Church at large. Their preoccupation in other fields of endeavor during that critical period of American life no doubt made both them and their fellow Presbyterians quite content with this strong, though unofficial position.

As the political upheavals that were eventually to bring on the Revolutionary War began to agitate the colonists, the Presbyterians found themselves in a very strong position. Their membership in the three great middle colonies, New York, New Jersey, and Pennsylvania, was approximately equal to that of the Anglicans, Baptists, Lutherans, and the other Reformed bodies combined. In the colonies of Delaware,

Maryland, and Virginia, their strength was significant. Even in the Carolinas, they had strong roots and could wield considerable influence. The vast majority of these American Presbyterians were wholly colonial in their attitudes. Their clergy were well educated, discipline and morale were very good as colonial standards went, and a great proportion of these ministers had traveled and preached in more than one of the middle colonies. Some were well acquainted with several of the colonies. In their presbyteries and in the synod they possessed strong official bodies transcending colonial boundaries and uniting them across all geographical and political lines, as well as across all differences in European and British origins. Though the Church represented a good cross section of colonial society, a large part of its strength came from the better educated and more prosperous middle and upper classes where most of colonial leadership rested. The Church's strong position on the frontier as well gave to it a firm basis in the entire area of the middle colonies. The Church had, therefore, religious vitality, competent organization, good resources, and strategic position. These all came quickly to be thrown into the cause of colonial independence.

12

THE WAVERING OF DESTINY

At the time of the reunion of the two synods in 1758, the clergy of New England origin, or education, were the large majority. A significant proportion of the congregations also were of English origin, with blendings of other stocks, Huguenot, Dutch, Welsh, Scotch, and Scotch-Irish. Of solidly Scottish churches there were none, and churches made up wholly of Scotch-Irish were to be found only on the Pennsylvania-Virginia frontier. In the period just after 1758, a number of influences were to be set in motion that would carry the New England group within reach of complete control of the Church. Another set of forces, however, was also to play a part. By a series of events, some planned and some seemingly accidental, the upsurge of New England influences was to be first deflected and later contained. By the close of the Revolutionary War, the Presbyterian Church of the new nation was to be so apparently a Scotch-Irish Church that later generations were to assume that it had always been such.

The College of New Jersey had since its founding been the center and foundation of New England influences in the Presbyterian Church. Its founders and its first three presidents were New England men. Though the Log College group had joined with them at an early date, the New Englanders had been the acknowledged leaders of the school. The death of Jonathan Edwards in 1758 brought about a number of significant changes. Never again was the college to have a New Englander for a president. Moreover, although the next two presidents were to be great admirers of Edwards and true friends of the New England group, it was to be only a single decade until a president tacitly opposed to the New Englanders was to take office.

The trustees elected as Edwards' successor James Lockwood, of Weathersfield, Connecticut, a follower of Edwards' ideas. Lockwood, however, declined the office.[1] Thereupon, Samuel Davies, who had rendered the college such signal services on his journey to Great Britain, was chosen. The vote had not been unanimous, however, and the tutor who bore the notification of Davies' election to him was indelicate enough to tell Davies all, as were also a number of other persons.[2] Davies refused the offer at once. The minority group of the trustees had wanted Samuel Finley. No election was now possible, and Jacob Green, one of the trustees, filled the office of president *pro tempore* for a year. Davies was then persuaded to take the presidency. He was an admirer of Edwards' theology, and until his death was a close friend of Joseph Bellamy, upon whose shoulders Edwards' theological mantle had fallen. Samuel Finley, who succeeded Davies in 1761, was like-minded. Under both Davies and Finley most of the tutors were in close sympathy with the New England group.

Finley's death in 1766 brought about another great crisis in leadership. The college was definitely a New Side enterprise, and its trustees and patrons were determined to keep it such. However, the college had now devoured the leaders of both wings of the New Side party, leaving no one in the whole group capable of heading up the school. In this crisis the latent cleavage between an extreme New England group and a group predominantly Scotch-Irish within the New Side party began to be manifest. Alexander McWhorter and James Caldwell, both trustees and both close followers of Bellamy, joined with Jonathan Edwards, Jr. (a tutor at the college), in a determined move to bring the other great Edwardean, Samuel Hopkins, to the professorship of theology in the college. Hopkins was at that time reduced almost to destitution in his congregation, and desperately in need of a better call. It was John Rodgers, a Scotch-Irish trustee, pastor of the prominent New York Church, who finally swung the choice to John Blair rather than to Hopkins.[3] Had Hopkins come, it is quite likely that he would have become president during the long vacancy that followed Finley's death. The failure of the move to elect Hopkins marks the apex of New England influences in the college. Jonathan Edwards, Jr., Joseph Periam, and other strong New England men remained as tutors, but after this time the New England influences dwindled rapidly, though direct opposition was not yet apparent.

The desperate situation in the College of New Jersey seemed to offer an opportunity to the Old Side party. For some time theirs had been an unhappy lot. Following their failure to make a success of their synodical academy at New London under Alison, the Old Side had thrown their influence and support to the College of Philadelphia, where Alison was vice-provost. The college was nonsectarian, but during the whole colonial period the Anglicans, led by the provost, William Smith, and the Presbyterians, led by Alison, maneuvered for control of the school. Open strife, however, broke out in 1762 between the two factions. Since 1754 the Presbyterians had had a Fund for the Aid of Ministers' Widows and Orphans. It had been begun under Alison's sponsorship, in the Old Side Synod of Philadelphia. Alison had always regarded it as one of his major contributions to the Church. Following the reunion in 1758, the Fund had been incorporated, and plans set up for greatly expanding its functions. Among other things that were done, Charles Beatty, a very able Log College graduate, was sent to Great Britain in 1760 to solicit an endowment fund for the new corporation. Shortly after he reached Britain, William Smith arrived to solicit funds for the College of Philadelphia. Finding that Beatty's solicitations were producing very good results, and that his own chances of securing funds might therefore be reduced, Smith began a whispering campaign, designed to convince Britons that Beatty was raising funds under false pretenses. Beatty's fund-raising efforts were open to attack in that the articles of incorporation of the Fund, and the memorial setting forth the plea for financial aid, were far too broad. The Fund was a life insurance company for ministers, a benevolent society for augmenting the salaries of frontier preachers, a society for sending out missionaries to the frontier, and a charitable society for the granting of emergency aid to frontier ministers and congregations who had been plundered or driven away from their homes and holdings by the Indians. With such an omnibus program Beatty was very open to attack. Smith suggested, quietly and in important places, that Beatty was really seeking the money in order to Presbyterianize the middle colonies, and that the numerous benevolent and missionary aspects of the Fund were but a blind. This was the common accusation made against the Anglicans' S.P.G., hence Smith's whispered allegations were quite readily believed in many quarters. Beatty was just promoting a Presbyterian S.P.G., it seemed.

When word of Smith's activities reached Alison, a terrible furor broke out in the College of Philadelphia. The Fund was a favorite project of Alison's, and by striking at it Smith had torn open the whole seething mass of differences between the Episcopalian and Presbyterian parties in the college. The situation of the Anglicans in the school was precarious at the time, since Smith was the only Anglican on the faculty and in his absence his place was being filled by a young protégé of Alison's, John Ewing. In consternation, Philadelphia Anglicans wrote to Smith urging him to watch his actions lest everything be lost. Smith replied evasively that he had done nothing but speak to a few persons privately, and that the situation was not so serious.[4] Hardly had this fire broken out before the whole American seaboard was staggered by a newspaper report that the King had promised £1,000 to the College of Philadelphia, and a similar amount to King's College in New York on condition that every faculty member of each of these schools be a graduate of an English university. The College of Philadelphia was again in turmoil. Richard Peters, one of the Anglican trustees, wrote to Smith, who was still in England and from whom many thought the report had come:

"You never saw such a ferment as poor Dr. Allison and Mr. Ewing are put into by a paragraph of a News Paper wch says all the Masters for Philadelphia and New York Colleges are to come from England. Allison asked me seriously if it was so and that his Congregation was now importunate with him to return to them, if it was so, he would go to them again. He is a narrow jealous man and I am sorry to see this Temper blaze out as it does every now and then very high.

"You must be very prudent with this man. I assured him I knew of no such design but that both Mr. Penn and you had in all your Letters warmly recommended the broad Bottom on which we stood and had not mentioned any such thing. Notwithstanding this I hear all the Dessenters are allarmed. Certain it is that Dr. Allison woud not chuse to see a Professor or an Usher of ye Church in the Academy, and it is as certain y^t if we have not a proportional Number ye Academy System will soon be destroyed.

"What must be done as to a Mathematist Master. The Continent affords not one, and grave objection will be made by D. Allison and his friends against one's coming from England. . . ." [5]

That the Presbyterians held the whip hand in Philadelphia is confessed in Peters' letter. Soon he had to make this admission to the Archbishop of Canterbury. The latter had written saying that an S.P.G. missionary had reported that the College of Philadelphia was "dwindling away . . . into a mere Presbyterian faction." Peters had to tell the Archbishop that they were unable to find competent Anglican teachers on the whole American continent, and they had had to choose, therefore, between Presbyterian teachers and no teachers. [6] Barring royal intervention, the Presbyterians could control the school simply because they only could furnish a faculty. Strife and mutual jealousies increased during Smith's stay in Britain, so much so that Smith was soon accusing Ewing of trying to supplant him, instead merely of substituting for him. [7]

More trying to the Presbyterian backers of the college than Smith's maneuverings was the student problem. The school had become a bridge from the Presbyterian Church into the Church of England for many Presbyterian youths in spite of the fact that the faculty of the college was almost wholly Presbyterian. Alison wrote to Ezra Stiles in 1766: " I am ready to resign my place in the College, and retire to the country meerly thro chagrine. The College is artfully got into ye hands of Episcopal Trustees. Young men educated here get a taste for high life and many of them do not like to bear ye poverty and dependence of our ministers. Those that pass Tryals for ye ministry meet with hard Treatment from ye Brethren yt favor Jersey College, and can hardly find settlements, and under that discouragement they are flattrd and enticd by their Episcopal acquaintances to leave such biggots and to go to London for orders. Now two or three of our ablest young men are ready to sail for London for this purpose; this makes parents uneasy, and it gives me pain, as our enemys gathr strength by our loss, and Jersey College is so unfit to make scholars, that we would have no great pleasure to send them there; we would hope they will now put that Seminary on a better foundation; I would be glad of ye advice on this head (of my removal) by ye post. . . ." [8]

Other witnesses confirm the fact that a great proportion of the Presbyterian students for the ministry at Philadelphia went over to the Anglican Church. George Bryan, a lay member of First Church, the pastors of which were Alison and Ewing, comments that the Anglican clergy in Pennsylvania were principally " cast-off Presbyterians." [9] (Alison, in his letter to Stiles, ignored the fact that a number of his former students who turned Anglican had been legitimately convicted of censurable acts.[10]) Some Anglicans themselves voiced resentment against the large number of former Presbyterians who found their way into the Church of England.[11]

The Old Side party had, therefore, come to a most critical juncture in their relations with the College of Philadelphia just at the time when the death of Samuel Finley left the New Side desperate for a leader. Both parties were united at that time in a common effort against the establishment of an Anglican bishop in the colonies. Through the synod, of which all were members, both factions had supported the alliance with the Connecticut Congregationalists against the proposed episcopate. But, the controversy over the ministry, which was especially sore at this very time, revealed how far apart the two groups were. Nonetheless, the Old Side party made a very bold move to solve all the current issues in one stroke, by taking over the then leaderless College of New Jersey.

One of Alison's and Ewing's parishioners, Samuel Purviance, Jr., described the plan to Ezra Stiles: " Im now to inform you that a very strong and spirited Remonstrance is prepard and intended to be signed by the Leading Members of our Congregt[n] to be delivered by Commisn^rs who will attend the Trustees of Jersey College at their meeting ye 20 Novr to name a Presid^t. In this we propose to have the Institution put on a new Plan, to have 4 able Professors appointed and Dr. Alison at their Head, and even to offer (tho' I don't know how we could fill his Place) to give up Mr. Ewing if judg'd necessary for ye publick Good, as he is one of the ablest Mathematicians that we know of; we offer to make up by an Annual Subscription whatever their Funds fall short of supporting the proposed number of Professors, and to join all our Influence in Raising Funds sufficient to support the College and in general to throw our whole force into that one Channell. All these proposals are strongly enforc'd by every Reason of Interest, Necessity and peculiar Circumstances that we think can have any Weight with them. And in order to give our Remonstrance the utmost Weight we have privately engaged our emminent Friends the Lawyers at N.Y. to use their Influence in predisposing every Trustee they can influence to copporate in the Scheme, and have also eng^d three Gentlemen to meet our Commisn^rs at Princeton and back our proposals with their Presence and Oratory; a Copy of these Proposals is allready sent them with a very strenuous Letter, submitting ye Proposals to their Correction and Amendment. So sensible are we of the narrow Biggotry of our Brethren ye New Lights, that we dare not disclose these our benevolent and generous Views for fear of defeating our Intentions; by apprising them beforehand we know Schemes w^d be laid to oppose us in this most Salutary Measure; so that we hope to take our Freinds off their Guard; on this Acco^t the Design is inten^d to be kept private amongst a few until near the time of Election. If this looks like Cunning, Im sure its such as youle approve where the Intention is so good.[12] Its needless to point out to a Person who can so readily see, how many Advantages w^d naturally arise from this Scheme; it w^d in general kill ye Seeds of narrow Principles, Unite our at present divided Strength, Raise a number of able Labourers for ye Vineyard, and Render us a formidable Barrier agst both Civil and Religious Encroachers: I can hardly suffer myself to despair of Success in these noble Aims. If we are defeated we shall immediately turn our Attention to New Ark Schooll and endeav^r to make it at least a very valuable Academy. If we succeed in Uniting our Strength in the Jersey College, and the intended Union with our Friends in N. Eng., I shant much regard what our Enemies can do ag^st us. . . . I forgot to tell you, that whether we succeed in our Views in Jersey College or not, the Doctor [Alison] is fully determ^d to leave this College ag^st Spring and Remove to the Country, which will certainly ruin Phil^a College."[13]

In spite of the precautions of the Old Side party, news of the intended coup leaked out. When the trustees of the College of New Jersey met on November 19, 1766, they were forewarned. The five-man committee of the Old Side, all prominent laymen, were left outside while the trustees met. After electing John Witherspoon, of Scotland, to the presidency of the college, the trustees invited the Old Side delegation into their presence. Since control of the office of the president was essential to their plan, the Old Side committee found that they, not the trustees, were the victims of a coup. After protesting that the trustees ought not to have elected a president before hearing their proposals, the committee declared that since a president had been elected, they could do nothing further until they had consulted with their friends.

Shortly after the meeting, Alison wrote to Stiles describing more fully the ill-starred scheme. The Old Side had proposed that he and Ewing be taken onto the faculty, one as president and the other as a professor. If these two names were unacceptable, then Alexander Mc-Dowall, head of the Old Side's Academy at Newark, and Matthew Wilson, an Old Side minister in Delaware, should hold these two offices. The other two professorships were to go one to John Blair or Joseph Treat, New Side ministers, and the other to George Duffield, Robert Ross, or Jeremiah Halsey, graduates of the years 1751 and 1752.[14] To give the presidency and a professorship in the college to the Old Side, who had labored so earnestly against it, and who even then were irreconcilably opposed to all that the college stood for religiously, was a hopelessly large demand. In the Church at that time the New Side party exceeded the Old Side group by not less than four to one. Moreover, the New Side were enjoying a healthy growth while the Old Side were losing most of the few young men whom they were able to start toward the ministry. In return for control of the College of New Jersey the Old Side were offering to assist in the raising of funds. No definite promises were made beyond the offer to take up subscriptions toward any annual deficit caused by the expansion of the faculty. Since the Old Side had never been able to raise funds sufficient to make anything of their own academy, either under Alison or under McDowall, these assurances of support were not very impressive. For that matter when, in 1773, the Old Side did try to strengthen their Newark Academy, they were able to raise little from their own followers, and sought funds in Great Britain. Their mission to Great Britain brought them much less than what Davies and Tennent had secured.

The Old Side smarted furiously under the humiliation of their defeat. Alison wrote to Stiles: " They the trustees have chosen one

Wetherspoons, a minister in Paisley in Scotland; he is esteemed as a keen satirical writer, but they know nothing of his academic abilities, nor whether he will accept their offer; . . . whether he can teach anything but Divinity is hard to say. Should he accept their invitation and undertake this Province, this would be a likely way to unite us, but in the meantime the College is sinking in its reputation for the want of a head. Three young men bred in our College, are now gone home for orders, they are all men of Learning and abilities, and two of them excellent preachers. This has inflamed our people with indignation against our College (of Philadᵃ). Our students meet with hard measures from the ministers in ye favor of Jersey College, under a pretense of examining their stiles, so that they can hardly find settlements or pass tryals; and on the other hand, the Church advocates persuade them to leave such persecuting narrow biggots, and join with them; this disappointant excited our Gentlemen to come to a Resolution to send all their children to Jersey, being persuaded that were all our students bred under the same professors in the same College, all our disputes would have an end. Had this scheme taken place, I had resolved to withdraw from this College; for if I should do so, few Presbyterians would come here. But now I really do not know what is my duty." [15] Purviance shared Alison's gloom and discouragement. Writing to Stiles, he berates the trustees of the College of New Jersey for their " selfish views " and their inability to see the dangers of the times which call so loudly for a united front against the Episcopalians. " In this disagreeable Situation, encrooch'd on by our Adversaries, and rejected by our Freinds, whither shall we turn ourselves: By supporting ye College of Philadᵃ the Flower of our Youth are every Day perverted by the Intrigues of that designing subtile Mortal Dr. Smith; and if we attempt converting our flourishing Schˡ at New Ark into a Seminary for ourselves, we must unavoidably perpetuate the unhappy Parties that destroy our Common Interest and Strength, and feed the Flame that every Moderate Man wᵈ quench. . . . Doctor Alison seems determind on leaving the College of Philadᵃ in Spring which will in fact be giving up all the Interest we have therein." [16]

Thus, though neither side would admit it openly, the election of Witherspoon was an attempt to heal the breach between the two factions in the Church. How true this was may be seen in Richard Stockton's plea to Witherspoon after the latter had rejected the college's first offer: " Shall we turn to our old Antagonists and thereby let them in by Wholesale, or shall we make them greater Enemies than ever by totally neglecting them? I am pained when I think of the consequences of your determining against us." [17] The Old Side took a hand in matters by writing a letter to Witherspoon, ostensibly urging him to accept the invitation, but actually to give him such a picture of the college as to turn him definitely away from the call. Richard Stockton later declared that this " artful plausible, yet wickedly contrived letter " did more than anything else to turn Witherspoon against accepting the proffered position.[18] Witherspoon's wife was resolutely opposed to the move. Finally the offer was refused and the supporters of the college were in despair.

The Old Side then renewed their offer. When the trustees met in 1767, the same Old Side committee was present with the same plan. The trustees asked if the appointment of specific persons was of the essence of the proposals. The committee replied in the negative, and suggested that the scheme of the proposals be adopted, and that all faculty members be chosen on the basis of merit. The trustees thereupon elected John Blair, Hugh Williamson, and Jonathan Edwards, Jr., as professors. It was at this time that such strenuous efforts had been made to have Samuel Hopkins rather than John Blair called as professor of theology. The rejection of Hopkins was undoubtedly, at least in part, a conciliatory gesture toward the Old Side. Blair and Edwards were able, competent men, both strongly New Side. Williamson was a former ministerial candidate under the Old Side, who had turned to the study of medicine and been educated in that field in Great Britain. Thus these appointments were indeed justifiable on the basis of merit. For the presidency a young man of only twenty-six was chosen. He was Samuel Blair, one of the ministers of Old South Church in Boston. His late father had been one of the original leaders of the Tennent party and the founder of the famous Nottingham Academy. One of the Old Side's committee, George Bryan, was made a trustee. Then, since the college was without funds to support so large a faculty, the trustees voted that only John Blair should take office at once. The new president and the other professors were to take office a year later, at which time it was hoped that funds for their support would have been raised through the efforts of both the New Side and the Old Side parties.

The election of Samuel Blair as president, rather than Alison or Ewing, as proposed originally by their committee, incensed the Old Side. Blair had enjoyed a brilliant career, first as a tutor at the college, and then as minister in one of the greatest churches in the New World. He had prestige, therefore, among Presbyterians both because of his father and through his own attainments, and in New England he was held in high regard. His age, twenty-six, was bitterly commented upon by the Old Side, although it was at exactly the same age that Ewing had been brought to Philadelphia by Alison for the dual job of substituting for Provost Smith while he was in Great Britain and of being head pastor of the First Church of Philadelphia. Whatever Blair's fitness for the office may have been, Ashbel Green (Witherspoon's colleague and successor) is perhaps right in saying that the trustees may have had no thought of Blair's ever taking office. Many of them seem to have expected that Witherspoon would yet accept the presidency.[19] Outwardly the Old Side accepted these elections as an implementation of their scheme, even though they later freely revealed the depth of their anger and disappointment. Alison gave up his thoughts of leaving the College of Philadelphia, and he and Ewing, aided by the other Presbyterian members of the faculty, consolidated their hold upon that school. The plans for building up the Newark Academy were dropped.

Two months after this meeting of the trustees another special meeting was held. Word had come that Witherspoon was now willing to accept the presidency, and that Samuel Blair had refused the office. Blair had, of course, been told of Witherspoon's change of mind, and had withdrawn in the latter's favor. Witherspoon was unanimously elected, and in due time arrived in Princeton joyfully acclaimed by the supporters of the college.

While this struggle was taking place for control of the college at which, by this time, nearly two thirds of the ministerial candidates of the Church were being trained, other most significant events were taking place within the Church. The controversy over ministerial qualifications and discipline had been going on most vigorously, and was still continuing. More significant, however, was the gradual change in the leadership of the New Side party, as more and more men of Scotch-Irish ancestry came into the larger pulpits and fewer and fewer men of New England origin or training occupied these prominent posts. So great had been the prestige of New England men at the time of the reunion that when Cross retired from the First Church of Philadelphia in 1758, the Committee of the Congregation asked presbytery for permission to hear three possible candidates, all New Side men, two of New England background. Later, James Sproat, a Connecticut pastor and friend of the New Side, was actually nominated and elected. Only by herculean maneuvers was the pulpit finally saved for the Old Side by the warping in of John Ewing, who had studied under Alison, then gone to the College of New Jersey, and finally completed his work under Alison.[20] A decade later, Sproat came to Philadelphia as Gilbert Tennent's successor, but so advanced had been the shift away from New England leadership that he was then the only New-England-trained man in any large or important Presbyterian pulpit. Scotch-Irishmen held the three great pulpits that had long been the basis of New England prestige in the Church. Alexander McWhorter had succeeded Aaron Burr, James Caldwell had come into Dickinson's congregation at Elizabethtown, and John Rodgers had been installed in the New York church where the influential New Englanders, Pemberton and Bostwick, had previously ministered. In smaller places, New England men still were numerous. But the leadership of the Church was based upon the larger churches, and upon the heads of the schools. Graduates of the College of New Jersey were everywhere about the Church, and most of them were descendants of Scotch-Irish families.

Witherspoon had been sought for the presidency of the College of New Jersey in part because he would be a neutral in the still continuing Old Side, New Side controversy. But the New Side had been attracted to him for deeper reasons as well. He was the leader of a small group in Scotland who were vigorously opposed to the growing ecclesiasticism of the Scottish Church, and to the theological views of the regnant Moderate party in that Church. He came to the college knowing the situation in both college and Church, yet without any pledges or commitments. From his arrival he was his own master, as his acts soon revealed. He began a vigorous campaign for funds for the college. Most of the Church responded well. Even some of the less prominent Old Side men got behind the fund-raising campaign. The synod had since 1768 been giving aid to the college in order to maintain a divinity professor. The sum was less than a third of Blair's salary, and the college was soon unable to continue him in office. Witherspoon therefore, in 1769, assumed the teaching of divinity. Synod at once appealed for greater funds for a professor, and some disgruntled comments came from the Old Side's Second Presbytery of Philadelphia. They wished to know if Witherspoon was actually teaching divinity, if the students attended, and if not, why not.[21] Friction between the Old Side leadership and Witherspoon, however, did not become apparent until two years later.

For a long time the old First Church of Philadelphia, the citadel of Old Side influence, had had a strongly New Side minority. These were the members who had almost succeeded in calling a New Side New England minister after Cross's retirement. As the city had grown, the church had formed a collegiate congregation called the Third Church. Into this branch had gone most of the New Side group. Eventually they became the major part of that collegiate congregation. When a third pastor was needed to carry the load of the two congregations (Ewing and Alison devoted much of their time to the college where each carried a full-time responsibility), these New Side people in the Third Church sought to call a man of their own kind. A long, bitter battle ensued as Alison and Ewing sought to place an Old Side man in the pulpit. Finally the Third Church broke away from the collegiate relationship, and called George Duffield, a New Side man from Donegal Presbytery. The Old Side fought the move in Donegal Presbytery and in the synod. Losing their case in these courts, they sought to bar the congregation and Duffield from the church by force. A near riot ensued, and eventually the Old Side fought a long battle in civil court (in defiance of the synod's order to desist), which they also lost.[22] Duffield, a Scotch-Irish graduate of the College of New Jersey, became the pastor of the church, and soon made it one of the great churches of the denomination. By the time of the Revolutionary War he was the dominant Presbyterian leader in Pennsylvania. In deep bitterness the Old Side reported their defeat to Ezra Stiles, even before they had conceded it openly. Significantly enough they blamed none other than Witherspoon for their discomfiture. Evidently his influence had been instrumental in the synod's ruling against the Old Side. Stiles comments that neither Ewing nor Alison had welcomed Witherspoon's coming to America, and that Ewing was " a great enemy to Witherspoon." [23] Witherspoon had seen in Alison, Ewing, and others of the Old Side, something very much akin to Scottish Moderatism.[24] A few years later, in 1776, he rather fully demolished a brief philosophical paper published by Matthew Wilson, a protégé of Alison's who had once been urged for a chair at the College of New Jersey by the Old Side Philadelphia committee of 1766.[25]

However opposed Witherspoon may have been to the personnel and views of the Old Side, much more far-reaching in significance was his coolness toward the " New Divinity " of the Edwards-Bellamy-Hopkins school, which had hitherto exercised such a great influence in the New Side. The part that Edwards and Bellamy had played in the Great Awakening had opened the hearts and minds of the New Side Presbyterians to receive the New Divinity with scarcely any qualms. Gradually, however, as the New Divinity became " newer " and " newer," some men began to be uneasy. One of the earliest evidences of an anti-New-England spirit in an old Puritan area came from a branch of the Newark Church called Newark Mountains. The church there was seeking a minister, and had asked the aid of a Connecticut minister. This man in turn wrote to Bellamy: " In that country, they insist very much on a man's being a good speaker, and they hate the New England tone (as they call it). They insist likewise upon one that is apt to be familiar. But most of all 'tis necessary that a man be a man of religion and good principles in order to be useful among them. . . ." [26] Much more serious than the dislike of "New England tone" was the dislike of the New England theology which now began to appear, and with which Witherspoon later quietly aligned himself.

Many of the New England group had not been very happy about the trial of Samuel Harker. They were not persuaded that he was guilty of major heresies, and sought to have him treated with lenience. During this trial McWhorter had written to Bellamy much perplexed by all the ado about the esoterics of predestination. What avail, he asks, is the use of the means of grace to an unregenerate man? Why should we ask him to pray, read, or hear, seeing the carnal mind is enmity against God? [27] The great stress upon predestination and the divine sovereignty in the New Divinity bothered many. Under the influence of it, however, many of the numerous Presbyterian churches of New England background threw off the old Congregationalist usages in connection with the sacraments. But in other ways the New England theology met with growing opposition. "We begin," writes James Caldwell to Bellamy, "to be suspected of refining too far and of using that thing called Metaphysics or Common Sense. . . . I have just finished a dissertation for tomorrow [his monthly midweek service] on this question: Is it virtuous to love self as self? or is relative affection as such virtuous? I have answered in the negative." [28] To worshipers brought up under Dickinson, Burr, and others of the original New Side, such fare must indeed have seemed much too refined and metaphysical.

Witherspoon made no hurried assault upon the Edwards-Bellamy-Hopkins theology or its supporters in the Church. However, those tutors who were most devoted to it, Jonathan Edwards, Jr., and Joseph Periam, left the school after Witherspoon's first year. In his philosophical lectures, Witherspoon labored against all forms of idealism, and therefore against the philosophical system of Edwards. "Dr. Witherspoon has a sad time of it," wrote Charles Chauncy, of Boston, to Ezra Stiles, "as the New Jersey College is the fountain of their corruption [the New Divinity]. He will do what he can to purge it, but begins to have his enemies, and they will soon, it is possible, openly appear agt him." [29] On the campus the advocates of the New Divinity developed a full-grown persecution complex, which in turn gave rise to a zealous underground movement. A student named Bradford confided to Bellamy that the cause was being zealously prosecuted even though opposed. Outwardly, he said, Witherspoon was cool, but at heart he was against Bellamy's views. Bradford and his cohorts, aided by Chapman, the pastor of Newark Mountains Church, had circulated

Bellamy's books (with their title pages cut out) among the students under a pledge of secrecy. When the student readers were convinced by this reading of the truth, Bradford and his friends would tell them who the author was. In this manner converts were being snatched from under Witherspoon's influences.[30] Before long, however, Witherspoon had eliminated most of the New Divinity from the school. No doubt he was aided in his task when Joseph Periam, who upon leaving the school had studied theology under Bellamy, then applied to New York Presbytery for entrance into the ministry. Even the stanchest of the Presbyterian supporters of the New Divinity were thrown into consternation as Periam assured his presbyterial examiners that God was the author of sin. Several other equally astounding statements, each an exaggeration of the New Divinity, made Periam wholly indefensible in the presbytery. He was rejected and withdrew, bringing a great deal of discredit upon all the New England party.[31] About this time, 1773, Stiles notes that Witherspoon and most of the Presbyterians were against the New Divinity.[32]

Thus fifteen years after the reunion, the New England element in the Presbyterian Church had lost heavily in position and influence. They were gradually being supplanted in the larger pulpits by men of another nationality, they were out of favor with the faculty of the College of New Jersey, and the New Divinity of Bellamy and Hopkins, with which many of them were at least somewhat in sympathy, was beginning to alienate them even more from the leading clergymen of the Church and the faculty of the college. The New England group, principally in the Presbyteries of New York, Suffolk, Dutchess, and New Brunswick, were still numerous and powerful in the aggregate. No open conflict had appeared, and the over-all spirit of the New Side party still held them together. They were weakened, however, in the Church at large by the indifference of many of their number to their responsibilities as members of presbyteries and of the synod. Year after year Suffolk Presbytery sent not one minister or elder to the synod. Dutchess Presbytery was not much better. Frequently nearly a full half of New York Presbytery's clergy were absent from synod's sessions, and few of their elders attended. This intense preoccupation with their own local affairs greatly reduced their effectiveness in the denomination as a whole. Those New Englanders who exercised any real influence in the Church at large were the clergy of that group who were settled in New Jersey. The two factors, however, that made the decline of the New England group irremediable came not from within but from without. These were the land policies of the various colonies and the continuing Scotch-Irish immigrations.

Confined as it was to the middle and southern colonies, the Church was conditioned in its expansion by the manner in which these colonies expanded. New York colony grew in population, but not in area. Long Island became more thickly settled, and the east bank of the Hudson increased in population. In these regions Suffolk and Dutchess Presbyteries slowly gained. No great numbers of new immigrants came in and the areas were populated largely by the descendants of the earlier settlers. West of the Hudson River, however, few settlements were made until after the Revolutionary War. The great manors held by a few wealthy landowners were unattractive to settlers, and the colony made no effective efforts to settle the interior until the colonial government was overthrown in the war. Expansion for the large New York Presbytery had, therefore, to go southward. Upper New Jersey was its strongest area all through the colonial period. New Jersey was strongly Presbyterian, with the three largest presbyteries working in its borders, New York, New Brunswick, and Philadelphia. Yet as the colony settled up, its western borders were quickly reached. Again, expansion took place largely to the south. Delaware, belonging in part to New Castle and Lewes Presbyteries, was in a similar situation. Pennsylvania, because of its vast area and its land policy, was able to absorb thousands of settlers. Virginia, the two Carolinas, Kentucky, and Tennessee also had large regions that were available to settlement on relatively easy terms. Maryland was dotted with large semifeudal baronies and was not an attractive colony to immigrants who entertained any hopes of achieving economic independence.

The pattern of growth in the middle colonies during the colonial era was, therefore, roughly that of a right triangle whose apex was in the region of New York City and whose sides spread, one down the seaboard, and the other farther and farther, year by year, southward and westward. Under such circumstances the New England group, centered in the presbyteries situated in the apex of this triangle, were inevitably destined to absorption into the expanding portions of the colonies. The second large wave of Scotch-Irish immigrants, who came in during the years beginning about 1760 and up until the outbreak of the Revolutionary War, settled largely on the western frontier of Pennsylvania, in the Valley of Virginia, and in the hill country of the Carolinas, and during the war penetrated even into Kentucky and Tennessee. Very few ministers came with these immigrants. This great wave of tens of thousands of nominal Presbyterians contributed little of a positive nature, therefore, to the shaping of the Church in the colonial era. In another way, however, their influence was enormous. Their rapidly increasing settlements constituted a missionary responsibility into which the synod threw every minister upon whom they could lay a claim. New Side, Old Side, New England, and Scotch-Irish clergy all were pushed out westward and southward, missionizing the new frontiers. In this great missionary drive the New England group's destiny was finally fixed. In their own areas expansion was limited by conditions beyond their control. In responding wholeheartedly, as they did, to the call to church those frontiers that could expand, they aided in bringing into the Church so large a part of the immigrating Scotch-Irish that the character of the Presbyterian Church was radically altered. By the close of the Revolutionary War there were literally hundreds of churches among these Scotch-Irish on the frontiers. As their many sons turned toward the ministry there was not one school, among the then several schools and colleges that were preparing Presbyterian youths for the ministry, that was staffed by New-England-trained men, or by men sympathetic to New England views. Yale and Harvard men still came into the Church in small numbers, and some young followers of the New England way remained unconvinced by their Scotch-Irish teachers, but even so, the future of the Church belonged to the descendants of the Scotch-Irish. In this situation the former New Side and Old Side distinctions among the Scotch-Irish gradually dwindled away after the Revolutionary War, and before many years of the nineteenth century had passed, a Scotch-Irish party arose within the Church in whose eyes the New England group were interlopers, who had somehow crept into a Church that had always been essentially Scotch-Irish.

13

THE THREAT OF ANGLICAN ESTABLISHMENT

Relations between Presbyterians and Anglicans in the American colonies were never good. The memory of each Church was long and heavily studded with the scars of incidents around which had gathered feelings of lasting bitterness. The Presbyterians of Puritan background had much to remember. Many of them owed their presence in the colonies to their forefathers' determination to escape once for all from the Anglican Church. The memories of the Scotch-Irish group of Presbyterians were even more vivid. The larger percentage of these Presbyterians had themselves quitted Ulster but a few years earlier because of the intolerance of the Anglican hierarchy. To the Anglicans the Presbyterians were a keen reminder of Nonconformity, Cromwellianism, the Solemn League and Covenant, and many another expression of determined hostility and opposition. Both groups early sensed the strategic importance of the middle colonies in the religious life of the New World. That they came quickly into conflict is therefore not at all surprising.

The first exchange of blows had come the year after the founding of the first presbytery, when Lord Cornbury imprisoned Francis Makemie and John Hampton. Later he had seized the property of a number of Puritan churches and had attempted to crush all Dissent in the area under his jurisdiction. Even after Makemie had won his case against Cornbury, and the latter had been recalled in disgrace, the Anglicans continued to hold the churches illegally seized by Cornbury's connivance. Makemie's successful defense had been based upon the contention that he was, according to the terms of the Toleration Act, a regularly licensed Dissenting minister. In his trial he had the aid and support of New England Congregationalists, who in turn had secured the help of prominent members of the United Brethren of London. This array of forces, the Presbyterianism of the middle colonies and New England Congregationalism, together with the aid of

228

London Dissenters, was to be employed again and again in opposing every direct or indirect attempt at increasing the power of the Anglican Church in the colonies. Before long the Presbyterians were refusing to classify themselves as " tolerated " in any of the middle colonies. They were claiming an unlimited freedom of worship, based upon the contention that the Act of Establishment referred only to England proper. The Anglican Church, therefore, was no more established in the middle colonies than it was in Scotland. It was the English Church, not the Church of the Empire. The Anglicans of the middle and New England colonies, on the other hand, never ceased to struggle for an establishment of their Church in these colonies. Their argument was that the American colonies were a part of England, and that the Church of England had identical rights in every part of English territory, unless, by specific exemption, as in the case of the Scottish Church, certain exceptions were granted to other bodies.

The Society for the Propagation of the Gospel in Foreign Parts was chartered in 1701. Though organized for the purpose of propagating the Gospel among the unchurched and the heathen, it quickly became the organ of the Anglican cause in the middle colonies and New England. There its efforts were aimed at supplanting the Dissenters and securing Anglican establishments. Hence, when Governor Cornbury illegally seized several Puritan properties on Long Island, he gave them to S.P.G. missionaries. William Vesey, the Puritan minister of Hempstead and New York City, was persuaded to conform to the Anglican Church, as were also several French Huguenot ministers. After Cornbury's disgrace and recall, the Anglicans lost the official support of the governor and their progress became much slower. In order to strengthen their cause, the Anglicans, led by the S.P.G., began an urgent attempt to secure the appointment of an Anglican bishop for the colonies. George McNish had appealed to Cotton Mather for assistance in getting back his church from the S.P.G. missionary to whom Cornbury had given it. Mather had written about the case to Thomas Reynolds, a Presbyterian minister in London. Reynolds, writing on June 9, 1715, had little encouragement to offer. Not only had he failed to gain any assurance of redress for McNish's congregation, but, he writes, " And I must now with sorrow of heart tell that the society [the S.P.G.] are not without hopes of gaining bishops to be sent unto his Majesty's plantations." [1] Fortunately, however, the Whig government of Sir Robert Walpole, which had just taken office, rejected the plans of the S.P.G. Only a few months before, Queen Anne had approved the plan, but her death had made its presentation to Parliament impossible. [2]

Though for the time being the colonial Dissenters were freed from the dangers of a resident bishop, it was not long before the Presbyterians were again made to feel the political power of the Anglican hierarchy. In 1721 the Presbyterian Church in New York City applied for a charter in order that it might be empowered legally to hold property. The request was rejected. It repeated its attempts to secure a charter in 1734, 1759, and 1767. Each time Anglican political power brought their efforts to naught, even though the Church of England was not legally established in New York.[3]

Perhaps the most explicit and open clash of Presbyterian and Anglican that came in this early period was the long pamphlet war which Jonathan Dickinson waged with several S.P.G. missionaries. In 1723, John Checkley, a Massachusetts Anglican partisan as yet unordained, published *A Modest Proof, of the Order and Government Settled by Christ, in the Church*. His earlier efforts had stirred a controversy in New England,[4] and his *Modest Proof* now brought a reply from Dickinson entitled, *A Defence of Presbyterian Ordination*. Other Anglicans joined in the fray and until Dickinson's death pamphlet followed pamphlet. Several of these publications dealt with the ministry, and therefore with episcopacy, others with baptismal regeneration, and other doctrinal topics. Dickinson became through these works the intellectual leader of the Presbyterians and the leading theological opponent of the Anglicans in the middle colonies. Indicative of his spirit is his reminder to a Newark audience, when delivering his *The Vanity of Human Institutions,* directed against the Anglican position, that the thirteenth chapter of First Corinthians must be applied even to theological debates.

Dickinson again came into conflict with the Anglicans when he and his colleagues sought to secure a charter for the College of New Jersey. The Anglicans of the middle colonies opposed the granting of the charter successfully at first, and later fought vigorously to have the charter of 1746 annulled. The bitterness between the two groups had, of course, been heightened by the Anglican opposition to the Great Awakening. For a time their mutual hatred of the revival had brought the Old Side Presbyterians and the Anglicans closer together. Under William Smith, the Anglican Provost of the College of Philadelphia, and Francis Alison, the Presbyterian vice-provost, a number of co-operative ventures were carried out. The relationship, however, was strictly one of convenience, and their bonds were either a common detestation of the revival or common political aims in the colony of Pennsylvania. No lasting good came, therefore, to either Church from the co-operation. The Old Side Presbyterians were soon to complain that the Anglicans were enticing away from them their ministerial candidates.[5] On the other hand, not all the Anglicans welcomed this large influx of Presbyterian converts.[6] A rather amusing complaint came from one S.P.G. missionary from Virginia. His Old Side Presbyterian neighbors were causing him very real trouble. "The greatest harm that the Presbyterians do us, is by mixt marriages and by this means they draw away many of our young people so that we have but few of them that stay with us after they get married, and how to remedy this misfortune I know not, for if I offer to say anything against mixt marriages, tho' I am as cautious in speaking as I can be yet I shall incur the displeasure of both sides; if there be any small tracts upon that subject, I should be glad if the Society would favour us with some. . . ."[7] Within the College of Philadelphia tensions between the Anglican and Presbyterian factions continued all through the colonial period.

The founding of King's College in New York was the occasion of another conflict between Presbyterian and Anglican forces. This conflict was very significant in that it was waged primarily by Presbyterian laymen, and was fought largely in civil or political terms. In 1751 the first moves were made to found a college established by government funds. The Anglicans moved quickly to secure that the president of the college should be Anglican, and that the liturgy of the Anglican Church should be used in the worship of the school. A group of laymen connected with the Presbyterian Church in New York, William Livingston, William Smith, and John M. Scott being the leaders,[8] conducted a vigorous campaign for an out-and-out nondenominational college under the control of the New York Assembly. In the course of this controversy a great many other issues were brought in. Several series of articles, under the names of " The Independent Whig," " The Independent Reflector," and " The Watch Tower," were published in the New York papers. Most of these dealt primarily with the college, but also brought into question the whole status and ambitions of the Anglican Church in the colonies. One long article took up the question, " Was the Church of England ever established in New York? "[9] Smith wrote a history of the colony of New York, which gave him much opportunity to reflect upon Anglican policy. Livingston reissued Makemie's account of his imprisonment and abuse by Lord Cornbury and his Anglican cohorts. Though the battle for a nondenominational college was lost, a powerful political party began to take form which was of great importance in the struggle for American independence a few years later.

Elsewhere in the colonies also Presbyterians and Anglicans were at loggerheads. The growing work of Samuel Davies in Virginia was giving the Anglicans great concern. A very rigorous movement was set on foot to contain the Presbyterian revival and its attendant growth. Davies contended that though the Church of England was established in Virginia yet the Act of Toleration gave him, as a regular Dissenting minister, the right to preach and organize Presbyterian churches. The Anglicans brought pressure to bear upon the Virginia authorities and succeeded in holding Davies to his present gains. He was unable to expand his work. When he went to England shortly thereafter, 1756, to solicit money for the College of New Jersey, he took this matter up with the home government. With the aid of English Dissenters, he succeeded in securing a ruling from London to the effect that the Act of Toleration did give the Presbyterians full toleration in Virginia. After this victory Presbyterianism in Virginia grew rapidly.

During the brief period of co-operation between Anglicans and Old Side Presbyterians these two groups had organized a movement to Anglicize the vast numbers of German immigrants in Pennsylvania. These Germans had made little or no effort to become a part of the New World. They lived in colonies apart from the other groups, maintained their own languages and customs, and could, it seemed to some, become a danger to the colony through falling prey to clever but bad leadership. Money was secured from Great Britain to establish a series of English schools among these Germans. Graduates of the College of Philadelphia could be secured as teachers. Several schools were started, but the movement gained little headway.[10] Behind it lay, of course, the growing competition among Presbyterian, Anglican, and Quaker politicians for the German vote.

Their common opposition to the Quaker party long held the Presbyterians and Anglicans together in Pennsylvania. The strain of fighting the French and Indian War was a severe test for the ruling Quaker party in Pennsylvania. The two opposing groups, Presbyterians and Anglicans, made so much of the Quakers' difficulties that the latter were forced finally to withdraw from power during the war. The growing Scotch-Irish immigration greatly increased Presbyterian strength during this same period. When, therefore, after the Peace of Paris in 1763, which brought the war to a close, the Quakers attempted to regain power, a very sharp controversy arose. In due time the Quakers won, but during the controversy a Presbyterian party was formed that later bore a decisive part of the battle for American independence.

The Quaker power in the colony was based upon a cleverly arranged system of inequities in representation in the colonial legislature. Those counties where the Quaker party was strong had more representatives than those where the party was weak. The popular majority of the Quakers' opponents, therefore, could not defeat them. The frontier counties where the Scotch-Irish group predominated, and the city of Philadelphia, where the middle and lower classes were very hostile to the dominant upper-class Quaker party, all had very meager representation. The popular party in the city and the frontiersmen, accordingly, united against the Quakers. In rapid succession this conflict passed through several phases.

The Quaker party had long sought to maintain good relations with the Indians by purchasing lands from them by treaty, by maintaining fair trade relations with them, and by keeping the German and Scotch-Irish settlers between the Indians and themselves as buffers. When the British Government, following the Peace of Paris, divided the lands on the frontier that were conquered from the French, they assigned the Indians a reserved belt of lands on the very fringe of the Scotch-Irish settlements in Pennsylvania, and left a vast " free " territory west of the Indian reservation for exploitation by itself. This act caused recriminations among the Quakers and Presbyterians of Pennsylvania, as each blamed the other for this strange act. The Quakers had planned to sell the lands now assigned to the Indians at a handsome profit, and the Scotch-Irish had planned to drive the Indians far west of their frontiers. The Quakers sought redress for their losses by trying to overthrow the proprietors of the colony in order to secure greater favors as a royal colony. The Presbyterians sought their redress in direct action against the Indians. Vigorous controversies were fought in the press and the Assembly as each party opposed the other's attempts at redress. The Presbyterians clung to the proprietary government, not so much because they favored it, but because they feared an increase in the Quaker power under crown control. The Quakers, in turn, adopted a policy of virtual indifference toward the frontiersmen's plea for protection against the Indians. The Assembly, now controlled once more by the Quakers, made no provision for military protection against the Indians. Furthermore, the Assembly forbade the governor to take any action, and refused to allow the frontiersmen to organize for their own defense. In Quaker eyes the Scotch-Irish were responsible for the Indian attacks and could halt them at any time by a better treatment of the Indians. The British Government refused to use any regular troops as garrisons against the Indians. Their reason perhaps was that they wished to keep on friendly terms with the Indians, leaving to the colonists the matter of frontier defense. No doubt the Scotch-Irish were unduly harsh in their treatment of the Indians. However, other factors entered in which were beyond the control of the frontier settlers. Much of the Indian depredations were due to long-standing attitudes built up in the days of the French and Indian War, to injuries done the Indians by traders, to the demoralizing influences of contact with the worse sort of white people, and especially to the sale of rum among the Indians.

Late in 1763 certain members of a volunteer frontier troop called the Paxton Boys received word from a scout that an Indian murderer had taken refuge in a Christian Indian village at Conestoga Manor, a Moravian missionary project. For some time this small group of "partially Christianized" Indians had been under criticism. During the war against the French it had been necessary to buy their allegiance with presents. Commissioners from the Colonial Assembly had investigated these Indians and found that some had been in arms against the English and were allied with tribes still hostile to the colony. Yet because they were few in number and were the objects of missionary endeavor, and because of the prevalent Quaker attitude, no move had ever been made to shift them back into Indian territory. When, therefore, the report came that an Indian murderer had been hidden in this Indian village, the Paxton Boys marched on the village. They murdered such of the Indians as they found in the village (only six were there at the time) and dispersed. The authorities quickly rounded up the remainder of the Conestoga Indians and placed them in the Lancaster jail for safety. A few weeks later the Paxton men marched on Lancaster. John Elder, the Presbyterian minister who had been active in the organization of the Paxton troop for the defense of the colonists, attempted to dissuade the men from their contemplated crime. At length he rode his own horse across the path of the men and retired only when their leader threatened to shoot his horse. At Lancaster fourteen unarmed Indians were brutally murdered in the jail. A general alarm was now sounded all through the colony and other Moravian Indians were hurriedly rushed into Philadelphia for safety. A large troop of frontiersmen marched on the city, compelling even Quakers to take up arms in defense of their city. At the time it was reported that large numbers of the lower classes in the city were prepared to join the Paxton men against the hated Quaker party. Franklin was able to persuade the Paxton men to lay their grievances before the Assembly and not resort to further violence. The Quaker-controlled Assembly made no effort to grant the frontiersmen any redress, but sought rather to punish them for the murder of the Indians. Popular sympathies were too strong, however, and the Paxton men went unpunished. Eventually the governor offered a bounty for Indian scalps, but nothing came of the entire incident save that it revealed the terrible weakness of the Quaker government. A long pamphlet war followed, in which the Paxton incident was made a Presbyterian venture by the Quakers. The Presbyterian party replied by citing the sufferings of the frontiersmen and the Quaker refusal to grant them any aid. Also the Presbyterian group continued to oppose the Quaker party's attempt to make Pennsylvania a royal colony. Franklin was appointed by the Assembly as agent for the colony in London. Since his mission was to secure a royal charter, the Presbyterians vigorously opposed his appointment. Franklin answered them in two pamphlets, accusing them of opposing him for his part in quelling the Paxton uprising, and charging also that the Presbyterians were seeking to become the established Church of the colony. During these struggles the Presbyterian party in the colony emerged as a faction strong enough to trade blows with the ruling Quaker party. Though still somewhat allied with the Anglicans, they were soon finally alienated from them by the renewal of the strife over an American bishop, and by the controversy over the Stamp Act.

The Anglicans had seen in the Presbyterian-Quaker contest some hopes for themselves. Thomas Barton, an S.P.G. missionary, wrote to London that both the Quakers and the Presbyterians were now in favor of an American bishop because each thought that it would weaken the other.[11] Barton's optimism was badly founded. From another quarter came a new call to battle against the bishops. For some time the S.P.G. had been under fire in the colonies and in Great Britain. It was being accused of violating its charter by devoting its efforts to the political interests of the Anglican Church in the colonies and not to the heathen and the unevangelized. In 1758, Archbishop Secker had written a long letter on the subject to President Johnson, of King's College, and he reverted to the subject again in 1763: " But indeed I fear the world will think we have settled too many Missions in New England and New York: and therefore it may be best, not absolutely to justifie, but to excuse ourselves in that respect, as prevailed on by Intreaties hard to be resisted, as having rejected many applications and resolved to be hereafter more sparing in the admission of them; instead of making it our business to *episcopize* New England, as Dr. Mayhew expresses himself. Our adversaries may be asked, whether they have not made as great mistakes in some points as we in this: and whether bitter Invectives against Them would not be unchristian." [12] By 1763 the American Dissenters, led by Jonathan Mayhew, of Boston, had aroused a very considerable controversy over the activities of the S.P.G., and in so doing had ushered in the final stage of the conflict over an American bishop.[13] Except in New York, where the S.P.G. was very active, the Presbyterians did not figure prominently in this controversy, although no doubt most of them followed its course with interest.

As the trend of colonial affairs brought the interests of the colonists and the home government more and more into conflict, the Presbyterians found themselves increasingly on the side of the colonial interests. Although the British Government had not given the Anglican Church much support in the colonies for some years, the Church had powerful connections with the London government, and was intent upon securing establishment, as Archbishop Secker plainly stated, in all the colonies. Whatever gains the Anglicans made in the middle colonies depended almost wholly upon London. They were a small minority in these colonies and could hope for little popular support for their plans. Inevitably, therefore, they had to cast their lot in with the Tory cause. The Whig opposition to an American episcopate and the growing agitation against the S.P.G., upon which so many of the Episcopal clergymen depended for support, only drove the Anglicans deeper into the Tory camp. Some of them went so far as to advocate the annulling of all the colonial charters and placing all the colonies in one nonchartered government directly under the crown. (This was later largely accomplished. Only Connecticut, Rhode Island, Pennsylvania, and Maryland escaped becoming crown colonies.) In 1763, Samuel Johnson urged Archbishop Secker to permit public agitation by the colonial Anglicans for such a program. "Is there then nothing more that can be done, either for obtaining Bishops, or demolishing these pernicious charter Governments, and reducing them all to one form, in immediate dependence on the King? I can't help calling them pernicious, for they are indeed so, as well to the best good of the people themselves, as to the interest of true Religion, as Your Grace remembers I formerly intimated in some Queries and Letters. I would hope Providence may some how bring it about that things may be compromised respecting the Ministry, and would it not now be a proper juncture for some such general address from the Clergy of these Provinces to the King, as I once mentioned to Your Grace? or is there not probability enough of success yet, with regard both to Bishops and Governours, to make it worth while for a Gentleman or two, (who I believe might be procured) to go from hence, to solicit the gaining these points? for I doubt nothing will do without solicitation from hence. Regard to these things, as soon as may be. — It is indeed too much to trouble Your Grace with these affairs, in your present infirm state; I therefore humbly beg your pardon that I am thus importunate. — I remember you once mentioned his Grace of York, as having an extraordinary Talent for Business, could not he be engaged to be active in these affairs?" [14]

Under such a crown government Johnson expected that the Church of England would be fully established. The loyalism of the colonial Anglicans, and their constant efforts to secure through the English hierarchy privileges that they could never secure from the people in the middle colonies, gave to the Whig cause a certain degree of religious sanction. A triumph for the London government could mean an intolerant Anglican establishment. A triumph for the Whigs would mean religious freedom. The support of American liberties against the government of George III became, therefore, for the Presbyterians a holy cause.

The first open identification of the Presbyterians, *as a Church,* with the cause of colonial liberties came during the Stamp Act controversy. The Presbyterians of Pennsylvania, who worked through the Proprietary Party, had taken a prominent part in the opposition to the act. The unhappy distributor for the stamps, John Hughes, reported to his London superiors: " When I received information, that the ship with the stamps was come up to the town that day, and that a mob would be collected, by beating muffled drums through the street, and ringing the state-house and church-bells muffled, which was accordingly done all afternoon, but at two o'clock the post arrived with the mail and packet, and, among other things, my Commission; . . . Accordingly the mob collected, chiefly Presbyterians and proprietary emissaries with the Chief Justice's [Mr. William Allen] son at their head, animating and encouraging the lower class. . . . Common justice calls upon me to say, the body of people called Quakers, seemed disposed to pay obedience to the stamp-act, and so do that part of the Church of England and baptists, that are not some way under proprietary influence. But presbyterians, and proprietary minions, spare no pains to engage the Dutch and lower class of people, and render the royal government odious, but at the same time profess great loyalty to the best of kings, and yet insinuate that his immediate government is intolerable." [15] In the New York and New Jersey areas Presbyterians had participated vigorously in the organizing of the Sons of Liberty. The Church officially took no action, however, until *after* the repeal of the Stamp Act.

In 1766 the synod took three very important steps to bring the Church as a Church into the struggle for American liberties. The first step was the approval of a motion by Francis Alison " that an address should be made to our Sovereign, on the Joyful occasion of the repeal of the Stamp Act, and thereby a confirmation of our liberties. . . ." [16] The Church placed itself on record in this address as considering the repeal of the Stamp Act as " a confirmation of our liberties." In other words, the repeal of the act was an admission that the act had been wrong. The Church was taking the stand of the Stamp Act Congress and the radical colonial party.

Next the synod sent out a pastoral letter to all the churches under their care. Deeply religious in tone, the letter was essentially a call to repentance and spiritual renewal. Implicit all through it, however, was the assumption that the justice of the colonial cause was a matter of common agreement among all Presbyterians.[17] The third step in the furtherance of the cause of colonial liberties was perhaps the most significant of all the three. The synod had met that year in New York City, convening on May 21. That very day the Anglican clergy also opened a small but very important gathering in the city. For some time the controversy over an American bishop had been going on at a white heat in New England, New York, and old England. The Anglicans had come to feel that time was running against them and that urgent steps must be taken. United action was required, it seemed, and so, the clergy of the Province of New York sent out a call to their brethren in New Jersey and Connecticut inviting them to a meeting in New York City.[18]

It was in answer to this call that fourteen Anglican clergymen from New York, New Jersey, and Connecticut had gathered to plan for such an intercolonial Anglican convention. They agreed to work together and in concert with other colonial Anglicans, and with British churchmen, in order to gain an American episcopate and other ends. How soon knowledge of this meeting reached the ears of the Presbyterian synod is not known. On the last day of the synod's sessions, May 30, "an overture was brought in to endeavour to obtain some correspondence between this Synod and the consociated churches in Connecticut. A copy of a letter from this Synod to them was also read and approved." [19] This move must have been under consideration at least long enough to have prepared a plan, and a letter, which could be accepted without debate. Word of this plan soon got abroad, in a garbled fashion evidently, for in August, Archbishop Secker wrote to William Smith, the Anglican leader in Philadelphia: "The clergy at New York have been alarmed with a Report that the American Dissenters are uniting themselves with the Kirk of Scotland, in hopes of obtaining by their means some new privileges from our Parliament. I do not apprehend any danger of that sort." [20]

In November the first convention of Presbyterians and Connecticut Congregationalists met at Elizabethtown, just a week after the first regular meeting of the Anglican convention in the same city. The Anglicans had drawn up petitions to be sent to the King, the archbishops, the bishops, the S.P.G., and the universities of Cambridge and Oxford, all praying for the granting of an American episcopate. They had also commissioned Thomas Chandler to write a popular pamphlet setting forth their case for bishops. The Congregationalist-Presbyterian " General Convention of Delegates " drew up a number of bylaws, stating that by this united effort no organic union was intended, and " that the general design of this Convention be to gain information of the public state of this united cause and interest; to collect accounts relating thereto; to unite our endeavors and counsels for spreading the Gospel and preserving the religious liberties of our Churches; to diffuse harmony and keep up a correspondence throughout this united body and with our friends abroad, to recommend, cultivate, and preserve loyalty and allegiance to the King's Majesty, and also to address the King or the King's Ministers from time to time with assurances of the unshaken loyalty of the pastors comprehended in this union and the churches under their care, and to vindicate them if unjustly aspersed." [21]

The convention sought to secure the co-operation of the other Congregationalists and Presbyterians of New England, and of the Dutch churches. Interestingly enough, the Anglican convention also had voted to invite the Dutch churches to align themselves with their convention. Letters were sent to the English Dissenters too, informing them of the founding of the General Convention and asking their aid in matters relating to the religious freedom of the colonies. No formal actions or resolutions on the issues discussed are recorded in the Minutes of the General Convention, but two letters written by individuals from it, intended as sample letters which others might follow in writing to their friends, give some idea of the attitudes of the delegates. No objection was being made to a wholly spiritual episcopate for the Anglicans. But, the delegates did not believe that the Anglicans really intended to stop with wholly spiritual bishops. If bishops were to be sent, some very strong Parliamentary guarantee of the religious freedom of non-Anglicans was utterly essential.[22]

All the forms of propaganda were now brought into play by both parties. Chandler's *Appeal to the Public* appeared in 1767 and touched off a hot pamphlet war. The New York Presbyterians continued " the American Whig " and other controversial literature. Also they renewed their appeal for a charter for their Church. The Bishop of London personally interceded to have the petition denied at the very time when the Anglicans were assuring one and all that American bishops would have no political interests or influences, and would respect fully the religious liberties of all non-Anglicans. In Philadelphia, Alison began the publication March 24, 1768, of a series of articles in the newspapers under the name "The Centinel." These two newspaper series, "The American Whig" and "The Centinel," attracted the attention of a much more popular audience than did the pamphlets that others were issuing. Also, these series, which were reprinted in several colonial newspapers, were much more political in tone than were the pamphlets.[23] William Smith, of Philadelphia, who had been answering his colleague Alison's "Centinel" in his own the "Anatomist," wrote to the secretary of the S.P.G. in London that the Presbyterians were attacking the Church about American bishops from one end of the continent to the other. A few months later he wrote again, saying that he wished the issue might never have been raised. Even so, he thought, all groups except the Presbyterians now favored American bishops, and even the Presbyterians might eventually be brought into line.[24] Smith was, however, quite mistaken in his hopes.

From New York, Alexander Mackrabie wrote to Sir Philip Francis: "Among the many disputes in this and the more northern parts of America, the religious are not the least. The zealous members of the Church of England are full of Apprehensions at the great and growing power of the Presbyterians. Don't imagine that I mean in any matters that regard Salvation; that Affair might have been left to shift for itself at Doomsday. The Alarm was taken at an Election lately; since which the Parties have raged with tolerable violence. The Church People, conscious that the Presbyterians, who have the Appointment of their own Ministers, must always outnumber them, are desirous of having some Person here vested with the Power of Ordination — but they don't like a Bishop, nor Ecclesiastical Courts, in short they don't know what they want. You remember Dean Swift was to have been made Bishop of Virginia. The Presbyterians should not be allowed to grow too great. They are all of Republican Principles. The Bostonians are Presbyterians."[25] Samuel Auchmuty wrote a few months later in a similar vein to Sir William Johnson: "The presbyterian party are determined (S——y, is one) to try all their Strength at this Election — Scot and others here, oppose the Delancey's Crugers, & the Church Interest."[26]

In New York a group of Presbyterian and Baptist laymen formed a "Society of Dissenters" in 1769. They planned to organize similar corresponding societies in other places and to keep the movement unified by committees of correspondence. The project lasted but a few months, however.[27]

The colonists of both parties and their friends in England fought most vigorously for some years over the episcopate. The issue was finally settled by the British government's desire to avoid any unnecessary antagonizing of the colonies. The Anglicans were greatly in the minority, and their opponents greatly in the majority, in the colonies. The Anglicans frequently argued that if their cause in the colonies was strengthened, they would bind the people more fully to the crown. Though they were quite mistaken in this,[28] it does reveal the close connection in the minds of colonial Anglicans between their cause and the cause of the British government. By promising to support the crown and Parliament in the colonies they were in effect asking also for bishops powerful enough to fulfill such promises. Almost the entire urge for American bishops had come from the middle and New England colonies where the Anglicans were very weak, and the Dissenters had a great many strong churches. From the southern colonies, where the Anglican Church was established, either opposition or little or no enthusiasm greeted the proposals for an episcopate. Nearly all those involved in pleading for bishops were missionaries supported by the S.P.G. in strong Presbyterian and Congregationalist areas. Here they also used all possible means of opposing legitimate Dissenting interests, such as the chartering of colleges, churches, and benevolent funds (the New Jersey fund for ministers' widows and children). If, therefore, the attitude of the S.P.G. missionaries who were campaigning for bishops was a criterion of what the bishops' attitudes would be, no mere spiritual episcopate was intended. Moreover, the intense loyalism of many of these Anglican missionaries was not without significance. In fact, both Archbishop Secker and Thomas Chandler, to say nothing of others, rather plainly hinted that they had no intention that the bishops should *remain* purely spiritual, and that they should never have authority under an establishment which would include all the colonies. An American bishop devoid of the power of his English fellows would be hazardous even for the English bishops. English Dissenters would soon be asking that the American plan of the wholly spiritual episcopate be adopted for England.[29] The most important result of the controversy over the episcopate was that the Presbyterian and Congregationalist Churches had become fully convinced that religious liberty for them stood or fell with the civil liberties of the colonies.[30] As the tension between London and the colonies increased, the Presbyterians became more vigorous in their support of all organizations and plans for the " preservation of our liberties." The close working arrangements with the Connecticut Congregationalists were continued, as were also those with the British Dissenters.

14

IN FREEDOM'S HOLY CAUSE

While among the Presbyterians there was general agreement that the liberties of the colonies must be defended, great differences soon began to appear among them as to the ultimate meaning of that defense. In each of the middle colonies, by the year 1770, three rather distinct parties were forming among colonists of all backgrounds. One group was outright loyalist, desiring a complete victory for the London government, and not averse to seeing the British take drastic action to compel obedience. Another moderate, or conservative, group, usually drawn from the upper classes of the seaboard areas, hoped for a solution that would give the colonies great local autonomy under a modified British rule. This group feared the local demands of the frontiersmen, and the restless lower classes of the cities, more even than they did the British. The third party, the radicals, were found among the working classes of the cities, and on the frontiers. This group had grievances against both the British government and the ruling classes of the colonies. The moderate group feared to be left at the mercy of the radicals, and clung, therefore to the British government as a means of keeping the radical party's colonial program in check. The radical party, enjoying a large popular majority, was in favor of a complete revolution, in which control would pass from the conservatives to themselves. Presbyterians were represented in all these parties, though less than half a dozen of their leading laymen and clergymen were loyalists. The Presbyterian problem was the choice between conservative and radical.

In New York, the three leading lay Presbyterians all through the struggle had been William Livingston, John Morin Scott, and William Smith. Livingston moved to New Jersey and became an active radical. Scott was a New York radical, and William Smith was soon to become an outright loyalist. The colony of New York was so torn by its various parties that it alone of the thirteen colonies declined to vote on the Declaration of Independence on July 4, 1776. Presbyterian sentiment was divided between conservative and radical. Smith's position was shared by very few.

John Witherspoon had reached American shores in 1768. Yet, within a few years he had joined with Livingston, Abraham Clark (a layman from Elizabethtown), and ministers such as Jacob Green, Elihu Spencer, and Alexander McWhorter, in the radical independence party in New Jersey. The conservative Presbyterian layman, Elias Boudinot, was greatly dismayed by the activity of the Presbyterian ministers. In June of 1776 he wrote to James Caldwell, a Presbyterian minister soon to distinguish himself for unusual radical activities: " Our clergy unhappily have gone distracted, and have done us more injury than I am afraid they will do us good, in a great while. They have verified what our Enemies have so often prognosticated. We have been quarreling with the Ch. of England these 40 years past, about uniting Civill and Ecclesiastical Power, and now at the moment we have the shadow of Power in our Hands, we are running into the same extreme. Six or seven clergymen set up for candidates at the late election among whom three were elected viz: Dr. Witherspoon (who is at the Bottom of it) Mr. Green and Dominie Hardenburg. This has given amazing offence and has raised a cry agt our clergy that must ruin their influence in every station." [1] Boudinot had had a brush with Witherspoon earlier that year, in March, when the latter had tried to swing a county delegation to espouse outright independence from England.[2] Witherspoon, as Boudinot complained, early became the leader of the radical group in New Jersey, and by 1776 was the most prominent Presbyterian Revolutionary leader. Under his administration the College of New Jersey had become a hotbed of radical sentiment. (The college was the least localized of any in America at the time, both in the sources of its students and in the distribution of its alumni. Roughly one fourth of its alumni were resident in New England, one half in the middle colonies, and one fourth in the southern colonies.)[3] The British troops on Long Island, on July 30, 1776, did him the honor of burning him in effigy as though haranguing a row of effigies of no less important colonials than Washington, Lee, and Putnam!

The struggle between conservative and radical was nowhere greater than in Pennsylvania, where it sorely divided Presbyterians. Of loyalist sentiment there seems to have been little, although Chief Justice William Allen, who was a member of the old First Church, became a loyalist. A strong conservative party led by James Wilson, also a member of First Church, was matched with a strong party of radicals, among whose most ardent leaders was Daniel Roberdeau, an elder in the Second Church. Charles Thomson and Thomas McKean, of the First Church, were also active in the conservative party. George Duffield's prayers and preaching in Third Church vastly pleased the New England ultraradical John Adams. Perhaps it was Duffield who preached on Esther 4:3: "And in every province, whithersoever the king's commandment and his decree came, there was great mourning," on June 1, 1774, the day the Boston Port Bill was put in force.[4] So keen was the struggle between conservative and radical that as late as June 8, 1776, Wilson joined with four other conservatives to vote the Pennsylvania delegation in the Continental Congress five to two against independence. Not until the night of July 3 was Wilson finally persuaded to vote for independence. The power of the conservatives in Pennsylvania was broken only when the Continental Congress moved to recognize the radical party as the power in control of Pennsylvania. The entire movement toward independence was delayed for some time by the intransigence of the Pennsylvania conservatives.[5]

Of the sentiments of Presbyterians in Maryland, where a ruling conservative party halted between a radical party, to whom they had long denied many legitimate rights, and a dislike of British policy, no clear record remains. The Church was, for that matter, not strong in the colony. Patrick Allison, of Baltimore, was later very active in the cause of independence, and may also have been at this time.

Virginia was very early forthright in demanding total independence from Great Britain, in spite of the fact that the colony had some disaffected inhabitants in its back country. Though these, heavily Presbyterian, early forced their grievances into the foreground, both the internal and the continental revolutions were allowed to develop simultaneously. In Hanover Presbytery, and among the Presbyterians of the Valley of Virginia, radical sentiment was strong.

Trouble of long standing existed between the coastal areas of the two Carolinas and the interior. The ill-fated Regulator Movement of 1768 had involved many Scotch-Irish Presbyterian settlers in North Carolina. The handling they had received from Governor Tryon and the seaboard conservatives had left many bitter memories. During the struggle four prominent Presbyterian ministers had publicly appealed to the Regulators to abandon their tactics, and had been of real support to Tryon and the conservatives.[6] In this same colony were a rather large number of settlers from the Scottish Highlands, all of whom were loyalists. For the conservatives, therefore, the situation in 1775 was most precarious.

South Carolina also had contingents of Regulators, some of whom were Presbyterians, in its back country. To these were sent, in 1775, two clerical ambassadors, William Tennent, III, and William Henry Drayton. Their task was to win the people of the back country to the support of the Continental Congress. The mission was not particularly successful. Ministerial eloquence had little effect upon minds and hearts in which still flamed the memories of the ruthless beating down of the Regulators, and a total disregard of their claims.[7]

Even though the mission of Tennent and Drayton was no great success, Joseph Hewes, a delegate to the Continental Congress from North Carolina, felt that a similar effort should be made in his colony. Through his efforts the Congress asked the German Reformed, the Lutheran, and the Presbyterian Churches to send ministers to urge these people of the back country to take the colonial side.[8]

In November of 1775 the Continental Congress resolved, " That two ministers of the Gospel be applied to, to go immediately amongst the regulators and highlanders in the colony of North Carolina, for the purpose of informing them of the nature of the present dispute between Great Britain and the colonies; that the gentlemen to be employed be allowed each forty dollars a month for their services, and that the delegates of the said colony be empowered to apply to and procure persons proper for this business." [9] George Duffield, a chaplain to the Congress, was asked to nominate the two emissaries. The day after Christmas an emergency meeting of New Brunswick Presbytery was held in order to permit Elihu Spencer to go on this mission. The presbytery noted that he was " immediately to take a Journey thither [N. C.] and preach, and converse some time among those People, as their Case is extremely critical. The Presbytery most chearfully aquiesced with the motion." [10] Spencer's companion was Alexander McWhorter, of Newark, whose views were thoroughly radical. The men had been on missionary journeys in these areas before, and therefore had some established contacts. For nearly six months these two men labored at their assigned task, but they seem to have had little success. Hewes also got the four Presbyterian ministers of Philadelphia to write to the disaffected North Carolinians.[11]

In Mecklenburg County, North Carolina, however, the Presbyterians were early in the radical fold. Even though the so-called Mecklenburg Declaration of Independence has been proved spurious, the " Resolutions " put out by that body on May 31, 1776, are ample witness of extreme radical sentiment among these Presbyterians.

In the struggle, therefore, all through the middle and southern colonies, between the conservative and the radical parties, Presbyterians were found in both camps. Moreover, no very clear pattern seems to have existed by which the allegiance of a given individual or group might be forecast. Presbyterians of New England and Huguenot backgrounds were found in each party, as were also those of Scottish and Scotch-Irish descent. The simple assumptions often made that the Presbyterians were colonial patriots because they were Scotch-Irish in origin is not borne out by a study of the period.[12] Neither were all those affected by the liberalizing influences of the Great Awakening to be found in the radical camp. When the war for independence finally did come, Presbyterians of every origin were in the patriot ranks, and again no pattern of racial background can be successfully demonstrated.

The synod of 1775 was very poorly attended. It met in New York City on May 17, and numbered but thirty members, twenty-four ministers and six elders. A few late-comers straggled in, and a number of members left early. From areas south of New Brunswick Presbytery only four ministers were present. The battles of Lexington and Bunker Hill had been fought, and feeling was running high throughout the colonies. Yet even in the Continental Congress, which had reconvened seven days earlier, with more radical members than ever before, outspoken desires for independence and separation from Great Britain were still very few. The synod issued a pastoral letter which reflected quite accurately the opinions of most Presbyterians at that time. Witherspoon and a rather capable committee had drafted it. The letter opened by stating that the synod felt " that they could not discharge their duty to the numerous congregations under their care, without addressing them at this important crisis." Civil war seemed imminent and only God's hand could stay it. Repentance, and a return to God seeking his mercy, were urgently called for. " The Synod cannot help thinking that this is a proper time for pressing all of every rank, seriously to consider the things that belong to their eternal peace. Hostilities, long feared, have now taken place; the sword has been drawn in one province, and the whole continent, with hardly any exception, seem determined to defend their rights by force of arms. If, at the same time, the British ministry shall continue to enforce their claims by violence, a lasting and bloody contest must be expected. Surely, then, it becomes those who have taken up arms, and profess a willingness to hazard their lives in the cause of liberty, to be prepared for death, which to many must be certain, and to every one is a possible or probable event.

" We have long seen with concern, the circumstances which occasioned, and the gradual increase of this unhappy differnce. As ministers of the gospel of peace, we have ardently wished that it could, and often hoped that it would have been more early accommodated. It is well known to. you, (otherwise it would be imprudent indeed thus publicly to profess,) that we have not been instrumental in inflaming the minds of the people, or urging them to acts of violence and disorder. Perhaps no instance can be given on so interesting a subject, in which political sentiments have been so long and so fully kept from the pulpit, and even malice itself has not charged us with labouring from the press; but things are now come to such a state, that as we do not wish to conceal our opinions as men and citizens, so the relation we stand in to you seemed to make the present improvement of it to your spiritual benefit, an indispensable duty.

" Suffer us then to lay hold of your present temper of mind, and to exhort, especially the young and vigorous, by assuring them that there is no soldier so undaunted as the pious man, no army so formidable as those who are superior to the fear of death. There is nothing more awful to think of, than that those whose trade is war should be despisers of the name of the Lord of hosts, and that they should expose themselves to the imminent danger of being immediately sent from cursing and cruelty on the earth, to the blaspheming rage and despairing horror of the infernal pit. Let therefore, every one, who from generosity of spirit, or benevolence of heart, offers himself as a champion in his country's cause, be persuaded to reverence the name, and walk in the fear of the Prince of the kings of the earth, and then he may, with the most unshaken firmness, expect the issue either in victory or death.

" Let it not be forgotten, that though for the wise ends of his Providence it may please God, for a season to suffer his people to lie under unmerited oppression, yet in general we may expect, that those who fear and serve him in sincerity and truth, will be favoured with his countenance and strength. It is both the character and the privilege of the children of God, that they call upon him in the day of trouble, and he, who keepeth covenant and truth for ever, has said, that his ears are always open to their cry. We need not mention to you in how many instances the event in battles, and success in war, have turned upon circumstances which were inconsiderable in themselves, as well as out of the power of human prudence to foresee or direct, because we suppose you firmly believe that after all the counsels of men, and the most probable and promising means, the Lord will do that which seemeth him good; nor hath his promise ever failed of its full accomplishment; ' the Lord is with you while ye be with him, and if ye seek him he will be found of you; but if ye forsake him he will forsake you [II Chron. 15:2].' "

Following this pastoral exhortation the synod offered a few advices. The first was a plea for loyalty to the King, " who has merited well of his subjects on many accounts, and who has probably been misled into the late and present measures by those about him; neither have we any doubt that they themselves have been in a great degree deceived by false information from interested persons residing in America." Coupled with this plea was a forthright disavowal of any "desire of separation from the parent state. . . . Let it ever appear, that you only desire the preservation and security of those rights which belong to you as freemen and Britons, and that reconciliation upon these terms is your most ardent desire."

The second "advice" was a plea for solidarity among the colonies. "And in particular, as the Continental Congress, now sitting at Philadelphia, consists of delegates chosen in the most free and unbiased manner, by the body of the people, let them not only be treated with respect, and encouraged in their difficult service — not only let your prayers be offered up to God for his direction in their proceedings — but adhere firmly to their resolutions; and let it be seen that they are able to bring out the whole strength of this vast country to carry them into execution. We would also advise for the same purpose, [i.e., colonial solidarity] that a spirit of candour, charity, and mutual esteem, be preserved and promoted towards those of different religious denominations." Union of the various religious groups in this cause is necessary, the synod said, "for there is no example in history, in which civil liberty was destroyed, and the rights of conscience preserved entire."

Advices three and four called for a reformation of manners, and for "a regard to order and the public peace," for the conscientious payment of just debts, and mutual service to one another, "so that the evils inseparable from a civil war may not be augmented by wantoness and irregularity."

The fifth advice pleaded for humanity and mercy in the struggle: "We think it of importance, at this time, to recommend to all of every rank, but especially to those who may be called to action, a spirit of humanity and mercy. Every battle of the warrior is with confused noise, and garments rolled in blood. It is impossible to appeal to the sword without being exposed to many scenes of cruelty and slaughter; but it is often observed, that civil wars are carried on with a rancour and spirit of revenge much greater than those between independent states. The injuries received, or supposed, in civil wars, wound more deeply than those of foreign enemies, it is therefore the more necessary to guard against this abuse, and recommend that meekness and gentleness of spirit, which is the noblest attendant on true valour. That man will fight most bravely, who never fights till it is necessary, and who ceases to fight as soon as the necessity is over."

Lastly, the synod urged the Church to frequent public and private seasons of prayer, and closed with their own prayer "that the present unnatural dispute may be speedily terminated by an equitable and lasting settlement on constitutional principles."

The spirit and tone of this letter are notable. There is about it a sincerity and a calmness springing from a conviction that, whatever lies before them, the event is in God's hands. Their problem is to carry out their part as befits Christians. Loyalty to the King is asked, but the British Parliament is ignored. Colonial solidarity is stressed, and confidence in, and obedience to, the Continental Congress are called for. Repentance, reform, legal and orderly procedures, humanity and mercy, and prevailing prayer are urged upon all as they face the oncoming civil war.

The letter was approved, though one minister, Jeremiah Halsey, was hardy enough to enter his dissent from the "declarations of allegiance." Others very probably also had their doubts on the matter, but the letter did represent the general position of the entire Presbyterian Church. Politically it was abreast of most colonial opinion.[13]

During the next few months the failure of the colonial conservatives' "Olive branch petition," the King's proclamation of rebellion, and the Continental Congress' "Declaration of Causes and Necessity of Taking Up Arms" brought the radical party's hopes closer to fulfillment. Thomas Paine's *Common Sense* appeared, and served to spur the radicals to redoubled efforts. Witherspoon was especially active.[14] On the fast day appointed by the Congress for May 17, 1776, he for the first time brought his political views into the pulpit. Two months earlier he had urged total independence at a meeting of political leaders, but in this sermon he took the more moderate stand of the Pastoral Letter of 1775. He did, however, give the enormous weight of his prestige to the bringing of politics into the pulpit. Others had, of course, done it before, but they were lesser men in influence than he. In its printed form this sermon had appended to it a plea to the colonials of Scottish descent. He notes that the name "Scotch" is becoming a term of reproach "these days," because it is felt that the American Scots are far less concerned for liberty than are the colonists from England and Ireland. He urges his Scottish brethren to support the American cause because: (1) It is necessary; (2) It will be honorable and profitable; (3) It will in all probability work out to the final advantage even of Great Britain. The American cause is not just another Wilkes affair. Throughout the Revolutionary period the indifference and loyalism of the Scots weighed upon Witherspoon's mind.[15]

In July he returned to the Continental Congress just in time to vote for the Declaration of Independence. (Unfortunately the widely celebrated "nick of time" speech which he is supposed to have delivered on this occasion is, according to his biographer V. L. Collins, "a legend.") Thereafter he was seldom out of the government until the critical phases of the war were over. He was the only clergyman, and the only college president, who occupied any significant position in the Continental Congress and the government which it established. His character as a minister was ever apparent both by the full clericals which he always wore and by his carefully expressed ideas.

Once the colonies had decided to declare their independence, the conservative Presbyterians swung behind the Congress almost to a man. Charles Inglis, an Anglican clergyman, writing from New York in October 31, 1776, found Presbyterian opinion quite solid: " I have it from good authority that the Presbyterian ministers, at a synod where most of the middle colonies were collected, passed a resolve to support the Continental Congress in all their measures. This and only this can account for the uniformity of their conduct; for I do not know one of them, nor have I been able, after strict inquiry, to hear of any, who did not, by preaching and every effort in their power, promote all the measures of the congress, however extravagant." [16] Since the synod of 1776 took no formal notice of political affairs, the memory of the plea for the support of Congress contained in the Pastoral Letter of 1775 must have lingered long in loyalist minds. Ambrose Serle, a newly arrived respresentative of Lord Dartmouth, may have caught something of the New York Anglican attitude, for in November he wrote to Dartmouth: " The war is . . . at the Bottom very much a religious War; and every one looks to the Establishment of his own Party upon the issue of it. And indeed, upon the Issue, some one Party ought to predominate, were it only for the Conservation of Peace. It is perhaps impossible to keep the ecclesiastical Polity out of the Settlement, without endangering the Permanency of the civil." Later, Serle wrote (April, 1777), " When the war is over, there must be a great Reform established, ecclesiastical as well as civil; for, though it has not been much considered at Home, Presbyterianism is really at the Bottom of this whole Conspiracy, has supplied it with Vigor, and will never rest, till something is decided upon it." [17]

The Virginia Presbyterians now moved to secure full liberty for their colony. After Davies' victory over intolerance in 1755, rather liberal toleration of Presbyterians had been obtained. But it was still only toleration by the grace of an established Church. Beginning in 1768, the Anglicans had adopted very severe measures against the Baptists, and all Dissenters became restless. In 1773, 1774, and 1775 remonstrances were sent up to the Assembly asking for religious freedom. When in 1775 the full benefits of the English Act of Toleration were offered to Dissenters by the Assembly, the Presbyterians flatly demanded freedom. To the first meeting of the Virginia General Assembly under the new constitution, which met on October 7, 1776, the Presbytery of Hanover presented a memorial asking for full religious freedom. After citing the Declaration of Rights in the new constitution, and the unfairness of the present establishment of the Anglican Church, the presbytery said, " In this enlightened age, and in a land where all, of every denomination are united in the most strenuous efforts to be free, we hope and expect that our representatives will cheerfully concur in removing every species of religious, as well as civil bondage." They argued that the basic theory of an established religion would be as valid for a Mohammedan or Roman Catholic establishment as for any. The Virginia establishment had seriously handicapped the colony, by making settlers hesitant about entering it. The Gospel needed not the aid of the State, and for themselves the Presbyterians desired none. They did desire the disestablishment of any and the freedom of all.[18] It was not until after much toil that this freedom came, ten long years later.

The attitudes of the North Carolina Presbyterians stirred Governor Martin to write Lord Dartmouth: "I cannot therefore, help observing to your Lordship the Congeniality of the principles of the Church of England with our form of government. To the reproach of the professors of Christianity on both sides . . . distinctions and animosities have immemorially prevailed in this country between the people of the established Church and the Presbyterians on the score of the difference of their unessential modes of Church Government, and the same spirit of division has entered into or been transferred to most other concernments; at present there is no less apparent schism between their Politics than in matters appertaining to religion, and while Loyalty, Moderation and respect to Government seem to distinguish the generality of the members of the Church of England, I am sincerely sorry to find that they are by no means the characters of the Presbyterians at large, whence . . . the people of this denomination in general throughout the continent are not of the principles of the Church of Scotland, but like the people of New England, more of the leaven of the Independents, who according to the English story have ever been unfriendly to Monarchical Government."[19]

There was indeed something inherent in Presbyterianism that made the cause of colonial independence congenial to it. Apart from the issue of religious freedom which played so large a role, and from the Puritan-Scotch-Irish dislike for much that England had hitherto meant to them, and from the various social and economic factors which had come to the surface in the conservative-radical controversy in the middle colonies — apart from all these, there was in the underlying current of colonial political thought a basic note which the Presbyterians could recognize as their own. The idea that a people suffering under a tyrant had the right to resist him through their legally constituted representatives was traditional Calvinism. It was in fact rooted in certain views of John Calvin himself. Calvinism had coupled with that conviction two others, namely, that there is no lawful government without a mutual compact freely entered into by king and people, and that government must be based upon a fundamental written law. These three tenets were founded upon natural law, and were therefore considered as God-given natural rights. For their elucidation and application to specific historical circumstances reason and conscience (enlightened by the Scriptures) were the divinely provided guides. This scheme of thought had been further developed by many thinkers before Locke gave to it the form that played so great a part in the thinking of American Whigs.[20] When, therefore, Jefferson wove these ideas into the Declaration of Independence, Presbyterians recognized at once their Calvinistic theology and their Whig political theory. This recognition only fortified their conviction, previously drawn in their struggle against the appointment of an Anglican bishop for the colonies, that the cause of American independence had become a holy cause.

Though the struggle for independence was thus wholeheartedly sanctioned as a Christian " calling " by the Presbyterians, bounds were always set beyond which the Church would not go. Church and State were two separate and distinct entities, and this separation was not only to be observed but also to be most jealously guarded. Therefore, little or no action referring to the war appears in any extant presbytery or synod record. Pastoral letters, summons to fast days and prayer meetings, commissions for chaplains, and other such official acts are frequent, but seldom does an official body seem to have gone further. All other activity in the war was on an individual and civic level. Even the most ardent patriots among the clergy withdrew from politics, Witherspoon among them, at the close of the war. True, three or four did not, but neither did they continue as ministers.

The complete record of the Presbyterian contribution to the Revolutionary War can never be reconstructed. Laymen and clergy alike bore a share in the struggle disproportionate even to their great numbers. From Generals Morgan and Roberdeau to the humblest drafted private who mutinied with the Pennsylvania line in 1781 or shouted in triumph at Cowpens, Presbyterians saw action from Quebec to North Carolina. Elias Boudinot, who at one time had charge of caring for the prisoners of war, advanced over $30,000 for their care. Though many a heroic deed is now forgotten, records do remain of significant participation in the struggle for independence of over one third of the clergy. Their services range from active duty in the line of battle, on through service in the chaplaincy, in colonial and state assemblies and conventions, in the Continental Congress as chaplains, and into such fields as recruiting, buoying up the morale of civilian and soldier, and the work of propaganda. The chaplaincy of the Continental Army was quite haphazard at first, and never did become particularly well organized. Yet many Presbyterian ministers served tours of duty with the Army. Some of the leading clergymen of the Church, such as John Rodgers, as well as young ministers ordained in haste for the purpose, shared the hardships of field and camp with the Army.[21] A number of the clergy lost their lives in the war. James Caldwell and John Rosbrough were murdered while on noncombatant duty. Both were known as ardent patriots. Their murders, and that of Caldwell's wife, were among the worst of the war's atrocities. No less than forty commissioned officers during the war are said to have come from Caldwell's congregation. Charles McKnight died of the effects of a brutal imprisonment. Others met with similar fates, though perhaps none met with quite the same vengeance as did Ebenezer Prime, who died while the British were in occupation of his Long Island parish. The British commandant, later Count Rumford, Undersecretary of State, had come so to hate the patriot clergyman that he placed his headquarters in the church graveyard, and made Prime's tombstone his doorstep, in order, he said, " to have the pleasure of treading on the old rebel as often as [I] went in and out." [22] Jacob Green had more to do perhaps with the drafting of the New Jersey constitution than any other man. Some clergymen, such as Hugh H. Brackenridge and Joseph Montgomery, became so involved in political affairs that they never returned to the ministry.

One of the great contributions of the Presbyterian clergy during the war was made through printed sermons and addresses. Here, of course, Witherspoon's part was the most impressive, but many others made useful contributions. These publications served to nerve the troops and to steady the morale of the populace, by instilling in all a sense of the rightness before God of the American cause, and of its final victory. The irresponsibility, extreme individualism, and selfishness of the colonial party, both in the Army and at home, were vigorously attacked from a Christian point of view. Also the fair picture was held out of the nation that was to be beyond the struggle. Seldom, though at times, did the preacher forget to sound an authentic Christian note of the Gospel, its call for repentance, renewal, and godly living. Hugh H. Brackenridge closed one of his sermons as a chaplain by saying: " Lastly, [the war] suggests to us a motive to repentance. It seems to me our cause shall prosper, and be finally successful; yet cloudy days of suffering may be in reserve before us. I do not by any means expect a sudden issue to the contest. . . . What will it profit [an American], if he escape the taxation of Great Britain; but in the meantime, must lie down in sorrow, and pay the debt, due to God's justice in the flame of hell. In time of war, or in time of peace, there is no safety but in Christ. As some countryman, who travels in the stormy night, when the wind shakes the forest, and the rain beats upon him, would hasten to the shelter of a rock, where he may be safe from the hurricane, and the forked lightnings, which play above the mountain; so it becomes every one in the day of storm and sore commotion, to fly swiftly to the rock Christ Jesus, and seek for refuge, in the merit, and peace speaking blood of a redeemer." [23]

As the line of battle moved up and down through the middle colonies, the orderly life of the Church was badly broken up. The synod were able to bring off their annual meetings by shifting the locale according to the prevailing military situation. Attendances, however, were often very meager. The Presbyterians on Long Island were severely harassed by the long occupation. The Suffolk Presbytery ceased to function during the occupation. Dutchess Presbytery, lying in the Hudson Valley, likewise were unable to carry on. New York Presbytery managed to function largely in their New Jersey area. Their records previous to 1775 disappeared, a serious loss in view of the great importance of that presbytery in the history of the Church. The territory of New Brunswick Presbytery saw some of the fiercest fighting of the war, yet the presbytery maintained a fairly regular schedule of meetings. Philadelphia First Presbytery, led by men such as Sproat and Duffield, showed an amazing vitality. Though they were forced at times to meet in distant places, this presbytery continued their usual functions, going on with their examination and ordination of candidates, ordering of supply preaching and other functions in spite of all odds. Philadelphia Second Presbytery, hardly a presbytery but rather a political bloc in the Church, ceased functioning for the entire war period. New Castle and Lewes Presbyteries were in regions that were often the scenes of heavy fighting, yet they found it possible to maintain some form of organization. Lewes Presbytery enjoyed a distinction, perhaps unique among all the presbyteries, in that on March 26, 1776, a military company attended the session of presbytery in order to hear Matthew Wilson preach. Donegal Presbytery, situated in an area that was seldom a battleground, went on their way much as usual. In Virginia, Hanover Presbytery enjoyed a similar freedom, as did also Orange Presbytery.

In the regions that at one time or another were occupied by the British the Presbyterians' reputation cost them sorely. In most of these areas Presbyterian churches were desecrated, and often wantonly destroyed. Only hatred of the Presbyterian denomination as such can account for many of these acts of vandalism. The Huntington, Long Island, church was wrecked, and its stones used to build a blockhouse in the midst of its cemetery. Tombstones were used to floor ovens in such a manner that the bread would show the inscription marks. The First Church in New York was used as a stable, as was also the New Brunswick church. The Pennington and Hopewell churches were needlessly violated and wrecked. The Elizabethtown church was burned to the ground. At Princeton the college suffered severely, and the church as well. Wherever British troops came in the course of the war, the results for Presbyterians were the same.[24]

Beyond the physical destruction of property, the war created great difficulties for the churches financially. Inflation destroyed much of the whole basis of church finances. First Church, Philadelphia, in 1779, voted to make pew rents fifteen times what they had formerly been. Ewing, the pastor, received no salary from May 1, 1777, to January 31, 1780. Fortunately, he had also his position at the College of Philadelphia, and thus was able to subsist. James Sproat, at Second Church, found his salary badly in arrears as early as June, 1776. Similar conditions prevailed all through the Church. The load of these past arrears, plus the cost of rebuilding ruined churches and manses, laid a staggering burden upon the Presbyterians. They were years in liquidating these debts.

Though entered into slowly, and eventually prosecuted with a zeal born of the conviction that it was a holy cause, the struggle for American independence had been a costly one for the Presbyterians. That they would demand a high price for their contribution seemed only too likely to some Americans who disliked them. During the radical-conservative debates of 1775 the Pennsylvania Quaker party had charged that the Presbyterians and Congregationalists were seeking for themselves the status of established Churches.[25] As the war drew on to a victorious conclusion, these old charges were renewed by various parties so insistently that the synod of 1783 made an explicit and official disclaimer of any such desire or plan. The minute had actually been recorded in 1781, expunged in 1782, and finally restored in 1783.[26] No one desired an establishment. The issue during these three years had been whether or not it was consistent with the dignity of the synod to take official action aimed at mere rumors.[27]

It has often been said that the Presbyterian form of government greatly influenced the formation of the American form of representative government. A more careful examination of the evidence fails to vindicate the claim as such. Rather is it true that Calvinistic ideas of the State had become thoroughly blended into current political theory, especially that of Locke, and that the framers of the Constitution leaned heavily upon those political theorists who had been influenced most by Calvin. Of direct influence of American Presbyterian ecclesiastical polity upon the framers of the Constitution none can be traced.

A number of Presbyterian elders and laymen did serve in the Continental Congress and in the Constitutional Convention. A considerable body of the writings of these men has been preserved, and in these there is no indication that Presbyterian polity influenced their political thinking. The two men most responsible for drawing up the Constitution of the United States were James Wilson and James Madison. Wilson, who had been a Presbyterian until about 1782, and perhaps an elder, was an Episcopalian at the time when he did his definitive work on the Constitution. His writings show no influence from Presbyterian ecclesiastical polity.[28]

James Madison was also an Episcopalian, but since he had been a student at the College of New Jersey under Witherspoon, some have asserted that he had been influenced by Presbyterian ideas of polity under Witherspoon. Unfortunately, Witherspoon himself is a witness against this view. In May of 1776, while seeking money and students from non-Presbyterians in Bermuda, he gave his solemn word and pledge that no discussion whatever of the topic of Church government was allowed in the school, much less was the Presbyterian form promoted. "Every question about forms of church government is so entirely excluded, that, . . . if they [the students] know nothing more of religious controversy than what they learned here, they have that Science wholly to begin." [29] He asserts that not then, nor ever in the history of the school, has there been any denominational bias expressed. As further proof of his plea, he cites the fact that there have been many Episcopalian graduates of the school, including a number then serving as Anglican clergymen. Men like Madison and the other students of Witherspoon who served on the Constitutional Convention had, therefore, not learned Presbyterian polity from him. As in the Declaration of Independence, so in the Constitution, Calvinistic political theory had influenced all political thought of the day. The theological doctrine of natural law and the political theory of natural rights provided the meeting place for Presbyterian and citizen rather than the Presbyterian form of Church government. New England Congregationalists and Virginia Episcopalians stood with American Presbyterian laymen in this political theory, and with this common heritage they were able to work together although their heritages in ecclesiastical polity still separated them widely.

15

THE CHURCH IN THE CONFEDERATION

The closing of the Revolutionary War brought on a period of readjustment for which many of the colonists were ill-prepared. The Presbyterian Church, rooted as it was in areas where the war damage had been great and where the difficulties of readjustment became very serious, suffered severely during this period. Beyond the physical losses and the financial handicaps lay the Church's most appalling problem, the destitution of spirit. Most of the clergy had entered vigorously into the war, whether on the war front or on the home front, and not a few had seen service in the lines of battle. The war had become a holy cause. In sermon and in political address the justice of the colonial cause had been maintained, the assurances of God's favor exhibited, and a future for the Americans big with promise had been foretold. Not only because of the clergy's influence but from the deepest motives of their own, the lay Presbyterians had entered into the war with zeal. It was peculiarly difficult, therefore, for this Church to face the situation that prevailed in the early years of the Confederation.

Many of the Presbyterians felt deeply that the triumph of the colonies against the mother country was due to God's providence. Yet on the other hand the war had brought on a loosening of the moral tone of the colonists, and a severe decline in their spiritual life. Some of the greatest of the colonial leaders were avowedly deists. Thomas Jefferson, Thomas Paine, Ethan Allen, and many lesser lights had played a significant role in the winning of independence, yet they were openly opposed to much that was dearest to the Presbyterians. The French, to whose timely aid so great a part of the colonial victory was due, had been a baneful influence indeed upon the religious life of the new nation. Skepticism and cynicism had become the marks of " breadth " and " culture." Furthermore the inevitable concomitants of civil war had opened up great seams in the social life of many communities, revealing the enormity of the greed and pettiness of many Americans, who smuggled, profiteered, betrayed, sold and were sold, according as the fortunes of war and inflation dictated.

While, therefore, the Presbyterian Church emerged from the war years with a deep sense of gratitude to God for the victory won against England, there was no mistaking the fact that for it the spiritual warfare of those years had been a decimating defeat. Though it was highly respected throughout the thirteen colonies for its contributions to the winning of independence, this respect did not carry with it any particular interest in the Gospel which the Church proclaimed. In the great war the Church had done no more than had Jefferson, Paine, Allen, or the rankest of the colonial unbelievers or the French infidels. Gratitude to the Church for its contributions to the war did not necessarily include any concern for Christianity.

Only a few of the Presbyterian clergy had boldly prophesied a new utopia beyond the war, and even to these men such visions splendid may have been, at least in great part, oratorical flights in the interests of the war effort. But there is ample evidence that most of the clergy were unprepared for the postwar conditions. Disillusionment, discouragement, and war weariness laid a heavy toll upon their morale. All knew that before them lay the severest struggle in the life of the American Church. In spite of the temporary letdown in the general spirit of the colonists, every minister realized that sooner or later the new American life would spring up with resistless vigor and go on to create a new nation. But, in doing so, would America utterly forsake the Gospel and traditional morals, and create a godless nation?

A number of the clergy, even of the abler of them, after spending themselves wholeheartedly in the war effort never again took their place behind the pulpit. Perhaps to Caleb Wallace, later Justice of the Supreme Court of Tennessee; Joseph Montgomery, prominent in Pennsylvania politics; Hugh Brackenridge, famous as an essayist and editor; and others, political endeavor seemed to offer greater possibilities for immediate results in such troublous times than did the Christian ministry.[1]

The poverty of spirit born of discouragement, war weariness, and disillusionment brought far-reaching changes into the Church. The tense years during which the various states were drawing up their constitutions were difficult for the Church. As in the years leading up to the war, so in the years after the war radical and conservative groups in each state strove for the right to control the formulation of governmental policy. Three of the states in which this tension was the greatest were also the three states in which the Presbyterian Church had its main base, New York, New Jersey, and Pennsylvania.[2]

During these troubled years, also, some who had been prominent Presbyterian laymen left the Church. This was especially true in Philadelphia, the largest city in the new nation. Men like Charles Thomson, James Wilson, and Benjamin Rush withdrew, some because of religious differences, some because of social and political reasons. As the new nation struggled to the birth, intense political convictions claimed the attention and allegiance of the leading laymen of the Church, many of whom were now as well-educated as the clergymen. In the distraction of their times, the leaders of the Church could not see any one clear Christian solution to the questions of the day behind which all might be urged to rally. The war for independence had become a holy cause, but no holy cause now appeared.

The doctrine of the separation of Church and State came more and more to be held in such a way as to require that the Church be neutral on all issues on which its members were disagreed. John Rodgers, who had been very active in the war, soon came to doubt whether a clergyman ought to vote in any civil election.[3] Other ministers, like Samuel Miller, Samuel Doak, and John Ewing, continued a vigorous personal activity in some one political party, as individuals, but most of the clergy did not. Before long, Samuel Miller completely changed his mind and ceased all political endeavor, regretting seriously his earlier activity and becoming quite uncertain that a minister ought to vote.[4] John Witherspoon's preoccupation with the abject poverty of the College of New Jersey, and his advancing years, drew him out of his former direct participation in social and political affairs. However, he and fellow Presbyterian clergymen did not at all, in another sense, cease either their interest in or their influence upon the social and political life of the new nation. They were pre-eminently the educators of the middle states. In their schools, as distinguished from their pulpits, their concern for the shaping of the new nation's forms appeared. The schools, academies, and colleges that the Presbyterian clergy conducted, scattered all over the new nation, contributed a number of the local, state, and national political and social leaders who shaped the rise of the new republic, in excess of the number produced by all other educational institutions of the middle states combined. The withdrawal generally of the Presbyterian clergy from political and social activities, therefore, was intended to mean no more than that the ministers of the Church were to be neutral while the laity were obligated as Christians to be active. That a Christian should, or might, be unconcerned about these phases of life would have been roundly denied. Simply because Christians generally ought to be concerned, it was argued, the laity had a right to expect neutrality on the part of the clergy lest the Church should cease to be composed of all sections of society.

One clear need that the Church did see in the years immediately following the war was the struggle against infidelity and deism. So far had the Christian Church as a whole been thrown back that the total Christian strength in the entire nation during the critical years just after the war was not more than five per cent of the population. So confident and strong did the deistic movement become that the Christian Church was indeed in no small danger of a crushing defeat.[5] The Church was the more vulnerable to the attacks of deism because of the rationalistic character of its own theology. Natural law, general revelation, natural philosophy, and moral philosophy were deeply interwoven into the orthodox as well as the heterodox theologies of the day. At the College of New Jersey the earlier Edwardean theology with its idealistic philosophical basis had been replaced, under Witherspoon's influence, by a system based upon the then regnant Scottish philosophy of natural realism, or common sense. In the University of Pennsylvania the Hutchesonian philosophy introduced by Francis Alison had been developed by three of Alison's pupils, John Ewing, Samuel Magaw, and John Andrews, to a point little short of deism.[6] Ewing was a prominent Presbyterian minister, though Magaw and Andrews had left the Church. Since the actual basis of all systematic theology in the Church during that period was philosophical, deism was a matter of degree or quantity, a matter of emphasis.[7] The attack upon deism, therefore, assumed the nature of a holding operation, a containing maneuver. Bounds were set beyond which rationalism must not be carried. These bounds were usually the bounds found in some older, traditional formulations of current acceptance.

Not only the clergy, but laymen as well, were engaged in the struggle against deism. William Livingstone, now governor of New Jersey, wrote against it his *Thoughts on Deism*. So actively did the Presbyterians generally combat infidelity and deism that a recent scholar has credited them with being the backbone of the movement that finally crushed these forms of unbelief.[8] The struggle, however, brought about some profound effects upon the Church.

The pressure of infidelity and deism stirred up an abnormal interest in theological polemics. Against such errors new ideas were not considered safe or sure antidotes. Greater and greater reliance was, therefore, placed upon the " system of sound doctrine " as the only infallible guard against the new irreligion of the day. Tampering with, or improving upon this traditional system became highly suspect and utterly undesirable. Any attempt at re-examining the inherited symbols was rejected as a weakening of the front against error, a sapping of the inner strength of the Church. Edwardean theology fell into even greater disrepute because it departed from the older norms. The feeling against it soon took on a great part of the feeling directed toward deism and infidelity. Orthodox theology looked upon itself as fighting for its very life, and hence drew less and less distinction between anti-Christian deism and those movements within the Church that it considered heretical. By pooling its enemies, in its own thinking, the current orthodoxy simplified its polemical work. Any deviation from the system was heretical.

How the Church came to fall into this oversimplification of its problem it is difficult to explain. Scarcely any significant movement, gain, or achievement in colonial Presbyterianism had come through its ultraconservative party, the Old Side. The working out of a wise attitude toward the creedal responsibility of the Church, the quickening of the Church's spiritual life, the cleansing and revitalizing of the Church's ministry, and the securing for the laity of a greater part in the life of the Church, had all come from those whom these conservatives had fought as not being true Presbyterians. Each time the conservatives had been wrong both in fact and in practice. Only in the civic or political realm had their contribution been significant. In the French and Indian War, in the controversy over an American bishop, and during the Revolutionary War, these conservatives had been prominent. However, even in these, their contributions had been less than the contributions of the New Side, since they lacked both the numbers and the leadership of the latter.

Several factors entered into paving the way for this conservative reaction. The Great Awakening itself, while originally a radical movement, left behind it the seeds of a new orthodoxy. An excellent witness to this is provided by one of Samuel Davies' converts from Virginia: "The subjects of conversation were usually such as the following. What is the difference between conviction of sin and mere terror of conscience? What is the evidence of true evangelical repentance, and how is it to be distinguished from false repentance? What is the difference between true love to God and the Redeemer, and that self-congratulation of which hypocrites may be the subjects? What is the difference between true love of the brethren and that which arises from self-love and party spirit?"[9] The necessity of establishing some norms and standards for Christian experience always carried with it the danger that the resulting approved form would become more and more fixed, and more and more official, until it would defy the very spontaneous spiritual life of faith, for whose protection it was first elaborated.

Catechetical instruction also contributed to the re-establishment of the older conservative attitudes. The Great Awakening had brought in many converts from outside the Church. These converts, and the children of the Church also, needed instruction. Catechetical teaching was the accepted method. Since it put a premium upon mere memorization and made little or no place for reflective thinking or practice in the Chris.ian life, this method of instruction made for rigidity of form and disinterest in the freer and more unpredictable aspects of the Christian life of faith. Preaching also, as it became more polemical and defensive, took upon itself thereby more and more the character of instruction in, or transmission of, a fixed system of correct ideas. The enunciation of right doctrine required that a minister give ever greater heed to the accepted standards and less and less attention to Christian life. The accepted standards were tangible and abstract, hence always predictable and easy to formulate into polemical and sound sermons. The life of the spirit, contrariwise, could hardly be standardized. Therefore, in that realm it was only too easy to depart from the accepted standards. The risks which the men of the Great Awakening constantly took were not frequently taken in the years just after the war. Attempting to do for 1785 what the Log College men had done for their generation, namely, to reinterpret the Christian life, was not done.

Although Witherspoon had been a radical in the midst of Scottish ecclesiasticism, and a radical in colonial politics, his influence in American Presbyterianism was on the conservative side. He had opposed quietly but successfully the Edwardean theology in the College of New Jersey. No great theological thinker himself, he tended to follow the standard authors who had become the traditional authorities. At no time was he a theological leader in the American Church. His contributions were on the practical side. Through his close connections with the ultraconservative Scottish Secession Church in America he drew his own Church in that same direction. For several years he led an attempt to unite the synod with the Seceders. The very approach to such a venture demanded and brought forth great conservative assurances from the synod.[10] Witherspoon also led a move to unite the Dutch Reformed Church and the synod. Here again, very express conservative guarantees were demanded of the synod by the Dutch Church.[11] Both union moves failed, but they left their impress upon the Presbyterians.

The growing influence of the Scotch-Irish in the Church also played its part. Many of those who came in during the vast immigration after 1760 were not greatly affected by the Great Awakening and its liberalizing influences. As they, and especially those of their youths who entered the ministry after the war, began to exercise an influence on the Church, it was on the extremely conservative side. The remnants of the Old Side, purged now in large measure of immoral clergymen, came, through John Ewing, Robert Davidson, Patrick Allison, and other strong, able men, to play a greater part in the leadership of the Church, especially among and through their countrymen, the Scotch-Irish.

The most important contributing factor to this conservative reaction, however, was the rationalism which pervaded the theology of both the conservative and the more liberal groups in the Church, and which provided the bridge by which many former New Side men crossed over to the conservative side under the pressure of the times. During the Great Awakening the New Side had broken somewhat with the current static theology, but had been unable to transcend this older system and go beyond it. For a time the Edwardean theology had seemed to provide a new way, but it had proved abortive in Presbyterianism. The New Side, both its Log College wing and its New England wing, had been unable to break out of the rationalistic method and to achieve a Biblically based theology. Their differences with the Old Side conservatism became, therefore, more and more a matter of emphasis and of personal conscience, as the impact of the Great Awakening grew fainter with the lapse of time.

It was out of this conservative reaction that the Old School Presbyterianism of the early nineteenth century grew. Sensing that it was essentially a reaction, it took as one of its major tasks the elimination of all the older liberalizing influences in the Church. This required eventually the discrediting of the entire Great Awakening and of the Log College men as destroyers of due form and order. It also required the derogation of the New England antisubscription group as opponents of strong doctrinal standards. Thus the Church, which owed its very life, purity, and strength to the stress upon the free, spontaneous, though adequately responsible, Christian life born out of the New Side in the Great Awakening, was taught to abhor the very springs of its greatness.

Whatever its desires might have been, the Church was not given much leisure after the Revolutionary War in which to plan any such thing as a postwar program. The inflation and other economic distresses of the years 1783–1786 wrought havoc in the congregations. Ministers were driven to the wall financially as their people were utterly unable to pay them. Not only did ministers have to give up churches, only to go on to other equally uncertain fortunes, but old established congregations were broken up as whole communities trekked out to the frontier in hopes of finding some degree of economic security. In the schools and colleges the number of students studying for the ministry shrank to an alarming degree. Wartime destruction and depletion of the colleges, and the effects of inflation reduced the total enrollments a great deal. The religious conditions, however, reduced the numbers of ministerial candidates far below the proportions of previous years. Princeton, which had sent seventy-five men into the ministry in the seven years before 1776, was to send only one half that number (thirty-nine) in the next eighteen years, an average of little more than two per year. With such conditions the Church made slow progress under great pressure in the first few years after the war.

In view of these difficulties, the determination with which the Church faced its new responsibilities was remarkable. A concerted push was made to evangelize the frontier regions. As economic conditions became more stable, after 1786, the tempo of this work increased steadily. Even while the over-all conditions in the colonies were very depressing, ambitious plans for the reorganization of the Church's ecclesiastical structure were gotten under way, beginning in 1785.[12] Born of the need of greater formal strength, this step carried with it conservative tendencies which were becoming manifest all through the Church's life, and which were profoundly to influence its later development.

The population of the middle and southern states rose from about one and three quarter millions in 1783 to slightly over two and three quarter millions in the next seven years.[13] This rapid increase of population in the areas where the Presbyterian Church was rooted, and where it was the only Church that had a well-spread pattern of congregations radiating throughout these states from one central governing body, placed a heavy responsibility upon the Church. The distribution of this approximately sixty per cent increase was not calculated to ease the Church's problem of evangelization. The strength of the Church lay in New York, New Jersey, and Pennsylvania. Of these three states, only New York had an increase in population equal to the national average. The increase in the other two states was approximately forty per cent, with New Jersey slightly exceeding Pennsylvania in percentage of increase. In these areas where the Church was best organized, and where most of the congregations were small, increases of even one hundred per cent would not have caused any great strain upon the available supply of clergy and funds. Individual churches would have grown and strengthened under their existing leadership. However, the massive increases in population occurred in Maryland, Virginia, North Carolina, and Georgia, where the framework of the

Church could not bear the added load of missionizing the newly settled areas. These new settlers included many who were earnestly desirous of having Christian ministrations. Some were Presbyterians from the older areas, who had migrated to the frontiers. Others were from Ulster or Scotland and, if at all religiously inclined, they looked to the Presbyterians for ministers. The Church was faced with the task of maintaining itself in the older areas even while extending itself to the utmost in an endeavor to follow the rapid expansion of the country on the distant frontiers. When under the current economic stress many of the older congregations were decreased as their members moved out to the frontier in search of better conditions, the plight of these churches became desperate. Many of them could no longer support a minister, and gradually died out.

From time to time restlessness over the Church's high and rigid educational requirements for entrance into the ministry had appeared. This, in part, was responsible for the withdrawal of Jacob Green and others from the Church in 1779 to 1780.[14] As the number of places that appealed in vain to the presbyteries and to the synod for ministers soared into the hundreds, some ministers began to demand a system based upon the immediate needs of the new republic rather than upon the Old World's standards. In 1783, and again in 1785, attempts were made in the synod to relax the educational requirements for candidates. The attempt of 1783 was made as a request for an exception to the rule for one individual, and was led by Sproat. Witherspoon took the lead in opposing the measure in synod and the request was not granted.[15] The second attempt was, however, more general in scope. " An overture was brought in [i.e., into the synod] in the following terms, viz: 'Whether in the present state of the church in America, and the scarcity of ministers to fill our numerous congregations, the Synod, or Presbyteries, ought therefore to relax, in any degree, in the literary qualifications required of entrants into the ministry?' And it was carried in the negative by a great majority." [16] Not quite content with this, two days later some members of the synod moved to add one full year to the study requirements. The motion gained some support but was put off for a year.[17] Discussion of it was not resumed for several years.

Some means had, however, to be found for holding services in the many vacant congregations. In 1783 the First Presbytery of Philadelphia, situated in one of the oldest areas of the Church, voted that inasmuch as the shortage of ministers was so serious and the prospects of securing more clergymen were so dim, laymen should be urged to assemble for worship under their own leadership. They should conduct the usual services and appoint some of their own numbers to read printed sermons and expositions.[18] Three years later the synod itself adopted these measures and urged them upon the whole Church. "The Synod earnestly recommend to all the vacant congregations under their care, to meet together every Lord's day, at one or more places, for the purposes of prayer and praises, and reading the Holy Scriptures, together with the works of such approved divines as they may be able to procure, and that the elders be the persons who shall pray, and select the portions of Scripture and other books, to be read by any proper person whom they may appoint."[19] Such expedients, largely futile in the end, were deemed preferable to the relaxing of the standards of ministerial education.

So stubbornly did the synod hold to these traditional standards that in 1785 they rebuked New Brunswick Presbytery for having allowed a man to deliver one of his parts of trial in English instead of in Latin. The easement had been granted three years earlier while the war was still on, and the practice had become no longer unusual among most of the presbyteries. None the less, this deviation was now flatly forbidden by the synod.[20] In the records of the various presbyteries instances become rather frequent after 1785 of men studying theology with some older minister two and even three years after leaving college. While part of this longer period of study was due to a higher standard of work being required in these presbyteries, the economic factor no doubt played a part also. Men were becoming reluctant to accept licensure and to become "supplies" under the direction of a presbytery. The presbyteries pleaded with their vacant congregations to use their young supplies more generously. New Castle Presbytery protested to its people that these men must "be able to subsist" or they will go elsewhere and take "other employments, as some have already done, by which means our Congregations are threatened with a Famine of the Word of God."[21] New Brunswick Presbytery likewise appealed to their vacancies, pointing out the high cost of living, the expense these men had been to in securing an education, the high qualifications desired in such men, and the imminent danger in which the whole Church would stand if the situation of young licentiates became too difficult and discouraging.[22] The presbytery asked 40/s per Sunday for these young supplies, about the equivalent of the weekly cash earnings (not including perquisites, manse, wood, and use of farm) of the pastor of a weaker rural church. Efforts were made also to raise funds for the aid of ministerial students in colleges.

The Presbyterian Church, accordingly, took up its mission in the new republic with a small, highly select, and well-trained clergy. The adoption of such a policy was to have a profound effect upon the whole future of the Church. Numerically the policy was to cost the Church its position as the largest denomination in the middle and southern states. Moreover, pre-eminence on the new frontiers was to pass from the Presbyterians. On the other hand, leadership in American education, leadership in theological thinking, pre-eminence in the pulpits of the major cities, and a powerful influence in republican affairs were long to be Presbyterian prerogatives. For some years this dynamic leadership made up in great part for the lack of numbers of ministers. What notable results comparatively few men, and most of them young men, were able to accomplish on the frontiers it is difficult even to grasp.

The Presbytery of Redstone, organized in 1781, ministered to an undesignated area, beyond the mountains in southwestern Pennsylvania and northwestern Virginia, larger than some of the smaller states of the Union.[23] In 1783 it had six members; in 1788, eight. With only this handful of ministers, western Pennsylvania had twenty-three congregations in 1783 and thirty-four in 1789.[24] Few of these congregations had even log churches. They met in barns, in homes, or in the open air. In spite of the most primitive conditions, three of these ministers, John McMillan, Thaddeus Dodd, and Joseph Smith began classical schools in their own homes. Dodd's and Smith's schools passed away, but McMillan's became an ancestor of Jefferson College. In his school men studied both arts and theology, and were licensed and ordained without going on to other institutions.[25]

Kentucky was settled originally by people from Virginia. Until 1783 no Presbyterian minister had settled in the area although settlement had begun even before the Revolutionary War. Hanover Presbytery assumed jurisdiction over the area, and David Rice, who in his youth had been under Samuel Davies' influence, went out there in 1783. He found religious conditions anything but good. " After I had been here some weeks, and had preached at several places, I found scarcely one man and a few women who supported a credible profession of religion. Some were grossly ignorant of the first principles of religion. Some were given to quarrelling and fighting, some to profane swearing, some to intemperance, and perhaps most of them totally negligent of the forms of religion in their own houses.

" I could not think a church formed of such materials could properly be called a church of Christ. With this I was considerably distressed, and made to cry, where am I! What situation am I in? Many of these [settlers] produced certificates of their having been regular members in full communion and in good standing in the churches from which they had emigrated, and this they thought entitled them to what they called Christian privileges here. Others would be angry and raise a quarrel with their neighbours if they did not certify, contrary to their knowledge and belief, that the bearer was a good moral character. I found indeed very few on whose information I could rely respecting the moral character of those who wished to be church members." [26] To make matters worse, whereas the pioneer clergy of western Pennsylvania were of unusual character, Rice comments that those who joined him in Kentucky " were men of some information, and held sound principles, but did not appear to possess much of the spirit of the Gospel." [27]

A later historian, Robert Davidson, comments on Rice's strictures: " That this picture is not overcharged, must appear from the melancholy fact, gathered from an inspection of the records, that nearly half the entire number of preachers were, at one time or other, subjected to church censures more or less severe; several being cut off for heresy or schism, two deposed for intemperance, one suspended for licentiousness, several rebuked for wrangling, and others for other improprieties unbecoming the gravity or dignity of the clerical character. . . . This is a development fraught with solemn instruction, warning the Church that instead of sending to new and promising settlements her weakest men, as if anything were good enough for such stations, it would be far wiser to send the most efficient laborers, picked men, who would leave the impress of their own commanding virtues upon succeeding generations." [28]

Through the period up to 1789, Kentucky Presbyterianism had a stormy career. The territory was perhaps more deeply infected with the current infidelity and irreligion than any other part of the American frontier. Through Caleb Wallace, formerly a Presbyterian minister and now a prominent figure in Kentucky legal and political life, and others, Transylvania University had been organized, in 1785, under Presbyterian auspices but with some state aid. Control of the school was lost by the Presbyterians in 1794, as the board of trustees no longer had a majority of Presbyterians.[29] Within the Church itself the undying intransigence of a few, led by Rev. Adam Rankin, caused a controversy in 1789 over the use of Watts's hymns. This led to a local schism some years later, and the founding of the " Rankinites." [30] Rice, together with a few able and godly ministers, held on, doing what they could to build a true Church. Eventually they triumphed in the period after 1789.

All during the war the Dissenters in Virginia, particularly the Presbyterians and the Baptists, fought for a greater degree of religious liberty. Some progress was made from time to time, especially in 1779, when the established Episcopal Church was deprived of its right to levy and collect taxes on all for its own support. A year and a half later it lost its exclusive right to perform marriages and to collect fees therefor. Even so, the Dissenters remained dissenters, and the Episcopal Church remained established, with all its properties intact, and retaining the right to tax all citizens for the support of the poor. In 1784 and 1785 a determined effort was made by the Dissenters to achieve complete religious freedom in the state. The Episcopal clergy and their followers clung tenaciously to their former pre-eminence and tried by various means to salvage at least a part of its old position. At one time during the struggle it seemed as though public sentiment were swinging toward a policy of imposing a religious tax upon all citizens of the state, allowing each person to designate the Church to which his tax should go. The Presbytery of Hanover agreed once to such a compromise, only to reverse themselves just a few months later. One of the great points of contention was that of the disposition of the large property holdings which the established Church had built up during the colonial period, when it enjoyed the right to tax all citizens, including Dissenters. At length, in 1785, full religious liberty was granted to all, the Episcopal Church was reduced to the same position as any other, and the property of the Episcopal Church was sold for the benefit of all denominations in the state.[31] Once freed of the incubus of a dissenter status, the Presbyterian Church in Virginia was able to forge ahead.

Before the war Hanover Presbytery had been instrumental in founding and encouraging two good schools. In 1774 the presbytery had taken over the Academy at Augusta, and later reconstituted it as Liberty Hall at Timber Ridge. Another move brought the school to Lexington, where it was to become first Washington College, and finally Washington and Lee. Hanover Presbytery also founded Hampden-Sydney College in 1776 and secured a charter for it in 1783. The effects of the irreligion that prevailed after the war were marked upon both these schools. Each was led by an able devoted man, but the spirit of the age seemed too strong to be overcome. In the years 1786 to 1788 these two schools were swept by revivals, remarkable alike for thoroughness and for lack of objectionable accompaniments.[32] A host of young converts, including Archibald Alexander, later the first professor of Princeton Seminary, streamed from these schools to strengthen the Church in the South and in the West. The revival affected a number of the congregations near these schools, but did not become general. The evangelization of Kentucky, Tennessee, and western Pennsylvania was markedly aided by men from Virginia. A number of ministers also were furnished to the Carolinas.

North Carolina, which with Virginia had very large increases in population between 1783 and 1789, was the scene of strenuous missionary effort. At Charlotte an academy had been founded some time before 1770. In that year an unsuccessful attempt had been made to charter the school as a college. Alexander McWhorter, who had twice visited North Carolina as a missionary of the synod and again in 1776 as an emissary of the Continental Congress, became head of this school for a brief time after 1779. David Caldwell's justly famous classical school at Guilford was continued, and numerous smaller schools were active. In addition to evangelizing the new immigrants within its own borders, North Carolina furnished several able leaders in missionizing Tennessee, Kentucky, and Ohio. James McGready, the great revivalist of the early nineteenth century, was one of them.[33]

By 1784 the Presbytery of Orange, which had at one time included both Carolinas, was divided so as to make a new Presbytery of South Carolina. The old independent Presbytery of South Carolina, which had existed since before 1724, had ceased to exist during the war. Its successor, the Presbytery of Charleston, was not finally organized until about 1790. To this presbytery belonged only four churches, all in and around Charleston. It was too weak to evangelize the new state, and the task fell to the Presbyterians who were pushing down from North Carolina. Georgia also became the territory of this new Presbytery of South Carolina.

Work on the frontier, therefore, followed a rather uniform pattern. A small group of well-trained and earnest ministers (Kentucky offering some exceptions) were, by means of incessant itinerating, preaching the Gospel in widely scattered settlements, conducting schools, establishing colleges, and training a new generation of ministers born and raised on the frontier. Great as their efforts were, and considerable as their successes were, they could not, it is true, keep pace with the swelling tide of immigration and the rapid growth in population. What they were doing, however, was work of the most solid kind — well-organized congregations, local schools, classical academies and colleges, all ably supervised by democratically functioning presbyteries. Other more loosely organized denominations might outstrip the Presbyterians in the rapid sending out of frontier missionaries, but none could equal them for decades in the building of both Church and society on the frontier.

In the older areas of the Church new congregations were also springing up. More noticeable, however, is the changing character of the older congregations. Lists of elders and trustees, together with other notices of lay members, indicate that these older churches were maintaining their background of mixed origins. More and more, however, their ministers were being drawn from among the Scotch-Irish. Spiritually the Church in these areas was not flourishing, though congregational life was regular and, in spite of the irreligion of the times, there was a solid core of faithful members. Out of their means they supported their own churches and provided, often liberally, for the churches, schools, and ministers of the frontier. One of the interesting phases of this activity was the Church's effort to send Bibles and other Christian literature to the frontier settlers. Collections for this purpose were taken up in 1785 all through the Church. The synod specifically ordered that "Mr. Aitken's Bible" be sent. Aitken, a Presbyterian elder in Philadelphia, had, at great risk financially, published a Bible during the war, when British Bibles could no longer be secured. It was the first complete Bible in English to be published in America. Aitken never recovered his investment.[34] Concern for the spiritual life of the Church led the Presbytery of New Castle to draft and publish a plan for reviving religion, but no significant religious quickening was to take place in the older areas until early in the nineteenth century.[35]

Before the war little concern had been expressed among Presbyterians regarding slavery.[36] Jacob Green, however, took the occasion of the fast day appointed in 1779 by the Continental Congress in the interests of American liberties to preach on "The Acceptable Fast." The sermon was a powerful protest against the enslaving of Negroes. His effort aroused great opposition, but eventually he won out among his own people to such an extent that no slaveholder was allowed membership in their church.[37] Sentiment continued to develop in the Church, fostered by others also, including Benjamin Rush, until in 1780 the issue was brought up in synod. This body noted that in 1774 the problem had been before them, "but [was] by some means passed over the following Synods, and not since resumed."[38] Unfortunately, this time also the issue was debated "to considerable length" and then dropped.

The issue had been debated to considerable length no doubt because by this time a demand for the abolition of slavery had been built up in the Presbyterian Church, though largely among the laity. In Pennsylvania "The Act of 1780, which was principally the work of George Bryan, was the final, decisive step in the destruction of slavery in Pennsylvania."[39] Bryan was a Presbyterian elder, though during the fight for the Act of 1780 he complained that the Presbyterians as a whole seemed to be against his bill. Benjamin Rush, "than whom the Negro had no better friend in Pennsylvania," [40] was still a Presbyterian and very active in the abolition cause.

Other laymen, such as Ebenezer Hazard, Elias Boudinot, and Governor William Livingston of New Jersey, were actively campaigning against slavery. In 1778, Livingston had failed to get an antislavery bill through the New Jersey legislature, but at the time he served notice on his opponents that he was determined " to push the matter till it is effected, being convinced that the practice is utterly inconsistent with the principles of Christianity and humanity; and in Americans who have almost idolized liberty, peculiarly odious and disgraceful." [41] Not for another seven years did the synod again return to consider the lot of the Negro slave. In 1787 a Committee on Overtures made up of the rank and file of the synod's membership, one member from each presbytery, brought in a remarkable overture:

" The Creator of the world having made of one flesh all the children of men, it becomes them as members of the same family, to consult and promote each other's happiness. It is more especially the duty of those who maintain the rights of humanity, and who acknowledge and teach the obligations of Christianity, to use such means as are in their power to extend the blessings of equal freedom to every part of the human race.

" From a full conviction of these truths, and sensible that the rights of human nature are too well understood to admit of debate, Overtured, that the Synod of New York and Philadelphia recommend, in the warmest terms, to every member of their body, and to all the churches and families under their care, to do every thing in their power consistent with the rights of civil society, to promote the abolition of slavery, and the instruction of negroes, whether bond or free." [42]

This overture was evidently far too radical for the synod. In its stead the synod " came to the following judgment ":

" The Synod of New York and Philadelphia do highly approve of the general principles in favour of universal liberty, that prevail in America, and the interest which many of the states have taken in promoting the abolition of slavery; yet, inasmuch as men introduced from a servile state to a participation of all the privileges of civil society, without a proper education, and without previous habits of industry, may be, in many respects, dangerous to the community, therefore they earnestly recommend it to all the members belonging to their communion, to give those persons who are at present held in servitude, such good education as to prepare them for the better enjoyment of freedom; and they moreover recommend that masters, wherever they find servants disposed to make a just improvement of the privilege, would give them

a *peculium,* or grant them sufficient time and sufficient means of pro-
curing their own liberty at a moderate rate, that thereby, they may be
brought into society with those habits of industry that may render them
useful citizens; and, finally, they recommend it to all their people to
use the most prudent measures, consistent with the interest and the
state of civil society, in the counties where they live, to procure eventually the final abolition of slavery in America." [43]

This action, cast in the form of a judgment or opinion, rather than
passed as an overture, was the more remarkable since the majority of
those present at synod were from areas in which slave labor was a
minor factor. From states north of Maryland forty-one ministers were
present; only fourteen were from Maryland and other southern states.
The cautious approach to the issue, basing " the final abolition of slavery " upon the hopes of individual slaveowners' being willing to pay
for the training of their slaves to a degree where they would be prepared " for the better enjoyment of freedom," or being willing to allow
slaves to buy " their own liberty at a moderate rate," was quite in keeping with a growing body of American opinion on the subject. The ban
imposed during the war on the importation of slaves, and the local
successes in several states of the antislavery cause, had led many American people to believe quite sincerely that slavery was being progres-
sively rooted out and that no national or radical action was either necessary or advisable. [44]

To this period also belong the beginnings of other social reforms,
such as better education for women, an interest in temperance, and reforms in penal legislation and administration. In all these Benjamin
Rush was the leader, though Boudinot, Bryan, Daniel Roberdeau, and
other Presbyterian laymen also were very active. [45]

A greater place began to be given to the elders of the Church in the
years between the war and 1789. For the first time they were placed
upon a special commission of the synod in 1787. Jeremiah Greenman,
of the Pittsgrove, New Jersey, Church, was disciplined by the First
Presbytery of Philadelphia in 1779 for trying to dismiss his session. He
was straitly told that " we judge that the very being of a Presbyterial
Government, & the Peace & Order of Congregations depends on the
keeping up a Session, & Seasonably calling & consulting them." [46]

The position of the trustees also was becoming stronger in the
Church. In First Church, Philadelphia, John Ewing protested when
the trustees assumed full charge of the " secular affairs " of the Church,
relegating the minister and the session to the care of only the " ecclesiastical affairs." Ewing insisted that trustees and session be one body under the moderatorship of the minister. The controversy lasted all dur-

ing Ewing's pastorate.[47] However much Ewing, and other ministers also, disliked the idea of a separate board of trustees under its own chairman, the policy was becoming more and more common in the larger churches and was soon to become standard. Financial control of the churches was thus coming into the hands of laymen, who, since they were not elders and therefore not of the session, were often quite independent of the ministers' influence. This control of the finances was to become one of the major bases of lay strength in the Church.

It had long been traditional in the Churches of Great Britain and America to require that marriages be entered into only within those relationships stipulated in the Levitical law of the Old Testament. Marriages contracted between persons to whom that law forbade marriage made those persons guilty of incest or adultery. Litigations over such cases harassed the Presbyterian courts constantly all through the colonial period. Yet until toward the close of the eighteenth century the Church refused to yield to any demand for a re-examination of its rules. Again and again the Church ordered persons who had married a brother or sister of a deceased spouse to separate on pain of excommunication. Other cases involved the marriage of a half-sister or half-brother, of a niece, and other odd relationships.

Finally, in 1787, the Church relented on the issue of marrying a deceased spouse's brother or sister, by saying that such an act need not necessarily deprive the persons of Church privileges. Such marriages were imprudent, contrary to the Levitical law, against the common practices of all Churches, yet once entered into ought probably to be maintained. Upon proper expressions of penitence, therefore, the persons, still married, could be restored to the Church. A sizable minority dissented from this ruling, and brought the issue up the following year. Synod then substantially reiterated their previous ruling, but added a clause forbidding their clergy to celebrate such marriages.[48] James Finley published a pamphlet against the synod's ruling,[49] but no great move against it took place. Some years later New Brunswick Presbytery's records show that the synod's guarded attitude was being adopted in that judicature.[50] The issue, however, remained controversial in many parts of the Church.

During the war strict supervision of the clergy by the presbyteries was well-nigh impossible. As soon as hostilities ceased, however, presbyteries began to check up on their members. Most of them had without supervision acquitted themselves well. Only a few had ill-used the freedom from control. The presbyteries' greatest problem was that of bringing men back into orderly regular relations with the Church's courts. Some men wandered about doing secular work yet seeking to retain some form of ministerial office. Others had irregularly assumed charge of vacant churches in their own or in other presbyteries. A number of men had moved away without giving notice to any other minister or to their former congregations. Slowly the presbyteries began to regularize pastoral relations, to bring up their fringe members, to compel men who were no longer actual ministers to give up using their former office as a means of augmenting their income or prestige, and to discipline or drop those who had proved unworthy. A former minister in Delaware was finally found teaching school in Kentucky. Another was found to have left his church because of a face wound, although he was still utilizing his ministerial capacity in ways of his own choosing. A former pastor of one of the largest city churches failed to report after the city was liberated from the British. Later it was learned that he was in moral difficulties. One man naïvely wrote to his old presbytery, asking them to forward his credentials to a certain minister in another state from whom in turn he would later pick them up. The presbytery called the request " unprecedented "!

Very few Scotch-Irish clergymen had accompanied the great waves of immigrants from Ulster in the two decades preceding the war. As the ministry of the Church became more and more native-born, and largely trained in schools where the spiritual and ethical tone was good, the problem of ministerial discipline had become vastly simplified. Also the stringent rules applied by the synod, just on the eve of hostilities, regulating the reception of men from abroad, especially those from Ireland, had restrained presbyteries from admitting any who might be about the colonies during the war years. With the coming of peace, and the resumption of immigration, the old problem of renegade clergy from Great Britain returned to plague the Church courts. This time the synod acted with drastic severity. In 1784 they ordered:

" The Synod having reason, by information given since their present meeting, to apprehend the churches under their care in imminent danger from ministers and licensed candidates of unsound principles coming among us, do hereby renew their former injunction to the respective Presbyteries within their bounds, relative to this matter, and do also strictly enjoin on every member of this body, under pain of censure, to be particularly careful in this respect. And the stated clerk of the Synod is hereby directed to furnish each of our Presbyteries with an attested copy of the said injunctions, together with a copy of this minute." [51] This order seems to have been quite conscientiously observed by the presbyteries. Under its terms (i.e., subject to the synod's approval) a number of men from New England, Scotland, England, and Ireland were admitted. Unfortunately several of these men, one from

England and others from Scotland and Ireland, caused trouble. As the colonial period of the Church drew to a close, some of the presbyteries, notably New Castle, were making synod's rule even more stringent by their application of it.

A genuine and remarkable catholicity marked the Church's attitude toward other denominations. Though they had left no stone unturned in the decade before the war to prevent the Anglicans from securing an American bishop, the Presbyterians now took no notice whatever of the ordination of three bishops for the Episcopal Church. The General Convention of the Presbyterian and Congregational Churches, which had been formed for the purpose of defending religious liberty against the Anglicans, and which had ceased to meet when the war broke out, did not now resume its meetings. Its work had been accomplished. Relations with the Congregationalists remained intimate, however, and were shortly to give rise to another co-operative venture in 1801. A number of conferences were held, over the years from 1784 to the founding of the General Assembly in 1789, with the Dutch Reformed Church. These conferences began as a means of healing some complaints of that Church against New York and New Brunswick Presbyteries. Gradually these talks were broadened out to include the topic of union between the two bodies. In the end the fears of the Dutch group that the Presbyterians were not strict enough in doctrine and worship brought defeat to the idea of organic union.[52] Some measure of co-operation was, however, achieved. New Brunswick Presbytery sought to have at least one of their small churches unite with the nearest Dutch Church. A committee of the two denominations on work on the frontier also functioned for a time.[53] The Roman Catholic Church was not very often thrown into contact with the Presbyterians in the period. However, when Bishop Carroll, of Baltimore, assumed the title "Bishop of Baltimore," Patrick Allison engaged in a newspaper controversy with him over his right to so ambitious a title.[54]

The best indication of the Church's real attitude toward other Protestant denominations may be had again from the preface to the first draft of the Directory for Public Worship, submitted in 1787. While never officially adopted (for reasons not connected with its sentiments[55]), it was the work of a broadly representative and influential committee. Regarding other denominations, it said:

" This Church firmly believes, that her doctrines, and modes of worship, are most agreeable to the Word of God; to the Practice of the Primitive Church in the three first Centuries; and to the best reformed Churches. She thinks it the indispensible duty of all her people to use their utmost endeavours, to have regular settled Ministers of their own persuasion; and stated worship, in their own way, every Lord's day.

"At the same time, the Presbyterian Church maintains a high respect for the other Protestant Churches of the Country, though several of them differ from her in some forms of government and Modes of worship: particularly for the regular Congregational Churches to the eastward; for the Associate, Low Dutch, and German reformed Churches; and for the Lutheran and Episcopal Churches.

"In places where there are only a few Presbyterians, and they are not able to have worship usually in their own way; it is recommended to them, to attend with the Christian brethren of any of the above denominations, which may be most convenient, rather than spend their Sabbaths without public worship. But this Church warns all her People against illiterate, vagrant, and designing persons, who, under pretence of greater zeal, and strictness than others, only go about to make a party. It is much better for them, to stay at home on the Lord's day with their families, than to encourage those men, who, by condemning regular, known and pious Churches, give too much reason to suspect that their own views are dangerous and wrong." [56]

To the committee it seemed better that men should worship God than that they should serve only the Presbyterian Church.

THE FOUNDING OF THE GENERAL ASSEMBLY

Even before the Revolutionary War, and as early as 1774, it had become evident that some changes were needed in the structure of the Church in order to keep pace with its rapid growth. It had become increasingly necessary to depend upon committees to discharge certain functions during the intervals between the synod's meetings. A commission of the synod had been appointed from year to year with undefined powers, but it seems seldom to have met. On such occasions as it did meet, it assumed powers practically equivalent to those of the full synod. As the result of a decision by the Commission of Synod in 1770, which ruled against Alison, Ewing, and the First Church of Philadelphia, and in favor of Duffield and the Pine Street Church, the issue of the commission's authority was raised.[1] Joseph Montgomery, an Old Side party man, had been on the commission for that year, had cast a dissenting vote against its proceedings, and protested them later in synod. Accordingly, the synod in 1772 appointed Ewing and Montgomery to draw up an overture defining the powers of the commission. These two men brought in an overture, whose nature is not recorded. The synod rejected it on the vote.[2] Two years later, the question was put in synod as to whether to discontinue appointing a commission each year, or to continue the practice and officially define the powers of these commissions. The latter alternative was adopted, and a predominantly New Side committee reported in an overture vesting in the commission all the powers of the synod. Furthermore, the overture stipulated, " And let it also be duly attended to, that there can be no appeal from the judgment of the Commission, as there can be none from the judgment of the Synod; but there may be a review of their proceedings and judgments by the Synod." This strongly worded deliverance was " carried by a large majority." [3] Concurrent with these deliberations there had been a bitter New Side, Old Side battle over the coming of Duffield to Third Church, Philadelphia, and over the reception of any further ministers or candidates from Ireland.

Other factors also were calling for some structural changes in the Church's government. Hitherto, the synod had not been a delegated body. For a few years, 1724 to 1728, a plan whereby one half the members of each presbytery were to be delegated to attend synod every first and second year, and all were to attend each third year, had been in operation. After the controversy over subscription in 1729, the idea of a delegated body was dropped.[4] So generally distasteful was the idea of a delegated synod that, when, in 1748, Suffolk Presbytery asked of the Synod of New York the right to be represented in synod only by delegates (because of their great transportation problem), the synod refused. Rather, the presbytery should send ministers when they could, and when they could not, the synod would reckon them as excused absentees.[5]

In 1774 two moves toward a reorganization of the Church were made. Matthew Wilson, an able Old Side man of rather independent judgments, proposed to the synod some kind of plan of government. Whatever the plan he proposed was, it drew forth no more comment than, "The Synod recommend it to their members to make themselves well acquainted with the fundamental principles of the Presbyterian constitution." [6] Another overture was introduced calling for the breaking up of the synod into three smaller synods.[7] The proposal was postponed until the following year, when, no doubt because of the war, it was not again taken up.

After the war, the rapid expansion of the Church made it wholly impractical to continue governing the Church through the large undelegated synod. Members were now being expected to journey once a year to Philadelphia, New York, or Elizabethtown from places as remote as South Carolina and Tennessee. Attendances at the synod were very poor. Often two or more entire presbyteries were absent, and others were represented by only one or two men. Few elders were able to come. The old colonial form of Presbyterianism was outmoded.

Not all Presbyterians, however, looked to the strengthening of a central authority as the proper and desired development. Jacob Green, and a number of other ministers in New Jersey and New York, felt that a decentralized form of Presbyterianism ought to be adopted. They objected that the synod was assuming too much authority over the presbyteries. They would have the presbyteries enjoy a far greater measure of autonomy, and make the synod increasingly an advisory or consultative body. This, they asserted, would be true Presbyterianism — in which the presbytery was the real unit of government. The trend of opinion in most of the Church was against them, although many shared their uneasiness over the movement toward a more and more powerful, and more and more imperious, synod. Finally Green and a few of his friends withdrew peacefully from the Church, in 1779, and founded the Presbytery of Morris County. This group quietly went their own way for a number of years alongside the larger denomination. Gradually their churches dwindled away or were reabsorbed into the main body toward the close of the century.[8]

By 1785 the poor attendance at synod was made a matter of real concern. Only 30 ministers were present, and 6 elders, from the 13 presbyteries then forming the synod. New York Presbytery had 4 present and 16 absent; New Brunswick, 2 present and 11 absent; First Philadelphia, 7 present and 7 absent (the synod met in Philadelphia); Second Philadelphia, 2 present and 3 absent; New Castle, 7 present and 7 absent; Donegal, 5 present and 20 absent; Lewes, 3 present and 4 absent. Six presbyteries — Hanover, Orange, Dutchess, Suffolk, Redstone, and South Carolina — were wholly absent. In other words, nearly 100 ministers were absent, and of the several hundred congregations of the Church, only 6 were represented by elders. The first item on the order of business, after the election of Matthew Wilson as moderator, was to excuse the newly elected moderator for not having been in synod for the past eleven years. The war had, of course, been responsible for the poor attendance in synod during the years of its duration. Attendance from 1775 to 1783 inclusive had been, in order: 24, 18, 26, 11, 19, 15, 20, 30, 43 for the clergy; 5, 3, 4, 3, 7, 4, 4, 9, 10 for the elders. The years 1784 and 1785 had seen a drop in the attendance of both ministers and elders. The figures were 30 ministers and 6 elders for each year. When the attendances for the years from the reunion of 1758 through to 1774 inclusive are studied, it becomes evident that from 1758 to 1785 the entire theory on which the synod was supposedly based had been false. The theoretical basis of the synod was that it was an annual gathering of all the presbyteries for the discharge of such functions as the individual presbyteries, as individual bodies, were not able to perform. Every minister of every presbytery was obligated to attend, and each church was under obligation to send an elder. The synod was merely a " presbytery of the whole." In practice this had not worked out. From 1758 to 1774 over half the clergy had been absent every year but 1761, when 56 out of a total of 105 had been in attendance. In 1764, 1769, 1770, 1771, 1772, and 1774, less than one third of the ministers had been in attendance. Not one of the presbyteries had a good record for attendance. Of an average of over 22 ministers, New York Presbytery had had an average attendance of nearly 8; of 12 ministers, Suffolk had had an average attendance of less than 2, and had been unrepresented in six of the fourteen years. Dutchess Presbytery had been represented four times in the nine years of their existence, usually by 1 minister. (In 1775 they had 11 members. Their earlier reports are vague.) New Brunswick, with an average membership of 14, had an attendance average of less than 6; First Philadelphia, membership average 16, attendance average 8; Second Philadelphia, membership average 7, attendance average just over 3; New Castle, membership average 14, attendance average under 7; Donegal, membership average 11, attendance average under 4; Lewes, membership average 5, attendance average under 3; Hanover, membership average 11, attendance record, eight years all absent, five years 1 present, one year 2 present. The average attendance of the elders had been very low. Since the synod usually met at Philadelphia, the centrally located presbyteries had attendance averages of about one half, and the other presbyteries less, according to their distance from that city.[9]

When the synod of 1785, therefore, expressed great concern about the falling off in attendance at synod, they were not discussing an unfamiliar problem. However, when the synods of 1784 and 1785 were each attended by scarcely one fourth of the ministers, the problem could hardly be avoided longer. The synod sent a pastoral letter to the presbyteries of Hanover, Orange, Suffolk, and Dutchess, urging their attendance and expressing the synod's " great concern . . . that for several years past, very few have attended from some of our distant Presbyteries; and that some others have been entirely unrepresented in our meetings. . . . The Synod wish also to suggest their fears, lest a habit of neglect should be insensibly introduced, to the weakening of each other's hands, the discouraging the comparatively few that attend, and the great injury, if not entirely mouldering away of the body; events, which they rest assured, you would by no means wish to take place, and will, therefore, they persuade themselves, endeavour, so far as in your power, to prevent." [10] Nothing seems to have been done about the numerous absentees from the other presbyteries. The regular form of requiring excuses from absent members upon their next appearance no doubt was allowed to stand in their behalf.

Of much greater importance were two motions passed the day before synod broke up. One required that every candidate for the ministry be subjected " to an accurate examination on the discipline of the Presbyterian Church." The other motion appointed a committee to draw up an American compilation of this said Presbyterian discipline. " On motion, Ordered, That Dr. Witherspoon, Dr. Rodgers, Mr. Robert Smith, Dr. [Patrick] Alison, Dr. [Samuel S.] Smith, Messrs. Woodhull, Cooper, Latta, and Duffield, with the moderator, Mr. Wilson, be a committee to take into consideration the constitution of the church of Scotland, and other Protestant churches, and agreeably to the general principles of Presbyterian government, compile a system of general rules for the government of the Synod, and the several Presbyteries under their inspection, and the people in their communion, and to make report of their proceeding herein at the next meeting of Synod." [11] No mention was made of a General Assembly; these rules were to be for " the Synod, and the several Presbyteries."

Later in the day, " an overture was brought in, that for the better management of the churches under our care, this Synod be divided into three Synods, and that a General Synod, or Assembly, be constituted out of the whole. The Synod agree to enter on the consideration of this overture, on the first Friday after their next meeting, and appoint Dr. Smith to transmit a copy of this overture to such of the Presbyteries as are not at present represented in Synod, and earnestly urge their attendance at our next meeting." [12] Next, an overture was introduced enjoining it upon every minister, and supply in the Church, to be very faithful in the work of catechizing.

Among the papers preserved from the meetings of the synod of 1785 is a memorandum containing verbatim both of these two last-mentioned overtures. On the memorandum, between these two overtures which were spread upon the minutes of the synod, was another most significant section regarding which the minutes are silent. It seems to have been prepared as an elaboration of the first overture. It read as follows: " There shall be also a general assembly of the whole church consisting of deputies from each of the presbyteries, colleges, & universities in the same proportion, & after the same manner as in the general assembly of the Church of Scotland." A note referring back to the words " three Synods " in the first overture amends that overture by adding, " These Synods to hold such intercourse & communication with each other as is at present held by the Synods of the Church of Scotland — and the general assembly exercising the same government & directed by the same rules of proceeding as those that exist in the general assembly of that church; excepting such as arise solely out of its civil establishment, & its political connexion with the state." [13] Who in the synod was, or were, responsible for such an all-out adherence to the Scottish system, it seems impossible to say. The Committee on Overtures was headed by McWhorter, who had deep attachments to the New England Congregationalists and was an intimate friend of Joseph Bellamy. He had once been called to the Old South Church in Boston upon the death of Alexander Cumming, his brother-in-law. Cumming and Ebenezer Pemberton had left the Presbyterian fold to assume charge of that famous Congregational pulpit. The other members of the committee were none of them influential leaders of thought at any time. The overture must have been prepared outside the committee, then passed to it, and while in its hands suffered the loss of the section ordering the Church to be modeled on the Scottish plan. When it is noted that the overture as passed included an order that Dr. [Samuel Stanhope] Smith transmit copies of the overture to the various presbyteries, it seems quite likely that the whole overture originated in the recently appointed committee on Church government of which Smith was a member. That being so, the overture was probably an attempt by that committee to get through the synod, at once, some preliminary statement of policy upon which they could build in drawing up a plan of government. They could hardly design a plan of government without knowing whether or not they were to design it for a general assembly or for no general assembly. Furthermore, some on the committee were evidently deeply attached to the Scottish ways, and also much concerned that colleges and universities should enjoy the special privileges to which the Scottish Church admitted them. Smith was Witherspoon's colleague at the College of New Jersey, and Patrick Allison was head of the Academy at Newark which had long been sponsored by the Old Side. In the absence of further evidence it seems likely that some one or more of these men may have been the leaders of the move. The College of New Jersey was at this time in a deplorable financial condition. Appeals to the Church for collections had brought little money, and Witherspoon's trip to Great Britain the previous year in quest of funds had not gained him enough to pay his expenses. Allison's school had always been weak financially. If a powerful position in the General Assembly were accorded to "colleges & universities," would not the securing of money from the Church be rendered far easier? Whoever made the move was disappointed. Not only was the Scottish scheme deleted, but action on the balance of the overture was deferred until all the presbyteries could study it, and vote on it the following year.

A very wise motion was made to have a committee draw up a new book of psalmody for the Church. The proposal was discussed at some length, and was carried "by a small majority." A committee, predominantly Scotch-Irish of Old Side leanings (because, no doubt, of the conservatism of that group on the subject of psalmody) was appointed: Patrick Allison, Robert Davidson, John Ewing, Samuel Blair (II), and Daniel Jones. The committee reported the next year "that they had paid attention to the affair, but had not yet completed it." They were ordered to continue their work, and to report the following year. The committee made no report in 1787, but the synod that year sanctioned

the use of an American revision of Watts's hymns, edited by Joel Bar-
low, and published in New England.[14] With that action the matter of
a Presbyterian book of psalms was dropped.[15]

In spite of the urgency with which the synod had pleaded for a good
attendance at the synod of 1786, in view of the gravity of the business
contemplated, only 38 ministers and 9 elders answered the roll call.
The following day, 4 more ministers came, and a day later 8 more ministers and 1 elder. Five whole presbyteries — Suffolk, Dutchess, Orange,
Redstone, and South Carolina — were absent. The influential New
York Presbytery had only 4 ministers present; even Alexander Mc-
Whorter was absent. One man represented Abingdon Presbytery. Donegal had 5 present and 22 absent, including Dr. Robert Davidson. Hanover had 4 present and 15 absent, among whom were some of their
best men. The largest delegations were from: First Presbytery, Philadelphia, 11 ministers; New Brunswick, 8; New Castle, 9; and Donegal, 5.
It was with great caution, therefore, that the synod proceeded with their
critical sessions. Considerable courage was required to proceed in the
face of such evident disinterest in, if not opposition to, the idea of a reorganization.

As the debate on all phases of the proposed reorganization got under
way, the first vote taken was on the resolution, " The Synod considering the number and extent of the churches under their care, and the
inconvenience of the present mode of government by one Synod, resolved, that this Synod will establish, out of its own body, three or more
subordinate Synods, out of which shall be composed a General Assembly, Synod, or Council, agreeably to a system hereafter to be adopted."
This motion carried, and a committee chaired by Dr. Rodgers was appointed to draw up a plan for dividing the synod.[16] The committee
recommended that sixteen presbyteries be created, and grouped into
four synods. It also presented a plan for a General Assembly.[17] For
some reason, the synod approved only that section of the report which
ordered the creation of sixteen presbyteries. Action on the erection of
the four synods and the General Assembly was put off for another
year.[18] Perhaps the thin attendance made the synod reluctant to take so
important a step. A concrete plan was now before the Church, and a
year of thought upon it might settle many qualms and questions as to
the ultimate scope and authority of the proposed new bodies.

The committee to draft a system of discipline and Church government submitted a report, the nature and extent of which was not entered upon the minutes. The records state that part of the report was
read (and presumably discussed) at a session which occupied the short
afternoon and evening session.[19] In an official letter, written the follow-

ing day to the Dutch Reformed Synod and the Associate Reformed Synod, with whom union negotiations were being carried on, the synod said, "They [the Synod] have now under consideration a plan of church government and discipline." The plan was Matthew Wilson's and from him there came soon after a graphic account of the debate which had taken place:

"The Scottish Gentry could not, (they durst not) attack our Discipline, but they show'd their low and dirty Spite in Abusing us for some small & trivial Inaccuracies of the Transcriber of our Minutes E G Charging us with *Impiety* and *Want of Religion,* because the Transcriber left out a U P P S which He understood not. . . .

"As for Discipline, after that Evening, when I read Part of my MSS; and Dr. Smith insisted that we should adopt Pardovan, or the Scots Discipline, before he would read it (a curious Maneuver indeed) We had no more of it, but a Committee is appointed in September to meet, and consult & print one. I am one of the Ten Ministers, (tho' my Name was not printed in the List by some Mistake or Design) & Drs. Alison, Sproat and Ewing insist very hard on me to attend. I know not how I can. However I intend to abridge my Plan, & come as near them, as the Constitution of the first Churches would admit. . . . I think they will publish Scotts Discipline with some Abatements. It is wholly a human Creature, I cannot approve it. What should we do? Ought we not to offer a Modest Dissent, & annex our strong Reasons? — to be published with their Book, if they permit it; if not, by itself, to exonerate our Consciences . . . ?"[20] A trivial squabble over the omission of the Latin abbreviation indicating that the committee had not failed to open its meetings with prayer had given a clear indication of the bad spirit prevailing in the synod. Accordingly, when at the evening session Wilson began to read his proposed sketch of a Discipline, Samuel Stanhope Smith, Witherspoon's colleague at the College of New Jersey, not only refused to study Wilson's manuscript, but also tried to have it set aside at once, by calling for an immediate vote on a proposal to adopt the entire Scottish system of government and discipline (of which "Pardovan" was the current handbook, compiled by Walter Steuart, of Pardovan). The synod voted not to adopt the Scottish system, but consideration of Wilson's proposed system was also dropped. "We had no more of it," as Wilson put it.

So warm indeed had been the debate on Wilson's plan that the synod "on motion resolved, that the book of discipline and government be recommended to a committee to meet in the City of Philadelphia on the second Tuesday of September next, who shall have powers to digest such a system as they shall think to be accommodated to the state of the Presbyterian Church in America, that they shall procure three hundred copies to be printed and distributed to the several Presbyteries in proportion to the number of their members under the engagement of this Synod, to have the expense of printing and distribution reimbursed to the committee at their next meeting; and every Presbytery is hereby required to report, in writing, to the Synod at their next meeting, their observations on the said book of government and discipline." [21] The committee on the book was superseded by a new committee, consisting of some of the old committee and some new members. The appointees were: Witherspoon, McWhorter, Rodgers, Sproat, Duffield, Patrick Allison, Ewing, Wilson, S. S. Smith, and three elders — Isaac Snowden, Robert Taggart, and John Pinkerton. Their instructions, according to the motion, were exceedingly broad. Wilson's book was "recommended" to them, and they were given "powers to digest such a system as they shall think to be accommodated to the state of the Presbyterian Church in America." In spite of Wilson's angry cry, the synods of 1785 and 1786 had made it plain that neither a slavish imitation of the Scottish system nor an individualistic system such as Wilson's would be acceptable.

The new committee met as ordered in September. The chairman, Dr. Witherspoon, did not attend. Neither did Dr. Allison. Of the surviving members of the old committee only Rodgers, S. S. Smith, Duffield, and Wilson were in attendance. Of the new members, all but McWhorter were present. It is difficult not to see in all this some significance. If Witherspoon and Allison had been behind the plan for a Scottish imitation presented in 1785, it is quite probable that their influence against the virtually rejected book of 1786 had also been in that direction. That two such prominent men, and one of them the chairman, were absent from this meeting of the reshuffled committee, is too singular to have been accidental. McWhorter had, of course, been chairman of the Committee on Overtures which was probably responsible for the removal of the Scottish scheme from the original overture on the reorganization of the Church. During the meetings of this committee in September, 1786, a complete book of government and discipline was produced. The committee's account of their labors gives no indication of how they worked. "The Committee . . . met according to appointment, except Dr. Witherspoon, Dr. McWhorter, and Dr. Allison; and although the members were divided in sentiment on several parts of the Draught, it was finally agreed to, by the majority, as it now stands." [22] At first, this minute might seem to say that the basis of their work had been Wilson's earlier draft. However, Wilson himself indicates that this did not happen. Writing after the committee meeting and before printed copies of the resulting book had reached him, he said: "Yours by Eq Wiltbank came safe to hand. The Contents give me *too much Suspicion.* . . . What I wrote you when I came home was the Truth, for then the whole Matter & Disputations were fix'd on My Mind. . . . Dr. Duffield was Clerk of the Committee, and totally *Erastian* in Principle, Allowing *no Scripture Discipline,* & therefore Choosing the Scottish, as allowing him perpetuity of Wrangling. Dr. Sproat and Dr. Ewing were to assist in preparing for the Press, the former has been sick as I hear, & the latter otherwise engaged, & not in the greatest cordiality with our Clerk. The minutes were strongly intermingled with *Dr. Smith's Book,* how they are separated or managed I long to know." [23] The committee had elaborated a new book, based partly on Scottish usages, and owing a strong debt to a book drafted by Samuel S. Smith. The committee printed their finished draft as instructed, and sent it out to the presbyteries, under the title, *Draught of a Plan of Government and Discipline.*

It is disappointing to note from the minutes of the various presbyteries how little attention was given to this momentous transaction, involving as it did the reorganization of the entire Church. Not all of these minutes are preserved, but such as are extant reveal less interest than seems desirable. True, since the synod were merely all the presbyteries met as one presbytery, many of the clergy may have felt that their presbytery had already adequately expressed their mind in the sessions of the synod. New Brunswick Presbytery appointed Witherspoon and Armstrong, plus two elders, to study the draft and prepare a report for the synod. At the next synod the committee reported that they had met, but since the two elders did not attend, the ministers decided to take no action.[24] The minutes of the presbytery do not indicate that the plan was ever discussed in the presbytery. Whether Witherspoon's failure to attend the meeting of the reconstituted committee on the book was in any way connected with his attitude on the presbytery's committee is not known. The Philadelphia Presbytery, composed (after 1786) of the former First Presbytery of Philadelphia and those members of the old Second Presbytery who lived within the area of Philadelphia, discussed the proposed plan with some care. They asked, principally, that greater authority be given to the people in electing elders, and that the elders not serve for life: "that the people should be allowed the privilege of choosing their Elders annually or triennially if they see meet; the former [elders] still continuing in office till such election be had, and being re-eligible." The presbytery also asked "that some method should be prescribed for setting apart elders to that office"; and "that in allowing vacant congregations a seat in judicatures care be taken to preserve an equality of representation between the Clergy and laity."[25] Hanover Presbytery likewise were concerned that there should be some method prescribed for setting apart elders. Ordination of elders at this time seems seldom to have been practiced. The synod had ruled some years earlier that election in itself made a man an elder. It added that some public acceptance of the office by the man was desirable, but did not prescribe how the man should perform this public acceptance. The case was notable since it involved one of the most rigorous of the Scotch-Irish Old Side ministers, who had contended against his people that no public acceptance of the eldership was necessary. In the synod the appeal was brought in by New Side party men. Also the case was notable since the whole stress of the controversy fell on whether or not the newly elected elder ought to be required to accept the office in the presence of the congregation. The idea of the man's not being fully vested with the office until something beyond election had been done to him in the name of the Church (i.e., ordination) was not mentioned in the controversy, and was not adverted to or required in the synod's ruling.[26] Scottish practice on the point was also ambiguous at this time. Ordination by the laying on of hands was not used. Elders and deacons alike were asked certain constitutional questions, and then " set apart " by prayer. Presbyterian and Reformed practice generally has varied a great deal on both the theory and the exercise of the office of the elder.[27] Strong sentiment in Philadelphia and Hanover Presbyteries for some clarification of the issue was therefore not surprising.

Of the then sixteen presbyteries, thirteen were represented at the synod of 1787. Suffolk, Orange, and Transylvania were absent wholly. Fifty-four ministers, barely one third of the total number, answered the roll, together with 7 elders. Once again the attendance from all but Philadelphia and New Castle Presbyteries was spotty. During the next few days of the synod's sessions, which lasted from May 16 to May 28, with the Sundays off, another 15 ministers and 7 elders straggled in. Since the synod's sixteen presbyteries had then about 177 members,[28] the reorganization of the Church was to be transacted by two fifths of its clergy and a fraction of its eldership. The meeting therefore was again marked by great caution.

Early in the synod's deliberations attention was turned to a letter from the Suffolk Presbytery " praying that the union between them and the Synod may be dissolved." The presbytery had not been represented in synod since 1772 (a synod marked by fearful strife[29] including an overture: " Overtured, whether the state of the Presbyteries belonging to this Synod is such as contributes most to the interest of religion and the honour of this body. Deferred till next year." [30]) The synod appointed a committee to confer with the Suffolk Presbytery and drafted a letter to them as well.[31] If in addition to the withdrawal of those ministers who had left the synod to form the Presbytery of Morris County, the entire Presbytery of Suffolk were to withdraw, the loss would be serious indeed. The Church would almost cease to exist in the Hudson Valley, Long Island, and parts of northern New Jersey.

As debate on the draft of the plan of government and discipline was taken up, most other business was laid aside for six days. Thereafter, other items as well as the draft were handled. The minutes of this debate are too skeletal to provide much knowledge of what went on. Only one formal presbytery report is mentioned (and that no more than mentioned), although each of the sixteen presbyteries had been ordered to submit a written report. The proposed plan was discussed section by section in the full synod, and seems to have been voted on section by section. In only four sections is explicit mention of debate recorded. A comparison of the draft of 1786 with the draft of 1787, however, indicates that a great many changes were made or ordered made.[32] The synod laid aside until the end of the debate the issue of what representation to grant to vacant churches in the Church courts. Also a committee of Witherspoon, Rodgers, S. S. Smith, and Latta was appointed to " prepare an overture respecting the setting apart of ruling elders and deacons to their respective offices." Later " it was moved and carried, that the Form of Process [in the Judicatures of the Church of Scotland, with Relation to Scandals and Censures. Ratified and approved by act of the Assembly 18th April 1707] in Steuart of Pardovan's Collection[s and Observations Concerning the Worship, Discipline, and Government of the Church of Scotland] be read and considered as a basis of deliberation, along with the draught." [33] The following morning this order was revoked. Walter Steuart's *Collections and Observations,* a digest of the various deliverances of the Scottish Church on worship, discipline, and government was generally regarded as an authoritative compilation of Scottish practice. Evidently the desire for adherence to Scottish models still had strong backing in the synod, but not a conclusive majority. S. S. Smith no doubt made the motion, for Wilson states that he made a similar move a year earlier.

In the midst of this debate a paper from the Widows' Fund was brought in. The Fund had presented its case to the synod the previous two years as well.[34] Declining membership had brought it to such a state that annuities could not be paid. Moreover, serious differences of opinion had arisen over its treatment of two widows, one of whom had appealed to the synod for "interposition" at this session. The synod tabled the papers sent up by the Fund.[35] In the 1786 Draught of a Plan of Government it was stipulated that every minister must join the Fund, but this was eliminated in the 1787 draft. In 1784 and 1785 the synod had recommended the Fund to their members. After its incorporation, which was initiated on the eve of the reunion and while it was still under the Old Side control, the Fund had continued to be controlled by officers who were predominantly Old Side. A long struggle had been waged between the synod and the Fund over certain missionary monies to which the Fund had tried to lay an exclusive claim. At one time the Fund was attempting to operate virtually as a missionary society.[36] This had led, among other things, to the organization of a rival Presbyterian Widows' Fund in New Jersey. Its petition for a charter was still pending when the war broke out in 1775, and this fund was never brought into being. No doubt some of these matters, together with dissatisfaction with the current management, had contributed both to the decline of the Fund's memberships and to the synod's unwillingness again to enter into close relations with it. It was unfortunate that because of such a series of events the reorganization of the Church was carried through without any plan for the assisting of the widows and orphans of ministers. From the synod of 1788, however, the Fund secured the privilege of publishing as an Appendix to the new constitution of the Church a statement of its purposes and the requirements for membership.

At length on May 28, " the Synod having gone through the consideration of the draught of a plan of government and discipline, Dr. Rodgers, Dr. McWhorter, Mr. Miller and Mr. Wilson, junior, were appointed a committee to have a thousand copies thereof printed as now amended, and to distribute them among the Presbyteries for their consideration, and the consideration of the churches under their care." [37] No vote was yet taken on whether or not to adopt the plan. Rather, it was approved only for sending down to the presbyteries.

Attention was now directed to the Confession of Faith and to the Directory for Public Worship. " The Synod took into consideration the last paragraph of the twentieth chapter of the Westminster Confession of Faith; the third paragraph of the twenty-third chapter; and the first paragraph of the thirty-first chapter; and having made some alterations, agreed that the said paragraphs, as now altered, be printed for consideration, together with the draught of a plan of government and discipline. The Synod also appointed the above named committee to revise the Westminster Directory for public worship, and to have it when thus revised, printed, together with the draught, for consideration. And the Synod agreed, that when the above proposed alterations in the Confession of Faith shall have been finally determined on by the body, and the Directory shall have been revised as above directed, and adopted by the Synod, the said Confession thus altered, and Directory thus revised and adopted, shall be styled, ' The Confession of Faith, and Directory for public worship, of the Presbyterian Church in the United States of America.' " [38]

The committee to whom the Plan of Government and the Confession of Faith were given, and to whom the revision of the Westminster Directory was entrusted, were John Rodgers, Alexander McWhorter, Alexander Miller, and James Wilson. Rodgers had been on every committee that had had anything to do with the drafting of the Plan of Government, and had attended each meeting. No other individual had had the same continuous connection with this task. Witherspoon had been on the original committee of 1785, but had missed the crucial special meeting of 1786. Matthew Wilson had been on the original committee, and had attended the special meeting of 1786. He had not been in the synod in 1787 and was now dropped from the committee. S. S. Smith and Duffield, who had been on the original committee and at the special meeting, were also dropped, though they were at the 1787 synod. McWhorter had been a new appointee for the year 1786, and had missed the special meeting of that year. Alexander Miller and James Wilson had not been connected with the plan previous to their appointment at the 1787 synod. Circumstantially, it would seem that Rodgers had been the leader in the enterprise all along. Further hints of this appear in that he was named first (in the letter) of the committee mentioned as about to visit the Suffolk Presbytery, in an effort to persuade them not to withdraw from the Church. As the one who had had the most to do with the drafting of the plan, he would have been the best one to head the delegation sent to explain it.

There is a tradition to the effect that Witherspoon was the chief architect of all the plans for the reorganization of the Church. His biographer, Collins, adopts the tradition, and cites as authority for it an unpublished life of Witherspoon by Ashbel Green.[39] This life of Witherspoon was written sometime after 1835, at a time when Green was over seventy-three years old, and over half a century after the reorganization of the Church.[40] Green states in this biography: " In forming the present Constitution of the Presbyterian Church his [Witherspoon's] agency & influence were all but dominant. The propriety of an Introduction to this Formula in which should be specified the general principles on which the Synod had proceeded as the ground work of the whole system which they adopted was first suggested by

him, was prepared solely by himself. An attempt was made by one influential member to modify some of the statements, but the original
draught was finally & unanimously adopted, with scarcely an alteration. The writer [Green] was a personal witness of what he states on
this topic." [41] Green says, therefore, two things, that Witherspoon's
voice was all but dominant in all the deliberations, and that he composed by himself the short preface to the Plan of Government. The
first of these claims is almost impossible in view of Witherspoon's
record on the committee, but the second may well be true. The preface,
a remarkable piece of work, remained substantially unchanged from its
first known form, that of the special committee's report of 1786,
through to the end. Some changes were made, and the document is
the poorer for them, but in the main it was not greatly altered. If
Witherspoon prepared this draft, and submitted it to the synod of May,
1786, it might well have been part of the uncompleted book which
was then turned over to the reshuffled committee upon which he
seems never again to have served. [42] When the debate of which Green
writes took place, it is difficult to conceive. From 1786 to 1788 changes
were made in the document, and its text was not fixed until Rodgers'
committee finally reported it in in 1788. Then it was not voted upon
except as a part of the entire Plan of Government and Discipline. It
was certainly not unanimously adopted in May of 1786 when Witherspoon reported it in. Whatever Green's errors in memory may have
been, he was guilty of less than Collins, who, leaning on Green's
" dominant influence " statement, credited Witherspoon with almost
the entire reorganization of the Church. [43]

To another committee, the synod of 1787 gave the task of breaking
up that body into three synods. The committee were S. S. Smith, Mc-
Whorter, Duffield, Powers, Casson, Kerr, Simpson, J. B. Smith, Temple-
ton, and Balch. [44] Representation of the various presbyteries seems to
have influenced the choice of this committee. S. S. Smith, McWhorter,
and Duffield had previously served on the Committee on the Plan of
Government, but only McWhorter now held a position on both committees. Later this committee reported, " and after considering their
report, the Synod agreed that the arrangement of the Presbyteries under four Synods should, for the present, remain as determined last
year." [45] Just before adjournment an overture was brought in: " Resolved, that the division of the Synod be postponed until next year,
and that the Synod be then divided." [46] What difficulty lay back of this
repeated deferring of the division of the synod is a mystery. It may
have been that many were fearful that if the synod were broken up,
and four equally autonomous synods were created while there was in

existence no body superior to them, some of these synods might choose to stay independent.

To those who had borne the burden of reorganizing the Church, the synod of 1788 must have been somewhat anticlimactic. Twenty-nine ministers answered the roll call. Over 140 ministers were absent.[47] One half of the sixteen presbyteries were wholly absent, and three were represented by only 1 minister. Nine elders answered the roll call. Stragglers raised the attendance record by only 9 ministers and 1 elder. From the initiation of the move to found a general assembly, the attendance had steadily dwindled, in spite of synod's pleas for large attendances in view of the importance of the reorganization. The synod of 1788, including stragglers, had an attendance of less than twenty per cent of their ministerial membership. The percentage of churches represented by the 10 elders must have been poor indeed. At no time since the reunion of 1758 had so small a percentage of presbyteries, ministers, and elders attended the sessions of the synod. A probable explanation is that psychologically the time for a system of delegated representation was long past. Or it may be even more likely that as the Church had grown, local ties and local interests alone seemed vital, and the problems of synods and general assemblies were being left to whoever were interested in them. Such essentially independent attitudes had always had some vogue in the Church, and frontier conditions would both justify and intensify them in the minds of many.

Real satisfaction is reflected in a minute of the synod recording the fact that Dr. Rodgers' committee to the Presbytery of Suffolk had been able to persuade that body to withdraw their request for the dissolution of their ties to the synod. A member of the presbytery was present as their representative.[48]

From his home, where he was detained by illness, Matthew Wilson made a final effort to have the draft of the Plan of Government laid aside. His own personal copy of the draft of 1786, heavily annotated in his own hand, gives some clue as to his feelings. Upon the title page he had written, " Teaching for Doctrines the Commandments of Men." Among his many notes is one upon a mellifluous passage in the preface to the Plan. Occurring in the passage were the words, " The whole system of the internal government which Christ hath appointed." In the margin Wilson wrote: " An: Has Xt appointed these Laws? — Are they not stolen from the Kirk of Scotland? " On the back of his copy of the Plan Wilson notes: " See a much better Book of Discipline by Mr. [Thomas] Cartwright, A.D. 1584, Neal's H[istory of the Puritans] Vol 1, Appendix, [II]. Also Willson's *Scripture Discipline*." Wilson's final plea to the synod of 1788 was tabled. From several congregations, one in New York Presbytery, one in Baltimore Presbytery, and one in Orange Presbytery, memorials were sent up, but were merely tabled.

After four days of discussion, the draft of the Plan of Government and Discipline was completed. When it is noted that these discussions for so many days during a four-year period finally resulted in a forty-six-page duodecimo publication, it becomes evident that few corners of the document had been left unexplored. An earnest effort had been made to create a plan that would be truly American, and yet also in harmony with general Presbyterian and Reformed usages. The changes in the Confession of Faith also were discussed in detail.

May 28, 1788, " the Synod having fully considered the draught of the form of government and discipline, did, on a review of the whole, and hereby do ratify and adopt the same, as now altered and amended, as the Constitution of the Presbyterian Church in America, and order the same to be considered and strictly observed as the rule of their proceedings, by all the inferior judicatories belonging to the body. And they order that a correct copy be printed, and that the Westminster Confession of Faith, as now altered, be printed in full along with it, as making a part of the constitution.

" Resolved, That the true intent and meaning of the above ratification by the Synod, is, that the Form of Government and Discipline and the Confession of Faith, as now ratified, is to continue to be our constitution and the confession of our faith and practice unalterable, unless two thirds of the Presbyteries under the care of the General Assembly shall propose alterations or amendments, and such alterations or amendments shall be agreed to and enacted by the General Assembly." [49]

Constitutionally then, the synod, which was an annual gathering, undelegated, of all the presbyteries, a presbytery of the whole, adopted the Constitution of the Church by its own authority, after advice and consultation had been received from the presbyteries acting separately. The presbyteries, in so far as their records are preserved, did not vote upon the question of ratifying or adopting the Constitution except when each presbytery was, legally, present as a whole in the synod. In other words, the synod, as the presbytery of the whole, was granted the authority by the presbyteries to adopt the Constitution and make it binding upon all. Since the Church hitherto had not as yet adopted any explicit form of government, and had made its rules " as circumstances should from time to time show to be expedient," [50] this procedure was logical. Lest, however, it give rise in the future to an authoritarian and all-powerful General Assembly, the ratification was explicitly given an official interpretation.

This ratification of the Constitution by the synod was not to set a precedent for future constitutional changes by the General Assembly. Hereafter changes in the Constitution could be proposed only by the presbyteries, with two thirds of them concurring in the proposal. Enactment of these proposed changes was subject to the agreement of the General Assembly. Since the Assembly hereafter was to be a delegated body, with representation based upon the numerical strength of each presbytery, a system of checks and balances was thus provided.

Relatively short work was made of approving the Directory for Worship which Dr. Rodgers' committee presented. Two sections of it were quickly revised by Witherspoon, S. S. Smith, and Woodhull, and the whole approved in three sessions lasting less than two days.

" The Synod having now revised and corrected the draught of a directory for worship, did approve and ratify the same, and do hereby appoint the said directory, as now amended, to be the directory for the worship of God in the Presbyterian Church in the United States of America. They also took into consideration the Westminster Larger and Shorter Catechisms, and having made a small amendment of the larger, did approve, and do hereby approve and ratify the said Catechisms, as now agreed on, as the Catechisms of the Presbyterian Church in the said United States. And the Synod order, that the said Directory and Catechisms be printed and bound up in the same volume with the Confession of Faith and the Form of Government and Discipline, and that the whole be considered as the standard of our doctrine, government, discipline, and worship, agreeably to the resolutions of the Synod at their present sessions." [51]

Strictly interpreted, this adopting act would mean that the Directory was adopted in the same sense as were the Plan of Government and Discipline, the Confession of Faith, and the two Catechisms. The book was wholly one of advice and counsel on the manner of conducting the acts of worship. It did not even include set forms for celebrating either sacrament, or for the performing of marriage ceremonies. Adoption of the Directory meant therefore that the long-standing tradition of completely free worship was to be continued.

When the three extant plans of government, those of 1786, 1787, and the one adopted in 1788, are compared, two trends are quite clearly apparent. Certain distinctly American aspects, though not all, become more strongly expressed with each revision; and a greater degree of formality was brought about in each revision.

The preface, or " Introduction," as it was officially titled, to the Plan of Government was intended, it said, to set forth the basis upon which the synod had proceeded in drawing up this plan. Under eight heads the synod reaffirmed:

I. "That 'God alone is Lord of the conscience, and hath left it free from the doctrines and commandments of men; which are in anything contrary to his word, or beside it in matters of faith or worship.'" Therefore, the synod reassert the rights of private judgment in matters of religion, repudiate all ties to the civil government, and call for full freedom of religion for all.

II. Every Christian Church, accordingly, is free to declare the terms of admission to its body, and to declare what it thinks are the rules laid down by Christ for his Church. If in doing this it makes the laws too lax or too narrow, it wounds, not outsiders, but only itself.

III. Christ has appointed officers in his Church who are to preach, administer the sacraments, and exercise discipline in the Church.

IV. "Truth is in order to goodness and the great touchstone of truth, is its tendency to promote holiness." (This statement was weakened in 1787, but the 1786 version was restored in 1788.) Nothing is more absurd than to say that it does not matter what a man thinks.

V. While it is necessary to make effectual provision that all who are teachers be sound in the faith, the synod say that there are both truths and forms about which "men of good characters and principles differ." Here mutual forbearance is asked in the 1787 and 1788 drafts. (The draft of 1786 had a far nobler spirit, much akin to the preface which the Rodgers committee prepared for the Directory.[52] The 1786 draft included this passage: "Teachers [, this Church believes, should] be sound in the faith, and hold the essential doctrines of the gospel; they also believe that there are truths of less moment, and forms as to practice or omission of which men of the best characters and principles may differ, and in all these they think it the duty . . . [to exercise] forbearance, and neither to judge rashly nor refuse such communion as may shew that they look upon all such as brethren who in the judgment of charity love our Lord Jesus Christ in sincerity, and that they believe in the unity of the catholic church." (It is regrettable that this confession of the unity of the Church Universal and the plea for the joining in worship with other Christian Churches were both deleted from the later drafts.)

VI. All phases of Church government are laid down in the Scriptures, but the applying of these rules to any particular Church is the right of that Church itself.

VII. All Church power is only ministerial and declarative. The Bible is the only rule that is infallible in matters of faith and practice. It is the only authoritative constitution, and no Church may make rules

binding upon men's consciences. More danger lies in a Church's grasp-
ing of legislative power than in a Church's failure to judge aright what
are the Biblical laws.

VIII. Understood in the light of the above principles, strict Church
discipline "will contribute to the glory and happiness of any church.
Since ecclesiastical discipline must be purely moral or spiritual in its
object, and not attended with any civil effects, it can derive no force
whatever, but from its own justice, the approbation of an impartial
public, and the countenance and blessing of the great Head of the
Church universal."

From 1786 to 1788 only two significant changes had been made in
this preface, that in section IV, which was restored later, and the unfortunate deletion in section V. No doubt the licking of wounds from
bygone days before the Revolutionary War, and the intensive missionary activities of the Baptists and Methodists at this time, plus memories
of Ireland, made only a few great souls able to confess the Church Universal.

The Form of Government itself is essentially an American document.
In general, it shows the influences of the Form of Government and the
Directory prepared in London by the Westminster Assembly, and
adopted later for the Church of Scotland, but even where the similari-
ties are the greatest, a new spirit is at work.

If in any section the two Forms should have shown great similarity,
it ought to have been in the section on the presbytery, the very heart
of the Presbyterian system. Yet here the contrast is great. The British
document was written when the "due right of presbyteries" needed
defense. The American document is largely concerned with how a
presbytery are to conduct their functions.

The draft of 1786 had been concerned to restrict drastically the
power of the General Assembly by denying it the right to "assume the
business of a presbytery, to issue processes for scandal or misdemeanor,
or try any matter *de novo;* unless, so far, as to determine any matter of
dispute, *in thesi,* submitted to them, by any synod, presbytery, or
bishop." [53] The Plan of 1787 (retained in 1788) made this restriction
more general, but included a provision that no act of a General Assembly
could become a standing rule without first being referred to the presbyteries, and securing the consent of at least a majority of them.

The Westminster Form was almost wholly silent on the General
Assembly because of the British situation at the time. The development of the Scottish General Assembly had been quite different from
that in America. When Presbyterianism was established in Scotland,
Parliament created a General Assembly. This body adopted its own

laws, created the synods and presbyteries under its authority, and determined their scope, powers, and general rules. The Scottish Church was, therefore, organized from the top down, and all ultimate authority rested in and came from the Assembly. Some curbs had from time to time been put upon the Assembly's exercise of this power, but the basis has never been changed. In the American Church the presbytery came first and created the synod; then the synod, acting as little more than the presbytery of the whole, created the General Assembly, but did so in such a manner as to leave ultimate authority in the presbyteries, and to make the synods and the General Assembly agencies for unifying the life of the Church, considering appeals, and promoting the general welfare of the Church as a whole.

At least two of the presbyteries had expressed dissatisfaction with the draft of 1786, because it contained no explicit section on the election and ordination of elders and deacons. Usage both in Great Britain and America was not stable, and guidance was needed. The Plan of 1787 provided for election of both these officers by any method desired by the individual congregation. Scottish usage was choice by the existing session, with permission for the congregation to object if they desired.[54] This was the pattern of the Westminster system. The growing American practice was nomination by the session, with election the sole right of the people. Trouble over this clash of patterns had been common. The Plan of Government side-stepped the whole issue. Also, no stand was taken on whether or not the eldership was for life, or for a term. Philadelphia Presbytery had asked for such a declaration. The Westminster system prescribed a life term, as did also the Scottish Second Book of Discipline. But actual practice in Scotland until the beginning of the eighteenth century had tended to make the eldership an annual office. As late as 1718 a Scottish synod came in conflict with the General Assembly because they had tried to compel the use of limited period eldership.[55] As for the ordination of elders and deacons, neither the Westminster Form and Directory nor any Scottish act set out fixed forms. The Plan of 1787 (and 1788) provided the same constitutional questions for the elders and deacons (on the Bible, the Confession of Faith, and the government and discipline of the Church) as were used for the ordination of ministers. Both elders and deacons were to be set apart by prayer, without the laying on of hands, after they had publicly answered these questions and expressed their willingness to accept the offices. The one form was to be used for either office.

The office of the ministry no doubt received most careful consideration by the founding fathers in all their deliberations. The subject was naturally dear to them, and, furthermore, many of them had formed rather sharp opinions on the ministry during the pre-Revolutionary controversies with the colonial Anglicans. Moreover, many more would remember the controversy over the ministry that had burned so fiercely within the Presbyterian Church itself from 1760 to the opening of the war.

The sole and total right of licensure and ordination was vested in the presbyteries, contrary to Scottish law, but in conformity with the New Side's policy earlier in the century.[56] Following again the lead of the New Side, the Plan of Government provided: " And it is the duty of the presbytery, for their satisfaction with regard to the real piety of such candidates, to examine them respecting their experimental acquaintance with religion, and the motives which influence them to desire the sacred office." It was " recommended " that a candidate have a college diploma, " or at least authentic testimonials of his having gone through a regular course of learning." Moreover, the requirement of two years in the study of theology, rejected in the synod of 1785, was now incorporated into the Plan of Government. Certain tests or " trials " before the presbytery were also prescribed, in Latin, Hebrew, and Greek (the first official requirement of Hebrew in American Presbyterianism), the arts and sciences, theology, and church history. This requirement was in keeping with general Reformed usage everywhere.[57] It was, however, more explicit than the statements of any other Presbyterian Church of that day.

The American Presbyterians, accordingly, followed the lead of the Scottish Church in making the licentiate a distinct office with a continuable status. Not all the Reformed Churches did so. The Westminster Form and Directory did not provide for licensure, and many of the Continental Reformed Churches did not. Since the Scottish Church, and the American also, disliked intensely the idea of ordaining men who did not have calls to specific churches, the status of the licentiate provided a sort of halfway office. The licentiate could preach, catechize, and evangelize while seeking a call to a congregation, and the Church as a whole had some control over him in the period between his leaving off his studies and his securing a call. The other Reformed Churches tended to ordain a man after he left school, and to allow him thereafter to find a call.[58] If, however, they followed the Scottish pattern in adopting the office of a licentiate, the Americans did so with a difference which is nowhere better revealed than in the questions propounded by the two Churches to candidates for licensure:

AMERICAN CHURCH

" 1. Do you believe the scriptures of the old and new testament, to be the word of God, the only infallible rule of faith and practice?

" 2. Do you sincerely receive and adopt the confession of faith of this church, as containing the system of doctrine taught in the holy scriptures?

" 3. Do you promise to study the peace, unity and purity of the church?

" 4. Do you promise to submit yourself, in the Lord, to the government of this presbytery, or of any other presbytery in the bounds of which you may be? "

SCOTTISH CHURCH

" 1mo, Do you believe the Scriptures of the Old and New Testaments to be the Word of God, and the only rule of faith and manners?

" 2do, Do you sincerely own and believe the whole doctrine of the Confession of Faith, approven by the General Assemblies of this National Church, and ratified by law, in the year 1690, and frequently confirmed by divers Acts of Parliament since that time, to be the truths of God, contained in the Scriptures of the Old and New Testaments; and do you own the whole doctrine therein contained as the confession of your faith?

" 3tio, Do you sincerely own the purity of worship presently authorised and practised in this Church, and asserted in the 15th Act of the General Assembly, 1707, entitled, ' Act against Innovations in the Worship of God;' and do also own the Presbyterian government and discipline now so happily established in this Church; and are you persuaded that the said doctrine, worship, discipline, and Church government, are founded upon the Holy Scriptures, and agreeable there?

" 4to, Do you promise, that, through the grace of God, you will firmly and constantly adhere to, and in your station to the utmost of your power assert, maintain, and defend the said doctrine, worship, and discipline, and the

SCOTTISH CHURCH

government of this Church, by Kirk-Sessions, Presbyteries, Provincial Synods, and General Assemblies?

"5to, Do you promise, that in your practice you will conform yourself to the said worship, and submit yourself to the said discipline and government of this Church, and shall never endeavour, directly nor indirectly, the prejudice or subversion of the same?

"6to, Do you promise, that you shall follow no divisive course from the present establishment in this Church?

"7mo, Do you renounce all doctrines, tenets, or opinions whatsoever, contrary to or inconsistent with the said doctrine, worship, and government of this Church?

"8vo, Do you promise that you will subject yourself to the several judicatories of this Church, and are you willing to subscribe to these things?" [59]

In addition to answering these questions the Scottish candidate had to sign the following subscription formula:

"I   do hereby declare, that I do sincerely own and believe the whole doctrine contained in the Confession of Faith, approven by the General Assemblies of this National Church, and ratified by law in the year 1690, and frequently confirmed by divers Acts of Parliament since that time, to be the truths of God; and I do own the same as the confession of my faith: As likewise, I do own the purity of government and discipline now so happily established therein; which doctrine, worship, and Church government, I am persuaded are founded on the Word of God, and agreeable thereto: And I promise, that, through the grace of God, I shall firmly and constantly adhere to the same, and, to the utmost of my power, shall, in my station. assert, maintain, and defend the said doctrine, worship, discipline, and government of this Church, by Kirk-sessions, Presbyteries, Provincial Synods, and General Assemblies; and that I shall in my practice conform myself to the said worship, and submit to the said discipline and government, and never endeavour, directly nor indirectly, the prejudice or subversion of the same; and I promise, that I shall follow no divisive course from the present establishment in this Church; renouncing all doctrines, tenets, and opinions whatsoever, contrary to, or inconsistent with, the said doctrine, worship, discipline, or government of this Church." [60]

The requirement of some such formula had been one of the chief aspects of Old Side Presbyterianism, but the American Church did not adopt any form of subscription. The Westminster system had no such formula. In Scotland subscription, with the same formula as was required of the licentiate, was exacted from the candidate for ordination. No subscription formula was required by the American Church. Procedure for ordination followed in most respects the usage that had by then become common in Reformed Churches, i.e., by the laying on of hands by the ministers of the presbytery only. Earlier Reformed usage had wavered on this matter.[61]

The call and election of a licentiate as minister to a congregation in a free Church in America was already very different from that in the established Church of Scotland. The American pattern was thoroughly democratic, providing for election by the members of the congregation who were in good standing, and who contributed to the necessary expenses of the congregation. Because of the popular structure of the Church, some detailed instructions were laid down for the calling of a minister. (The 1786 Plan required minister and congregation to join the Widows' Fund, but this section was eliminated in the later plans.) All calls had to pass through the presbytery.

The Westminster Form closed with the section on ordination, and gave over to the Directory for Church Government, Church Censures, and Ordination of Ministers a number of matters on Church government. The Americans placed all topics relating to Church government in their Plan of Government and Discipline. Most of these matters in the American plan are based wholly on American conditions and ways.

The same pattern of the greatest freedom in the following of English, Scottish, and Continental Presbyterian and Reformed usages prevailed in the Form of Process, and the Directory for Worship. Instead of the long twenty-page Form of Process of the Scottish Church, which some of the synod had wished to adopt, a very concise six-page document was produced by the Americans. The Scottish book was deeply rooted in the Scotland of 1707, and would have been anachronistic in the new republic of 1788. Yet there is a certain similarity between the two books. On the procedure for the trial of a minister the American book leans heavily on the Scottish Form. Yet again even where they are most alike formally, the spirit is different.

An examination of the first draft of the Directory for Public Worship, which the Rodgers committee reported in in 1787, makes it quite clear that, although the committee must have had the Westminster Directory for Public Worship before it, the book is essentially a new compilation. For the most part it is a vastly inferior book liturgically. Its ideas are not much different from those of the older English Directory, but the excellent phrasing, appropriate cadences, and stateliness of the seventeenth century Puritan Directory are not to be found in the product of the raw new world. No doubt the American book was too hastily gotten up. As did the Westminster Directory, the American edition of 1787 suggested pattern prayers, but they were not of great stature. In the 1788 edition all these were omitted, and quite rightly so. Furthermore, the 1787 book was rather loosely framed, and verbose. The revised edition of 1788, shorn of the long suggested prayers and made much more terse, was little more than a book of counsel for the clergy. Even in this regard it lacked the depth of the older Puritan document.

The suggestions for the celebration of the two sacraments, as proposed in 1787, were retained in the final edition, with no great change except for the elimination of the suggestions regarding the prayers. No forms were outlined for either sacrament. This, in general, was identical with the uses of the Westminster Directory. Set forms were anathema. Admission to the sacraments, however, in the 1787 Directory required assent of all to a rather full doctrinal statement. The edition of 1788 dropped this, preferring merely to say that persons should be examined as to their knowledge and piety.

The resistance to all set forms appears again in the section on marriage. Only the vows themselves were given as explicit words to be used. The section on the burial of the dead, occupying less than half a page in the 1788 edition, by indirection permitted a funeral service. The draft of 1787 allowed a funeral service, but forbade any ceremony whatever at the interment. The 1788 edition remains silent regarding any ceremony at the interment. Here the 1787 book followed the Westminster Directory, as it did also in granting that "it is decent and proper, that persons be interred, in a manner suitable to their rank and condition while living" — a direction omitted from the later definitive edition. The draft of 1787 also strictly condemned the custom of serving liquor at funerals. This condemnation the book of 1788 omitted.

A rather large (twenty-five pages) section of suggested forms of prayers for use in the home and family was appended to the 1787 edition. By omitting this from the 1788 edition, the synod seem to have carried resistance to forms farther than was for the best interests of the Church. The holding together of the worship in the home and the worship of the sanctuary by means such as the book of 1787 intended had real merit. Other differences between the 1787 and 1788 editions, or between these and the Directory, might be mentioned, but suffice it to say that while the Westminster pattern was in large measure used, the American book was quite independent of, and often inferior to, its British predecessor. This inferiority, however, was no doubt more than compensated for by the fact that the new American book was truly of the American Church, and not merely a traditional book inherited from the Old World.

The Westminster Confession of Faith had since 1729 been the confession of the Church. It was not necessary, therefore, to deliberate long about it. The sections that connected the Church with the State were revised so as to make the church wholly a free church, Chs. XX.4, XXIII.3, XXX.1. Hitherto, the American church had never adopted either the Larger or the Shorter Catechism. After Question 109 of the Larger Catechism had been revised, by deleting from it the statement that "tolerating a false religion" was a sin against the Second Commandment, the two Catechisms and the Confession were included in the Constitution.

In all these constitutional symbols, accordingly, the American presbyteries sought to continue their communion with the other Churches that shared the Presbyterian and Reformed heritage in faith and life. This they did freely and in conformity with what they considered the genius and needs of their own Church.

The statistics published by the Church in 1788 listed the number of ministers and the number of congregations.[62] (See page 306.)

Its work completed, the synod of 1788 appointed John Witherspoon to open the first session of the General Assembly with a sermon, and to preside during the election of the Moderator.[63] It set the dates on which the new synods were to meet, and then dissolved. Its career had been at times stormy, but it had never failed to have a solid core of godly ministers and faithful congregations. Under the guidance of this synod the Church had grown both in grace and in size. The future

Church bodies might alter in the years to come much of what the synod had enacted, but nothing could dim the luster of the synod's solid achievements.

Synod	Presbytery	Ministers	Congregations with Pastors	Congregations Without Pastors	Licentiate
New York and New Jersey	Suffolk	11	9	3	1
	Dutchess County	6	5	4	—
	New York	22	20	19	3
	New Brunswick	16	17	9	—
		55	51	35	4
Philadelphia	Philadelphia	23	15	6	—
	New Castle	15	21	5	1
	Lewes	6	15	4	—
	Baltimore	6	9	3	—
	Carlisle	26	35	22	1
		67	95	40	2
Virginia	Hanover	7	13	8	1
	Redstone	8	14	17	—
	Lexington	10	11	16	—
	Transylvania	5	No report	No report	—
		30	+38	+41	1
Carolinas	Abingdon	4	4	19	1
	Orange	10	16	37	—
	South Carolina	11	10	34	3
		25	30	90	4
Totals, 1788		177	+214	+206	11

RETROSPECT

For all Americans the colonial era had been stormy. In this respect the Presbyterians had fared neither better nor worse than their fellows. The storms had been well-nigh inevitable, because the forming on a frontier of a Church, within a new nation, and out of a clergy and a people emigrating from various homelands traditionally hostile toward each other, could not have been accomplished with urbane serenity. The storms themselves are now of no significance, that they should be recalled to memory. But those men and women who in the midst of the storms built the foundations of the Church, the true pioneers of American Presbyterianism, may not be remembered apart from the struggles they endured.

The greatness of a Church is in its understanding of the Gospel and the Christian life. The pioneers of American Presbyterianism understood the nature of the Christian life as a communion with God in the fulfillment of his purposes in themselves and in their times. This communion was won and maintained at great cost and agony to man, and yet it was not man's act. It was God who redeemed sinners in and through the means of grace which he had given solely to the historical Church. For these colonial Presbyterians the Gospel was to be known only through the Biblical revelation, of which no ecclesiastical council or historic creed could be the final interpreter. Yet the common heritage of many of diverse origins in a common creed and a common ecclesiastical loyalty was to them a divinely provided means of corporate Christian life and witness. It is therefore impossible to interpret American Presbyterianism apart from the Great Awakening, in which, and out of which, this understanding of the Gospel and the Christian life came.

The greatest contribution of a Church is its own integrity as the Body of Christ in history. No other contribution, whether in the religious, the social, the political, the cultural, the economic, or in any other field, can vindicate a Church that has lost that integrity. Far-reaching as had been the contributions of colonial Presbyterianism in these fields — it was the largest, best organized, and most virile of the Churches in its areas, the most discerning of all the Churches in its grasp of the total social mission of the Church, the ablest and most consistent among the colonial Churches in the defense of both religious and civil liberty, the greatest single educational factor in its areas, and the least stratified economically of the colonial Churches — far-reaching as these contributions had been, the deepest concern of the pioneers of the Church who had led the way in all of this had been the maintenance of the Church's true character as the Body of Christ. Consequently its contributions had been but the Church's duty, and the God-given right of all to whom these contributions came. They were but a part of the Church's proclamation of the Gospel, for which function alone it existed.

The relevance of a Church is found in its character as the Body of Christ in history. Never since the colonial era has American Presbyterianism been so much a Church in history. Nothing in colonial life was alien to the pioneers of this Church. No part of human life fell outside the reign of God and the responsibility of the Church. Therefore, for these Presbyterians, the birth, though in agony, of a new nation on a savage frontier was according to the purpose of God. To live, then, 's the Church of some distant homeland, the perpetuator of orders foreign to this new land, the Church of a select origin, was to deny that the new nation was the creation of God with a destiny of its own. To be the Body of Christ in history meant to be an American Church, with a divinely directed mission in American history, and not a mere colonial offshoot of some foreign Church which had neither part nor lot in American life. Again, it was in and through the Great Awakening that the vision was caught of making all aspects of the life of the new nation conformable to the reign of God.

The true pioneers of the Presbyterian Church in the colonial era were the group commonly known as the New Side, a group that drew their immediate inspiration from such men as Jonathan Dickinson and William Tennent, Sr. Led by such men as Gilbert Tennent, Aaron Burr, Samuel Davies, John Rodgers, and John Witherspoon, they had shaped the growth of a Church which was both one with the Church of all the centuries and peoples and yet as new as the world within which it was growing.

Bibliography

BIBLIOGRAPHY

The bibliography of colonial Presbyterianism has never been brought together with any degree of completeness. During the research for this volume more than one thousand works by, or concerning, American Presbyterians, published prior to the year 1789, were found in various libraries. It is difficult to say how many more may be in existence in those libraries that it was not possible to visit. However, almost every discernibly Presbyterian item listed as being from this period in Charles Evans' *American Bibliography,* and in Sabin's *Dictionary of Books Relating to America,* was located, together with a number not found in either of these great bibliographies. A few publications mentioned in the colonial literature, however, could not be found. It is hoped that the list of the items found can shortly be published elsewhere as a trial bibliography of colonial Presbyterianism.

The bibliography here published is confined to the items quoted or cited in this work. Some abbreviated titles have been used in order to save space. Each entry, however, concludes with that number under which complete bibliographical information may be found in the bibliographies of either Evans or Sabin, e.g., E 1167, S 2542. Many of the publications cited or quoted in the text were reprinted at different times. An effort has been made to cite consistently that edition which is listed in this bibliography, although over the period of years during which this study was made several editions of a single publication were sometimes used.

No bibliography of the secondary materials used in this study has been attempted. In citing some of the older works which have been reprinted from time to time, an effort has been made either to cite from the original edition, or to include in the note the date of the reprint used. Very few abbreviations have been used, and most of these should be obvious, e.g., P.H.S., for The Presbyterian Historical Society; H.S.P., for The Historical Society of Pennsylvania; L.C.P., for The Library Company of Philadelphia.

Manuscript materials relating to the Presbyterian Church in colonial times were found in greater profusion than had been anticipated. The materials were of varying degrees of usefulness or importance. Here again, only those items cited or quoted in the text are included in this bibliography. A thorough bibliographical study of the manuscript sources of the colonial Church would be a useful contribution to the entire field of colonial American history.

I. Manuscript Sources		Depository or Location
A. Minutes and Records of the Official Courts		
1. The Higher Court [1]		
a. The Presbytery	1706–1716	P.H.S.
b. The Synod	1717–1745	P.H.S.
c. The Synod of New York (New Side)	1745–1758	P.H.S.
d. The Synod of Philadelphia (Old Side)	1745–1758	P.H.S.
e. The Synod of New York and Philadelphia	1758–1788	P.H.S.
2. The Presbyteries [2]		
a. Long Island	1717–1738	Lost
	1738–merged with #f to form #i.	
b. New Castle	1717–1731	P.H.S.
	1732–1758	Lost
	1758–1788	P.H.S.
c. Philadelphia	1717–1732	Lost
(from 1761–1786 called	1732–1746	P.H.S.
First Presbytery of Phil-	1747–1758	Lost
adelphia)	1758–1781	P.H.S.
	1782–1788	Lost
d. Snow Hill	1717– ? (Unknown, presbytery probably never met)	
e. Donegal	1732–1745	P.H.S.
	1745–1747	Lost
	1748–1751	P.H.S.
	1751–1758	Lost
	1759–1765	P.H.S.

[1] These minutes are cited from the revised published edition, *Records of the Presbyterian Church in the U. S. A.*, ed. by William H. Roberts, Philadelphia, 1904. They are cited under the abbreviated title, *Records*.

[2] For completeness' sake the records of all the presbyteries are here given.

These minutes are cited as follows, Ms. records, Presbytery of ——, with the date of the entry cited abbreviated thus, 1/12/[17]42. The bibliography of these presbyterial records is carried up only to the year 1788. For further records of these bodies, see the *Minutes of the General Assembly*, 1789 ——.

DEPOSITORY
or
LOCATION

	1765–broken up to form #o and #p	
	1766–reconstituted as before	
	1766–1786	P.H.S.
	1786–merged with #n to form #o	
f. East Jersey	1733–1738	Lost
	1738–merged with #a to form #i	
g. Lewes (Lewestown)	1735–1742	Lost
	1742–merged with #b until 1758 reunion of synods	
	1758–1788	P.H.S.
h. New Brunswick	1738–1788	Clerk, Presbytery of New Brunswick, N. J.
i. New York	1738–organized by merger of #a and #f	
	1738–1775	Lost
	1775–1788	Clerk, Presbytery of Newark, N. J.
j. New Castle, New Side	1745–1759	Lost
	1759–merged with #b	
k. Suffolk	1749–1788	P.H.S.
l. Abington	1751–1758	P.H.S.
	1758–merged with #c	
m. Hanover	1755–1788	Library, Union Theological Seminary, Richmond, Va.
n. Philadelphia, Second Presbytery	1762–1771	P.H.S.
	1772–1781	Lost
	1782–1786	P.H.S.
	1786–merged with #e to form #o	
o. Carlisle	1765–1766	P.H.S.
	1766–merged with #p to reconstitute #e	
	1786–reconstituted from merger #e and #n	
	1786–1788	Clerk, Presbytery of Carlisle, Pa.

<table>
<tr><td></td><td></td><td>DEPOSITORY
or
LOCATION</td></tr>
<tr><td>p. Lancaster</td><td>1765–1766
1766–merged with #o to
   reconstitute #e</td><td>P.H.S.</td></tr>
<tr><td>q. Dutchess County</td><td>1766–1788</td><td>Missing since c. 1844</td></tr>
<tr><td>r. Redstone</td><td>1781–1788</td><td>P.H.S.</td></tr>
<tr><td>s. Orange</td><td>1770–1788</td><td>Lost</td></tr>
<tr><td>t. South Carolina</td><td>1785–1788</td><td>Historical Foundation,
Montreat, N. C.</td></tr>
<tr><td>u. Abingdon</td><td>1785–1788</td><td>Lost</td></tr>
<tr><td>v. Baltimore</td><td>1786–1788</td><td>Clerk, Presbytery of
Baltimore, Md.</td></tr>
<tr><td>w. Lexington</td><td>1786–1788</td><td>Union Theological Seminary, Richmond, Va.</td></tr>
<tr><td>x. Transylvania</td><td>1786–1788</td><td>Clerk, Presbytery of
Transylvania, Ky.</td></tr>
</table>

B. Other Sources

Alison, F., Ms. sermons — P.H.S.

The Bellamy Papers, transcripts of correspondence between Joseph Bellamy and various Presbyterian leaders, copied by Richard Webster — P.H.S.

The Brinton Collection, especially the Penn-Peters Correspondence — H.S.P.

Journal of the Charitable Corporation for the Relief . . . Presbyterian Ministers . . . , 1759–1797, 3 vols. — Photostat Copy P.H.S.

First Presbyterian Church, Philadelphia, Ms. records — P.H.S.

The Simon Gratz Collection, American Colonial Clergy, Autographs — H.S.P.

Green, Ashbel. Ms. Life of the Revd John Witherspoon . . . — Microfilm Copy, Princeton University

The Presbyterian Church, U. S. A., The General Assembly, Misc. Ms. not of record — P.H.S.

The Rush Mss., especially correspondence of Benjamin Rush — L.C.P.

Second Presbyterian Church, Philadelphia, Ms. records — P.H.S.

William Tennent, Sr., Ms. sermons — P.H.S. and H.S.P.

DEPOSITORY
or
LOCATION

The Webster Mss., numerous transcripts of documents, letters, etc., relating to colonial Presbyterianism, copied by Richard Webster   P.H.S.

II. PRINTED SOURCES

Alison, Francis: *Peace and Union Recommended;* and, Bostwick, David: *Self disclaim'd, and Christ exalted* . . . ; 1758; pp. 53, 54   E 8070

Beatty, Charles: *The Journal of a Two Months Tour* . . . ; London, 1768; pp. 110   S 4149

Blair, J.: *Essays on I,* . . . *Sacraments, II,* . . . *Regeneration, III,* . . . *Means of Grace;* 1771; pp. 89   E 11997
The New creature; 1767; pp. 32   E 10562

Blair, S.: *The Great Glory of God;* 1739; pp. 42   E 4340
A Particular consideration of a piece, entituled, The Querists . . . ; 1741; pp. 63   E 4675
Persuasive to repentance . . . ; [1743]; pp. 40   E 5132
A Vindication of the brethren who were unjustly . . . *cast out of the Synod of Philadelphia* . . . ; 1744; pp. 63   E 5343
Works; 1754; pp. 407   E 7152

Brackenridge, Hugh M. [H]: *Six political discourses founded on the Scripture;* [1778]; pp. 88   E 15748

Brainerd, David: *Mirabilia Dei inter Indicos* . . . ; [1746]; pp. viii, 253   E 5748

Carmichael, John: *A Self-defensive war lawful* . . . ; 1775; pp. 34   E 13862

Cross, Robert, *et al.*: *Protestation presented to the Synod of Philadelphia, June 1, 1741;* 1741; pp. 16   E 4704

Davies, S.: *Little children invited to Jesus Christ* . . . ; 1798; pp. 16   (cf. earlier ed., E 8337)
Religion and publick spirit . . . ; 1762; pp. 17   E 9101
Sermons . . . , 3 vols., ed. Albert Barnes, 1864   S 18766
The Method of salvation through Jesus Christ . . . ; 1793; pp. 32   S 18771
The State of religion among the Protestant Dissenters in Virginia . . . ; 1751; pp. 44   E 6657

Dickinson, Jonathan: *A brief Illustration and confirmation of the divine right of infant baptism* . . . ; 1781; pp. 52, iv   E 17136
The Danger of schisms and contentions . . . ; 1739; pp. 41   E 4358
Defense of . . . *Display of God's special grace* . . . ; 1743; pp. 46   E 5161

Display of God's special grace . . . ; 1742; pp. vi, iii   E 4931
Second ed., 1743; x, 74   E 5162
Familiar Letters . . . ; 1745; pp. 424   E 5572
*Remarks upon a discourse intituled An Overture presented
to the Reverend Synod of Dissenting Ministers sitting in
Philadelphia, in the month of September, 1728* . . . ; 1729;
pp. 32   E 3156
*Remarks upon a Pamphlet, entitled, A Letter to a friend in
the country* . . . ; 1735; pp. 32   E 3897
*A Sermon preached at the opening of the Synod at Philadel-
phia, September 19, 1722* . . . ; 1723; pp. 24   E 2428
*True Scripture doctrine . . . election . . . sin . . . conver-
sion . . . justification . . . perseverance* . . . ; 1741; pp. 253   E 4710
Witness of the Spirit . . . ; 1740; pp. 28   E 4504
Edwards, Morgan: *Materials towards a history of the Ameri-
can Baptists* . . . [Vol. I, Pennsylvania]; 1770; pp. 134   E 11641
Materials towards a history of the Baptists in Jersey . . .
Vol. II; 1792; pp. 155   E 24294
[Anon.] *An Examination and refutation of Mr. Gilbert Ten-
nent's remarks upon the Protestation* . . . ; 1742; pp. 152   E 4946
Finley, James: *An essay on the gospel ministry* . . . ; 1763;
pp. viii, 144   E 9387
Finley, Samuel: *The approved Minister of God* . . . ; 1749;
pp. 23   E 6317
A Charitable plea for the speechless . . . ; 1746; pp. viii, 115   E 5769
Clear Light put out in obscure darkness . . . ; 1743; pp. 71   E 5179
Satan strip'd of his angelick robe . . . ; [1743]; pp. xiii, 48   E 5180
A Vindication of the Charitable Plea for the Speechless . . . ;
1748; pp. viii, 113   E 6137
Foster, William: *True fortitude delineated* . . . ; 1776; pp. 24   E 14758
Franklin, Benjamin: *A Defense of the Rev. Mr. Hemphill's
Observations* . . . ; 1735; pp. 47   E 3901
*A Letter to a friend in the country . . . the Rev. Mr. Hemp-
hill* . . . ; 1735; pp. 40   E 3902
*Some Observations on the Proceedings against the Rev. Mr.
Hemphill* . . . ; 1735; pp. 32   E 3904
Gellatly, Alexander: *A Detection of injurious reasonings* . . . ;
1756; pp. 240   E 7671
Gilbert, Benjamin: *Truth vindicated, and the Doctrine of
Darkness manifested: Occasioned by the Reading of Gilbert
Tennent's late Composure, intituled, Defensive War De-
fended* . . . ; 1748; pp. 48   E 6148

Gillespie, George: *A letter to the Rev. Brethren of the Presbytery of New-York . . . ;* 1742; pp. 23 — E 4520

Gillespy, George: *Remarks upon Mr. George Whitefield, proving him a man under delusion;* 1744; pp. 24 — E 5405

[Husbands, Herman] *Some Remarks upon Religion . . . ;* 1761; pp. 38 — E 8885

Jenkins, Obadiah: *Remarks upon the Defence of the Reverend Mr. Hemphill's Observations . . . ;* 1735; pp. 22 — E 3917

Linn, William: *Military discourse . . . ;* 1776; pp. 23 — E 14828

Makemie, Francis: *An Answer to George Keith's Libel . . . ;* 1694; pp. 103 — E 693

A Good conversation . . . ; 1707; pp. 36 — E 1298

A Narrative of a new and unusual imprisonment of two Presbyterian ministers . . . ; 1707; pp. 47 — E 1300

[Anon.] *The Mechanick's Address to the Farmer . . . ;* 1761; pp. 14 — E 8927

Montgomery, Joseph: *A sermon, . . . at Christiana Bridge and Newcastle, the 20th of July, 1775. . . . a day of fasting . . . ;* 1775; pp. 30 — E 14261

Morgan, Abel: *Anti-Paedo-Rantism; or Mr. Samuel Finley's Charitable plea for the speechless examined and refuted . . . ;* 1747; pp. 174 — E 6013

Anti-paedo-rantism defended . . . ; 1750; pp. x, 230 — E 6555

Pemberton, E.: *Duty of committing our souls to Christ . . . ;* 1743; pp. 41 — E 5267

Knowledge of Christ recommended . . . ; 1741; pp. 28 — E 4779

Practical discourses on various texts . . . ; 1741; pp. 199 — E 4780

Salvation by grace . . . ; 1774; pp. iv, 143 — E 13514

A Sermon preach'd . . . at Philadelphia. April 20th, 1735; 1735; pp. 21 — E 3945

Sermons on several subjects . . . ; 1738; pp. 94 — E 4295

[Presbyterian Ministers of Philadelphia] *An address of the Presbyterian Ministers of the City of Philadelphia to the ministers and Presbyterian congregations in the County of [?] in North Carolina . . . ;* 1775; pp. 8 — E 14411

[Presbytery of New Brunswick] *The Apology . . . ,* 1741, in G. Tennent, *Remarks upon a Protestation.*

Presbytery of New Castle, William Smith, Moderator: *An Address from the Presbytery of New-Castle to the Congregations under their Care: Setting forth the Declining State of Religion in their Bounds . . . ;* 1785; pp. 62 — E 19199

[Anon.] *Prior Documents; A Collection of interesting, authen-*

DEPOSITORY
or
LOCATION

The Divine government over all considered . . . ; [1752]; pp. 78 [imp.] — E 6940

The Divinity of the Scriptures . . . ; [1739]; pp. 27 — E 4431

Duty of self-examination . . . ; 1739; pp. 20 — E 4432

The Espousals . . . ; [1735]; pp. 66 — E 3965

The Examiner, Examined . . . ; 1743; pp. 146 — E 5297

Funeral Sermon . . . *John Rowland* . . . ; *A Narrative of the revival* . . . *Hopewell* . . . ; 1745; pp. 72 — E 5698

The Gospel a mystery . . . ; [1750]; pp. 20 — Not in E or S

The Happiness of rewarding our enemies . . . ; 1756; pp. 32 — E 7798

The late Association for Defence, encouraged, or the lawfulness of a Defensive War . . . ; [1748]; pp. 46 — E 6245

The late Association for defence, farther encourag'd, or The Consistency of Defensive War, with True Christianity . . . ; [1748]; pp. 56 — E 6246

The Late Association for defence, farther encourag'd: Or, defensive war defended; and its consistency with true christianity represented . . . ; 1748; pp. iv, 183 — E 6247

The Legal Bow . . . ; 1739; pp. 38 — E 4433

Love to Christ a necessary qualification . . . ; 1744; pp. 37 — E 5497

The Necessity of holding fast the truth . . . *errors* . . . *Moravians* . . . ; 1743; pp. 110, 37, 31 — E 5299

The Necessity of praising God for mercies received . . . ; [1745]; pp. 40 — E 5700

The Necessity of Religious Violence . . . ; 1735; pp. 45 — E 3966

Remarks upon a Protestation presented to the Synod of Philadelphia, June 1, 1741. . . . The Apology of the Presbytery of New Brunswick . . . ; 1741; pp. 68 — E 4820

A Sermon preach'd at Burlington in New-Jersey, November 23, 1749; 1749; pp. 28 — E 6424

A Sermon preached at Philadelphia January 7, 1747.8. . . . Day of fasting and prayer; 1748; pp. 34 — E 6248

Sermons on important subjects . . . ; 1758; pp. xxxvii, 425 — E 8266

A Solemn warning to the secure world . . . ; 1735; pp. xiii, 205 — E 3967

The Substance and scope of both Testaments . . . ; 1749; pp. 27 — E 6426

The Terrors of the Lord . . . ; 1749; pp. 10 — E 6427

Twenty-three sermons . . . ; 1744; pp. 465 — E 5500

Two Sermons preach'd at Burlington, in New-Jersey, April 27th, 1749 . . . a Provincial Fast . . . ; [1749]; pp. 40 — E 6428

The Unsearchable riches of Christ . . . ; 1739; pp. vii, 59 — E 4437

DEPOSITORY
or
LOCATION

Tennent, John: *The Nature of regeneration opened* . . . ;
1735; pp. xv, 78   E 3968
Tennent, William, III: *God's sovreignty no objection to the
sinner's striving* . . . ; 1765; pp. 20 (By error Evans attrib-
utes this item to William Tennent, Jr.)   E 10182
Thomson, John: *Doctrine of convictions* . . . ; 1741; pp. 80   E 4827
*An Overture presented to the Reverend Synod of dissenting
ministers sitting in Philadelphia,* . . . *September, 1728* . . . ;
1729; pp. 32   E 3223
An Explication of the Shorter Catechism . . . ; 1749; pp. iv,
190, 14   E 6429
The Government of the Church of Christ . . . ; 1741;
pp. xiv, 130   E 4828
Whitefield, George: *A Letter from the Reverend Mr. White-
field, to some Church members of the Presbyterian persua-
sion* . . . ; 1740; pp. 13   E 4644
Witherspoon, John: *Address to the inhabitants of Jamaica, and
other West-India Islands* . . . ; 1772; pp. 27   E 12627

NOTES

CHAPTER 1

1 This primitive Congregationalism was soon modified, and ordination by a council of ministers became the pattern. The Congregationalists of New England were slower than those of old England in allowing a minister to exercise the functions of his office outside the bounds of his own congregation, *A Letter of Many Ministers in Old England Requesting the Judgment of their Rev'd Brethren in New England . . .*, 1643, Positions VII, VIII. As late as 1770, Ezra Stiles complained of a Congregationalist minister's celebrating the Lord's Supper while temporarily without a charge, *Diary*, I, pp. 37 f.

2 W. Walker, *Creeds and Platforms of Congregationalism*, Ch. XIV.

3 H. M. Dexter, *Congregationalism of the Last 300 years . . .*, p. 463.

4 C. A. Briggs, *American Presbyterianism*, pp. 100 f.; J. Macdonald, *Two Centuries . . . Presbyterian Church, Jamaica, L. I.*, pp. 65 f.

5 *Ibid.*, pp. 56–76.

6 The other old churches of Long Island that later became Presbyterian, such as Easthampton, Setauket in Brookhaven, and Huntington, were founded as Congregational churches.

7 J. Morgan, *History of the Kingdom of Bassaruah . . .*, ed. R. Schlatter, 1946, pp. 12 f.; P. B. Heroy, *Brief History of the Presbyterian Church at Bedford . . .*, pp. 4–6.

8 *Ecclesiastical Records . . . State of New York*, I, p. 709.

9 *Ibid.*, II, pp. 879 f.

10 J. F. Stearns, *First Church of Newark*, pp. 21 ff.

11 *Ibid.*, pp. 86 ff.

12 N. Murray, *Notes . . . Concerning Elizabethtown . . .*, pp. 45 ff.; Briggs, *op. cit.*, p. 121.

13 W. A. Whitehead, *Contributions to East Jersey History*, p. 386; J. M. McNulty, *Historical Discourse . . . 200 Anniversary First Presbyterian Church Woodbridge*, New Jersey, pp. 7 ff.

14 Charles Hodge, *Constitutional History*, I, p. 65.

15 E. Whitaker, *Bicentennial Celebration of Suffolk County*, New York, p. 13.

16 W. S. Perry, *Historical Collections*, II, p. 8.

17 Morgan Edwards, *Materials for a History of the Baptists . . .*, I, pp. 104–109.

18 Perry, *op. cit.*, II, p. 15.

19 He could hardly have been ordained by Makemie and other Scotch-Irish Presbyterians as has often been asserted, there being no presbytery in existence to bring them together for that purpose. Had any Scotch-Irish group assembled for his ordination, they would have had to meet as a temporary ordaining council acting wholly on their own authority, exactly in the form of a Congregational council. Moreover, all Andrews' connections at this time were with the New Englanders. A few years later Nathaniel Wade was ordained at Woodbridge, New Jersey, by a council called from Newark, Elizabethtown, and other churches of New England Puritans. Andrews' ordination no doubt took place under similar auspices.

20 J. W. McIlvain, *Early Presbyterianism in Maryland*, Johns Hopkins University, *Studies*, 1890, No. 3, pp. 20–22.

21 J. B. Spotswood, *Historical Sketch . . . Presbyterian Church, Newcastle, Delaware*, pp. 13–15; Briggs, *op. cit.*, pp. 126 f.

22 Quoted in McIlvain, *op. cit.*, p. 5.

23 Briggs, *op. cit.*, p. 111; M. P. Andrews, *The Founding of Maryland*, p. 305.

24 Hill's letter to Richard Baxter (printed in Briggs, *op. cit.*, Appendix, pp. xli ff.)

seems to indicate that he had been some time in Maryland. He had left England for the West Indies at an unstated date after 1664. Cf. A. G. Matthews, *Calamy Revised*, 1934, pp. 265 f.

[25] Briggs, *op. cit.*, p. 113, states that he was one of the ejected Nonconformists of 1662, though Calamy does not list his name.

[26] Andrews, *op. cit.*, p. 306.

[27] Briggs, *op. cit.*, p. 114.

[28] No copy of Makemie's catechism has as yet been discovered.

[29] Makemie dated the preface July 26, 1692, but he added materials to the manuscript later, e.g., an account of the Quaker yearly meeting of September, 1692. (Cf. E. W. Kirby, *George Keith, 1638-1716*, p. 75; F. Makemie, *An Answer to George Keith's Libel* . . . , 1694, pp. viii, 83.)

[30] Several of these letters are in Briggs, *op. cit.*, pp. xlv ff.

[31] Briggs, *op. cit.*, p. 118.

[32] *Ibid.*, p. 119; McIlvain, *op. cit.*, pp. 23 f.

[33] A. Hewat, *Historical Account . . . Colonies of South Carolina and Georgia*, 1779, I, pp. 52 f.; D. Ramsay, *History of the Independent or Congregational Church in Charlestown* . . . , 1815, pp. 4 ff.

[34] Cf. A. Blaikie, *Presbyterianism in New England*.

[35] C. F. Pascoe, *Two Hundred Years of the S.P.G.* . . . , pp. 7 f., tends to minimize this, and is able to quote from a sermon preached before the society in 1702, in which evangelization of the heathen is brought in as an objective, though as but a secondary objective. E. B. Greene, "The Anglican Outlook on the American Colonies in the Early Eighteenth Century," *American Historical Review*, XX, October, 1914, pp. 64–85, shows that in the first decade of the S.P.G. its *activities* were centered chiefly upon the reclamation of the Dissenters in the middle and southern colonies.

[36] See Increase Mather's protest, quoted in Walker, *op. cit.*, p. 478.

[37] See further the discussions in Walker, *op. cit.*, and Dexter, *op. cit.*

[38] That these churches were organized in 1683 shortly after Makemie came to

America is a tradition of long standing. It rests in the last analysis upon, I. Spence, *Letters on the Early History of the Presbyterian Church*, 1838, pp. 80 f. Spence's evidence, however, is most unconvincing.

[39] Briggs, *op. cit.*, p. 139.

[40] Increase Mather, *Order of the Gospel*, p. 136.

[41] The case of the nineteenth century "Old School" Presbyterians, as stated by Samuel Miller, provides a good example of this line of argument. The Presbyterian Church in America, he states, was founded by ministers and members chiefly from Scotland and the North of Ireland. After the organization of presbytery, "some who had been bred Congregationalists in South Britain, or in New England, acceded to the new body, and consented to hear the name and act under the order and discipline of Presbyterians. . . . In a few years, however, . . . [they] wished for many abatements and modifications of Presbyterianism, and were found frequently encroaching on the order of that form of ecclesiastical government." *Letters to Presbyterians*, 1833, pp. 4 f. Francis Alison, the eighteenth century leader of the Old Side Presbyterian party which Miller and his Old School associates professed to follow, and who had good occasion to know the facts, presents a much truer picture:

"That Pensylvania, a Province Distinguished for civil & religious Liberty has been peopled with numbers from England, Scotland, Ireland, Wales, Sweden, Germany & Holland & some French refugees. That those in general who held a parity among all Gospel Ministers (the Dutch excepted) united and formed Churches after Presbyterian Plan, both in this & the neighbouring Provinces of New York, New Jersey, Maryland & C and at length their Ministers agreed to hold a Synodical Meeting once a Year in the City of Philadelphia." *Minutes of the Corporation for Relief of Poor and Distressed Presbyterian Ministers, and of the Poor and Distressed Widows and Children of Presbyterian Ministers*, I, p. 16. (The above representation was signed "the 4th Day of March 1760" by Francis Alison, D.D., Secretary of the Corporation.)

The Old School, New School controversy over the origins of American Presbyterianism may be studied further in: C. Hodge, *Constitutional History;* R. Webster, *History of Presbyterian Church;* E. H. Gillett, *History of the Presbyterian Church, U.S.A.;* William Hill, *History of Rise . . . American Presbyterianism.*

42 *Records of the General Synod of Ulster,* I, pp. 275–296.

43 F. Makemie, *A Narrative of New and Unusual Imprisonment,* and *A Good Conversation;* William Smith, *History of New York,* pp. 111, 116; Briggs, *op. cit.,* pp. 152 ff., xlix.

44 Guy S. Klett has made a most valuable detailed study of the expansion of Presbyterianism in the colony of Pennsylvania, *Presbyterians in Colonial Pennsylvania.*

45 These figures are based on Briggs, *op. cit.,* through p. 173.

46 The best account of William Tennent, Sr., is the *Documentary History of William Tennent and the Log College,* by T. C. Pears, Jr., and G. S. Klett.

47 *Records of the General Synod of Ulster,* I, p. 52.

48 For this period, see: A. Phillips, ed., *History of the Church of Ireland,* III, Ch. 5; W. D. Killen, *Ecclesiastical History of Ireland,* II, Ch. 7; J. S. Reid, *History of the Presbyterian Church in Ireland,* III, Chs. 22, 23. A few Presbyterians conformed during this period of severe measures.

49 James Logan's letter to J. Greenshields (both relatives of Tennent's) in Pears and Klett, *Documentary History,* p. 39a.

50 *Records, Presbyterian Church, U.S.A.,* p. 51.

CHAPTER 2

1 The Scottish Church at this time was also finding it very difficult to get presbyteries to discipline immoral clergy. Cf. R. Wodrow, *Analecta,* IV, pp. 55 f.

2 Ms. records, Presbytery of New Castle, 9/27/30; *Records,* p. 63.

3 *Records,* p. 68.

4 Ashbel Green, "Letters to Presbyte-

rians," *Advocate,* XI, pp. 363 f.

5 The two catechisms and the Directory are not mentioned in either of the two acts of the Scottish Parliament upon which the Establishment rested, viz., the Act of 1690 and the Act of 1707.

6 *Acts of the General Assembly of the Church of Scotland,* p. 253.

7 For accounts of the two trials of Professor Simson, see H. F. Henderson, *The Religious Controversies of Scotland,* Ch. I; R. H. Story, ed., *The Church of Scotland,* III, pp. 617 f., 632–640; IV, pp. 249–251, 261–266; *Acts of the General Assembly of the Church of Scotland,* p. 604.

8 *Acts of the General Assembly of the Church of Scotland,* p. 519.

9 *Op. cit.,* pp. 534–536.

10 On the "Marrow Controversy," see Henderson, *op. cit.,* Ch. II; Story, *op. cit.,* III, pp. 620–625; IV, pp. 253–261; and W. G. Blaikie, *The Preachers of Scotland,* Ch. VIII.

11 For a survey of this struggle, see R. W. Dale, *History of English Congregationalism,* pp. 528 ff., and A. H. Drysdale, *History of the Presbyterians in England,* pp. 499–507. Also C. A. Briggs, *American Presbyterianism,* pp. 194–208.

12 *Records of the General Synod of Ulster,* I, p. 34.

13 *Ibid.,* p. 100.

14 *Ibid.,* p. 110.

15 *Ibid.,* p. 20.

16 *Ibid.,* p. 403.

17 *Ibid.,* p. 419.

18 This became evident when the whole matter was finally left to the individual presbyteries, after some discussion, in 1736. *Records of the General Synod of Ulster,* II, p. 214.

19 For this controversy over subscription, see T. Witherow, *Historical and Literary Memorials of Presbyterianism in Ireland;* and J. S. Reid, *History of the Presbyterian Church in Ireland,* III, Ch. XXV.

20 *Records of the General Synod of Ulster,* I, p. 522.

21 Printed in R. Webster, *History of the Presbyterian Church,* pp. 99, 100.

22 J. Dickinson, *A Sermon Preached at the Opening of the Synod at Philadelphia,* September 19, 1722.

[23] Ms. records, Presbytery of New Castle, 5/2/22.

[24] *Records*, p. 76. The minister was a chronic invalid who took the bath in hopes of alleviating an attack of illness.

[25] "Minutes of Presbytery of New Castle," in *J. P. H. S.*, XV, pp. 98, 207.

[26] Reid, *op. cit.*, III, pp. 243–249; and *Records of the General Synod of Ulster*, II, pp. 103–109.

[27] This overture was not inserted in the minutes. Thomson printed it with additions shortly thereafter: *An Overture presented to the Reverend Synod of Dissenting Ministers sitting in Philadelphia, in the month of September 1728. . . .* The text of the overture is reprinted in C. Hodge, *Constitutional History*, I, pp. 162–167.

[28] "Minutes of Presbytery of New Castle," in *J. P. H. S.*, XV, pp. 166, 175, 178.

[29] J. Dickinson, *Remarks upon a Discourse intituled An Overture presented to the Reverend Synod of Dissenting Ministers sitting in Philadelphia, in the month of September, 1728. . . .*

[30] Quoted in Hodge, *op. cit.*, I, pp. 168, 169.

[31] "Gillett and Liberal Presbyterianism," *Princeton Review, 1868,* XL, p. 609.

[32] This Adopting Act is entered in *Records*, pp. 94, 95.

[33] These parallels have been well set out in tabular form in Briggs, *op. cit.*, pp. 217–220.

[34] Green, *op. cit.*, pp. 365 f.

[35] No one saw this more clearly than so ardent an advocate of unqualified subscription as Ashbel Green, who utterly rejected his fellow Old-Schoolmen's attempt to set their truncated Adopting Act against their so-called "preliminary act," with its concessions. Green saw clearly that the Adopting Act was a single agreement and denounced it in entirety. "We consider the foregoing Adopting Act as one of the most curious compositions that we ever read. It seems to us to give and take, say and unsay, bind and loose, from the beginning to the end." Green, *op. cit.*, pp. 365 f., 413.

The literature on the Adopting Act is large. Besides the accounts in the histories of Briggs, Gillett, Hodge, Thompson, and Webster; Green's *Letters;* and Miller's *Letters to Presbyterians,* see the following articles: "Adoption of the Confession of Faith," *Princeton Review, 1858;* "Dr. Gillett and Liberal Presbyterianism," and "Presbyterian Reunion," *Princeton Review, 1868;* "Remarks on Dr. Cox's Communication," *Princeton Review, 1831;* "Spirit of American Presbyterianism," *American Presbyterian Quarterly Review, 1853;* Canfield, "Reunion of the Synods of New York and Philadelphia," *American Presbyterian Quarterly Review, 1859;* Gillett, "Men and Times of the Reunion of 1758," *American Presbyterian Quarterly Review, 1868;* Gillett, "True Character of the Adopting Act," *American Presbyterian Quarterly Review, 1869;* Loetscher, "Adopting Act," *Journal, Presbyterian Historical Society,* XIII.

[36] *Minutes of the Sessions of the Westminster Assembly of Divines;* especially the debates discussed in the Introduction, liii–lxvi, and the debates recorded, for instance, pp. 150–160, or pp. 284–294 where ten formal dissents are recorded in a short space, some by the prolocutor himself.

[37] "Anthony Tuckney, one of the best theologians in the Westminster Assembly, tells us: 'In the Assemblie, I gave my vote with others that the Confession of Faith, put outt by Authoritie should not bee eyther required to bee sworn or subscribed too; wee having bin burnt in the hand in that kind before, but so as not to be publickly preached or written against.'" Briggs, *op. cit.*, p. 200. How fully this view is in line with the New England group's feeling is seen in Andrews' letter to Colman during the controversy before the Adopting Act: "Our countrymen say they are willing to join in a vote to make it the confession of our church, but to agree to making it a test of orthodoxy, and term of ministerial communion, they will not." Quoted in Hodge, *op. cit.*, I, p. 168.

CHAPTER 3

[1] T. C. Pears, Jr., and Guy S. Klett, *Documentary History of William Ten-*

nent and the Log College, pp. 39a, 46, 51, 52.

2 Ibid., p. 40, and R. Webster, History of the Presbyterian Church, pp. 387 ff.

3 A. Alexander, Log College, pp. 25 f.

4 "Records of the Presbytery of New Castle," in J. P. H. S., XV, pp. 114-116, 195, 198 ff.; Records, p. 83.

5 For the details of this revival, see the accounts by P. H. B. Frelinghuysen, Theodorus Jacobus Frelinghuysen, and C. H. Maxson, The Great Awakening in the Middle Colonies.

6 Quoted from Whitefield's Fifth Journal by J. Gillies, Historical Collections, p. 327.

7 Frelinghuysen, op. cit., pp. 17, 34. In this account, the best extant, it is said, "[He] must have been affected, while getting his religious education, by [Pietism] . . . The influence of Pietism on [him] is unquestionable, but we have no accurate means of gauging his interest in the movement."

8 In all the long lists of accusations against Frelinghuysen to the Classis of Amsterdam, the most frequent epithets are "Koelmanite" and "Labadist." Cf. Ecclesiastical Records of New York, pp. 2249, 2252, 2263, 2267, 2275, 2283, 2307, et passim. In the Klagte, by his enemies, he is called "Labadist," "Koelmanite," and "Mennonite," ibid., pp. 2325, 2334. The Dutch do not call him a Pietist.

9 T. J. Frelinghuysen, Sermons, p. 373.

10 Koelman was a disciple of Voetius, who in turn had been a disciple of the English Puritan William Ames. W. Goeters, Die Vorbereitung des Pietismus in der reformierten Kirche der Niederlande bis zur labadistischen Krisis 1670, Leipzig, 1911, pp. 17 f., 81-84. For accounts of Labadie and Labadism, see H. Heppe, Geschichte des Pietismus und der Mystik in der reformierten Kirche, namentlich der Niederlande. Leiden, 1879, pp. 240-370, and Goeters, op. cit., pp. 139-270.

11 A. Messler, Memorial Sermons, p. 181.

12 Frelinghuysen, Sermons, p. 4.

13 Ibid., pp. 5, 6, 153, 299.

14 A chance meeting with Sicco Tjadden is sometimes cited as evidence of Frelinghuysen's connection with German Pietism. However, it was a chance meeting of two strangers, when Frelinghuysen was a mature man. (De Witt, in Frelinghuysen, Sermons, p. v, and Frelinghuysen, T. J. Frelinghuysen, p. 13.) Furthermore, Tjadden was not in sympathy with German Pietism. He had written a good deal against it during his lifetime. A. Ritschl, Geschichte des Pietismus in des reformierten Kirche, I, pp. 308-317, 411; Heppe, op. cit., pp. 417-420.

15 Alexander, op. cit., p. 14.

16 G. Tennent to Thomas Prince, Jr., in The Christian History, II, p. 293, quoted in J. Tracy, The Great Awakening, p. 34.

17 G. Tennent, The Legal Bow . . . , pp. 17 ff.

18 T. Prince, The Christian History, quoted in J. Gillies, Historical Collections, p. 350.

19 G. Tennent, Preface to John Tennent's Regeneration Opened.

20 E. Boudinot, Life of Wm. Tennent, Jr.; and "Revival at Freehold," in Christian Advocate, 1824, pp. 401 ff.

21 Cf. pp. 189 ff.

22 G. Tennent to G. Whitefield, in Gillies, Historical Collections, p. 334.

23 G. Tennent, Danger of an Unconverted Ministry, p. 9.

24 S. Finley, The Approved Minister of God . . . , p. 6.

25 Cf. Ch. 10.

26 Records, p. 105.

27 Records, p. 107.

28 Records, p. 109. The political nature of the subscriptionist movement was to become plain a few years later. Cf. pp. 141 f.

29 Form of Presbyterial Church Government, . . . in The Confession of Faith, . . . etc., of Publick Authority in the Church of Scotland, . . . Edinburgh, 1725, p. 127.

30 Records, pp. 110 f.

31 Records, p. 115.

32 On the Hemphill trial, see Franklin's pamphlets: A Letter to a Friend . . . Mr. Hemphill . . . ; Some Observations on the proceedings against Mr. Hemphill . . . ; and A Defense of the Rev. Mr. Hemphill's. . . . Also An Extract of the Minutes of the Commission . . . Hemphill . . . ; O. Jenkins, Remarks upon the Defence . . . Hemp-

hill; E. Pemberton, *A Sermon Preach'd
. . . at Philadelphia, April 20th, 1735;*
J. Dickinson, *Remarks upon a Pamphlet . . . ;* and *A Vindication of the
Reverend Commission of the Synod
. . .* Briggs and Webster also have accounts.

33 S. B. Canfield, "Reunion of the Synods of New York and Philadelphia,"
*American Presbyterian Quarterly Re-
view,* VII, p. 533.

34 Pears and Klett, *op. cit.,* pp. 83–88.

35 No contemporary record of Tennent's
pupils is known. For a suggestive attempt at a list, see Pears and Klett, *op.
cit.,* p. 174; and this author's comments on that list, see p. 330, Ch. 7, n. 4.

36 H. G. Graham, *Social Life of Scotland
in the XVIII Century,* Ch. XII; G. D.
Henderson, *Religious Life in XVII
Century Scotland,* pp. 123 ff.

37 T. Witherow, *Historical and Literary
Memorials,* pp. 80, 149, 324, 330, 345,
et passim.

38 On Hutcheson's school, see W. R.
Scott, *Francis Hutcheson,* Ch. II. Of
these Irish academies, Scott writes,
"These were in fact small denominational colleges — little side-currents in
the advanced education of the time,
necessarily fleeting individually, but
accomplishing valuable work as a
whole."

39 I. Parker, *The Dissenting Academies
of England.*

40 S. B. Canfield, "Reunion of the Synods . . . ," *American Presbyterian
Quarterly Review,* VII, p. 537.

41 *The Danger of Forgetting God . . . ;
The Espousals . . . ; The Necessity of
Religious Violence. . . .*

42 *A Solemn Warning to the Secure
World. . . .*

43 *The Nature of Regeneration Opened
. . . ;* by John Tennent, with an appendix by Gilbert Tennent.

44 *Records,* pp. 126 f.

45 Quoted in C. A. Briggs, *American
Presbyterianism,* p. 265.

46 Charles Hodge's contention in his *Constitutional History,* I, pp. 183 ff., that
the Act of 1736 only interpreted what
was actually meant in 1729 is unten-
able. He admits, p. 180, that the Act of
1729 was a compromise between two
extremes. Certainly the only meaning

and intent of the Act of 1736 was to
eliminate the element of compromise
in the Act of 1729. Hodge, of course,
was trying to show that unqualified
subscription had always been demanded in Presbyterianism until the
rise of the New School against whom
he planned and wrote the *Constitutional History.* Ashbel Green, as ardent an advocate of unqualified subscription as Hodge, proves the fallacy
of views such as Hodge's in his denunciation of the 1729 Act, cf. p. 332, n. 35.

47 *Records,* pp. 121 f.

48 *Records,* pp. 124–126, 129.

49 G. H. Ingram, "Biographies of the
Alumni of the Log College, William
Tennent, Sr. The Founder," *J. P. H. S.,*
XIV, p. 14.

50 *Records,* p. 127.

51 This is made quite plain in the presbytery's handling of the case of the
Woodbridge congregation in 1708. *Records,* pp. 18, 24, 29 ff.

52 Cf. p. 38.

53 Ms. records, Presbytery of Donegal,
11/15/32; 5/16/33; 9/17/33, *et passim.*

54 *Ibid.,* 6/23/37.

55 Andrews had been in trouble with his
congregation, Thomas Craighead likewise with his, and Samuel Gelston the
same; cf. their biographical sketches
in R. Webster, *History of the Presbyterian Church.*

56 *Records,* pp. 133 f.

57 *Records,* pp. 134 f.

58 R. Webster says, "Who these persons
were is unknown." *History of the Presbyterian Church,* p. 138. Maxson, *The
Great Awakening in the Middle Colonies,* pp. 34 f., thinks that the order
was aimed at the evangelistic efforts of
the Tennent group.

59 Ms. records, Presbytery of Donegal,
10/5/37; 11/7/37; *Records,* p. 139;
Webster, *op. cit.,* pp. 457 ff.; W. H.
Foote, *Sketches of Virginia,* I, p. 119.

60 *Records,* pp. 132, 137. Morgan's trial
before his presbytery is described by
the Quaker preacher, Elizabeth Ashbridge: "During our stay, we went to
a large meeting of Presbyterians, held
not only for worship, but business, in
particular, the trial of one of their
priests, who had been charged with
drunkeness was to come on. I per-

ceived such great divisions among the people, respecting who should be their shepherd, that I pitied them. Some insisted on having the old offender restored; others wished to have a young man they hâd on trial for some weeks [? John Rowland]; others again, were for sending to New England for a minister." *Some Account of the Early Part of the Life of Elizabeth Ashbridge . . . ,* 1807, p. 37.

CHAPTER 4

[1] G. H. Ingram, *175th Anniversary of the Presbytery of New Brunswick,* p. 13. The same author, in "The Erection of the Presbytery of New Brunswick," *J. P. H. S.,* VI, p. 221, gives the number of New Englanders as twenty-three.

[2] Ms. records, Presbytery of Philadelphia, 3/1/37-38.

[3] C. H. Maxson, *The Great Awakening in the Middle Colonies,* pp. 70-72.

[4] S. Blair, *Vindication of the Brethren . . . , Works,* p. 228. A note on a contemporary issue is of interest in this connection. "Is it really so very terrible if a local congregation calls in the aid of the Brothers from Chrischona [a well-known Evangelical Brotherhood near Basle], if the alternative is to be condemned to years of listening to rationalistic morality, and never a Gospel Message at all? Is it quite certain that loyalty to the National Church should be bought at such a price?" E. Brunner, *The Divine Imperative,* p. 542, n. 1.

[5] *Records,* p. 138.

[6] A. Alexander, *Log College,* p. 19.

[7] G. H. Ingram, "History of New Brunswick Presbytery," *J. P. H. S.,* VII, p. 167.

[8] *Records,* pp. 141 f.

[9] Ashbel Green rightly calls Samuel Miller to account for saying in his *Letters to Presbyterians,* p. 8, that the Tennents had a "disposition to license almost any young man who offered himself, however great a novice he might be, and however defective in literary acquirements, provided he appeared pious." This statement, Green declared, was utterly unfounded. He assigned two reasons for the attack on the Log College — an attempt to stop the revival, and personal jealousy on the part of Alison, who wished to head a school for the Scotch-Irish party. A. Green, "Letters to Presbyterians," *Advocate,* XI, pp. 458, 461 f. The fathers of both Green and Miller had been active in the Presbyterian ministry during the colonial period. Miller himself knew better than he wrote, for he had been the colleague and biographer of John Rodgers. As pastor of the important New York church, leader in the founding of General Assembly, active in the Revolution, Rodgers was one of the ablest of the colonial clergy. He had been educated under Samuel Blair and Gilbert Tennent. From him, as well as from other sources, Miller had had ample opportunity to know the record of the Tennents, and in his biography of Rodgers, Miller had himself unreservedly praised the educational attainments of the Log College men. *Memoirs of the Rev. John Rodgers,* pp. 20 ff. Cf. p. 320, n. 41.

Robert Smith, a pupil of Tennent's at the Log College, and himself the conductor of the splendid Pequea Academy, said that a few of Tennent's pupils finished their studies in four or five years, but "most of us have taken a much longer Space of Time to learn." *Detection Detected,* p. 124. For a more recent estimate of the training received at the Log College, see Maxson, *op. cit.,* pp. 28-30.

[10] R. Webster, *History of the Presbyterian Church,* p. 453, says "he may have been educated at the Log College." A. Nevin, ed., *Presbyterian Encyclopedia, ad loc.,* is taken almost verbatim from Webster, but is less cautious and gives no evidence. D. K. Turner, in Thomas Murphy's *Presbytery of the Log College,* p. 508, lists Alexander as an alumnus, but gives no sources. G. H. Ingram, "Alumni of the Log College," *J. P. H. S.,* XII, p. 493, n. 15, lists him as a probable alumnus on the basis of the three works noted above. T. C. Pears, Jr., and G. S. Klett, *Documentary History,* p. 174, list him as an alumnus (following Webster). There is, therefore, no evidence beyond Web-

ster's conjecture. Maxson, *op. cit.*, pp. 71 f., is more likely correct in calling him an "independent sympathizer of the Tennent group, whom Samuel Blair and Robert Smith evidently did not consider as being of their Log College group."

[11] *Records,* p. 139.

[12] Cf. p. 82.

[13] Cf. William Haller, *Rise of Puritanism,* pp. 93 ff.; and M. M. Knappen, *Tudor Puritanism,* pp. 342, 387–390, 391–400, and *Two Puritan Diaries;* W. G. Blaikie, *Preachers of Scotland,* pp. 102–120; and T. Witherow, *Historical and Literary Memorials,* pp. 7–25. As to the accompanying phenomena of the revival, J. Gillies, *Historical Collections,* pp. 84–271, contains a whole series of incidents of a similar nature in England and Scotland during the previous century. These phenomena were therefore fairly well known in American Presbyterian circles. Some of these incidents were mentioned in sermons by the Log College men.

[14] S. Blair, "True and Faithful Narrative . . . ," in *Christian History,* II, ed., T. Prince, pp. 242 ff.; also in Blair's *Works.*

[15] Ashbel Green makes it quite evident that the revival as such, not its faults alone, was opposed. *Op. cit.,* pp. 414 ff. Cf. also Briggs, *op. cit.,* p. 259.

[16] S. B. Canfield, "Reunion of the Synods . . . ," *American Presbyterian Quarterly Review,* VII, p. 547; C. Hodge, *Constitutional History,* II, pp. 87, 95.

[17] Webster, *op. cit.,* pp. 363 f.

[18] Quoted in C. Hodge, *Constitutional History,* II, p. 125.

[19] Alexander, *op. cit.,* p. 52, well says, "In Scotland, the General Assembly existed before there were either presbyteries or synods, and all church power descended from that body; but not so with us, where presbyteries first existed, of which the higher judicatories were formed." William Hill had pointed this out as early as 1839, *History of the Rise . . . of American Presbyterianism,* pp. 117 ff.

[20] Tennent's argument is summarized in Hodge, *op. cit.,* II, pp. 128 f.

[21] G. Tennent, *Remarks upon a Protestation . . . ,* p. 6.

[22] Ashbel Green, *op. cit.,* pp. 458 ff., shows that Rowland's qualifications were considerable in the light of contemporary requirements and standards.

[23] *An Examination and Refutation . . . ,* pp. 14, 21.

[24] Hodge, *op, cit.,* II, p. 121.

[25] *Records,* p. 144.

[26] Pears and Klett, *op. cit.,* p. 156.

[27] Green, *op. cit.,* p. 461.

[28] Cf. J. Rowland, *Narrative of the Revival in Hopewell. . . .*

[29] Ms. records, Presbytery of Philadelphia, 10/25/38; 10/26/38; *Records,* pp. 147 f.

[30] Ms. records, Presbytery of Philadelphia, 9/19/38; 10/25/38; 9/18/39.

[31] Two of the New England men, Pemberton and Pierson, thought well enough of Rowland to defend him. *Examination and Refutation . . . ,* p. 22; Andrews' letter to Pierson in Webster, *op. cit.,* p. 180.

[32] *Records,* p. 152 n.

[33] J. Dickinson, *The Danger of Schisms and Contentions with Respect to the Ministry . . . ,* especially pp. 15, 16, 40.

CHAPTER 5

[1] L. Tyerman, *Whitefield,* I, pp. 323, 348.

[2] G. H. Ingram, "Biographies of the Alumni of the Log College, William Tennent, Sr. The Founder," *J. P. H. S.,* XIV, p. 17.

[3] Tyerman, *op. cit.,* I, pp. 324–339.

[4] *Ibid.,* I, p. 341.

[5] *Pennsylvania Gazette,* December 13, 1739.

[6] *Boston Weekly News Letter,* 11/22/30; 11/30/39; 12/6/39. L. N. Richardson, *History of Early American Magazines, 1741–1789,* has a valuable treatment of the part that periodicals played in the Great Awakening.

[7] J. F. Stearns, *Historical Discourses,* pp. 152–160.

[8] Tyerman, *op. cit.,* I, pp. 107, 112, 275, 334. Since letters from Whitefield to the Erskines, and Whitefield's *Journals,* are the basis of a view that connects the Tennents very closely with the Erskines, two items may be noted in passing. Whitefield wrote to Ralph

Erskine in 1740, stating that Gilbert Tennent would soon be writing to the Erskines regarding their bigoted and narrow interpretation of Presbyterian government, *ibid.*, I, p. 352. Not long after, the Tennent group officially stamped as "unsound theology" Fisher's *Marrow of Modern Divinity*. The Erskines' ardent support of this book was one of the reasons for their secession from the national Church of Scotland.

9 R. Webster, *History of the Presbyterian Church*, p. 458; J. Rowland, "Letter to Thomas Prince," in J. Gillies, *Historical Collections*, pp. 337 f.; S. Blair, *Narrative . . .* , in *Works*, and also in Gillies, *Historical Collections*, pp. 343 ff. Cf. also pp. 77–80.

10 Ms. records, Presbytery of Donegal, 10/9/39; 4/1/40. During these two years Thomson was in serious trouble also with his own congregation. The presbytery tried in various ways to solve the difficulty, but without success. Finally they appealed to Thomson: "Ye Pby doe earnestly recommend it to our Bro. Mr. Thomson that he be strictly watchfull of his Conduct as a Pastor, & sincerely endeavour diligence in ye work of the Ministry." *Ibid.*, 10/30/39. On the eve of the fateful synod of 1741, the presbytery was still trying to resolve the controversy between Thomson and his people.

11 G. Tennent, *The Danger of an Unconverted Ministry*, pp. 5 ff.

12 S. Finley, *The Approved Minister of Christ*, p. 5 n. This is essentially in agreement with John Calvin's statement, *Institutes*, IV, iii, xi.

13 "A Protestation . . . 1741," *Records*, p. 158, item 5.

14 G. Tennent, *Remarks upon a Protestation*, pp. 23 f.

15 E. Pemberton, "An Exhortation to Minister and People," in A. Burr, *Sermon Preached at the Ordination of . . . David Bostwick*, p. 42. Burr's own statements are to the same effect, pp. 9–11.

16 S. Finley, *Clear Light . . .* , p. 52.

17 J. Thomson, *Doctrine of Convictions*, pp. 68 f.

18 E. Brunner, *The Divine Imperative*, p. 534, together with note 14, puts the

matter well: "The mere fact that something is done 'officially' does not mean that it has divine authority; an official position in the Church is no guarantee that the 'office-bearer' possesses God's Word." "On this point Luther and Calvin teach exactly the same thing."

19 S. Finley, *Clear Light . . .* , p. 59.

20 *Ibid.*, p. 61.

21 G. Gillespie, *A Letter to . . . Presbytery of New York*, pp. 6 f.

22 S. Davies, *Sermons* (1864 ed.), III, p. 514.

23 R. Webster, *History of the Presbyterian Church*, p. 147.

24 Charles Hodge, *Constitutional History;* R. Webster, *op. cit.;* R. E. Thompson, *History of the Presbyterian Church;* and many others. A much truer estimate may be found in C. A. Briggs, *American Presbyterianism;* C. H. Maxson, *The Great Awakening in the Middle Colonies;* and W. M. Gewehr, *The Great Awakening in Virginia.*

25 Cf. further, Chs. VII and X.

26 C. Hodge in *Constitutional History*, II, p. 119.

27 E. H. Gillett, *History of the Presbyterian Church*, I, p. 313.

28 *Querists*, Part III, p. 98.

29 *Boston Weekly News Letter*, June 19–26, 1740.

30 *Records*, p. 151.

31 *Ibid.*, p. 153.

32 S. Blair, *Vindication of the Brethren . . .* , *Works*, p. 219.

33 Blair, *op. cit.*, pp. 209 f., 211 f., 213 f., 217 f.; *Apology of the Presbytery of New Brunswick*, p. 53.

34 *Records*, p. 153.

35 *Ibid.*, p. 154.

36 *Ibid.*

37 *Examination and Refutation . . .* , pp. 11 f.

38 *Ibid.*, pp. 15 f.

39 G. Gillespie, *Letter . . . New York Presbytery . . .* , pp. 16, 18, 19.

40 *Apology of Presbytery of New Brunswick*, pp. 48 ff.

41 *Ibid.*, p. 51.

42 S. Blair, *Vindication of the Brethren . . .* , *Works*, pp. 225 ff. Hodge's view that Tennent's paper came first is not borne out by Blair's own later statement above. J. Tracy, *Great Awak-*

ening, pp. 64 f., says Blair made the first move. See also *Records,* p. 154.

43 Tracy, *op. cit.,* pp. 64 f., accepts Blair's version, in his *Vindication,* that the Scotch-Irish group only made it appear that they desired a trial. Hodge, *op. cit.,* II, pp. 150 f., adopts the Scotch-Irish party's contention that Blair and Tennent refused to make regular cases out of their general denunciations. Fairly good evidence is cited for each view.

44 Gillespie, *op. cit.,* p. 5.

45 For Dickinson's own account of this revival, see J. Gillies, *Historical Collections,* pp. 339 ff.

46 W. M. Gewehr, *The Great Awakening in Virginia, 1740-1790,* has an excellent account.

47 *New England Weekly Journal,* 6/24/ 40, in *New Jersey Archives,* I, XII, p. 33.

48 Ms. records, Presbytery of Donegal, 6/18/40.

49 *Ibid.,* 9/3/40.

50 *Ibid.,* 11/5/40.

51 *Ibid.,* 12/10/40.

52 *Ibid.,* 4/7/41.

53 Maxson, *op. cit.,* pp. 66 f.

54 S. Blair, *Particular Consideration . . . ,* p. 12.

55 G. Tennent, *Remarks upon a Protestation,* p. 8; *Querists,* Part III, p. 127.

56 Hodge, *op. cit.,* II, p. 221 n.

57 G. Whitefield, *A letter . . . to some church members of the Presbyterian persuasion. . . .*

58 *A Short Reply to Mr. Whitefield's letter . . . to the Querists.*

59 S. Blair, *A particular consideration of . . . the Querists.*

60 *The Querists,* Part III.

61 Thomas Prince, Jr., in Gillies, *op. cit.,* pp. 349-357.

62 Thomas Clap, *A letter . . . to . . . Edwards . . .* and *A letter . . . to a friend in Boston . . . ;* J. Edwards, *An expostulatory letter . . . to . . . Clap . . . ;* and *Copies of the two letters. . . .*

63 Cf. n. 6.

64 Ms. records, Presbytery of Donegal, 4/7/41.

65 *Ibid.,* 4/8/41; 6/1/41; 6/16/41; 7/2/41.

66 *Ibid.,* 4/9/41.

67 *Ibid.,* 5/6/41.

68 Maxson, *op. cit.,* p. 73.

69 G. Tennent, *Remarks upon a Protestation,* pp. 10 f.

70 Gillespie, *op. cit.,* p. 3.

71 This *Protestation* is found in *Records,* pp. 157 ff. It was also published in pamphlet form with a preface by Cross.

72 So Briggs, *op. cit.,* p. 263.

73 *Records,* pp. 158 f.

74 G. Tennent, *Remarks upon a Protestation,* pp. 32-35.

75 *Records,* p. 162 *et passim.*

76 Robert Cross, in a letter (by order of the committee of the synod on October 16, 1747) to Mr. Kennedy, of Rotterdam, Holland. Reprinted in J. I. Good, "Early Attempted . . . ," *J. P. H. S.,* III, pp. 130-134.

77 *Records,* pp. 186 ff.

78 Webster, *op. cit.,* pp. 175, 463.

79 *Ibid.,* pp. 409, 431.

80 Ashbel Green, "Letters to Presbyterians," *Advocate,* XI, p. 414.

CHAPTER 6

1 Figures are not available on the number of converts. For New England the most generally accepted estimates are that 10 per cent of the total population were added as new converts to the New England churches. The revival in the middle colonies was not less successful.

2 The situation of the Tennents paralleled in many ways that of the Reformers and the Puritans. Each of these reforming groups faced a corrupt, well-intrenched old order which controlled the ecclesiastical organization. Each was compelled to struggle, therefore, against the system as well as against the corruption. Consequently each found growing up within its own bosom a serious sectarian problem, largely laical in origin.

3 Ms. records, Presbytery of New Brunswick, 6/2/41.

4 Ashbel Green, "Letters to Presbyterians," *Advocate,* XI, pp. 413 f.

5 S. Blair, *Vindication of the Brethren . . . ,* p. 228.

6 R. Webster, *History of the Presbyterian Church,* pp. 185 f.

7 Ms. records, Presbytery of New Bruns-

wick, 7/31/39; 4/1/40; 4/30/40; 6/3/40; 6/24/41; 10/16/41.

[8] J. Bellamy to A. Burr, 1/13/41–42, in Webster Mss., I.

[9] *Boston Weekly News Letter*, 4/9 to 15/42; 7/15 to 22/42; also *Boston Evening Post* and other papers.

[10] B. Colman, *The Declaration of a number of ministers . . . Davenport . . .*; J. Davenport, *. . . Confessions and Retractions*, [with a letter from Solomon Williams to Thomas Prince]; Colman, *A letter . . . to Mr. Williams . . .*; Davenport, *A letter . . . to Mr. Jonathan Barber. . . .* In view of the prominence usually given to Davenport's excesses, Webster's summary is worthy of serious consideration: "Of the extravagancies charged on him, many are plainly untrue, coming from scoffers and worldly-wise men, to whom the great truths of Christ's redemption were far more odious than any error into which Davenport fell. If he had been the only. one assailed, we might receive the testimony of Chauncey and his intelligencers; but when we know that Pomeroy was carried to prison, and deprived of his salary for a year; that Allen and Robbins were accused and condemned on frivolous pretexts; that three ministers were suspended for ordaining Lee at Salisbury; that denunciations fell like hail on Whitefield, and that Buell and Brainerd were held up as strollers and fanatics whom it was not allowable to improve; that Pomeroy, Buell, Davenport, Moorhead, Blair, Croswell, and Rowland were classed as 'common railers,' 'men whom the Devil' drives into the ministry; that Dr. Cutler speaks with equal dislike of Dr. Cooper, Rodgers of Ipswich, Tennent, and Buell, styling Davenport a nonpareil, and lamenting that the enthusiasm is still (1743) breaking out; and that Finley was twice carried out of Connecticut as a vagrant, it seems reasonable to doubt whether Davenport may not have been greatly slandered. Who does not reject, with equal scorn, Chauncey's assault on Davenport's moral character, and Cutler's insinuation that Whitefield and Tennent embezzled what was collected for the poor, and repeated the enormities of Hophni and Phineas at the door of the tabernacle?" *Op. cit.,* p. 543.

[11] Ms. records, Presbytery of New Brunswick, 5/22/46.

[12] R. S. Field, "Trial of Rev. William Tennent," *Proceedings of New Jersey Historical Society,* VI, p. 35; E. Boudinot, *Life of William Tennent, Jr.;* G. H. Ingram, "History . . . , Part VII, The Trials of Rev. John Rowland and Rev. William Tennent, Jr., 1741–1742," *J. P. H. S.,* VIII, pp. 114–122.

[13] G. Gillespie, *Letter to. the Reverend Brethren . . . Presbytery of New York. . . .*

[14] G. Tennent, *Examiner Examined,* p. 90; *Some Account of . . . Moravians,* pp. 47, 51.

[15] S. Finley, *Satan Stripped . . . ,* pp. ix, x. Some of Zinzendorf's leading followers, among them David Spangenberg, who left the Count for a time because of his mystical and eccentric ideas, strongly disapproved of such theological notions, and later led the Moravian Church to repudiate them. J. T. Hamilton, *The Moravians, American Church History Series,* VIII, pp. 457 f.

[16] J. Dickinson, *Familiar Letters, . . . Important Subjects in Religion,* p. iii.

[17] G. Gillespie, *Remarks upon . . . Whitefield,* pp. 13 f.; G. Whitefield, *Expostulatory Letter to . . . Zinzendorf.*

[18] *Ecclesiastical Records, State of New York,* V, p. 3332.

[19] This letter was not made public until in the late summer, when it was published by President Clap (to whom Dickinson had given it) in the *Boston Evening Post* for July 27, 1742. The August 12, 1742, issue of the *Pennsylvania Gazette* reprinted it. The entire letter is to be found in Hodge, *Constitutional History,* II, pp. 111 ff.; and in Webster, *op. cit.,* pp. 189 ff.

[20] Webster, *op. cit.,* pp. 191 ff.

[21] *Records,* p. 162.

[22] Webster, *op. cit.,* p. 193 n.

[23] *Boston Weekly News Letter,* 9/16 to 23/42.

[24] Quoted in Webster, *op. cit.,* pp. 198–201.

[25] Ms. records, Presbytery of New Brunswick, 4/6/43.

[26] *Records*, pp. 168.
[27] Ms. records, Presbytery of New Brunswick, 8/10/43.
[28] [Herman Husbands] *Some Remarks On Religion, With the Authors Experience in Pursuit Thereof* . . . , p. 37.
[29] Morgan Edwards, *Materials for a History of the Baptists*, II, pp. 63, 71, 120.
[30] Quoted in Hodge, *op. cit.*, II, pp. 36 f.
[31] *Records*, pp. 233 f.

CHAPTER 7

[1] D. Brainerd to J. Bellamy, 3/26/43, in Webster Mss., I.
[2] S. Finley to J. Bellamy, 9/20/45, in Webster Mss., I.
[3] E. Wheelock to J. Bellamy, 3/13/49, in Webster Mss., I.
[4] No contemporary list of the Log College alumni exists. The following is the list suggested by T. C. Pears, Jr., and Guy S. Klett in *Documentary History of William Tennent and the Log College*, p. 174: "David Alexander, Charles Beatty, Hamilton Bell, John Blair, Samuel Blair, John Campbell, (Samuel Davies), William Dean, Samuel Finley, Daniel Lawrence, James McCrea, Charles McKnight, Dr. John Redman, John Roan, William Robinson, John Rodgers, John Rowland, Charles Tennent, Gilbert Tennent, John Tennent, William Tennent, Jr." It is exceedingly doubtful, however, whether David Alexander and Hamilton Bell should be included in this list. Cf. pp. 325, n. 10; 331, n. 18. It is also doubtful whether Samuel Davies should be included in the list.
[5] T. J. Wertenbaker, *Princeton 1746-1896*, 1946; and J. Maclean, *History of the College of New Jersey*, 2 vols., 1877.
[6] *New York Gazette — Weekly Post Boy*, 2/2/47, in *New Jersey Archives*, Series I, XII, p. 331.
[7] His election was announced 12/1/48 in the *Boston Weekly News Letter*, quoted in *New Jersey Archives*, Series I, XII, p. 503; Wertenbaker, *op. cit.*, pp. 25 n., 28.
[8] Wertenbaker, *op. cit.*, p. 32.
[9] The exact sum raised cannot be determined, since the records of the treasurer were lost during the Revolutionary War. Cf. Maclean, *op. cit.*, I, p.

152; C. A. Briggs, *American Presbyterianism*, p. 309.
[10] A. Burr to D. Cowell, 8/5/54, Webster Mss., I.
[11] Samuel Davies' "Diary," in W. H. Foote, *Sketches of Virginia*, I, p. 257.
[12] *Ibid.*, p. 246.
[13] *Ibid.*, p. 262.
[14] *Boston Evening Post*, 7/3/49, quoted in *New Jersey Archives*, Series I, XII, p. 550.
[15] S. Davies to J. Bellamy, 7/4/51; 7/13/51; S. Finley to J. Bellamy, 8/1/51, Webster Mss., I.
[16] Copies of a great many letters on this call are in Webster Mss., I, pp. 329-445, in the Presbyterian Historical Society.
[17] Ms. records, Presbytery of New Brunswick, 5/28/55.
[18] Cf. the accounts in Foote, *op. cit.*, Chs. VII ff.; W. M. Gewehr, *The Great Awakening in Virginia;* and G. Bost, "Samuel Davies," typed Ph.D. thesis, University of Chicago.
[19] Briggs, *op. cit.*, pp. 294 ff.; *Records*, p. 185.
[20] D. Brainerd, *Mirabilia Dei inter Indicos;* Briggs, *op. cit.*, p. 299.
[21] J. Tennent, *Regeneration Opened*, p. 27.
[22] S. Davies, *State of Religion in Virginia*, p. 7.
[23] S. Davies, *Sermons*, III, pp. 645, 650.
[24] G. Tennent, *Divine Government . . . Necessity of Gratitude*, pp. 45 f.
[25] A. Gellatly and A. Arnot, *A Detection of Injurious Reasonings;* S. Finley and R. Smith, *Detection Detected.* . . .
[26] Cf. p. 115.
[27] S. Finley, *Charitable Plea for Speechless . . . ;* A Morgan, *Anti-Paedo-Rantism . . . ;* S. Finley, *Vindication of the Charitable Plea . . . ;* Morgan Edwards, *Materials . . . History of Baptists*, II, pp. 18, 39.
[28] J. Dickinson, *Brief Illustration . . . Divine Right of Infant Baptism.* . . .
[29] M. Edwards, *op. cit.*, p. 17.
[30] Cf. pp. 277 f., 297.
[31] Some idea of the interest in this controversy may be gained from the number of publications issued during it. From 1745 to 1749, Tennent published six pieces, and several other publications appeared for or against his idea. G. Tennent, *Necessity of Praising God*

for Mercies Received; B. Franklin, *Plain Truth;* G. Tennent, *Late Association for Defence, Encouraged . . . ;* G. Tennent, *Late Association for Defence Further Encouraged . . . ;* John Smith, *The Doctrine of Christianity . . . ;* Samuel Smith, *Necessary Truth . . . ;* Benjamin Gilbert, *Truth Vindicated . . . ;* [B. Franklin] *Absolute and Obvious Necessity of Self-Defence . . . ;* William Currie, *Treatise on Lawfulness of War . . . ;* G. Tennent, *Late Association for Defence Further Encouraged . . . in Reply to the Doctrine of Christianity;* G. Tennent, *Sermon Preached . . . January 7, 1747, 8 . . . Day of Fasting . . . ;* G. Tennent, *Sermon . . . at Burlington, N. J.,* November 23, 1749; G. Tennent, *Two Sermons . . . at Burlington, N. J.,* April 27, 1749.

³² *New York Mercury,* 9/30/54, quoted in *New Jersey Archives,* Series I, XIV, p. 418.

³³ S. Davies, "The Curse of Cowardice," *Sermons,* III, pp. 160, 163, 153.

CHAPTER 8

¹ *Records,* p. 172.
² Robt. Jenney to the Bishop of London, 6/24/43, in W. S. Perry, *Historical Collections,* II, p. 235.
³ *Boston Evening Post,* 4/2/44, in *New Jersey Archives,* Series I, XII, p. 213.
⁴ J. I. Good, "Early Attempted Union of Presbyterians With Dutch and Reformed Churches," *J. P. H. S.,* III, pp. 122 ff.; C. A. Briggs, *American Presbyterianism,* pp. 284 ff.
⁵ R. Webster, *History of the Presbyterian Church,* pp. 243, 245.
⁶ Cf. pp. 84, 96.
⁷ *Records,* p. 188.
⁸ Alison's letter was perhaps the one referred to by Hutcheson in a letter to his friend, Thomas Drennan. He comments that he has recently had a letter from a presbytery in Pennsylvania: "The Pensilvanians regret the want of true literature: they wrote that Whitefield has promoted a great contempt for it among his followers and bewailing some wretched contention among themselves," quoted in James McCosh, *The Scottish Philosophy,* p. 467.
⁹ Cf. p. 126.

¹⁰ H. W. Smith, *Life of Wm. Smith,* I, pp. 101 ff.
¹¹ This lack of men was undoubtedly a strong factor in the Old Side's lenient handling of scandalous clergy. Too rigorous discipline would have seriously reduced their numbers.
¹² Ms. records, Committee of the Congregation, First Church of Philadelphia, 3/15/55; 11/25/57.
¹³ J. H. Colligan, *The Arian Movement in England,* pp. 108, 115, 122, 140; A. H. Drysdale, *History of the Presbyterians in England,* pp. 508, 530; O. M. Griffiths, *Religion and Learning,* p. 128.
¹⁴ Copybooks of Alison's students indicate that his method of teaching was to have his men compend Hutcheson's works. Hutcheson was a friend of the nonsubscribing Irish Presbyterians who made up the Antrim Presbytery. More than any other individual, he was the founder of the Scottish "Moderate" party. No category fits Alison so well as that of a "Moderate." His later hostility to Witherspoon, an avowed anti-Moderate, may well have had its roots in Alison's leanings toward the Moderates. On Hutcheson and the Moderate party, see J. McCosh, *op. cit.,* pp. 57, 63 ff., 83 ff., 463, 465; and W. L. Mathieson, *The Awakening of Scotland, 1747–1797,* Ch. V; O. M. Griffiths, *op. cit.,* p. 130, has pointed out the close affinity between Hutcheson's thought and Arianism.
¹⁵ Ms. records, Committee of the Congregation, First Church of Philadelphia, 7/28/58.
¹⁶ Cross, Zancky, Black, and Caven.
¹⁷ Ms. records, Presbytery of Donegal, 5/7/41; 5/30/41; 7/2/41; 11/10/47.
¹⁸ Webster, *op. cit.,* p. 469, states he "was a student at Neshaminy in 1738." This seems very odd since he was sponsored into Donegal Presbytery, after the schism, by John Thomson, one of Tennent's greatest foes. Ms. records, Presbytery of Donegal, 10/27/41. Moreover, a New Side pamphleteer in 1761 lists Bell as one of "that man's party" (i.e., the Old Side) and a man of "infamous character." *The Mechanick's Address to the Farmer . . . ,* pp. 10 f. If Bell ever was at Neshaminy, and

only Webster has this tradition, he had joined the Old Side during the revival controversy before 1741.

19 Ms. records, Presbytery of Donegal, 4/6/42; 3/6/44.

20 Ms. records, Presbytery of Philadelphia, 10/29/46; Webster, op. cit., p. 317.

21 Ms. records, Presbytery of Donegal, 4/8/41; 8/11/41; 6/16/42; 9/23/42.

22 Ms. records, Presbytery of Donegal, 9/4/39; 11/8/39; 11/17/39; 4/2/41; 6/1/41; 7/2/41.

23 Webster, op. cit., p. 462.

24 Ibid., p. 467.

CHAPTER 9

1 The synod's letter to President Clap, 5/30/46, in Records, p. 189.

2 Records, p. 241.

3 Ibid., pp. 203 f.

4 Ibid., pp. 246 f.

5 Ibid., pp. 207 f.

6 Ibid., pp. 253 f.

7 Ibid., pp. 269, 221 f.

8 Ibid., pp. 222 f.

9 Ibid., pp. 279 f.

10 F. Alison, Peace and Union, p. 51.

11 Ibid., pp. 18 f.

12 Records, pp. 285 ff.

13 S. Davies, Sermons, 1864, III, pp. 525 f. It is notable that after 1758 all presbyteries drop the terms " subscribe " and " sic subscribitur," which were generally used before 1741 when the subscriptionist party controlled all but New York Presbytery and Long Island Presbytery. (The records of these last named presbyteries are not extant.) After 1758 the terms used are " received," " adopt," " accept," and " assent to."

14 G. Tennent, Blessedness of Peacemakers . . . , p. 10.

15 [J. Blair] Synod of New York and Philadelphia Vindicated, quoted in Charles Hodge, Constitutional History, I, p. 202.

16 Cf. pp. 126 f. The New Side had in 1757 vigorously maintained the distinction between essential and nonessential doctrines in a long controversy with the Seceders. Cf. S. Finley in R. Smith, The Detection Detected . . . , pp. 41 ff. and 13.

17 E. H. Gillett, History of the Presbyterian Church, I, p. 99.

18 R. Webster, History of the Presbyterian Church, pp. 250 f.

19 C. Hodge, Constitutional History, II, p. 256 n.

20 Webster, op. cit., p. 272.

21 Records, pp. 288 f.

22 The synod's list of 1758 lacks two names, one N. S. and one O. S. Records, p. 285.

23 Records, p. 292.

24 Ms. records, Presbytery of Hanover, 3/18/55; 9/28/58; 4/25/59; 7/18/59.

25 Ibid., 6/5/66.

26 Ms. records, Presbytery of Donegal, 10/23/60; 1/1/61.

27 Ms. records, Presbytery of Philadelphia, 5/16/60.

28 Records, pp. 301 f.

29 Ibid., p. 305.

30 The name was spelled variously.

31 The fact that these men did not know what induction meant in Anglican usage has been pointed to as proof that no Anglican had a part in drafting the letter. Much of the correspondence relating to the McClenachan case has been reprinted in H. W. Smith's Life of William Smith, I, Ch. XVI.

32 Records, p. 306. The pamphlets were: The Conduct of the Presbyterian Ministers Who Sent the Letter . . . ; Letter of a Farmer in Answer to the Conduct . . . ; A Second Letter to the Congregations of the Eighteen Presbyterian Ministers . . . ; The Mechanick's Address to the Farmer . . . ; A True Copy of a Genuine Letter, sent to the Archbishop of Canterbury . . .

33 Ms. records, Presbytery of Philadelphia, 10/15/60; 12/17/60; 4/23/61.

34 D. Bostwick to J. Bellamy, 8/21/61; S. Finley to J. Bellamy, 10/?/61; J. Bellamy to John Graham, Jonas Lee, et al., 10/1/61, Webster Mss., I, pp. 179 ff. A few years later the Old Side party made a similar attempt but failed to gain any aid from New England, E. Stiles, Diary, I, pp. 248 ff.; Records, p. 435, et passim to p. 470.

35 Ms. records, Presbytery of Donegal, 6/24/61; 11/12/61. Webster, op. cit., p. 601.

36 The pamphlet was, no doubt, the anonymous The Mechanick's Address. The section of the pamphlet referred to by

Hazard was probably that (pp. 10 ff.) which gave the names of a number of scandalous Old Side ministers, licentiates, and students who had gone over to the Church of England. Why, asks the pamphleteer, do not these people who consider themselves the only true Presbyterians, and who are horrified because eighteen New Side party men intercede for one decent Anglican, express at least equal horror over all these their immoral former colleagues who have now become Anglicans?

37 N. Hazard to J. Bellamy, 6/5/61, Webster Mss., I, p. 177.

38 *Records*, p. 317.

39 *Ibid.*, p. 319, and note.

40 *Ibid.*, p. 321.

41 *Ibid.*, p. 321.

42 Hugh Williamson remained a layman; John Beard fell into serious disgrace; William Edmiston, a brother-in-law of Sampson Smith, joined the Anglican Church after three years of very indifferent service in the synod; Samuel Magaw, after much irregular conduct also became an Anglican.

43 *The Mechanick's Address*, pp. 10 f.

44 John Ross to Secretary [of S.P.G.], 7/6/71, in W. S. Perry, *Historical Collections*, II, pp. 456 f.

45 *Pennsylvania Journal*, 12/24/61, quoted in *New Jersey Archives*, Series I, XX, p. 653. The book was *Predestination Consistent with General Liberty; or the scheme of the covenant of grace....*

46 S. Harker, *Appeal to the Christian World*, p. 6.

47 [J. Blair] *The Synod of New York and Philadelphia Vindicated*, pp. 10, 11, 13.

48 Ms. records, Presbytery of New Castle, 6/23/63; 6/30/63. The presbytery was at that time predominantly New Side. *Records*, p. 349.

49 Ms. records, Presbytery of New Castle, 4/20/63.

50 Ms. records, Presbytery of New Castle, 4/8/60; 6/18/61; 10/20/64; 2/5/65; 4/25/65.

51 Ms. records, Presbytery of Lewes, 4/28/67; 5/26/67; 7/28/67; 11/5/67; 12/25/67; 11/14/69; 4/3/71.

52 Ms. records, Presbytery of Philadelphia, 5/8/64, and thereafter frequently until 6/18/66; 4/9/67. The manuscript

letters of Benjamin Rush, an elder of the church, are a valuable source on Murray. Also E. Stiles, *Diaries*, I, p. 193. A. G. Vermilye's "Memoir of John Murray," *Maine Historical Society Magazine*, 1857, does not face the whole evidence, and seeks to excuse him.

53 Ms. records, Presbytery of New Brunswick, 4/22/67.

54 J. Finley, *Essay on the Gospel Ministry*, pp. 60–63, 65 f.

55 S. Thomson, S. Smith, and J. Beard were soon out of the ministry on moral grounds. Steel, Tate, and McMordie never held any congregation for any length of time.

56 Ms. records, Presbytery of Donegal, 6/22/64; 6/24/67.

57 *Records*, p. 337.

CHAPTER 10

1 For an account of this revival, see R. Fleming, *Fulfilling the Scripture;* and G. D. Henderson, *Religious Life in Seventeenth Century Scotland*, p. 24.

2 Quoted in J. Gillies, *Historical Collections*, p. 202.

3 With the aid of R. Wodrow's *Analecta*, or Gillies' *Collections*, as a guide, earlier examples of the ways of the Log College men can be multiplied.

4 C. A. Briggs's use of the term "Methodism" for the Great Awakening in the Presbyterian Church was very misleading. He traced the origin of the movement to the Wesleys, though his own chronology denied the possibility of such an origin. When he stated that "Whitefield came over to head the movement in 1739," and that "American Methodism produced two great theologians, Jonathan Dickinson and Jonathan Edwards," the sheerly individualistic use which he made, for the purposes of his own point of view, of the term "Methodism" became evident. *American Presbyterianism*, pp. 239 f., 252, 260 f., *et passim*. R. E. Thompson, *History of the Presbyterian Churches in the U. S.; American Church History Series*, VI, made clear the independent origin of the Great Awakening, pp. 29 ff., but asserted that the views

of the Tennents and the Methodists were essentially alike, p. 37.

5 It is not possible within the limits of this work to present a discussion of the Federal theology as such. What is here intended is merely to show how the New Side adapted Puritan Federalism to their situation. The literature on the Federal theology is very inadequate. For its symbolic history, H. Heppe, *Reformierte Dogmatik,* rev. ed. by E. Bitzer, has certain materials. Perry Miller has traced its rise in Great Britain in "The Marrow of Puritan Divinity," *Publications,* The Colonial Society of Massachusetts, Vol. 32, pp. 247–300. G. Shrenck, *Gottesreich und Bund . . . ,* discusses the Continental Federal theology. Most of the literature on Puritanism directly or indirectly touches upon this their theology.

6 S. Blair, *Works,* Sermon II, p. 47.

7 Cf. the steps proposed in S. Davies, *Little Children Invited to Jesus Christ,* pp. 5–8; *Sermons,* I, pp. 152–154, 199 ff.; II, p. 617; J. Dickinson, *True Scripture Doctrine,* pp. 128–132, 138–145; *Defense of . . . a Display of God's Special Grace,* p. 5.

8 The picture presented by R. E. Thompson, *op. cit.,* pp. 37 f., of the New Side men's view of Christian experience is without any foundation in the extant sources from the period. According to Thompson, the view was that every experience must be identical, that every conversion was instantaneous, and included a joyful assurance, and that "religion must thus come into the man 'like a bolt from the blue.'" He also asserted that credible evidence of regeneration, understood in Anabaptist terms, not in the Reformed sense, was required for Church membership. "Christian nurture of the family, along with catechetical instruction of the young by their pastors, came to be regarded as relatively unimportant." Introspection, spiritual gloom, egocentricity, and a neglect of the relevance of the Christian faith in public life characterized the movement.

9 G. Tennent, *Twenty-three Sermons,* p. 339; *Necessity of Keeping the Soul,* pp. 7 f.

10 S. Blair, *Works,* Sermon I, pp. 40 f. Cf. also William Tennent, III, *God's Sovreignty No Objection to the Sinner's Striving,* p. 6.

11 William Tennent, III, *op. cit.,* p. 7; G. Tennent, *Twenty-three Sermons,* p. 341; S. Blair, *Persuasive to Repentance,* 1743, ed., "Premonition . . . ," p. 4.

12 J. Blair, *Essays,* p. 74.

13 William Tennent, III, *op. cit.,* p. 9.

14 G. Tennent, *Discourses on Several Important Subjects,* pp. 296 f.; S. Davies, *The Method of Salvation,* p. 29. Under the pressure of the "New Divinity," this issue again arose. In 1764, Alexander McWhorter wrote to Joseph Bellamy: "What is the use of means of grace to an unregenerate man? Why should we ask him to pray read or hear seeing the carnal mind is enmity against God?" Webster Mss., I, A. McWhorter to J. Bellamy, 1/28/64.

15 J. Blair, *op. cit.,* pp. 88 f. F. Alison, of the Old Side, stated that it was up to each individual seeker to find his own way to God, using of course the stated means of grace, the Bible, public worship, etc. No directions were given by the minister in preaching. Mss. Sermons, Sermon on Luke 15: 18 f., 9/3/58.

16 J. Blair, *op. cit.,* pp. 75 f.; S. Davies, *Sermons,* II, pp. 240 f., III, pp. 30 ff.; S. Blair, *Works,* Sermon IV, pp. 120 f.; G. Tennent, *Legal Bow,* p. 192; E. Pemberton, *Practical Discourses,* p. 92. Even the Bible itself is not savingly understood except by the Holy Spirit's agency, G. Tennent, *Gospel a Mystery,* p. 13.

17 For instance, S. Davies, *Sermons,* I, p. 295.

18 As late as Charles Hodge, this view was vigorously maintained, *Systematic Theology* [1871], I, p. 135; and *Church Polity* [1878], pp. 41, 55 ff., 73 n., 75.

19 J. Thomson, in presenting the overtures calling for strict subscription, in 1722 and in 1729, made this point very prominent. Cf. pp. 46 f.

20 J. Calvin, *Institutes of the Christian Religion,* IV, i, ii.

21 On Calvin's doctrine, see *ibid.,* IV, i, v, vi, and iii, i–xvi; together with J. L. Ainslie, *Doctrines of Ministerial Order in the Reformed Churches.*

22 S. Finley, *Approved Minister,* p. 9.

23 G. Tennent, *Divinity of the Scriptures,* p. 168. This is Calvin's doctrine also.

24 S. Davies, *Sermons,* II, pp. 144–154, 166 f.

25 G. Tennent, *Unsearchable Riches,* p. 14.

26 S. Davies, *Sermons,* II, p. 139.

27 G. Tennent, *Duty of Self-examination,* pp. 142–144, 132, 136; *Unsearchable Riches,* p. 21.

28 Strict discipline of unworthy members was insisted upon as a means of keeping the Sacrament from profanation, but that was only traditional Calvinism, *Records,* p. 111.

29 G. Tennent, *Solemn Warning to the Secure World,* pp. 191 f.

30 S. Davies, *Sermons,* II, p. 97.

31 William Tennent, III, *God's Sovreignty No Objection to the Sinner's Striving,* p. 4. Cf. Samuel Willard's *Compleat Body of Divinity,* p. 435, "The Spirit of God, in the Calling of a Sinner home to Christ, doth not deal with him, as with a stock or stone, but as a reasonable Creature." This work, published 1726, was the most massive yet attempted in New England. G. Tennent, *Duty of Self-examination,* p. 137 (preached 1737); *Sermons on Important Subjects,* 1758, pp. 157 f., has the same view. Since the object of this chapter is to indicate the manner in which the New Side reinterpreted the Christian life, no discussion of the concepts of reason, will, affections, etc., in Federalism is here attempted. The New Side and Old Side scarcely differed on these points. Typical New Side statements may be found in: J. Tennent, *Regeneration Opened;* G. Tennent, *Sermons on Important Subjects; The Gospel a Mystery;* S. Davies, *Sermons,* I, "Preaching Christ Crucified"; II, "Religion Wisdom, Sin Folly"; S. Blair, *Works,* Sermon VI. Perry Miller's *New England Mind* has an excellent discussion of the Puritan background of these tenets of Federalism.

32 S. Davies, *Sermons,* II, pp. 537 f. Cf. also William Tennent, III, *op. cit.,* p. 14; G. Tennent, *Duty of Self-examination,* p. 137.

33 William Tennent, III, *God's Sovreignty,* pp. 3 f.

34 J. Preston, *The New Creature,* p. 283.

35 S. Davies, *Sermons,* II, pp. 609–620.

36 G. Tennent, *Sermons on Important Subjects,* p. 201. Cf. S. Blair, *The Great Glory of God,* p. 94.

37 For example, John Cotton, *The Way of Life,* pp. 231, 246, 250, a typical Puritan exposition; G. Tennent, *Solemn Warning to the Secure World,* pp. 30, 49; and S. Davies, *Sermons,* II, p. 622, are typical New Side statements.

38 G. Tennent, *Solemn Warning to the Secure World,* pp. xiii, 3, 8, 9, 12–19.

39 G. Tennent, *Examiner Examined,* p. 46; R. Smith, *Detection Detected,* pp. 35 f. Cf. also A. Green, "Letters to Presbyterians," *Advocate,* ΧI, p. 418; C. Hodge, *Constitutional History,* II, pp. 87, 95. Richard Niebuhr has some fine comments on the religious and social significance of these emotional outbreaks in his *Kingdom of God in America,* pp. 106–126. Clarence E. Macartney's comment also is worthy of note: "The history of the [Old Side] Presbytery and Synod at this time shows that whatever may be the dangers of extreme evangelistic zeal and piety, they are less to be feared than the paralysis of dead formalism, and rigid adherence to doctrinal standards without grace and evangelizing zeal." "Period of the General Assembly," *Journal of The Department of History of the Presbyterian Church in the U.S.A.,* XV, p. 25.

40 Ms. sermon, "The Terrors of the Lord," preached six times from 1757–1777.

41 This was one of the accusations made in the schismatical *Protestation* of June 1, 1741.

42 For the New England group, see for example E. Pemberton, *Practical Discourses,* pp. 21–49, and *Duty of Com-*

mitting our Souls, pp. 5–8; J. Dickinson, *Display of God's Special Grace,* pp. 3–25.

43 S. Finley, *Clear Light,* p. 34; G. Tennent, *Discourses on Several Important Subjects,* p. 234, and *Legal Bow,* p. 203. For similar views in earlier New England theology, see S. Willard, *op. cit.,* pp. 443 ff.; J. Norton, *Orthodox Evangelist,* pp. 129–152.

44 On conscience in convictions, see S. Davies, *Sermons,* I, p. 361, II, pp. 547 ff.; J. Tennent, *Regeneration Opened,* pp. 19 f.; G. Tennent, *Twenty-three Sermons,* pp. 186 f.; J. Blair, *Essays,* pp. 77–79.

45 S. Blair, *Works,* Sermon II, p. 45; see also pp. 46, 64.

46 G. Tennent, *Legal Bow,* pp. 181–187; see also S. Davies, *Sermons,* I, p. 146.

47 G. Tennent, *Sermons on Important Subjects,* p. 194.

48 *Records,* pp. 140, 144, 148 f., 152.

49 C. Hodge, *op. cit.,* I, pp. 197 ff. Hodge says of the synod's ruling, "This is surely sound doctrine."

50 Quoted in R. Webster, *History of the Presbyterian Church,* p. 179.

51 J. Thomson, *Government of the Church,* pp. 11 f.

52 S. Blair, *Works,* Sermon I, p. 23.

53 W. L. Mathieson, *The Awakening of Scotland,* pp. 190 ff.; H. F. Henderson, *Religious Controversies of Scotland,* p. 5.

54 G. Tennent, *Twenty-three Sermons,* pp. 29–58. Samuel Davies has the same solution, *Sermons,* I, pp. 648, 650, II, p. 271. Cf. also R. Smith, *Bruised Reed,* pp. 12 f., 16 f.

55 G. Tennent, *Duty of Self-examination,* p. 137; *Discourses on Several Important Subjects, . . . Vindicae Operum,* pp. 311 f.

56 G. Tennent, *Twenty-three Sermons,* pp. 201 f.; J. Blair, *Essays,* p. 67.

57 J. Blair, *New Creature,* p. 15. J. Dickinson has the same view, *True Scripture Doctrine,* p. 150. This same general scheme is to be found in all the New Side literature. Cf. also E. Pemberton, *Practical Discourses,* pp. 77–84, *Duty of Committing,* pp. 10, 13, and *Knowledge of Christ,* p. 6.

58 J. Tennent, *Regeneration Opened,* p. 12; G. Tennent, *Sermons on Impor-*

tant Subjects . . . British Nation, pp. 214 f.

59 S. Blair, *Works,* Sermon IV, pp. 70 f.; S. Davies, *Sermons,* II, p. 528.

60 S. Davies, *Sermons,* II, pp. 514 f.; J. Blair, *Essays,* p. 64.

61 J. Thomson, *Doctrine of Convictions,* pp. 15 ff., and *Explication . . . Shorter Catechism,* pp. 67 f.

62 S. Davies, *Method of Salvation,* p. 23; and *Sermons,* I, p. 592; G. Tennent, *Sermons on Important Subjects . . . British Nation,* p. 7; *Discourses on Several Important Subjects . . . Justification,* p. 64; *Solemn Warning,* p. 21; E. Pemberton, *Sermons on Several Subjects,* p. 15; J. Dickinson, *True Scripture Doctrine,* pp. 141–206, *Familiar Letters,* pp. 120 f.

63 S. Blair, *Works,* Sermon III, p. 79. Cf. Sermon I, p. 21; cf. also S. Davies, *Sermons,* II, pp. 652, 654.

64 G. Tennent, *Discourses on Several Important Subjects, . . . Justification,* p. 63; E. Pemberton, *Salvation by Grace,* p. 59; J. Dickinson, *Familiar Letters,* p. 117; S. Davies, *Method of Salvation,* p. 22.

65 E. Pemberton, *op. cit.;* G. Tennent, *op. cit.;* J. Dickinson, *op. cit.*

66 R. Smith, *Detection Detected,* pp. 98 f.

67 J. Thomson, *Explication . . . Shorter Catechism,* p. 148; F. Alison, Ms. sermon on Jer. 50:5, 10/9/57.

68 S. Finley, *Clear Light,* pp. 40 f., 46, 56; J. Tennent, *Regeneration Opened,* pp. 71 f.; R. Smith, *Bruised Reed,* pp. 14, 24; J. Dickinson, *Witness of the Spirit,* pp. 3, 23; S. Blair, *Works,* Sermon III, p. 78; G. Tennent, *Duty of Self-examination,* p. 143, *Unsearchable Riches,* p. 52, *Brotherly Love,* p. 26, *Remarks upon a Protestation,* pp. 28 f. The Old Side caricature of the New Side position may be found in J. Thomson, *Doctrine of Convictions,* p. 14; *Querists, III,* p. 95, "A Protestation" Reason #7, *Records,* p. 159.

69 F. Alison, Ms. sermon on II Peter 1:10, 9/4/57.

70 J. Thomson, *Doctrine of Convictions,* p. 65; *Querists, III,* p. 95, *Short Reply of the Querists,* p. 10.

71 J. Dickinson, *Witness of the Spirit,* pp. 3–20; J. Tennent, *Regeneration Opened,* p. 71.

72 J. Thomson, *Explication . . . Shorter Catechism*, p. 79.

73 J. Dickinson, *Witness of the Spirit*, pp. 4–17.

74 F. Alison, Ms. sermon on II Peter 1:10, 9/4/57.

75 *Querists, III*, p. 95.

76 G. Tennent, *Duty of Self-examination*, p. 140. Cf. also S. Finley, *Clear Light*, pp. 47 f.

77 J. Dickinson, *Witness of the Spirit*, p. 25.

78 S. Finley, *Clear Light*, p. 41.

79 J. Dickinson, *Familiar Letters;* G. Tennent, *Necessity of Holding Fast the Truth . . . Appendix . . . Moravians;* R. Smith, *Detection Detected.*

80 J. Dickinson, *True Scripture Doctrine*, pp. 147 ff.

81 G. Tennent, *Discourses on Several . . . Vindicae Legis*, p. 174.

82 S. Davies, *Sermons, I*, p. 271.

83 S. Blair, *Works*, Sermon IV, p. 95; G. Tennent, *Unsearchable Riches*, p. 19; *Twenty-three Sermons*, pp. 268 f.; S. Davies, *Sermons, I*, p. 556.

84 G. Tennent, *Discourses on Several Important Subjects, . . . Vindicae Legis*, p. 217 f.; E. Pemberton, *Duty of Committing*, pp. 15 ff.; S. Blair, *Works*, Sermon VI, p. 165.

85 J. Blair, *Essays*, p. 678.

86 J. Dickinson, *Familiar Letters*, pp. 322–344. G. Tennent, *Discourses . . . Vindicae Operum*, pp. 253 ff., 262 ff., 269–273, 345, is to the same effect.

87 S. Davies, *Sermons, II*, p. 109. Cf. also III, p. 254; G. Tennent, *Two Sermons Preach'd at Burlington*, p. 7.

88 S. Davies, *Sermons, II*, p. 115.

89 S. Davies, *Sermons, II*, p. 108; also, I, pp. 513, 650 f.

90 G. Tennent, *Twenty-three Sermons*, p. 296.

91 G. Tennent, *Discourses . . . Vindicae Legis*, p. 225.

92 *Ibid.*, p. 104.

93 *Ibid.*, p. 149. Cf. also his *Substance and Scope of both Testaments*, p. 6. How typically Puritan this insistence was may be seen from Perry Miller's *New England Mind*, pp. 196 ff.

94 G. Tennent, *Discourses . . . Vindicae Legis*, pp. 104, 139, 228 f.; also S. Blair, *Works*, Sermon VI, pp. 163 f. On this identification of the moral law and the Decalogue in Puritanism, see S. Willard, *Compleat Body of Divinity*, p. 150, and Perry Miller, *op. cit.*, p. 196.

95 G. Tennent, *op. cit.*, pp. 147, 240 f.; on the example of Jesus, see also S. Davies, *Sermons*, I, p. 645.

96 G. Tennent, *Funeral Sermon . . . J. Rowland, . . . Narrative . . .*, p. 7.

97 S. Finley, *Satan Stripped . . .*, pp. 21 f.

98 G. Tennent's sermons on war are a very clear illustration of this general conviction.

99 G. Tennent, *Discourses . . . Vindicae Legis*, pp. 219 f.; and *Divine Government . . .*, pp. 38 ff.; S. Davies, *Sermons*, II, p. 625; S. Blair, *Works*, Sermon II, pp. 57 f., Sermon III, p. 84.

100 R. Smith, *Principles of Sin and Holiness*, p. 9; J. Tennent, *Regeneration Opened*, p. 20; S. Davies, *Sermons*, I, pp. 255 f.; G. Tennent, *Necessity of Keeping the Soul*, pp. 8 f.; J. Blair, *Essays*, p. 10.

101 G. Tennent, *Unsearchable Riches of Christ*, p. 12.

102 E. Pemberton, *Duty of Committing*, pp. 18 f.

103 S. Davies, *Sermons*, II, p. 394.

104 *Ibid.*, p. 399.

105 G. Tennent, *Twenty-three Sermons*, p. 311; S. Davies, *Sermons*, II, pp. 463 f.

106 R. Smith, *Bruised Reed*, pp. 17 f.

107 J. Tennent, *Regeneration Opened*, p. 25.

108 Quoted in L. Tyerman, *George Whitefield*, II, pp. 590 f.

109 S. Davies, *Sermons*, II, pp. 99 f., 110, 114 f.; *Religion and Publick Spirit*, pp. 4–6; G. Tennent, *Twenty-three Sermons*, pp. 177 f., 291.

110 G. Tennent, *Happiness of Rewarding . . . Enemies*, p. 21; even more explicit, *Brotherly Love*, p. 3.

CHAPTER 11

1 Ms. records, Presbytery of Lewes, 5/8/65.

2 *Records*, p. 361.

3 J. Johnston, *Letter to E. H. Gillett on Early Presbyterianism on the East Line of the Hudson*, 12/27/1844.

4 *Documentary History of the State of New York*, IV, pp. 362, 373, 383.

[5] J. McC. Blayney, *History of the First Church, Albany*, p. 13.

[6] H. A. Harlow, *History of the Hudson Presbytery.*

[7] S. Knapp, *History of the Brick Presbyterian Church*, p. 32.

[8] Ms. records, Minutes of the Fund, "Address to England and Ireland," 3/4/60, p. 18.

[9] J. Smith, *Old Redstone*, p. 12.

[10] C. Beatty, *Journal of a Two Months Tour.* . . .

[11] J. Smith, *op. cit.;* William W. McKinney, *Early Pittsburgh Presbyterianism;* and G. J. Slosser, "A Chapter from the Religious History of Western Pennsylvania," *J. P. H. S.,* XVI.

[12] W. H. Foote, *Sketches of Virginia, I,* and *II Series:* William Gewehr, *Great Awakening in Virginia.*

[13] Thos. Barton to Secretary of S.P.G., 10/18/68, in W. S. Perry, *Historical Collections,* II, p. 434.

[14] J. Green to J. Bellamy, Webster Mss., I, 11/22/75.

[15] J. Finley, *Essay on the Gospel Ministry,* pp. 45 f.

[16] C. A. Briggs, *American Presbyterianism,* p. 316.

[17] Ms. records, Presbytery of New Castle, 12/9/61.

[18] This Fund has continued in operation as an independent organization, still bearing its original name, "The Presbyterian Ministers' Fund, Philadelphia, Pa."

[19] As early as 1707, Joseph Yard, of the First Church, appears on the minutes of presbytery as an elder. Very likely he attended as the church's representative, and was received by the presbytery as such. (In the early years of the original presbytery such men were termed "assistants." *Records,* pp. 37, 41.) The church's records state very clearly, however, that a session of elders was first formed in 1770. At that time no mention was made of existing elders (though the church had often been represented in presbytery and synod), and some discussion was conducted as to the proper manner of choosing elders. Rules were agreed upon, and subsequently an election was held. Ms. records, First Church, Philadelphia, Committee of the Congregation, 8/13/70.

[20] Ms. records, Presbytery of Suffolk, 6/5/54.

[21] Ms. records, Presbytery of Donegal, 10/22/60. On an appeal from this decision by a number of former New Side men, the synod ruled that election was the essential act. *Records,* p. 345.

[22] Ms. records, Presbytery of Lewes, 5/11/68. The term "set apart" is used of the ordaining of ministers, and also of the installation of deacons, who were never ordained.

[23] Ms. records, Presbytery of New Brunswick, 8/12/78.

[24] D. Bostwick to J. Bellamy, 1/14/63, Webster Mss., I, p. 205.

[25] On scholasticism in the pulpit, see pp. 223 f.

[26] In E. Stiles, *Itineraries,* p. 434. The reference to "threatens us with slavery" is to the perilous conditions of the colonies.

[27] M. L. Locke, *Anti-Slavery in America,* pp. 52 ff., *et passim,* has a good discussion of Rush's contributions to the antislavery movement.

[28] N. G. Goodman, *Benjamin Rush,* p. 298.

[29] *Records,* pp. 456, 458 f.

[30] *Ibid.,* pp. 487 f., 539 f.

[31] J. Brainerd to Mrs. Smith, 8/24/61, Simon Gratz Mss., American Colonial Clergy, gives a long and detailed account of Indian missionary work at this time.

[32] J. Brainerd, "Letter to Pennsylvania Journal," 9/15/63, *New Jersey Archives,* Sermon I, XXIV, p. 231.

[33] D. McClure, *Diary,* ed. by F. B. Dexter.

[34] Colonel Babcock to Miles Cooper, 8/11/73, in *Documentary History of the State of New York,* IV, p. 490. Babcock may have included Congregational missionary work also in his use of the term "Presbyterian." Anglicans often considered the two denominations as one.

[35] J. Montgomery, *A Sermon . . . at Christiana Bridge, . . . the 20th of July 1775 . . . ,* pp. 24 f.

CHAPTER 12

[1] E. Stiles, *Diary,* I, pp. 253 f.; T. J. Wertenbaker, *Princeton 1746–1896,* p. 44.

[2] Bellamy Papers, Presbyterian Histori-

cal Society: S. Davies to D. Cowell, 9/14/58, 10/18/58; J. Ewing to D. Cowell, 11/6/58; D. Cowell to S. Davies, 12/25/58; S. Davies to D. Cowell, 3/12/59.

3 Bellamy Papers, J. Caldwell to J. Bellamy, 3/16/67; S. Hopkins to J. Bellamy, 4/4/68, 5/4/68.

4 William Smith Papers, Penn-Peters Correspondence, Brinton Collection: Smith to Peters, 5/22/62, 9/14/62, 11/23/62, 1/8/63, 8/25/63, 2/25/64; Peters to Smith, 10/12/62.

5 Ibid., Peters to Smith, 6/27/63.

6 W. S. Perry, Historical Collections, II, pp. 389 ff.: Archbishop to Duché, 9/16/63; Peters to Archbishop, 10/17/63.

7 William Smith Papers, VII, No. 8, Brinton Collection: Smith to Peters, 2/14/64; 2/25/64.

8 E. Stiles, Itineraries, p. 428, Alison to Stiles, 10/30/66.

9 B. A. Konkle, George Bryan, p. 37.

10 Magaw, Beard, Lyons.

11 Cf. p. 159.

12 Here Stiles inserted a quaere in the margin as he read this remarkable letter.

13 E. Stiles, Itineraries, S. Purvicance, Jr., to Stiles, 11/1/66.

14 Stiles, op. cit., Alison to Stiles, 12/4/66.

15 Ibid.

16 Stiles, op. cit., Purvicance to Stiles, 12/13/66.

17 Ms. letter, R. Stockton to J. Witherspoon, 4/14/67.

18 J. Maclean, College of New Jersey, I, p. 288; V. L. Collins, President Witherspoon, I, p. 79; A. Green, Ms. Life of John Witherspoon, pp. 99 f.

19 Maclean, op. cit., I, pp. 295 f.

20 Ms. records, First Presbyterian Church, Philadelphia, 9/4/58; 10/5/58; 3/5/67; 4/6/67; 1/21/68; 2/16/68; 4/15/68; et passim to 6/9/69.

21 Ms. records, Second Presbytery of Philadelphia, 5/10/70.

22 Ms. records, First Presbyterian Church, Philadelphia, passim, 8/12/71 to 5/1/80.

23 E. Stiles, Diary, I, pp. 249 f., 7/16/72.

24 A. Green, Ms. Life of John Witherspoon, p. 93.

25 I. W. Riley, American Philosophy, pp. 455 ff., 489-493.

26 Bellamy Papers, J. M. White to Bellamy, 12/29/63.

27 Ibid., A. McWhorter to Bellamy, 1/28/64.

28 Ibid., J. Caldwell to Bellamy, 3/16/67.

29 E. Stiles, Itineraries, p. 451.

30 Bellamy Papers, Bradford to Bellamy, 4/18/72.

31 Ibid., Chapman to Bellamy, 8/14/72; Caldwell to Bellamy, 12/29/73. Later it became evident that Periam was probably mentally ill. E. Stiles, Diary, I, p. 516.

32 E. Stiles, Diary, I, p. 363.

CHAPTER 13

1 Quoted in C. A. Briggs, American Presbyterianism, p. 157.

2 A. L. Cross, The Anglican Episcopate and the American Colonies, p. 101.

3 Ecclesiastical Records of the State of New York, pp. 2173-2176, 4046-4048, 4067, 4081, 4095-4096, 4098.

4 Cross, op. cit., pp. 67 ff.

5 Cf. pp. 215 f.

6 Cf. p. 159.

7 Quoted in W. S. Perry, Historical Collections Relating to the American Colonial Church, II, p. 215.

8 Only Scott was a communicant member. Smith and Livingstone were trustees but not members.

9 Printed in Ecclesiastical Records of the State of New York, V, pp. 3427 ff.

10 On these schools, see H. Smith, Life of Wm. Smith, I, pp. 94 ff. Records, pp. 219, 227 f., 231.

11 Quoted in C. F. Pascoe, Two Hundred Years of the S.P.G., I, p. 38.

12 Printed in Ecclesiastical Records of the State of New York, V, pp. 3716 f.; and p. 3889.

13 Cross, op. cit., p. 147. Cross's account must be supplemented by the letters between Samuel Smith and Archbishop Secker printed in Ecclesiastical Records of the State of New York, VI, passim, access to which Cross seems not to have had.

14 Ecclesiastical Records of the State of New York, VI, p. 3910.

15 In Prior Documents, pp. 46, 49.

16 Records, p. 360.

17 Records, pp. 362 f.

18 W. S. Perry, History of the American Episcopal Church, I, p. 415.

19 *Records*, p. 364.
20 Printed in H. Smith, *Life of Wm. Smith*, I, p. 397.
21 *Minutes of the General Convention*, p. 18.
22 *Ibid.*, pp. 19 ff.; E. Stiles, *Letters and Papers*, p. 158.
23 On this point, see Cross, *op. cit.*, p. 197.
24 Smith, *op. cit.*, I, pp. 427, 434.
25 *The Francis Letters*, I, pp. 98 f., quoted in C. H. Van Tyne, *Causes of the War of Independence*, p. 364.
26 S. Auchmuty to Sir Wm. Johnson, January, 1769. Simon Gratz Autograph Collection, American Colonial Clergy.
27 H. L. Osgood, "The Society of Dissenters," *American Historical Review*, VI, 1901, pp. 498 ff.
28 Cross, *op. cit.*, pp. 251 f., 258.
29 *Ibid.*, pp. 89, 104–110, 120 f., 168–172, 212.
30 John Adams' summary of the controversy's influences, though often quoted, is worth repeating since it is the testimony of a shrewd observer: "If any gentleman supposes this controversy to be nothing to the present purpose, he is grossly mistaken. It [the plan of episcopizing the colonies, especially New England] spread an universal alarm against the authority of Parliament. It excited a general and just apprehension, that bishops, and dioceses, and churches, and priests, and tithes, were to be imposed on us by Parliament. It was known that neither king, nor ministry, nor archbishops, could appoint bishops in America, without an act of Parliament; and if Parliament could tax us, they could establish the Church of England, with all its creeds, articles, tests, ceremonies, and tithes, and prohibit all other churches, as conventicles and schism shops." Cross, *op. cit.*, p. 159.

CHAPTER 14

1 Quoted in V. L. Collins, *Witherspoon*, I, p. 206.
2 *Op. cit.*, I, p. 185; J. J. Boudinot, *Life of Elias Boudinot*, I, pp. 13 ff.; E. Boudinot, *Journal of Events . . .*, pp. 4 ff.
3 E. B. Greene, *Revolutionary Generation*, p. 124.
4 C. H. Lincoln, *Revolutionary Move-*
ment in Pennsylvania*, p. 168.
5 Greene, *op. cit.*, Ch. IX; Lincoln, *op. cit.*, Chs. IX ff.; and A. Nevins, *American States During and After the Revolution*, Chs. I to IX, have good accounts of this struggle.
6 E. W. Caruthers, *Sketch of Life . . . David Caldwell*, pp. 97–181; P. Davidson, *Propaganda and the American Revolution*, pp. 85 f.
7 Tennent was now serving a Congregational Church in Charleston, and Drayton was a Baptist. R. W. Gibbes, *Documentary History of the American Revolution*, I, prints many of the reports of Tennent and Drayton.
8 Davidson, *op. cit.*, pp. 199 f.
9 *Journals, Continental Congress*, III, 1775, p. 388.
10 Ms. records, Presbytery of New Brunswick, 12/26/75.
11 Davidson, *op. cit.*, p. 90. "*An address of the Presbyterian Ministers of the City of Philadelphia to the Ministers and Presbyterian Congregations, in the County of . . . in North Carolina. . .* [by F. Alison, J. Sproat, G. Duffield, and R. Davidson].
12 C. A. Hanna, *The Scotch-Irish*, I, pp. 2 f., gives a much distorted picture, which is followed by E. F. Humphrey, *Nationalism and Religion*.
13 *Records*, pp. 466 ff.
14 Davidson, *op. cit.*, and L. N. Richardson, *History of Early American Magazines*, both give good accounts of Witherspoon's propaganda efforts.
15 Popular feeling against the Scots is well revealed in an account, published in a British newspaper, of what befell a troop of captured Highlanders as they were marched from the coast to the interior for internment: "On our journey no slaves were ever served as we were; through every village, town and hamlet that we passed, the women and children, and indeed some men among them, came out and loaded us with the most rascally epithets, calling us 'rascally cut-throat dogs, Murtherers, blood hounds,' etc, etc. But what vexed me most was their continually slandering of our country (Scotland) on which they threw the most infamous invectives; to this abuse they

added showers of dirt and filth, and now and then a stone." *Letters on the American Revolution,* edited by M. W. Willard, p. 334.

16 *Ecclesiastical Records of the State of New York,* VI, p. 4293.

17 Ambrose Serle to Lord Dartmouth, 11/8/76; 4/25/77, in Stevens, *Facsimiles of Manuscripts in European Archives Relating to America,* 1773 to 1783, XXIV, No.'s 2045, 2057, quoted in L. Lundin, *Cockpit of the Revolution,* pp. 99 f.

18 The entire text is in W. H. Foote, *Sketches of Virginia,* I, pp. 323 f. An abridgment appears in H. S. Commager's *Documents of American History,* pp. 124 f.

19 *North Carolina Colonial Records,* IX, 1086, quoted in G. H. Van Tyne, *Causes of War of Independence,* pp. 367 f.

20 H. D. Foster, *Collected Papers,* especially Chs. 3 and 5. C. Becker, *The Declaration of Independence.*

21 J. T. Headley, *Chaplains and Clergy of the Revolution,* lists a number of these; W. B. Sprague's *Annals,* III, mentions others; and notices of the ordination of men for the chaplaincy are not infrequent in the *Records* of the synod.

22 Sprague, *Annals,* III, pp. 33 f.

23 H. H. Brackenridge, *Discourses,* pp. 60 f.; M. C. Tyler, *Literary History of the American Revolution,* II, pp. 210, 294, 297, 308, 311, 312, 319, discusses a number of Presbyterian publications. Headley, *op. cit.,* pp. 115, 300, 376, mentions others. John Carmichael, William Foster, William Linn, also published sermons on the war.

24 E. H. Gillett, *History of the Presbyterian Church,* I, pp. 189 ff., has a summary of the damage.

25 Lincoln, *op. cit.,* p. 192.

26 *Records,* p. 499.

27 Gillett, *op. cit.,* I, p. 200.

28 A good view of his political thinking is given by R. M. Dummere, "Classical Precedents in the Writings of James Wilson," *Publications,* Colonial Society of Massachusetts, Vol. 32, pp. 525–538.

29 J. Witherspoon, *Address to the Inhabitants of Bermuda . . . ,* p. 25.

CHAPTER 15

1 E. B. Greene, *The Revolutionary Generation,* Chs. XII–XV, and A. Nevins, *The American States During and After the Revolution,* have good accounts of this period.

2 A. Nevins, *op. cit.,* especially Ch. VII.

3 S. Miller, *Memoir . . . John Rodgers,* p. 129.

4 S. Miller, *Life of Samuel Miller,* I, pp. 122 ff., 136.

5 H. M. Morais, *Deism in XVIII Century America,* and G. A. Koch, *Republican Religion,* are the best accounts of deism in this period.

6 I. W. Riley, *American Philosophy, the Early Schools,* pp. 234 f.

7 Morais, *op. cit.,* has a good treatment of this fact.

8 Koch, *op. cit.,* pp. 13 f. According to Koch, however, it was by means of the early nineteenth century revivals primarily, rather than by means of theological polemic, that deism was broken.

9 "Memoirs of David Rice," in R. H. Bishop, *Outline of the History of the Church in . . . Kentucky,* p. 63.

10 *Records,* pp. 398, 406, 436, 442, 460, 541. Witherspoon also sponsored into the synod a number of Seceder ministers from Scotland and Ireland. His second wife was the daughter of Rev. William Marshall, the clerk of the Seceder presbytery, who finally closed the negotiations for reunion. Cf. also C. A. Briggs, *American Presbyterianism,* pp. 338 f.

11 *Records,* pp. 505, 508, 518–522, 541; Briggs, *op. cit.,* pp. 359 f.

12 Cf. Ch. XVI.

13 E. B. Greene and V. D. Harrington, *American Population Before the Federal Census of 1790.* In the Southern States, of course, a great deal of this increase was Negro slaves. Even these slaves, however, had some claim upon the Church's attention.

14 Cf. pp. 280 f.

15 *Records,* p. 499; Ms. records, First Presbytery of Philadelphia, 5/20/83; A. Green, *Memoirs of Joseph Eastburn,* p. 23.

16 *Records,* p. 511; "Considering the

growing extent of our Churches; the critical State of religious affairs, the great variety of Denominations multiplying in the State, the Danger of the Extinction of our own Churches, unless some speedy and effectual means be adopted to prevent the Evil, A Motion was made that our Pulpits may be rendered more easily accessible and more speedy by altering the usual Course of Education, at least with regard to those who are advanced in years." Ms. records, Presbytery of Hanover, 10/30/78.

[17] *Records*, p. 512.

[18] Ms. records, First Presbytery of Philadelphia, 10/22/83.

[19] *Records*, p. 526.

[20] Ms. records, Presbytery of New Brunswick, 4/23/82; 5/24/85.

[21] Ms. records, Presbytery of New Castle, 4/28/79.

[22] Ms. records, Presbytery of New Brunswick, 4/22/83.

[23] D. M. Bennett, " Life and Work of the Rev. John McMillan," *J. P. H. S.,* XV, p. 141.

[24] G. J. Slosser, " A Chapter from the Religious History of Western Pennsylvania," *J. P. H. S.,* XVI, pp. 112 f.

[25] Cf. Joseph Smith, *Old Redstone, or Historical Sketches of Western Presbyterianism,* p. 190.

[26] R. H. Bishop, *Outline of the History of the Church in . . . Kentucky, . . . containing the memoirs of Rev. David Rice . . . ,* pp. 67 f.

[27] *Ibid.,* p. 69.

[28] R. Davidson, *History of the Presbyterian Church in Kentucky,* p. 130.

[29] W. H. Whitsitt's life of Wallace has a good treatment of the history of this school. See also Davidson, *op. cit.,* Ch. XII.

[30] Cf. Davidson, *op. cit.,* Ch. III.

[31] Cf. W. H. Foote, *Sketches of Virginia,* I, pp. 307–348; and H. J. Eckenrode, *Separation of Church and State in Virginia.*

[32] Foote, *op. cit.,* I, pp. 408–430.

[33] W. H. Foote, *Sketches of North Carolina.*

[34] T. C. Pears, " The Aitken Bible," *J. P. H. S.,* XVIII, pp. 225 ff; *Records,* p. 500.

[35] *An Address from the Presbytery of*

New Castle . . . August 11, 1784. . . .

[36] Cf. pp. 207 ff.

[37] W. B. Sprague, *Annals of American Pulpit,* III, p. 138; R. Webster, *History of the Presbyterian Church,* p. 528.

[38] *Records,* pp. 487, 458.

[39] E. R. Turner, *The Negro in Pennsylvania,* p. 79.

[40] Turner, *op. cit.,* p. 180 n.

[41] Quoted in H. S. Cooley, *A Study of Slavery in New Jersey,* Johns Hopkins University Studies, XIV Series, 1896, pp. 9 f.

[42] *Records,* pp. 539 f.

[43] *Records,* p. 540.

[44] M. L. Locke, *Anti-Slavery in America,* pp. 72–87, 109.

[45] A. Nevins, *op. cit.,* pp. 455, 459; N. G. Goodman, *Benjamin Rush.*

[46] Ms. records, First Presbytery of Philadelphia, 4/8/79.

[47] Ms. records, First Presbyterian Church, Philadelphia, J. Ewing to the Trustees, 12/20/97.

[48] *Records,* pp. 495, 499, 500, 502. This case seems to have been brought before synod as early as 1775, and argued several times. *Ibid.,* pp. 475, 478, 484, 487.

[49] James Finley, *A Brief Attempt to Set the Prohibitions . . . Leviticus. . . .*

[50] Ms. records, Presbytery of New Brunswick, 11/7/87.

[51] *Records,* p. 504.

[52] Ms. records, Presbytery of New Brunswick, 5/10/84; *Records,* pp. 505, 518–522, 541, 547.

[53] Simon Gratz Autograph Collection, Letters of Solomon Freligh, 1/11/86; 12/23/83.

[54] Sprague, *op. cit.,* III, pp. 260 ff.

[55] The preface, rather long and directed wholly to immediate problems, was replaced by a much briefer one of a nature calculated to be applicable to any future time as well.

[56] *Draught of a Plan of Government . . . Directory for Public Worship,* 1787, pp. 51 f. The committee gave no indication who the " illiterate, vagrant and designing persons " condemned were.

CHAPTER 16

[1] *Records,* pp. 406 f.

[2] *Ibid.,* pp. 426 ff.

3 *Ibid.*, pp. 452, 457, 459.

4 *Ibid.*, p. 80, *et passim* to p. 99.

5 *Ibid.*, pp. 236, 238.

6 *Ibid.*, p. 460.

7 *Ibid.*

8 E. H. Gillett, *History of the Presbyterian Church,* I, pp. 207 ff.

9 Cf. the experience of the Continental Congress after the war. The various states became more and more absorbed in, and jealous of, their own interests and left the Congress and the Confederacy to become, as E. C. Burnett has said, a mockery. *The Continental Congress,* pp. viii f.

10 *Records,* p. 509.

11 *Ibid.*, p. 512.

12 *Ibid.*, p. 513.

13 General Assembly Mss., chiefly of 1785; motions, overtures, but not of record.

14 *Records,* pp. 513, 522, 535.

15 The first official hymnbook was formally approved in 1830.

16 *Records,* p. 517.

17 *Ibid.*, pp. 522 ff.

18 *Ibid.*, p. 526.

19 *Ibid.*, p. 524.

20 Matthew Wilson to John Miller, 6/11/86, Simon Gratz Collection, American Colonial Clergy. Miller's feelings are well revealed in a later letter to James Sproat, a New Englander who had become pastor of Gilbert Tennent's former congregation in Philadelphia: " Our Presbytery, I hear, by ye Authority vested in them, have made & constituted Dr. Wilson, a Commissioner to your General Assembly; at ye meeting of which he and another Doc I could name, rather of ye Yankee breed, will make but an awkward figure among a number of Gentlemen, who to use ye Phrase of my friend at Lewes [Wilson], are determined to cram ye Scotch Hierarchy down our throats. He probably will remonstrate but not assist at your Grand Council, which you are persuaded, by keeping high flying company, to believe by this time, was instituted by ye divine founder of Christianity. But my friend below, you will find true blue, a perfect infidel with regard to ye jure divine of your Synod & Genl Assembly. For my part, I am determined to love my Brethren, to live, as much as possible, in peace with all men, but not to adopt any plan of Church Government yt has no foundation in ye Christian institution." John Miller to James Sproat, 5/4/89, S. Gratz Collection, American Colonial Clergy.

21 *Records,* p. 525.

22 *Draught of a Plan of Government and Discipline . . . ,* 1786, p. ii.

23 Matthew Wilson to John Miller, undated, S. Gratz Collection, American Colonial Clergy.

24 Ms. records, Presbytery of New Brunswick, 4/25/87; 5/17/87.

25 Ms. records, Presbytery of Philadelphia, 4/13/87.

26 *Records,* pp. 330, 337, 344.

27 G. D. Henderson, *The Scottish Ruling Elder,* pp. 189, 211–220.

28 The synod's records are often incomplete regarding absentees, and exact computations are therefore impossible to make.

29 Over the Old Side's efforts to keep Duffield out of Philadelphia, and some disciplinary cases which involved party allegiances.

30 *Records,* p. 435.

31 *Ibid.*, pp. 532 f.

32 Cf. pp. 296 ff.

33 *Records,* p. 535.

34 *Ibid.*, pp. 508, 510.

35 *Ibid.*, p. 535.

36 *Minutes of the Fund,* 11/17/62.

37 *Records,* p. 539.

38 *Ibid.*, pp. 539 f.

39 V. L. Collins, *President Witherspoon,* II, pp. 160, 162.

40 *Op. cit.,* II, p. 237.

41 A. Green, Ms. Life of John Witherspoon, p. 172.

42 Though retained on the committee, he did not attend in September, 1786, and was dropped in 1787.

43 *Op. cit.,* II, pp. 160, 162, 256 f. Collins evidently made a most hasty examination of the synod's reorganization, for his account has numerous anachronisms and errors of fact. It is remarkable that W. B. Sprague, who compiled his *Annals* in 1857 with the aid of Green's Ms., and who quotes large portions of it, not only fails to quote Green's section on Witherspoon's contributions to the reorganization of the Church, but is himself silent on the

entire topic. *Annals of the American Pulpit*, III, pp. 288–300.

44 *Records*, p. 539.
45 *Ibid.*, p. 540.
46 *Ibid.*, p. 541.
47 The absentees listed were 141, but the list did not in every instance include the men ordained the previous year. *Records*, pp. 541 ff.
48 *Ibid.*, p. 544.
49 *Ibid.*, p. 546.
50 *Ibid.*, p. 409.
51 *Ibid.*, p. 547.
52 Cf. p. 277.
53 The term "bishop" is used very freely in the 1786 plan, in the sense of a minister as distinguished from a ruling elder.
54 Henderson, *op. cit.*, p. 216.
55 *Ibid.*, pp. 204 f.
56 The Scottish General Assembly retains for itself each and every several right of the lower judicatures. In the American church all undelegated, or "reserve," powers belong solely to the presbyteries.
57 Cf. J. L. Ainslie, *Doctrines of Ministerial Order in the Reformed Churches*, pp. 147 f.
58 *Ibid.*, Ch. VI.
59 *Acts of the General Assembly of the Church of Scotland*, Act X, 1711.
60 *Ibid.*
61 Ainslie, *op. cit.*, Ch. VII.
62 *Presbyterian Church U.S.A., Minutes of General Assembly*, 1789–1820, pp. 14–21. The totals for 1774 were 139 ministers, 153 churches with pastors, 180 vacant congregations, and five probationers. Cf. W. W. Sweet, *Religion on the American Frontier: The Presbyterians*, pp. 12–19, quoting Aitken's *General American Register*, 1774, pp. 182–191.
63 John Rodgers was elected the Moderator.

INDEX

Date Due